Religio

and Community
Cohesion

An exploration of challenges and opportunities

Edited by Michael Grimmitt

McCrimmons • Great Wakering, Essex

Dedicated with love to my granddaughter, Ellie-Mai.

First published in the United Kingdom in 2010 by
McCRIMMON PUBLISHING CO LTD
Great Wakering, Essex, England
info@mccrimmons.com
www.mccrimmons.com

ISBN 978-0-85597-710-8
Publisher's order reference: MB7108

British Library Cataloguing in Publication Data.
A catalogue record for this book is available from the British Library.

Cover design by Nick Snode
Typeset in Palatino 10pt roman
Printed and bound by Polestar Wheatons, Exeter, Devon, UK

J/J

CONTENTS

PREFACE

D URING THE FIRST ACADEMIC YEAR of my three year part-time Senior Research Fellowship at Oxford (2007-2010), I spent time investigating as much of the literature on social and cultural cohesion as I could find. There is a lot of it, much of it dating from after 9/11/2001. A careful search of the RE literature followed, especially from 2004 onwards, and this showed that there is a high expectation that RE can and should contribute significantly to social and community cohesion. The question is how?

At the beginning of my second year I began to formulate the outline of a book which would address this issue. With hindsight I now realise that it was over-ambitious and I was right to change it. I had wanted it to be a dialogue between educators, religious educators and representatives of the religious communities in Britain and their secular equivalents. The problem that I ran into was, whom could I approach to write the chapters which purported to represent the views of each of the communities? While there may be common agreements about social and community cohesion within and between communities, there are also fundamental differences of opinion. Indeed, it became clear that to find a consensus about which 'issues' actually lie at the heart of social and community cohesion and which are most in need of being addressed would be both difficult and controversial. Besides which, even if a possibility, such a book would need to be of a size way beyond my own time resources and beyond the costs that my publishers could reasonably be expected to bear.

In December 2008, using the questions that had emerged from my research, I decided to restrict the book to the expression of views by educators and religious educators. I drew upon the professional associations that I have formed over the years at the University of Birmingham and, more recently, at the University of Oxford, and included former students and others with whom I have worked. I wrote to potential contributors as follows:

'I envisage a 'Reader' enabling issues to be considered and reflected upon by trainee and practising RE teachers, members of SACREs, members of faith communities and those with responsibility for implementing DCSF Guidance (00598-2007) in schools as a duty and as an important focus of Section 5 school inspections. However, I am anxious not to include anything that has previously been published, but want to commission new, fresh writing which will stimulate reflection and discussion. I do not intend the book to adopt a particular stance on the subject but rather to include a range of views to stimulate and inform opinion, debate and decision-making.'

I wish to thank the contributors for the enthusiasm and skill with which they have responded to this request. I am deeply indebted to them for making their scholarship and expertise available so readily and for the interest that they have shown in contributing to this book. Readers will enjoy the contrasting positions which contributors have taken on issues while also discerning the identification of common concerns which transcend individual ideological standpoints. I am very hopeful that what is offered here will move the debate forward about the contribution that education and RE can make to social and community cohesion and encourage further developments in policy, curriculum and pedagogy.

I also wish to thank those who have contributed financially to my post at Oxford, namely, Dr David H. Lee – who has also given generously in other ways to the work of Harris Manchester College – and the Culham Institute and the Farmington Trust. I am especially grateful to the Revd. Dr. Ralph Waller, Principal, Harris Manchester College, and Professor John Furlong, the former Director of Oxford University Department of Education, for their encouragement of, and support for my work. I would like to add my thanks to the Revd. Dr. John Gay, Director of the Culham Institute, for reading my rather lengthy Extended End Piece (Chapter 16) in manuscript form and making some helpful suggestions.

For nearly 40 years I have enjoyed a very close and harmonious relationship with McCrimmon Publishing Co. Ltd. I would like to take this opportunity to thank Joan McCrimmon for the trust that she has shown in my work over the years and for the particular interest that she has taken in publishing this final book. It has been a considerable pleasure to work with her so successfully. Thank you, Joan.

To my family who, especially during this final academic year, have re-visited the bitter-sweet pleasures of being party to another book – that is, enduring my short temper and increasing isolation from things domestic – I record my humble thanks and deep appreciation for their patience. I promise them that things will improve after the 30th September – my retirement day!

Michael Grimmitt,
University of Oxford,
April, 2010.

UPDATE FOLLOWING THE GENERAL ELECTION ON MAY 11TH, 2010

The manuscript of this book was completed before the Conservative – Liberal Democrat Coalition Government took office on May 11th, 2010. As the legislative framework and statutory guidance of the previous Government(s) remain in place with regard to Religious Education and the requirement for schools to contribute to social and community cohesion, the book reflects the current legal position.

It is too early to predict how the Academies Act, 2010, may have an effect on the provision of Religious Education in those schools which choose to become Academies. Although these schools will not be required to follow the national curriculum (except in the core subjects and ICT), the requirement to provide a broad and balanced curriculum and adhere to the basic curriculum, of which Religious Education is a part, is currently being written into their funding agreements. Religious Education in Academies may therefore be expected to reflect the character of the subject as set out in the Non-Statutory National Framework for Religious Education (2004), and the Local Authority Agreed Syllabuses.

Irrespective of changes which may follow from the anticipated Department for Education's Curriculum Review in the autumn of 2010, the issues arising from Religious Education's obligation to contribute to social and cultural cohesion, examined in this book, will, of course, remain of vital significance to all those who support the subject's involvement in public education.

M. H. G
September, 2010

CHAPTER 1

INTRODUCTION

LIVING IN AN ERA OF GLOBALISED AND POLITICISED RELIGION:
What is to be Religious Education's response?

Michael Grimmitt

SUMMARY

CHANGES IN THE SOCIAL, political, religious, moral and ethnic landscape of the UK during the first decade of the twenty-first century are identified. The challenges and opportunities which these have created for RE are briefly considered. The need for further research and development in the theory and practice of RE is suggested as a necessary response to these new circumstances and one requiring international co-operation and collaboration.

INTRODUCTION

At the end of the twentieth century, thinking about RE in England and Wales and its provision in schools, largely through general, but not universal acceptance of its legislative basis in the 1988 Education Act, had achieved a certain commonality within the curriculum of general education. The challenge to assert the subject's educational value and legitimacy had been successfully met and an open, multi-faith RE had been enshrined in law, but not without dissent. There was common but not universal agreement about the need for RE to combine two forms of

8

learning – *learning about and learning from* religion(s). Examination syllabuses in Religious Studies, which enabled students at 16 years of age or younger to include the subject in their General Certificate of Secondary Education (GCSE), were devised in accordance with the same educational criteria which governed RE, with a focus on assessing students' knowledge and understanding of the beliefs and practices of religions and, significantly, their ability to evaluate the truth claims made by the religions. Various pedagogies were available for implementing the RE curriculum, all, with refinements and additions, based on a phenomenological method of study.[1] None required students to be of religious faith nor necessarily to agree with the orthodox teachings of the religions that they studied in order to demonstrate that their knowledge and understanding of the subject had reached one of eight requisite levels of attainment used generally, but not universally, to record and report progress in RE.

Within this situation the role of teacher-training institutions remained central to spearheading a thorough understanding of the educational basis of RE and in improving the overall quality of provision in schools through the production of well-trained, competent and enthusiastic teachers. As has always been the case, the essential link between training and research was maintained with one or two Universities in particular taking a lead in developing a coherent research base in the subject, especially one which continued to work on the establishment of RE's educational rationale, and the integration of religious subject knowledge with appropriate classroom pedagogies.[2] In comparison, the Government Teacher Training Agency, (TTA) placed its trust in a competence-based style of assessment to improve standards of classroom delivery without entering into a detailed consideration of how learning might be improved through changes in pedagogy. As a result, training institutions, dependent on receiving high grades during OfSTED inspections in order to continue to receive Government funding, gave rather more attention to achieving these outcomes than encouraging their student teachers to experiment with alternative pedagogies or engage in innovatory curriculum design. These pressures may have also inadvertently led to a period of complacency in the development of the subject with a pervasive belief that all that was needed was a continuing refinement and improvement of current practice which would then contribute to raising standards in teaching and learning in RE.

However, a seismic shift in the social, political, religious, moral and ethnic landscape of the UK in the last decade has presented RE with a new and still to be addressed challenge and has shown, in my view, that current theories and practices in RE are no longer entirely sufficient to address the very different circumstances created by the emergence of what I will call *'globalised and politicised religion'*. The main events which have caused this challenge may be briefly summarised under three headings: *world events and their consequences; the British Government's social and educational policies; and national and local issues and controversies.*

A NEW CONTEXT FOR THE DEVELOPMENT OF THE THEORY AND PRACTICE OF RELIGIOUS EDUCATION

World events and their consequences

This section, inevitably, is dominated by the events of 9/11 (2001) in New York and of 7/7 (2005) in London, the invasion of Afghanistan (in 2001) and Iraq (in 2003) and their aftermath, and the increase in anti-Muslim feeling associated with these events in the UK, Europe and the USA. It also includes the continuing conflict between Palestinians and Israelis in the Middle East and the increasing involvement of suicide bombers in pursuing ideological and religious goals there and elsewhere in the world. All these events have highlighted in a dramatic manner what has long been known to be the case, namely that the ideological power of religion often contributes to the world's longest-running conflicts.

However, with the number of British troops killed in Afghanistan since 2001 now in excess of 300, public awareness of this link between politics and religion has increased significantly, not least as a result of the almost daily expressions of personal loss and family grief depicted in the media.[3]. As a result, public support for a British military presence in areas of the world, especially where an Islamic agenda predominates, has waned. Invariably such circumstances have also contributed significantly to public awareness of religion being more associated with its negative influence than its positive values, especially in securing world peace and contributing to safe and harmonious relations between people of different faiths both globally and locally.[4]

The 9/11 aftermath, however, has been unique in establishing once and for all the absolute significance of religion to world order, international relations, intercultural understanding and co-operation, world trade, the economy and finance. In short, these events have forced the world to recognise that religion in the twenty-first century, rather than having a

10

decreasing influence, continues to have a major globalising impact on politics and world peace.[5] It has also reversed a previous trend for religious belief to become increasingly privatised. Religion and religious issues are now very public matters about which everyone has to become better informed and be prepared to address seriously. To exclude them from the public education system is now unthinkable; where else can young people gain a balanced understanding?

To relate this specifically to 9/11, the notion, initially entertained, that this event was an expression of inter-religious conflict was naïve and misleading. Many nations and cultures of Asia and the Middle East (largely Muslim) have felt exploited and disregarded by the west's power bids, especially for reasons of economic development and military security. The west's interventions in Afghanistan and Iraq both at the time and subsequently, have only served to reinforce this view and create further antagonism. It is this, among other factors, which provides one account for the ensuing willingness of some young Muslims to be prepared to respond to the call to combat what is seen as the moral decadence of western societies and western values by identifying with '*jihad*' – seen by some Muslims as a former 'sixth pillar' of Islam.[6] It continues to be one of the reasons – when Muslims see that, despite everything, the British and American foreign policies remain unchanged – why more young people are prepared to be radicalised in the name of Islam.[7] The conscious decision by many young Muslim women to wear *hijab* and by many young men to adopt Muslim dress styles is symbolic of their readiness to have their identity politicised and for them to be seen as Muslim first and British, or European, second.[8] This does not just include the radicalised Muslim but an increasing number of moderate, thoughtful young people seeking to identify both with the power of Islam to combat injustice but also with its traditional teaching of peace, compassion and tolerance. A guiding Qur'anic teaching is that nourishing justice brings the believer closer to the love and compassion of God.[9]

It is difficult to know how related to these events was the upsurge, in the first decade of the present century, in attacks by atheists – sometimes called the 'New Atheists' – on the intellectual status of religion, most notably by the Oxford Darwinian scientist Richard Dawkins, who has described religious belief as a dangerous delusion that continues to inflict grievous harm on society.[10] Initially aimed at British and American readers, Dawkins' book, *The God Delusion*, (2006) is now available in 31 languages,

11

and has been instrumental in the establishment of *The Richard Dawkins Foundation for Reason and Science* in both the UK and the USA with the aim to *'advance the public understanding of science and sponsor research into psychological unreason'* (the latter presumably being typified for Dawkins by religious belief and practice). Together with a tendency for the British press to present religious matters in a critical and often demeaning light, especially those relating to Islam or Christianity, there can be no doubt that as a result of writings by Dawkins and others the public perception of religion in the UK has undergone a negative change in the present decade, despite a robust defence by academics like Alister McGrath and Terence Eagleton.[11] Although religion may now have a higher profile it does not necessarily have a more popular one, although publishers have reported a 50% increase in the sale of books on religion in recent years. Whatever the context in which religion is currently encountered and discussed, however, it is most certainly one in which issues and controversies associated with religion are more to the fore than the systematic discussion of religious belief and practice itself. This is something that needs to be remembered when thinking about an appropriate basis for RE to have in schools.

Government social and educational policies

Here we will consider briefly the British Labour Government's social and educational policies (i.e. from 1997 to the present) as a major factor in bringing about changes in values and attitudes which have also had an impact upon religious and moral matters.[12] Like elsewhere in Europe, the British Government responded positively to the growing expectation that all Governments should be held accountable for the furtherance of human freedom from unequal opportunities and social, economic, educational, cultural and racial disadvantage and discrimination. This expectation is reflected in the following policies: the introduction by the 'New Labour' Government of a secularising, 'equality agenda' with social justice and human rights as its central concern and with education as a means of creating a society of equal opportunities; the pursuit of an anti-discrimination policy in terms of race, religion, gender, age, sexual orientation and disability; the encouragement of a diversity of educational provision, including faith schools and 'independent specialist schools'; the pursuit of a liberal and humane immigration policy towards refugees, asylum seekers and migrants, increasingly from Eastern European countries; the requirement that schools, through their policies and curricula, including citizenship education and religious education, will contribute to community and social cohesion; and the identification of links between social and educational policies and services, and, more recently, curricula, to ensure that every child is given the best possible support and encouragement to be *'healthy, stay safe, enjoy and achieve, make a positive contribution and achieve economic well-being'*.[13]

The aspiration to combat injustice and inequality and to build a society which offers equal access to all is not inconsistent with the values and teaching of all religions. In broad terms, therefore, secular and religious values should be able to cohere and support each other. This augurs well for a form of RE being able to be devised which encourages an effective dialogue to take place in the classroom about such values.[14] But, in the real world outside the classroom, the utopian vision for humanity which these values represent is dependent for its realisation upon a huge financial investment to counter the effects of all those factors which contribute to inequality – something which, like many other socially desirable aspirations, has become a victim of the current economic recession. Other factors may also contribute to hindering such aspirations; for example, the regrettable characteristic of contemporary social and political life, especially in a multicultural society like Britain, of 'scapegoating' – attributing to minorities, social classes, racial, ethnic and religious groups – the blame for the failings of society or of Government policy.[15] The following statements provide typical examples of scapegoating.

- 'Community and social cohesion has not been achieved in British society because the policy of multicultural education has failed as a result of some groups refusing to integrate and ascribe to a broader consensus of values than their own (e.g. Muslims).'

- 'Social, health and educational services are stretched beyond their capacity because the Government has admitted too many asylum seekers, refugees and immigrants (e.g. Eastern Europeans, especially Poles).'

- 'Employment opportunities have been taken away from white, British workers by the Government being ready to admit immigrants who are prepared to take lower wages and accept a lower standard of living.'

- 'Some schools have a disproportionately high number of children from ethnic minorities and their presence accounts for the lowering of standards and poor attainment levels in these schools as a whole.'

In response we might ask, how does a population in which the majority of the electorate only reads the popular press become better informed about the complexities which influence the success or failure of social, educational and economic policies which ultimately determine what sort of society we live in? Where and when do we begin to educate children to learn to look at the bigger picture of how a democratic society might achieve its goal of enabling everyone to have equal assess to good housing, an efficient health service, a successful school, a wide range of employment opportunities, and to economic and personal well-being, etc.? Can this be achieved solely within the present framework of Citizenship Education or is something more required?[16]

Finally we might consider the way in which one set of aspirations and values can conflict with another. Is it possible for community and social cohesion to be served by an educational system which favours 'diversity' in terms of the types of educational institutions it supports? Is it possible to argue that the presence of 'faith schools' in the system contributes to rather than detracts from this goal?[17] More to the point, what does an emphasis on social cohesion do to religions? In a society which values diversity and advocates and legislates for inclusivism, no religion is pluralist in matters of faith and belief and avoids making exclusivist claims to truth. While a democratic society seeks to prevent social fragmentation can it expect to achieve this by requiring religions to coalesce and 'accede to a relativist egalitarianism in which tolerance is the supreme, indeed the only virtue'?[18] This is a problem to be addressed and the outcome will have an effect upon what is thought possible and desirable in RE.

National and local issues and controversies

In this section we consider, very briefly, the impact of national and local events in the UK upon public conceptions of religion, culture and ethnicity. It is inevitable that the popular, tabloid press will seize upon tensions and conflicts of a religious and ethnic kind without necessarily conveying a balanced view of the situation. Unfortunately exposure to attention-catching headlines and biased reporting probably is the most powerful influence on how these events are interpreted, and parental attitudes are often quickly adopted by their children. The task of public education, and especially of RE, is to encourage a more critical and reflective interpretation of such matters, but many a well intentioned RE teacher has learned to their cost that their handling of controversial issues in the classroom can make them also the subject of newspaper headlines.[19] In brief the following issues and controversies are typical of those which exercise a major influence on the public mind and imagination in the UK and so affect attitudes to religion and to its portrayal in RE.

- The tensions between secular and religious values as exhibited by the negative response on the part of some religions or some of their adherents to the secular equality agenda, especially in matters relating to gender equality and sexual orientation. For example, opposition to legislation making homosexual relationships equal in law with heterosexual relationships; to the Adoption and Children Act of 2002 granting equal rights to same sex couples applying to adopt children; and to the Civil Partnership Act of 2004 giving same-sex couples rights and responsibilities identical to civil marriage. Typical examples are: the refusal of Roman Catholic Adoption Agencies to arrange adoptions for same-sex couples; the refusal of some Christian Registrars to conduct Civil Partnership ceremonies of same sex couples.[20]

- The tensions within religious communities as a result of religions and religious organizations being exempted by the Sexual Equality Regulations from compliance in their internal arrangements and procedures with some requirements of gender and sexual equality legislation because these are seen to be in conflict with strongly held religious convictions of a scriptural or doctrinal kind. The basis for restricting the law is because the European Convention of Human Rights guarantees the right to freedom of thought, conscience and religion as an absolute right which cannot be subject to limitation and restriction. A typical result of applying this exemption is the much publicised conflict within the Church of England and the Anglican Communion over the ordination of women bishops and the position of gay and lesbian clergy.[21] Concerning the latter, the controversy is made even more problematic by the Church's recognition of the rights of gay clergy to enter a Civil Partnership but not to have a sexual relationship within it.[22]

- The tensions which continue to be highlighted by the press between Christianity and Islam and between the 'British' way of life and other cultural values. A typical example from the press includes their denigrating and ridiculing the Archbishop of Canterbury's attempt to create a constructive dialogue with Islam by suggesting that

Sharia Law might, to the advantage of some Islamic family matters, be recognized within the English legal system.[23] Following this, the Archbishop's considered letter to Muslim scholars setting out the difficulties of Christians and Muslims having a shared view of God but seeking further dialogue to achieve this was greeted by such headlines as, 'How can the Archbishop lead the Church when he apologises for his faith?'[24]

- The tensions which the press continually highlights of disparity and unfairness exhibited by the Government and by Local Authorities in their treatment of, and regard for Christianity and the country's Christian heritage in comparison with their treatment of other religious and cultural traditions represented in Britain, especially of Islam. To take but one indication of this, the Church of England Report, *Moral, without a Compass* (2008), which expresses the view that the Church feels itself to be marginalized, excluded and neglected by the Government.[25]

- The tensions which are said to arise from the Government's position of 'moral neutrality' on matters of ethical significance, such as the 2008 Human Fertilisation and Embryology Bill (allowing for the creation of hybrid animal-human embryos which could be used in the cause of greater understanding and possible prevention of human disease) and the opposition of some religious groups for whom such procedures constitute a violation of the sanctity of human life.[26]

- Finally a further illustration of how political, economic and financial factors influence the treatment of religion, religious values and religious leaders. In May 2008, the Dalai Lama on his visit to Britain was welcomed by the Prime Minister Gordon Brown, not at 10 Downing Street, but at Lambeth Palace, the Archbishop of Canterbury's official residence. With important trade and economic policies between Britain and China then pending, and, not least, the Beijing Olympic Games, the political dimension was conveniently set aside and the religious significance of the visit heightened. This was in contrast to President Obama's meeting with him in February 2010 when the President pledged to 'revive the long-standing tradition of US support for Tibet in its quest for greater autonomy from Beijing.'[27]

RESEARCHING A FORM OF RELIGIOUS EDUCATION
TO MEET THESE CHANGED CIRCUMSTANCES

We come now to some fundamental questions. What form of RE in the general curriculum of state schools is best able to accommodate the globalised and politicised nature of religion today and the increased sensitivities which are associated with it? Can a descriptive, phenomenological approach to RE in schools enable these issues to be addressed and provide the basis for better dialogue, exchange and communication between young people from different religious and ethnic groups in the service of achieving greater community and social cohesion? Can all communities of faith be expected to support the notion that issues that are both sensitive and controversial should form part of children's RE, and feel confident that they can be addressed in the classroom with due regard for the interests and well-being of the communities of faith?

An *issues-related* form of RE which is prepared to encourage the *critical* discussion of religion and religions within their globalised and politicised context and which also addresses controversial local issues of the kind I have indicated is likely to be seen by the government of the day, Local Authorities, faith community leaders and teachers as unmanageable, undesirable and even dangerous. But on what basis and with what sort of understanding is RE being required to contribute to community and social cohesion? It is questionable whether the provision of information about religions is sufficient for this purpose, although it continues to have an important place in RE. As we have seen, the impact that the popular press has upon the public perception of religion is not so much about a religion's *internal agenda* (its theological or doctrinal beliefs, its modes of worship, its ethical teaching, etc., although these are sometimes included) but how this agenda affects its relations with others within a multi-faith society, especially as a result of its response to the equality agenda. Young people of secondary school age are especially aware of this and will quickly become impatient with a form of RE which avoids these issues. Teachers of RE may feel similarly, but it is important that they are safeguarded from accusations of political, theological or religious bias, indoctrination and even discrimination against the religions or religious content that are included within the curriculum. In this respect, what is prescribed in agreed syllabuses, including the use of appropriate pedagogies, becomes a necessary requirement for the implementation of a form of RE which, of necessity, must deal with points of tension as well as points of agreement between the religious faiths and other life-stances. The challenge to religious educators is to devise a suitable pedagogic framework for the exploration of controversial and divisive issues in RE in a way which avoids the press's tendency to polarize them and the faith communities' tendency to conceal or deny them. If such a pedagogy is not forth-coming the contribution that RE can make to community and social cohesion by dealing with religious and inter-religious issues within their globalised and politicised contexts will be greatly diminished.

Encouraging international collaboration in the research and development of RE

I have stressed the importance and necessity of RE in England and Wales continuing to be responsive to the challenge which changing social and political circumstances are having on values and attitudes in the UK. I have not attempted to identify parallels with events and circumstances outside the UK or to relate this to theories and practices of RE which have been developed elsewhere. My premise, however, has been that a purely descriptive phenomenological approach to the study of religion can no longer address the circumstances which now obtain in our society. I have accepted that a fundamental task which all societies face, and to which RE can contribute, is to improve inter-religious communication and inter-cultural understanding so that better social and community cohesion is achieved. But this is not the same as promoting appreciation of diversity and respect for difference. It requires members of different communities to commit themselves in an active manner to a framework of commonly shared values – to freedom from oppression and discrimination, to the practice and observance of human rights, to equal opportunities and a respect for all, to a common legal system, to shared responsibility for the poor and the dispossessed, to conserving the environment and world resources, to working for peace, and so on. This agenda requires that all groups in society, religious and secular, engage in ideological self criticism and are prepared to relinquish positions of power and privilege for the greater good. It also requires those groups who may know themselves to be disadvantaged and victimised to reject violence and terrorism and seek their goals through means which are consistent with their professed commitment to truth, reconciliation and peace. Finally it requires RE teachers and their classes to be encouraged to explore critically but constructively those aspects of religion and religious faith which stand in the way of social and community integration and cooperation.

The task of creating trust, mutual respect and co-operation between people holding many different viewpoints is an ambitious agenda for any society to contemplate but it is one to which RE can make a small but significant contribution. If, through the contributions made to this book, a greater understanding of this task can be achieved and a collaborative programme of research and development begun to achieve it, its publication will have been worthwhile.[28]

NOTES

1. See Grimmitt, M.H. (2000) 'Contemporary Pedagogies of Religious Education: What are they?', in Grimmitt, M.H. (ed) (2000) *Pedagogies of Religious Education*, Great Wakering: McCrimmon Publishing Co. Ltd., 24 – 52.

2. I mention here, in particular, the Universities of Birmingham, Exeter, King's College, London, and Warwick.

3. The televised procession of funeral corteges through Wootton Bassett in Wiltshire, England, of those troops killed in Afghanistan whose bodies have been flown into RAF Lyneham has undoubtedly influenced public attitudes to Britain's involvement in the war. In January 2010 the leader of 'Islam4UK', Anjem Choudary, said that he would try to persuade people in Wootton Bassett to back an anti-war parade along the main street. In an open letter on *Islam4UK's* website he denied the march was 'merely an act of incitement or provocation'. In the letter, addressed 'to the families of British soldiers who have fallen', Choudary writes: 'It is worth reminding those who are still not blinded by the media propaganda that Afghanistan is not a British town near Wootton Bassett but rather Muslim land which no one has the right to occupy, with a Muslim population who do not deserve their innocent men, women and children to be killed for political mileage and for the greedy interests of the oppressive US and UK regimes... The procession in Wootton Bassett is therefore an attempt to engage the British public's minds on the real reasons why their soldiers are returning home in body bags and the real cost of the war.' The march did not go ahead through the intervention of the Prime Minister and Home Secretary. On 15 March, 2010, (Mothering Sunday) 14,000 British bikers passed through the town to raise money for the charity '*Afghan Heroes*'. This appears to have been a response to the threatened parade from '*Islam4UK*'.

4. Recognising the link between politics and religion and incorporating it in a reformulated theory and practice of RE is likely to be a significant factor in the future development of the subject. With a continuous bombardment of 'breaking news' on the news channels and the internet, the context within which the public now perceive religion and religious belief and practice cannot be excluded from consideration when studying some aspects of religion in RE.

5. Liam Gearon refers to this as '...the re-emergence of religion as a force in global governance' in his chapter in this book (Chapter 6, 9).

6. There has been continuous internal debate among Muslims about the many meanings and the status of *jihad*. Some Shia Muslims, especially Ismaili, are more inclined than others to wish to raise it to the importance of a sixth pillar. Sunni Muslims regard such a view as heretical. The ethical and spiritual aspects involving control over personal behaviour – called the *Greater Jihad* – are given more emphasis and support than the *Lesser Jihad* which refers to the requirement to wage war against the enemies of Islam. But since 9/11 *jihad* has increasingly come to signify the political opposition between Islam and the West. For a detailed discussion, see Jalal 2008. However, please note the following observation on this statement by Dr Abdullah Sahin in private correspondence with me on 13 April, 2010:

> 'As you rightly note Jihad is a complex concept and there have been many discussions concerning its meaning among classical and contemporary Muslims. However Jihad has been important to both main stream Muslims, Sunnis, and the Shia. I am not sure about the information concerning the Ismaili attitude to Jihad.
>
> The Qur'an uses the concept of *Jihad* in many places to mean the totality of the personal and collective 'efforts' to engage with moral, spiritual self improvement and as an existential quest to search for meaning in life. For example, the Qur'anic verse says 'whoever makes an "effort" to reach God, He will guide them to the paths leading to Him'. Here the word *Jihad*, i.e. 'effort', is used in its original literal sense: to engage with personal struggle/effort in achieving salvation, spiritual purification.
>
> Obviously this struggle in God's cause takes many forms. For example, using one's intellectual faculties to discern Islamic guidance from the sacred text to solve social problems, namely *Ijtihad*, is recognized as a form of *Jihad* and in fact *Ijtihad* comes from the same verbal root. All sorts of sacrifices including defending the community against an act of military aggression can be seen as part of such an effort. However, crucially, the Qur'an uses the term *qital* for warfare and not *Jihad* thus making an important distinction. As such *Jihad* cannot be translated as 'holy war' as its primary and most common use in the Qur'an refers to the non military 'efforts' of contributing to cause of Allah. *Qital*, the military engagement, i.e. warfare, is used and Islamic law developed very strict conditions for the conduct of warfare and rules of engagement during the war. The expressions like *Jihadi ideology, Jihadism* etc.. are simply inaccurate modern political readings and cannot be reconciled with the Qur'anic use of the concept of *Jihad* or its mainstream reception/interpretation in classic Islamic religious thought.
>
> As I have said Jihad, as it is used within the broader Qur'anic context, has been recognized by the mainstream Sunni Islam as well as Shia as important as it refers to this constant effort that the faithful should exhort in remaining faithful to the Islamic values in the face of diverse challenges and personal temptations, etc,. Therefore, the mystical tradition in Islam, Sufism, championed a report attributed to the prophet which identifies this spiritual, existential struggle to remain faithful as *greater Jihad* in comparison to the actual bodily sacrifice during

a war which is depicted as a *lesser Jihad*. Although the authenticity of this report is questioned by the Hadith scholars its message is greatly shared by many scholars in mainstream Sunni Islam.' (Sahin, 2010)

7.   In her chapter in this book, Joyce Miller points out that 'there is a mistaken conflation of 'fundamentalism', 'radicalism', extremism' and 'violent extremism' for they are not part of a continuum… Radicalism can be defined in a variety of social and political contexts and is not intrinsically connected to violence.' (Chapter 14)

8.   See Coles, M. I. (2008) *Every Muslim Child Matters: practical guidance for schools and social services*, Stoke on Trent: Trentham Books, 23.

9.   Thorne, J. and Stuart, H. (2008) *Islam on Campus: A survey of UK student opinions*, London, The Centre for Social Cohesion. Report downloaded from www.socialcohesion.co.uk *Islam on Campus* claims to be the most comprehensive survey ever undertaken of Muslim student opinion in the UK, based on a specially commissioned *YouGov* poll of 1400 students, fieldwork and interviews. The report examines students' attitudes on key issues including killing in the name of religion, establishing a worldwide Caliphate, introducing Sharia law to the UK, setting up an Islamic political party in the UK, gender equality, the treatment of apostates and homosexuals and the compatibility of Islam with secularism and democracy.

10.   From 1995 until 2008, when he retired, Richard Dawkins was Simonyi Professor for the Public Understanding of Science in the University of Oxford.

11.   See also, Hitchens, C. (2007) who has described religion as 'the main source of hatred in the world'; and McGrath, A. (2004) and (2007) and Eagleton, T. (2009) who have both sought to counter the arguments of new atheism from a Christian perspective.

12.   These policies and those of the former Conservative Government are also addressed by Clyde Chitty in Chapter 5 of this book.

13.   The 'Every Child Matters' policy, enshrined in the Government's 2004 Children Act, came about as a result of the social services failing to prevent the torture and death of an eight-year old West African child, Victoria Climbié, in 2000.

14.   This a matter taken up by Audrey Osler in Chapter 4 of this book and also commented upon by Liam Gearon (Chapter 7), Andrew Wright (Chapter 89 and Matthew Thompson (Chapter 9).

15.   For a detailed discussion of the British Government's social and educational policies between 2003-2007, including scapegoating, see Tomlinson, S. (2008), *Race and Education: Policy and Politics in Britain*, Maidenhead: Open University Press, Chapter Six, '*Community cohesion, war and education* (2003-2007)', 151 - 175.

16. In 2002 Citizenship Education was introduced as a compulsory National Curriculum subject for all 11-16 year olds. The programme of study covers politics and government, the legal system, the media, identity and diversity, human rights and equal opportunities and global issues. The revised curriculum for 2007 states:

> 'Political, social and ethical issues and problems can be controversial and sensitive, and can lead to disagreement. They should not be avoided, but need to be handled so that pupils develop skills in discussing and debating citizenship issues and considering points of view that are not necessarily their own. Setting ground rules and using distancing techniques can help to manage the discussion of such issues.'

The programme of study can be downloaded from www.qca.org.uk/curriculum

17. This is an issue addressed by Geoffrey Walford in Chapter 6 of this book and, in the context of Northern Ireland, by Norman Richardson in Chapter 13.

18. John McDade SJ, (2008), *Religion and Social Cohesion*, College Publicity Leaflet: Heythrop College: The Specialist Philosophy and Theology College of the University of London, www.heythrop.ac.uk.

19. *Church Times*, 11 July, 2008:

> 'Islam lesson: teacher is suspended: Cheshire County Council this week suspended an RE teacher ... after complaints about a lesson in which children were asked to act out Muslim religious ceremonies (prayer). Two 12-year-old boys were disciplined for refusing to take part, leading to complaints from their parents, it was alleged. The Church of England's RE spokesman, the Revd. Dr John Gay, said that he suspected the incident was "a storm in a teacup". "It is common practice for children to take part in role-play, like dressing up for Sikh weddings. It helps them empathise with people from traditions other than their own," he said.'

20. *The Mail on Sunday*, 8 June, 2008:

> 'Catholic adoption agency to defy gay rights law', 15. Almost two years later, in the aftermath of serious objections to amendments which would remove exceptions for churches in Harriet Harman's Equality Bill, the *Daily Mail*, 18 March, 2010, announced: 'Catholics win fight to refuse gay adoption. Judge backs church over freedom of conscience.' 8

> 11 July, 2008:

> 'Victory for the Christian over gay wedding ban: A Christian registrar who refused to carry out gay 'weddings' won a landmark legal battle yesterday' 5, but *Daily Mail*, 16 December 2009, 'Christian who won't marry gay couples loses her legal fight' The Master of the Rolls in an Appeal Court ruling is reported to have said: 'The right to express a strong Christian faith must take second place to the rights of homosexuals under Labour's equality laws ... human rights law also puts the rights of homosexuals before the rights of Christians to hold to their beliefs.' 34

21. *The Times*, 1 July 2008:

> 'Clergy plan mass exit over women bishops: As the wider Anglican Communion fragments over homosexuality, England's established Church is moving

towards its own crisis with a crucial vote on women bishops this weekend ... More than 1,300 clergy, including 11 serving bishops, have written to the Archbishops of Canterbury and York to say that they will defect from the Church of England if women are consecrated bishops.' Front page.

22.   *The Times* 23 February, 2010, *Letters to the Editor; 'It's discrimination to stop gay couples taking vows in church'*: a letter signed by 20 leading academics, bishops and clergy:

'The amendment [to the Equality Bill] will be re-presented by Lord Alli on March 2. We urge every peer who believes in spiritual independence, or in non-discrimination, to support it.' 27.

23.   *The Times*, 9 February, 2008:

'Archbishop faces calls to quit over Sharia row: The Archbishop of Canterbury was facing a crisis of confidence in his leadership yesterday after calling for part of Islamic law, or Sharia, to be introduced into Britain.' Front page.

24.   *Daily Express*, 17 July, 2008:

'*How can the Archbishop lead the Church when he apologises for his faith?* On Tuesday he delivered a letter to Islamic scholars all but apologizing for the belief in the Holy Trinity – claiming the concept of a God consisting of Father, Son and Holy Spirit is "difficult, sometimes offensive to Muslims".' 12

Church Times, 18 July, 2008:

'*Let's talk modestly about God, Archbishop urges Muslims:* Christians and Muslims must not rush into agreement about God ... a more modest aim is to recognize that Christians and Muslims speak about God in ways that are not simply mutually unintelligible systems.'

25.   *The Times*, 7 June, 2008:

'*Church attacks Labour for betraying Christians'.* 'The policies of Tony Blair and Gordon Brown have helped to generate a spiritual, civic and economic crisis in Britain ... Labour is failing society and lacks the vision to restore a sense of British identity ... the Government has deep religious illiteracy and no convincing moral direction.' Front page.

Daily Mail, 4 February, 2010:

'*Christianity being squeezed out in the name of "equality"'*: Dr John Sentamu, [Archbishop of York] accused politicians and others of trying to sideline religion by promoting their false idea of 'tolerance' ... The Equality Bill had contained a clause which would have made it very difficult for a religious group to employ someone of the religion for a position within the organisation', 24

The Sunday Telegraph, 28 March, 2010:

'*Britain is persecuting Christians, say bishops'* 'Six prominent bishops and Lord Carey, the former Archbishop of Canterbury, describe the "discrimination" against churchgoers as "unacceptable in a civilised society"'... They were highlighting the plight of Shirley Chaplin, a nurse who was banned from working on hospital wards for wearing a cross around her neck.' Front page.

Daily Mail, 7 April, 2010:

> '*It's a very bad day for Christianity: nurse's verdict after tribunal rules she can't wear crucifix and work because it is not a "requirement of her faith"'*. 5

The Mail on Sunday, 4 April, 2010:

> '*Britain was built on Christianity. So why are our politicians so terrified of even a whiff of religion?:* '...their alibi is multiculturalism...[but] the people who are calling for the abolition of Christian values from schools are not members of other faiths, but politically motivated secularists using diversity to pursue their real agenda: to drive faith from the public sphere.' (Giles Fraser, Canon Chancellor of St Paul's Cathedral), 23

Daily Mail, 8 April, 2010:

> '*What has Britain come to when it takes a Muslim like me to defend Christianity?*': 'A strong society demands tolerance and integration. Yet the political class has made a tragic mistake in recent years by emphasizing cultural differences between migrant communities and normal Britons.' (Dr Taj Hargey, Imam of the Oxford Islamic Congregation.) 14

26. *Church Times*, 23 May, 2008:

> '*Embryology vote leaves lobbyists out in the cold*: ...the Government survived four attempts to amend the Human Fertilisation and Embryology Bill...attempts to reduce the upper limits for abortion from 22 weeks to 20 weeks were rejected by MPs. Anti-abortion and pro-choice campaigners demonstrated outside Parliament as the debate took place.'

27. *guardian.co.uk* 12 May 2008:

> The prime minister's spokesman said today that Lambeth Palace – the London residence of the Archbishop of Canterbury – was chose to reflect the fact that the Dalai Lama was a "respected spiritual leader".

The Times, 21 May 2008 '*The Lambeth Talk: Brown should be meeting the Dalai Lama in Downing Street*': A far larger group, outraged by the refusal of Gordon Brown to receive him at Downing Street, were bitterly scathing of what they saw as the Prime Minister's political cowardice and attempt to appease Beijing.'

The Times, 18 February, 2010:

> '*Obama revives US support for Tibet*'. 35

28. This Introduction draws on some of the content of my chapter, 'The Religious Education of the Religious Educator: An Exploration of Issues in the Education and Training of the Student Teacher of Religious Education', in Dommel, C. and Michell, G. (eds) (2008) *Religion Education*, Bremen, Kleio Humanities, 173 -188

REFERENCES

Coles, M. I. (2008) *Every Muslim Child Matters: Practical Guidance for Schools and Social Services*. Stoke-on-Trent: Trentham Books.

Dawkins, R. (2006) *The God Delusion*, New York: Bantam Books

Eagleton, T. (2009) *Reason, Faith and Revolution: Reflections on the God Debate*, London: Yale University Press.

Grimmitt, M.H. (ed.) (2000) *Pedagogies of Religious Education. Case Studies in the Research and Development of Good Pedagogic Practice in Religious Education*, Great Wakering: McCrimmon Publishing Co. Ltd.

Hitchens, C. (2007) *God is Not Great: How Religion Poisons Everything*, London: Atlantic Books

Jalal, A. (2008) *Partisans of Allah: Jihad in South Asia*. New York: Harvard University Press.

McDade, John. SJ (2008) *Religion and Social Cohesion*. College Publicity Leaflet. Heythrop College, The Specialist Philosophy and Theology College of the University of London. London. URL: www.heythrop.ac.uk.

McGrath, A. (2007) *The Dawkins Delusion? Atheist Fundamentalism and the Denial of the Divine*, London: SPCK

McGrath, A. (2004) *Dawkins' God: Genes, Memes and the Meaning of Life*, Oxford: Blackwell.

Thorne, J. and Stuart. H. (2008) *Islam on Campus: A Survey of UK Student Opinions*. London: The Centre for Social Cohesion. URL: www.socialcohesion.co.uk.

Tomlinson, S. (2008) *Race and Education: Policy and Politics in Britain*. Maidenhead: Open University Press.

CHAPTER 2

SEEKING SOCIAL COHESION THROUGH THE 'COMMON SCHOOL'

Richard Pring

SUMMARY

S CHOOLS AND COLLEGES need to address, as a central educational aim, the creation of a more cohesive society. This requires a careful balance between a common set of values and a deep respect for the different traditions within the wider community. In drawing upon the philosophical ideas of John Dewey, the paper argues for the strength of protecting diversity in order to ensure a richer sense of community – respect for cultural differences within a common culture of respect and enquiry.

INTRODUCTION

Imagine briefly standing in the great reception hall of Ellis Island – that small territory, near the Statue of Liberty and past Staten Island as the boat enters New York harbour. It was there that so many people from all parts of the 'old world' entered 'the new'. They were of different religions, different races, different countries – mainly poor, often illiterate and seeking a better life. They had little in common with each other, other than their common humanity. One could easily see them as an aggregate of diverse individuals, reflecting very diverse languages and cultures, having little in common.

Altogether, they could hardly be seen as a community. They were a collection of individuals, certainly, but also of very diverse small communities, tending very often to establish their own quarters within the cities. Such small communities would have, say, a common set of religious beliefs, or a common remembrance of the country from which they had come, or a common language. But such commonality within different groups could so easily be the basis of hostility between groups. The question therefore is and was: how might these different communities overcome their differences and their mutual suspicions, and come to live together in harmony and in cooperation for the good of the whole? How might one form a coherent, larger community coterminous with the state?

The problems occurring from mass immigration have by no means been confined to the exodus from Europe, Africa and the Far East to the United States of America. Recent years have seen mass movements of economically deprived or politically persecuted people throughout the world. In Britain, this is particularly evident in the big cities. The ethnic mix of the population is changing. The proportion from minority groups in 2001 was 4.5 million out of a population of 57 million (Social Trends, 2004). This proportion will grow (General Household Survey, 2004), with a strong correlation between such minority groups and poverty and thereby educational underachievement – thus exacerbating the feelings of alienation. The Ouseley Report (2001) warned of a socially segregated Britain and of a growing minority feeling alienated from mainstream society. Establishing social cohesion would seem to be of paramount importance. And therefore from 2007 all schools within the English maintained system are obliged to promote community cohesion, this being part of the inspection process.

However, the creation, or reinforcement, of separate and mutually alienated communities is not simply a product of immigration and ethnic differences. In Britain, the evidence of the Rowntree Foundation (2007) points overwhelmingly not only to the differentiation between extremely rich and extremely poor, but also to the physical isolation of the one from the other. It is increasingly a society with many divides and social barriers – lacking much needed cohesion.

This paper aims to do two things. First, it aims to look carefully at what we mean by 'community'. Second, it argues for the distinctive role of education and the school in achieving this larger and socially cohesive community. It does so through reference to the philosophical work of the American philosopher, John Dewey, because it was the kind of society, arising from the mass immigration referred to in the opening paragraph, which helped form Dewey's thinking about the nature and purpose of education. But, in so doing, he saw such diversity, not so much as a problem to be overcome, but as an opportunity for enriching the experience and understanding of all – as a source of education

COMMUNITY

A community is more than an aggregate of individuals. It is the social context in which these individuals relate and interact with each other in a meaningful way. That 'meaningfulness' is not necessarily explicit. It is embedded in common activities and social practices that embody shared beliefs and understandings. As Dewey argued:

> 'Men live in a community in virtue of the things they have in common. What they must have in common in order to form a community or society are aims, beliefs, aspirations, knowledge – a common understanding – likemindedness as sociologists say.' (Dewey 1916, 4)

What brings people together as members of the same community (the 'likemindedness') might be very different, for example, economic interests or religious beliefs or a shared history. And people might belong to other communities with which they share other values and aims. By contrast, people may live closely together in a neighbourhood without any reciprocity. They do not form a community, despite various kinds of interaction as, for example, in purely business arrangements. There is a kind of alienation between people who, despite their interactions, enjoy little reciprocity or shared understanding of the world.

A complex society like ours is, therefore, made up of families, voluntary associations and moral traditions. And such traditions are embedded in particular ways of life and social practices, with their own distinctive symbols and rituals. Such communities are referred to by Putnam (2000) as 'bonding communities'. That complex society, therefore, might be described, in the words of the Chief Rabbi of the UK, Jonathan Sacks, as a

> 'confusing mixture of reasons and associations which emerge, like a huge river, from its countless streams and tributaries out of a vast range of histories and traditions.' (Sacks, 1997)

Sacks argues for the importance of recognising the distinctiveness of the major and different traditions within the broader society, for each has its own distinctive narrative which has the potential to enrich that society – but only when that narrative is preserved, enriched and passed on to subsequent generations within which the individual finds his or her identity.

> 'This is a morality received not made. It is embedded in and reinforced by a total way of life, articulated in texts, transmitted across the generations, enacted in rituals, exemplified by members of the community, and underwritten by revelation and tradition.' (Sacks, *ibid*).

On the other hand, the preservation of these distinctive traditions (and here Sacks had in mind the main religious ones) can so easily be the source of alienation, suspicion and indeed hostility – undermining efforts at wider social cohesion. Surely, transcending these differences, there must be a shared set of understandings, beliefs and values – the basis of what Putnam refers to as 'bridging communities' – communities which go across the different social networks and enable those different communities to discover or create common interests and purposes.[1] As Halsey (1978) argued in his Reith Lectures:

> 'We have still to provide a common experience of citizenship in childhood and old age, in work and play, and in health and sickness. We have still in short, to develop a common culture to replace the divided culture of class and status.' (Halsey, 1978).

These words echo those of the social historian, R.H.Tawney:

> '... in spite of their varying character and capacities, men possess in their common humanity a quality which is worth cultivating and ... a community is most likely to make the most of that quality if it takes it into account in planning its economic organisation and social institutions—if it stresses lightly differences of wealth and birth and social position, and establishes on firm foundations institutions which meet common needs, and are a source of common enlightenment and common enjoyment.' (Tawney, 1938, 55-6)

Therefore, social cohesion within a society which is made up of so many smaller communities, each with a different narrative and each with its own distinctive beliefs, values and traditions, requires the recognition of this 'common humanity' with its 'common needs' and above all the possibility of 'common enlightenment'. We have, in short, as Halsey argues, 'to develop a common culture to replace the divided culture of class and status' – and he could have added 'religious divisions'.

What could be that 'common culture'?

COMMON CULTURE

It is important to distinguish between the descriptive and the evaluative senses of culture. In its descriptive sense, culture embraces those shared practices and understandings, referred to above, through which groups of people make sense of the social, economic and moral worlds they have inherited and inhabit. In that sense, one might equally talk of a religious, craft, socialist or capitalist culture.

Culture in the evaluative sense (of say 'a cultured person') refers to those values and understandings, embedded in certain practices, which are seen to enhance the distinctively human capacity for understanding and feeling. For instance, the literary culture of books, poetry and history and a scientific culture empower those within a purely 'folk culture' by putting them in touch with the fruit of others' work and achievements through which our knowledge and understanding are advanced.

But it is necessary to understand the tension here between that empowering 'common culture' and the diversity of cultures from which the different learners come and from which they gain a sense of identity, belonging and dignity. For Dewey, that creation of a common culture, upon which might be built social cohesion to the benefit of all, must be compatible with a deep respect for the diversity of traditions from which the young learners come. The benefits of the wider community and its inherited culture in this evaluative sense lie in the communication of differences, and thereby in the growth of that community through the seriousness with which those differences are addressed, reflected upon, learnt from by all – and no doubt modified through examination and criticism.

However, even that serious sharing and reflecting upon differences requires a sense of community, namely, a respect for each other despite differences, a recognition of 'common humanity', and a willingness to learn from those differences. And that has to be learnt, more often than not through immersion in a culture which embodies reciprocal respect and constructive criticism.

Therefore, intrinsic to this transcendence of differences through a common culture lie, first, a deep respect for the distinct cultures which the common culture transcends – 'the countless streams and tributaries out of a vast range of histories and traditions', which Sacks (*ibid*) speaks of, and, second, the 'democratic' values which enable that meaningful interaction between the different traditions to happen – whereby each might learn from and be enlightened by the other. That was why Dewey's *magnum opus* was entitled *Democracy and Education*. Education lay, not in the transmission of knowledge, but in the openness to further experience and in the adaptation of one's understanding of experience through the attempt to make sense of the experience of others. Such openness welcomed, rather than shunned, the experiences which others have, whether reached through books, papers or social interactions. Every tradition and every person had something valuable to say, and the attempt to grasp that could only enhance the understanding of one's own beliefs, as these inevitably evolve in reflecting upon, in the light of evidence and further experience, the social, physical, moral and religious worlds one inhabits.

For that purpose it was important to create the common school – where, in Dewey's Chicago and later New York, these diverse traditions might come together and benefit from the interactions between them.

THE COMMON SCHOOL

Dewey saw the common school to be crucial if the formal education of young people was to achieve this. A fundamental purpose of education was to prepare the next generation to live harmoniously together, despite the important differences in culture from which the students came. More positively, that intermingling of those differences in the community of the school would be seen as an enrichment of those very differences. In *Democracy and Education*, therefore, Dewey refers to 'education' as a 'social function, securing direction and development in the immature through their participation in the life of the group to which they belong' (Dewey, 1916, 81). The school was seen as an extension of the group to which the students belonged, enabling the kind of growth that the family and the village would be too limited to provide. The school, ideally, was a sort of model to anticipate the wider community into which young people were growing up, and should enable them to contribute to, to enrich and to shape that community:

> 'Roughly speaking, [schools] come into existence when social traditions are so complex that a considerable part of the social store is committed to writing and transmitted through written symbols … As soon as a community depends to any considerable extent upon what lies beyond its own territory and its own immediate generation, it must rely upon the set agency of schools to insure adequate transmission of all its resources… Hence, a special mode of intercourse is instituted, the school, to care for such matters.' (Dewey, 1916, 19).

School, therefore, is the agent of the community in order to make available what it, or the larger society and culture of which it is part, has accomplished. Part of that accomplishment lies in being able to live together and, despite differences, to have shared understandings, aims and interests, so that each can find support and sustenance in the other.

Behind this lies Dewey's distinctive view of education. Education lies in the growth of the capacity, through experience, 'to manage life intelligently'. That growth will lie in the constant challenge to the assumptions one has. For example, growth in moral understanding will lie in the challenge to received assumptions from the encounter with others' sincerely held beliefs. For Dewey, life lies in the constant accommodation to new challenges, new experiences and new acquaintances. Even the academic life of the school should, at its best, be seen in this way. The various subjects are what Dewey referred to as 'the accumulated wisdom of the race', and that wisdom, mediated by the good teacher, provides a challenge to the young person who comes to school with more simplistic and less adequate understandings.

Therefore, the purpose of the common school is not to 'homogenise' everyone's beliefs – to eliminate differences so that everyone thinks and believes in the same way – or to create a 'cultural sameness'. Indeed, there is a richness to a diverse society from which each and everyone might draw and benefit. Rather is the common school the place where young people will grow through their interactions with others. The Muslim will not only come to understand things from the Christian's perspective, but will gain a greater insight into his or her own beliefs through that interaction. Christians would gain greater insight into the significance of their beliefs and the need for greater depth of understanding through the conversations with those whose values are essentially secular. Furthermore, all would come to recognise the 'overlapping consensus' between different religious and humanist traditions.

That, however, depends on a broader understanding of the aims of education and the associated intellectual virtues. That broader understanding espouses openness to argument, respect for evidence, readiness to listen to different points of view, capacity to reflect on what is heard, the disposition to examine critically cherished views. These are the intellectual virtues too often neglected in the so-called pursuit of knowledge or in the defence of inherited positions. Thereby, people become entrenched in unquestioned positions, shut off from genuine communication with those who are different. It is difficult for the wider society to exist in such educationally impoverished conditions. Conflict and hatred find their roots in the ignorance of one's own culture and of that of others.

The common school, therefore, would seek to do three things: first, to understand and respect the different cultural traditions that the young people bring with them into the school; second, to reconcile those cultural differences, which, if ignored, fragment the wider community so that it is no community at all; third, to connect those with the more universal cultural traditions and achievements of the arts, crafts, sciences and humanities through which their own ways of thinking might be illuminated. But for this to happen, there has to be a connection between these more universally held cultural traditions and those that shape the present understandings, interests and aspirations of the school students.

The humanities and arts in particular would be the vehicle through which young people would be able to address matters of deep human and personal concern, and indeed the differences that, on the one hand, give a sense of identity to the individuals whilst, on the other hand, dividing them. There would be a central place for those matters of personal concern. In such an exploration understanding would be enriched by the diversity of beliefs within the school community.

For that to happen, however, the school would not only welcome diversity of moral tradition but also actively support it—nurturing the beliefs within the different traditions. If Muslim or Christian or Jewish or atheist students are to contribute intelligently to the exploration of matters of human importance, then they need to be helped to understand the richness of their respective tradition—the literature and poetry, the art and customs, the theology and historical evolution of its institutions and beliefs. The common curriculum requires also the support of diversity. It requires, too, the procedural values whereby the interaction of such diversity might be fruitful—a point developed very thoroughly by Stenhouse (1975) in the Humanities Curriculum Project that he led.

CONCLUSION

The problems of social cohesion have always been with us. There is a limit to how far individuals or different communities within the larger society can have shared understandings and aspirations where there are large inequalities in material conditions and seemingly major differences in what constitutes a valuable form of life. Furthermore, such differences are immortalised in inherited memories of differences, whether those be of a class struggle, religious persecution or political repression. To some extent, they have been exacerbated in recent years by massive movements of population and the consequent segregation of ethnic groups.

The argument of this paper is that there is a need to respect those cultural differences which embody a distinctive understanding of human nature and personal fulfilment. Indeed, so important are these for personal identity and dignity that the educational system must find ways of enabling the young people to gain deeper, more intelligent grasp of their beliefs and practices, for these different cultures often embody, referring back to what Sacks argued, a 'morality received not made ... embedded in and reinforced by a total way of life, articulated in texts, transmitted across the generations, enacted in rituals, exemplified by members of the community...'

That has implications for the organisation of the school, the content of the curriculum and pedagogy – the opportunity for the rituals and festivals of the different religious communities, prayer time timetabled, food needs met, and options for the deeper study of the respective cultures

However, although religious and other differences should be respected through separate provision, there should be timetabled opportunities for the different communities to come together to address, from their own distinctive perspectives, matters that affect the whole community – religious persecution, environmental change, poverty within society, relations between the sexes, terrorism, social and economic injustice, war between nations, and so on.

There are excellent examples of how this might take place through systematic and evidence-based discussion (for example, in the Humanities Curriculum Project, described in Stenhouse, 1975). Issues, which are controversial in the sense that they divide people within society, are opened up for discussion. That discussion, however, has to be evidence based. Such evidence would include theological and philosophical traditions to which the students belong, as well as the different historical perspectives. The 'humanities' at their best provide the framework in which matters of deep concern to society, and to these future citizens within that society, might be understood – illuminated by literature, poetry and drama and through the perspectives of theology and religious practices. Evidence would be drawn from the physical and social sciences where this is relevant to the questions being asked. Opinions are of little use unless they are grounded in argument and in evidence.

The role of the teacher – a very difficult one – is that of helping the students to articulate their beliefs and understandings in the light of such evidence, and to share them with others who may come from a different position, a different tradition. It is a search for the 'overlapping consensus', and for respecting the other's point of view when that is fully articulated. The teacher's job is to help each to articulate his or her views in the light of evidence and to ensure the procedures of rational reflection and respectful discussion in the light of relevant evidence.

NOTES

1. See Eaude, T. 2009, for a valuable commentary on and practical application of Putnam's distinction.

REFERENCES

Dewey, J. (1916) *Democracy and Education*, New York. The Free Press,

Eaude, T. (2009) *Bowling Alone? What can schools do to promote cohesive communities?*, London: National Education Trust.

General Household Survey. (2004) *Living in Britain*, London: ONS

Halsey, J.H. (1978) Reith Lectures

Ouseley Report. (2001) *Community Pride, Not Prejudice: Making Diversity Work in Bradford*, www.bradford2020.com/pride

Putnam, R. (2000) *Bowling Alone: the Collapse and Revival of American Community*, New York: Simon and Schuster.

Rowntree Foundation (2007) *Experience of Poverty and Educational Disadvantage*, www.jrf.org.uk/knowledge/findings/socialpolicy/2i23.asp

Sacks, J. (1997) *The Politics of Hope*, London: Continuum

Social Trends, (2004) No. 34, London: ONS

Stenhouse, L. (1975), *Introduction to Curriculum Instruction and Research*, London: Heinemann.

Tawney, R.H. (1931) *Equality*, London: George Allen and Unwin.

CHAPTER 3

RELIGIOUS EDUCATION AND SOCIAL COHESION:
Does history offer lessons?

Terence Copley

SUMMARY

I N THE 1940S NATIONAL SOCIAL COHESION in the UK might have been based not merely on the exigencies of war, but also on shared Christian values and assumptions, cohesion that a tradition of mainly biblical RE was intended to foster without controversy or sectarianism (c1870 to c1960). A concomitant hypothesis might be that social cohesion in a later multicultural and plural society also has the potential to be fostered by RE, this time predicated on a world religion basis, again presented with care to avoid controversy, confessionalism and indoctrination (c1975 to the present). In both cases, some politicians have been keen to emphasise the role of RE in this (alleged) role of fostering cohesion.

After considering methodological procedural issues arising from a historical approach to the possible connection between RE and social cohesion, we examine how far politicians at key times of educational planning looked to RE as an agent for promoting this. We consider in this context the (failed) Education Bill of 1917, the 1944 Education Act and the Education (Reform) Act (1988). Politicians have sometimes adopted an instrumentalist approach to education including religious education, i.e., they have expected it to deliver particular social goals. If the political intention has been to harness RE to promote social cohesion, the historical evidence does not demonstrate unambiguously that RE has delivered this. Indeed, such an attempt might create problems for the integrity of RE.

INTRODUCTION

'I would rather appoint King Herod to look after the Save the Children fund than give the government extra powers to control education...'[1].

Ashdown's words are a reminder of how polarised UK society and educational politics have been in the recent past and could become again. In such a divided society, social cohesion is chimerical. It is relatively easy to identify factors that produce social division. But what really produces social cohesion? War is one obvious candidate on the basis of which to unite a nation. In the 1940s the substantive unity of the UK was manifested in various ways. These included the need to co-operate in a wartime setting including the threat of imminent invasion and sustained bombing (this includes the 'Dunkirk spirit'); a coalition government working effectively and the rhetoric or mythology represented in the speeches of national figureheads like Churchill or the King. But if war is one potential contributor to social cohesion, can education, and religious education in particular, reinforce it?

The years from 1945 to the present day have witnessed many changes in the UK. Among these include the steep decline of institutional Christianity, the less heralded evaporation of the Sunday school movement, the arrival of different cultures and religions, secularisation, rampant consumerist individualism, and the wider publicity and increasing acceptability for atheistic and other secular rituals such as civic marriage ceremonies. In 1988 UK society was already deeply divided when the Thatcher government – its majority reinforced by victory in the Falklands War (1982) – took upon itself to reform education. According to prevailing government rhetoric, education had fallen into the clutches of professionals ('producer capture' in Conservative Party jargon of the time) and left-wingers who were dictating 'progressive' teaching methods.

It could be argued that in the 1940s and earlier there was social cohesion based not merely on the exigencies of war, but also on shared Christian values and assumptions underpinning British society, cohesion that non-denominational biblical RE was intended to foster. This hypothesis might pertain to the period c1870 to c1960. A second hypothesis might be that social cohesion in a multicultural and plural society has the potential to be fostered by RE, this time predicated on a world religion basis. Again, RE would have to be presented with care to avoid controversy and what had become known as confessionalism, i.e., presentation that assumed or attempted to promote a particular religious viewpoint above others. This second hypothesis might pertain to the period c1975 to the present. In both time frames, speeches by politicians sought to emphasise the role of RE in this (alleged) process of fostering social cohesion. It would therefore seem at first glance that whatever the complexion of society, the appropriate RE is at least theoretically capable of bolstering social cohesion within it. This case can be argued across cultures. For example we could examine Islamic Education (the curriculum subject rather than the whole education process, both of which are referred to as Islamic Education) as it is conceived and practised in Jordan. It fits without controversy into the fabric of a strongly Islamic culture in which other religions co-exist peacefully as very small minorities.

But there are questions and complexities that make these hypotheses less secure. War does not inevitably promote social unity. The Blair government's military adventures in Iraq (2003–2009) are ample evidence of this. However, being under threat of attack in the homeland (eg post-Dunkirk 1940 and the subsequent bombing of UK mainland targets by Nazis and later by terrorists) may promote a basic and temporary social cohesion engendered by a common struggle for survival. But has there ever been enduring or deep social cohesion in the UK in post-industrial times? If so, what evidence is there that RE or its classroom predecessor, religious instruction (RI) contributed to it? The evidence is not unequivocal. Moreover, when the subject is adopted by politicians as one vehicle for promoting social cohesion, this does not necessarily operate for the good of RE. What if the price imposed by this endeavour is the neglect of truth claims or the anodyne classroom presentation of religions in order to avoid potentially divisive differences (Copley 2008, 210-212)?

Not only are the two cohesion hypotheses identified above open to challenge in themselves, historical investigation of the possible relationship between RE and social cohesion is not free from methodological problems. Social cohesion produces, in research terms, variables that make the isolation of one possible factor (RE) and any assessment of its contribution, very difficult. Moreover, in identifying potential historical evidence, whose voice shall be viewed as authoritative or even reliable and how can it be accurately recovered? We might, for instance, consider the light shed on the relationship between RE and social cohesion by agreed syllabuses, which constitute apparently clear documentary evidence. We might go on to investigate how far the attempt at promoting cohesion is programmed into these syllabuses. But no definitive research data exists, at least before OfSTED inspection results of individual schools and generic reports, to show how far agreed syllabuses have been implemented at classroom level. Or again, we might analyse professional evidence and debate such as that in articles in the *Religion and Education Quarterly* in the 1930s, but we cannot know how far these represent typical or normative thinking and practice among RE professionals at that time. Or we might examine the statements of politicians, almost all of them amateurs in RE but who have collectively exercised decisive legislative power over it, often without acting on advice from professionals. Law is clear, at least in that documents exist (although interpretations still differ, e.g. over the Christian requirements in the RE provision in the Education (Reform) Act [1988]), but there is also a large gap between rhetoric in the speeches and intentions of lawmakers and reality as perceived by many classroom practitioners.

Then there is the attempt to hear the 'person in the street' undertaken by agencies such as Mass Observation during the Second World War. 500 people wrote journal entries and sent them to MO. We might read the MO diary writings by people such as Nella Last for glimpses of their attitudes to education or religion. Or we might turn to the work of academic historians, or the memoirs of some of the key players such as R.A. 'Rab' Butler, or Winston Churchill, perhaps tempering politicians' sometimes self-congratulatory retrospection with reference to Parliamentary Hansard. Then again we might attempt to evaluate some of the major events in the history of RE by providing a social or national historical context for the period under examination (as adopted by Copley 2008). McCulloch emphasises the importance of this method (McCulloch 1994, 17). For instance, when Herbert Fisher introduced the Education Bill into the Commons (10.8.1917) the Battle of Passchendaele was recent and 3rd Ypres had recently produced a quarter of a million British casualties. Questions were being asked about the purpose and progress of the War. The power of the German army had not quite peaked. So if we wish to penetrate received opinion or to question inherited generalisation, historical methodology is necessarily complex. Therefore whichever methodological procedure is adopted, or perhaps an attempt to combine or triangulate aspects of all of these, caution will still be required in deriving judgements from historical sources. Not only are we slow to learn the proverbial lessons of history, but academic rigour needs to be applied to attempts to deduce them.

POLITICIANS, RELIGIOUS EDUCATION AND SOCIAL COHESION

Within the limitations of one chapter and those imposed by methodology, this study will restrict itself simply to an examination of how far politicians over a period of time looked to RE as an agent for promoting social cohesion. We shall examine in this context the Education Bill of 1917, the 1944 Education Act and the Education (Reform) Act (1988). Quotations from speeches that follow are taken verbatim from Parliamentary Hansard. Hansard speeches are accurately reported, but their words are not neutral. They might be made to impress political party bosses, or lobbies, or the media, or the voting public. But in the case of education legislation we might reasonably assume that these speeches at least represent political aspirations. Sometimes speeches from the Floor of the Houses of Commons and Lords appear to be heartfelt pleas and not polished propaganda.

The 1917 and 1943 legislative processes were influenced or shaped by war, including their provision for RE. In the 1987-8 legislative process UK society was deeply divided, a social civil war made more graphic by the riots over the poll tax and by the coal miners' strike. But war with another country did not directly impact on the 1988 legislation, which has more in common with the circumstances surrounding the 1902 Act (see below).

The 1917 Education Bill

Opening for the government on the 1917 Education Bill was H.A.L. Fisher as President of the Board of Education in Lloyd George's coalition government. Fisher's was not then a high status post. He emphasised the direct connection between the measure and the war. It had been 'framed to repair the intellectual wastage caused...and to reduce industrial pressure on child life' [600,000 children had left school early to start employment]. But he clearly wanted to 'avoid what is known as "the denominational question"' i.e. the bitter denominational controversies that had dogged earlier legislation on school provision, religious teaching and worship for much of the nineteenth century. Prime Minister Arthur Balfour had referred to this when he introduced the 1902 Education Bill, mentioning the damage caused by militant denominationalists and militant anti-denominationalists. Leader of the Opposition in 1902, Henry Campbell-Bannerman, could only agree with Balfour that education had proved itself to be highly divisive. It was a history that influenced subsequent politicians strongly in their desire to avoid further battles on the issue of religion.

By 1917 the public and politicians, Fisher claimed, were most anxious not to fan into flame 'the old religious controversy.' Fisher emphasised repeatedly that the Bill was not revolutionary, neither was it intended to replace the landmark Balfour Education Act of 1902. No change in the provision for RE was proposed. But the government claimed not to be ignoring 'the spiritual aspects of education' and 'the increased feeling of social solidarity which has been created by the War.' 'We *assume* that education should be the education of the whole man [sic], spiritually, intellectually and physically' [my italics]. He appealed to common ground. The war, Fisher claimed, had brought the previously combative denominations closer together. The desire for better education was not about higher wages, or in order for people to rise above their class, 'always a vulgar ambition' (!). It was because people know that 'in the treasures of the mind they can find an aid to good citizenship, a source of pure enjoyment and a refuge from the necessary hardships of a life spent in the midst of clanging machines in our hideous cities of toil.' Was this genuine endeavour or mere rhetoric? Whichever it was, after orchestrated opposition by industrialists, LEAs and sections of the media, the Education Bill was withdrawn. A truncated version was passed in 1918. Out of this process emerges the commentary that religion was perceived by the politicians – with good reason from the past – as potentially divisive and that they were intent that Religious Instruction must take care to avoid this.

The 1944 Education Act

Introducing the 1943 Education Bill, President of the Board of Education R. A. 'Rab' Butler stated that the whole of his experience in working with collaborators 'whether in the country or at Whitehall, has been that personal, sectarian and political feelings have been subordinated to the interests of the children. This is a very remarkable fact to recall.' But his memoirs (Butler 1971) suggest that it was not a 'fact' at all and he had trouble especially with the Roman Catholic hierarchy about his proposed religious settlement. He had to placate them with dignity in several icy encounters. One of Butler's aims for the Act was to induce in children 'a new love for those spiritual values which makes the human personality.' Referring in the debate to 'the tragic history of [religious] misunderstanding and controversy', Westminster Abbey MP Sir Harold Webbe welcomed the Bill. He hoped it would help to revive spiritual and personal values in society and national life and 'open the way to a more closely knit society', in other words, social cohesion. But mismatch between 'fine talk and reality' was noted in the debate itself by a Mr Sexton, MP for Barnard Castle [forename not revealed]. He reflected on his 44 years as a teacher of classes of 40 children aged three to eight without any training or time for study. At the time of the 1902 Education Act when Sexton would have been teaching, 55% of the teaching force was untrained.

Richard Acland, Barnstaple MP, took issue with society itself: 'You cannot educate for citizenship when the standards of righteousness exemplified by the principles of your society are lower than the standard of righteousness accepted by the general mass of your people.' The real principle governing the past, Acland argued, has been the promotion of self-interest but the principle for the future ought to be the service of the community. His father, F.D. Acland MP, had spoken in the 1917 debate to support the training of the intellect as of benefit to the nation, not merely to army commanders. Speaking in the 1943 debate one such former commander, Lt Colonel Sir Thomas Moore, MP for Ayr Burghs, wanted primary school RI to be limited to 'the accepted Christian principles of truth, honesty, kindness, clean living and self-respect.' He represents a strand of thinking that saw Christian morality rather than Christian doctrine as the unifying key and RI as one agent for its delivery. Underlying this speech is the notion that behaviour counts more than belief and that while morality can unite, religion can easily divide.

Does this approach via Hansard triangulate with other evidence? Nella Last was a contemporary non-churchgoing 'ordinary' person who did not think of herself as a Christian, did not believe in Heaven or Hell, admired Jesus and did believe in a supernatural power she calls variously Force or Plan or Rhythm. She occasionally practised fortune telling and believed that people went on after death, 'somewhere where we got the chances we threw away, or never had, to grow' (Last in Malcolmson, P. and Malcolmson, R.[eds.] 2008, 291). In other words, a range of evidence of which hers provides an individual sample suggests that while Christianity and the established church were respected, profession of orthodox Christian doctrine was not a common denominator even at a time when the UK perceived itself as a 'Christian country'. Children were sent to Sunday school by parents who usually stayed at home and many people seemed content at most to adhere to what they considered the Christian ethic to be.

Corelli Barnett interprets the 1944 Act as merely carrying forward the prevailing outlook and beliefs of the establishment via the Norwood

Report, which had appeared ten days after the White Paper presaging the Act. Harold Dent, on the other hand, sees the Act as liberal-evolutionary reform, deservedly a landmark. Non-denominational religious instruction was for the first time made statutory, although this move was at least as much to do with a tidying up process from earlier legislation (1870 and 1902) that had omitted to do this.

Butler appealed to what he considered to be the wishes of parents, i.e. that their children should be given 'a grounding of the principles of the Christian faith as it ought to be practised in this country.' In other words, he saw himself as appealing to a unifying principle that already existed, not working to promote a new one. Opponents of the legislation would argue that by establishing separate types of schooling at age eleven – the tripartite system of grammar, technical and modern schools – it was the very opposite of social cohesion, with places at the much favoured grammar schools only for a minority of children. 'Failing' the eleven plus examination ensured inferiority of opportunity. In terms of RE, this legislation acknowledges that religion has a capacity to divide but also to unite around a non-denominational approach to teaching 'basic' Christianity. But Butler's phrase 'the Christian faith as it ought to be practised', i.e. not as it is actually practised, itself is indicative of a mismatch between reality and intention.

The 1988 Education Reform Act (ERA)

Jack Priestley has drawn attention to the paltriness of the intellectual thinking behind the Education Reform Act (1988) in contrast to the high quality of the education debates in the House of Commons in 1943, the latter held at a time when bombs were falling on London. [In Copley T. *et al* 1991, 8]. Commentary on ERA by religious educators has focussed mainly on the April 1988 House of Lords debates on the provision for religious education and collective worship (e.g. Copley 2008, 134 – 146). Other implications from the legislation have been less noted. First, that like the 1902 Education Act, ERA was pushed through Parliament by a government with a large Conservative majority in the face of considerable opposition inside and outside Parliament. In the case of the 1902 Act, this was one factor that led to the government's defeat in the 1906 general election.

ERA was pushed through without time for proper consultation and with opposition even from Conservatives. Kenneth Baker, Secretary of State for Education, by then a very high status post, introducing the Bill, quoted

Disraeli: 'Upon the education of the people of this country, the fate of this country depends.' He continued with a series of combative attacks on the other political parties followed by the call to reform, for a national curriculum, raising standards and extending parental choice. Edward Heath, Conservative MP for Old Bexley and Sidcup and a former prime minister, noted that Disraeli could appeal to a one nation philosophy – and so, he said, could Balfour and Butler. But, Heath argued, ERA was a travesty of that, 'a caricature of parliamentary government ...The extent of the Secretary of State's power [immensely strengthened in the Act] will be overwhelming.' It would be the enemy of unity and cohesion.

Ashdown estimated that by this legislation Secretary of State Baker would acquire 170 new powers. The proposals were seen by other opponents as crudely revisionist and instrumentalist (Dafydd Thomas, MP for Meirionnydd Nant Conwy) and a toxic mixture of free market ideas and centralism (Andrew Smith, MP for Oxford East). Norman Tebbitt (right wing Conservative MP for Chingford) saw it as 'a great reform bill.' At the Second Reading division, the Ayes were 348, the Noes 241. With such a split, it is clear that no consensus existed. The proposals for RE were confused. Baker said he was strengthening the 1944 Act by making RE provision mandatory, but it already was. In ERA RE was placed outside the national curriculum in the vaguely defined basic curriculum. Legally this was merely the national curriculum plus RE. So while the whole of the rest of the curriculum was centralised and altered, no change was proposed for RE. The House of Lords tried to influence its content but not its curriculum position. They did not seem to see that re-writing the curriculum map and leaving one subject unchanged effectively changes the position of that subject too.

There was no social or moral consensus in wider society to which legislators could appeal and there was no longer any consensus on religion. Those involved in framing the RE legislation seem to have been driven by the desire that children should not lose their right to a Christian heritage, or to hear the claims of Christianity. But the new legal requirement to teach 'the principal religions' represented in the UK was evidence of some awareness of pluralism and of a multicultural society. Social cohesion was not remotely on Baker's agenda, but by legislating to include world religion teaching in RE, the door was open to professionals to try to implement this in such a way as to promote understanding, tolerance and multicultural perspectives. What was to prove more crucial in ERA was how the RE professionals interpreted and applied the Act rather than any government commitment to the promotion of cohesion. But promotion of 'tolerance' had featured in some pre-Act deliberations, e.g. Keith Joseph's Department of Education and Science *Better Schools document* (1985).

The withdrawal clause

The parental withdrawal clause was retained in all the Bills and Acts we have surveyed. By 2009 it has become an archaic survival from bitter denominational controversies of the past and the days of religious *instruction* – from which in a democracy a protective opt-out provision is both logical and desirable. It has no defensible place within a context of religious *education* in world religions and secular alternatives and a culture in which complaints can easily be made about heavily biased teaching. There is no logic in parents being able to exclude their children from an inclusive curriculum area. Logic requires the right to withdrawal to be removed, otherwise extended to cover all curriculum subjects (Copley 2008, 226–228). But the right of withdrawal survives and is unlikely for political reasons to be removed in the foreseeable future. Proposals for its removal could be portrayed by defenders of the withdrawal provision as a human rights issue. That would be a misunderstanding of the purpose of 21st century UK RE. This debate lies outside the remit of this chapter. But the very existence and certainly the exercise of the right of withdrawal works against any contribution RE might make to social cohesion. Those who might most benefit from any cohesive aspects of religious education – the children of rabid sectarians in any religion or those of militant atheists – are the very ones whose parents are most likely to remove them from the RE classroom. History has on this occasion bequeathed a problem for the present.

CONCLUSION

Does evidence from the past, viewed through the political lens that we have chosen, support the view that RE can contribute to social cohesion? Gordon Brown certainly looked to RE to contribute in a parliamentary speech (14.11.2007) on preventing UK-born *terrorism* when he emphasised the role RE has in 'making sure children learn about all faiths.' He did not point out that this was to be accomplished on 5% or less curriculum time. The landmark educational Acts and the failed Bill examined in this chapter are multifarious. RE may have repeatedly been an essential component of educational legislation, but it has never been the primary or the driving one. It is easy for RE commentators to overlook that the key driving force in 1917 was the raising of the school leaving age to 14 and the attempt to achieve universal part-time education until the age of 16. In 1943 the key driving factors were the desire to implement the tripartite system and to establish the roles of LEAs and the dual system. In 1988 the drivers were an enforced national curriculum with national testing and the attack on LEAs by the creation of grant-maintained ('opted out') schools.

Politicians have understandably attended to the 'bigger picture' in education legislation and have sometimes seen religion as a lobby to be placated or resisted. Their control over education in the twentieth century moved relentlessly from finance to structure to detailed curriculum content. In addition, they have sometimes taken an instrumentalist approach to education including religious education, i.e. they have expected it to deliver particular social goals. Their speeches suggest that it is a case that better health education would mean fewer teenage pregnancies and sexually transmitted disease; better RE might mean more tolerance, less terrorism. Another recent example of instrumentalism in education was the introduction by the Brown government of cookery for all into Key Stage 3 in 2008 as part of moves to combat national obesity.

1988 was a watershed. Since then, politicians under Conservative and Labour administrations have continued to behave in a messianic and heavily prescriptive way in their forays into education. The underlying assumption has been that the education process is a machine or conveyor, which with adjustments as required can be programmed to deliver 'goods' i.e. things that are deemed to be socially good. In this dominating factory mindset, paradoxically growing ever stronger after the collapse of most of the manufacturing base in the UK, RE is likely to be expected to deliver socially cohesive values and to 'control' the religions that it deals with in the classroom by presenting them as socially harmless. But globally religions are volatile and vibrant, unable and sometimes unwilling to be defined and hemmed in by governments or syllabuses. So a clash of agendas might lie ahead, with curriculum RE caught into a vortex which might be part of the next defining phase of the social history of the UK.

NOTES

1. Paddy Ashdown, MP for Yeovil and Leader of the Liberal Democrat Party, speaking in the 2nd Reading debate on the Education (Reform) Bill, House of Commons, 1.12.1987.

REFERENCES

Barnett, C. (1986) *The Audit of War*, London: Macmillan.

Butler, R.A. 'Rab' (1971) *The Art of the Possible*, London: Macmillan.

Copley, T., Priestley, J., Wadman, D., Coddington, V. (1991) *Forms of Assessment in Religious Education*, Exeter: The FARE Project, University of Exeter.

Copley, T. (2008) *Teaching Religion: Sixty Years of Religious Education in England and Wales*, Exeter, University of Exeter Press.

Dent, H. C. (1944) *The Education Act 1944*, London: University of London Press.

Department of Education and Science (1985) *Better Schools*, London: HMSO.

Malcolmson, P. and Malcolmson, R. (eds.) (2008) *Nella Last's Peace*, London: Profile Books Ltd.

McCulloch, G. (1994) *Educational Reconstruction: The 1944 Act and the 21st Century*, Ilford: The Woburn Press.

Parliamentary Hansard, London: HMSO.

CHAPTER 4

PATRIOTISM, CITIZENSHIP AND MULTICULTURALISM:
Political discourse and the curriculum

Audrey Osler

SUMMARY

THIS CHAPTER EXAMINES the developing political discourse on patriotism, citizenship and multiculturalism in Britain since 1997, and particularly following the 2001 attacks in the US and the 2005 London bombings. These events and their aftermath, including wars in Afghanistan and Iraq, have shifted the focus of political and media discourse on race relations in Britain and given an international dimension to public debate about diversity and belonging. Their impact continues to be felt in the school curriculum.

In this period, there has been increased public debate in Britain on citizenship, national identity, multiculturalism and the integration of minorities. Here the focus is on the implications for citizenship and history education, on the one hand, and for faith-based schooling and for religious education, on the other. The inter-relationships between these curriculum areas are often implicit. This chapter seeks to explore and identify some specific contributions of each of these areas to community cohesion.

A range of commentators, including senior government ministers, have focused on the role of schools in creating a united and cohesive society and suggested how the school curriculum might be directed to strengthen 'Britishness' and 'British values'. This chapter focuses on the speeches of key government figures, notably Prime Ministers Tony Blair and Gordon

Brown, and on the ways in which they apply their ideas to the school curriculum. It explores the potential tensions which arise when history, citizenship and religious education are conceptualised so as to support a project of national unity.

Official concerns about the radicalisation of Muslim youth, and the policy implications of these concerns in education, add to the complexity of the situation. Such concerns arguably conflate fundamentalist religious belief and political extremism. This chapter reflects on discourses about separation and communication, applied to minorities in general, and to Muslims and to Muslim women in particular. Political discourse is contextualised within the race relations legislation of the period.

EDUCATION AND SOCIAL COHESION: CITIZENSHIP, HISTORY AND RELIGIOUS EDUCATION

Citizenship education, history and religious education are three distinct areas of the school curriculum, and the ways in which each is conceived and taught is likely to have a direct impact on social cohesion, both within and beyond the nation-state. An official report *Curriculum review: diversity and citizenship* (the Ajegbo report) (DfES 2007a), was published at a time of heightened media debate about national identity, security, and the threat of radicalisation among British Muslim youth. An official press release confirmed it 'was commissioned after concern about growing extremism and division in society after the London terrorist bombings' (DfES 2007b). Its main recommendation, an additional strand to the citizenship education framework for England on 'identity and diversity: living together in the UK' has since been adopted, complementing three pre-existing strands: social and moral responsibility; community involvement, including service to the community; and political literacy or the knowledge, skills and values to be effective in public life.

This official response to addressing extremism identified citizenship education as the primary curricular vehicle for promoting social cohesion, or what is more commonly referred to in Britain as 'community cohesion'. The vision is to promote cohesion at local and national levels through a strengthening of national identity. An injection of national history and the tying together of a national story and contemporary citizenship is part of this vision.

The Ajegbo report contains some examples of schemes of work which attempt to link citizenship learning with historical enquiry. One exemplar poses an interesting and no doubt legitimate question for the citizenship classroom: 'Should the UK pay compensation for the transatlantic slave trade?' (DfES 2007: 107). This is not, however, a historical question, in the same way as 'What impact did the slave trade have on eighteenth century Britain?' or 'What was the role of the English Church in the justification and maintenance of slavery during the eighteenth and nineteenth centuries?' These latter questions can be answered (in a variety of ways) by examining historical sources, but the answer to the question about government compensation for slavery cannot be answered simply by appealing to historical evidence. It also requires us to engage with today's social, economic and political issues; to consider the practical issues (who would benefit?) and examine the symbolic significance of compensation. It might equally be interpreted as a moral question, making it a legitimate issue for both political and religious education. Unfortunately, the scheme of work fails to distinguish historical questions from contemporary political ones.

Another sub-question: 'How important were British abolitionists in helping to end the transatlantic slave trade?' invites students to compare the UK abolitionist movement with 'pressure movements such as the African slave revolts' and to compare the revolts with 'contemporary groups that lobby for and promote social justice through human rights (e.g. Amnesty International and Human Rights Watch)'. That the 'slave revolts' can be described as 'pressure movements' distorts the sustained armed resistance which took place and to which the authorities responded with ruthless massacres (Fryer 1989). The scheme of work discusses the legacy of the slave trade, moving from 'the economic prosperity created' to the 'evolution of a "multicultural" UK' (DfES 2007: 107) ignoring more than a century of British imperial history.

There are a number of difficulties in seeking to harness history to serve the purposes of citizenship learning. While learners can study history to develop their thinking about moral issues, as Claire (2005) has so ably illustrated with reference to the education of young children, it is inappropriate to *distort* history, as in the above examples, in an attempt to develop moral thinking or understand modern democratic practices. Understanding history may strengthen democratic commitment, but an attempt to present one 'shared story' threatens historical enquiry, since there are generally competing sources of evidence which need to be analysed and many stories or perspectives to consider. A single story may serve to exclude and marginalise specific interests; presenting and analysing multiple sources is one of the strengths of history education in Britain. A study of history may foster democratic values and patriotism in some learners; equally, it may cause other learners to question those values.

Since 2001, the multicultural settlement reached in the final decades of the twentieth century is increasingly challenged in Britain and some other European nations, though it remains part of mainstream political discourse and policy in other nations, such as Canada, the United States and Australia (Reid *et al.*, 2010). Schools are required to address persistent inequalities, and the role of faith-based schooling has come under closer public and political scrutiny.

A Runnymede Trust project which set out to examine whether a school system which includes faith schools can promote equality and cohesion, in keeping with legal requirements (Berkeley, 2008; Osler, 2007) considered the role of religious education (RE) in realising this goal, in both faith-based and non-faith-based institutions. Respondents from a variety of faith communities were able to articulate how RE and the wider ethos of faith-based schools educated young people in line with their parents' specific religious convictions, but were less confident in articulating how the values prompted in such schools contribute to the wider community of citizens.

Berkeley (2008: 28) concludes that faith schools are 'more effective in educating for a single vision rather than opening dialogue about a shared vision' that would support community cohesion and build a common culture of human rights. Many respondents from faith-based schools felt that religious education was an adequate *alternative* to citizenship education, failing to see that citizenship learning extends beyond moral education to include political efficacy and political literacy. While teaching virtues such as compassion and generosity may be critical for learning to live together, practising these virtues in an unequal society is, in itself, insufficient. What is termed 'education for cosmopolitan citizenship' (Osler and Vincent, 2002; Osler and Starkey 2003 and 2005) centrally includes a deeper understanding of 'our global interconnectedness' which equips young people to 'contribute and engage constructively with difference at local, national and international levels, while at the same time acknowledging our shared humanity and human rights' (Osler, 2007: 15). Education for cosmopolitan citizenship inevitably involves addressing issues of power in our interdependent, interconnected yet unequal world.

51

Official guidance mentions religious education (RE) as a curricular tool which can support schools' efforts to promote community cohesion, whereby children can be taught to value differences and challenge prejudice, discrimination and stereotyping. The school inspection agency, OfSTED (2007), reports considerable variations in the quality of RE teaching and learning across schools in England, observing that RE cannot make an effective contribution to community cohesion without significant reform. In particular, RE needs to acknowledge diversity within faith traditions and to address the social realities of religion, rather than focus largely on ethics or ideals. Importantly, RE cannot ignore controversies and should not encourage young people to look uncritically at religion as a positive force.

Currently, the type of religious education a young person receives is dependent on the school s/he attends. In maintained, non-faith schools it is taught according to a locally agreed syllabus, and the government encourages the teaching of the tenets of Christianity and the five major religions represented in the UK (QCDA, 2009). Although many faith schools teach about other religions there is no obligation for them to do so. As there is no common standard or national framework and therefore no agreed entitlement for all children, it is particularly difficult to assess the degree to which young people have the opportunity to develop a proper understanding of society's secular and multi-faith characteristics. An agreed national framework would ensure a degree of transparency in all publicly funded schools.

In a multi-faith society concerned with promoting social cohesion, it is important that all professionals working with young people, including teachers, are confident in addressing issues related to faith and diversity. It would be insufficient to rely on RE teachers to take responsibility for handling questions relating to faith diversity. All teachers need skills in this field. Yet the Runnymede project confirmed that many feel uncomfortable and ill-prepared in handling questions of faith (Osler, 2007).

CITIZENSHIP, NATIONAL IDENTITY AND MULTICULTURALISM

In a lecture in December 2006, one of a series on 'our nation's future', Prime Minister Blair (2006) asserted the importance of multiculturalism, using the words 'multicultural' and 'multiculturalism' six times, all positively. This was significant, since other government ministers had questioned Britain's multiculturalism. Ruth Kelly (2006) then Secretary of State for Communities and Local Government, observed: 'we have moved from a period of uniform consensus on the value of multiculturalism, to one where we can encourage that debate by questioning whether it is encouraging separateness ... In our attempt to avoid imposing a single British identity and culture, have we ended up with some communities living in isolation of each other, with no common bonds between them?' Her sentiments echoed those of Trevor Phillips (2005), then Chair of the Commission for Racial Equality (CRE), who suggested Britain needs to abandon a model of multiculturalism which leads people to live separate lives. Phillips' warning, widely reported in the media, was that: 'we are sleepwalking our way to segregation. We are becoming strangers to each other, and we are leaving communities to be marooned outside the mainstream'.

Drawing on the US experience and on the example of the poor and predominantly African-American victims of hurricane Katrina, Phillips warned of the dangers of a segregated and unequal society in which the average black child attends a largely black school and the average white person returns home to a largely white suburb. Hurricane Katrina challenged the myth of integration based on black success stories revealing that poor black people were both invisible to and forgotten by powerful decision-makers. Phillips suggests that:

> '... for all of us who care about racial equality and integration, America is not our dream, but our nightmare. ... There I think the focus is purely on equal rights for different groups. Amongst America's hyphenated identities, the part of their identity that marks them out as different seems to have become as important, even more important, than the part that binds them together.' (Phillips 2005)

For Phillips, it is shared values which bind the British together. Calling for a focus on these values (defined as democracy, freedom of speech, and equality) and on common traditions (a common language, good manners, care of children, ironic humour targeting politicians, priests and do-gooders) Phillips argues that diverse lifestyles compatible with these common values are fully accepted in contemporary Britain: 'No-one tells us how to speak, how to dress, what we should eat or how we should worship'. He argues against a model of multiculturalism which is relativist and which permits behaviour such as child cruelty and abuse, in the name of cultural or religious freedom.

Phillips' critique of multiculturalism is that not only does it promote segregation but it also disguises and neglects structural inequality. One problem is that this critique has been taken up by media commentators to back a call for uniformity and assimilation. In a context in which Islamophobia flourishes, this call for uniformity amounts to an attack on Muslims, who are portrayed as a homogeneous group threatening 'our values' and 'our way of life' (Richardson 2004; Jawad and Benn, 2003). In fact, structural inequalities and poverty go a long way towards explaining the segregation that exists in some towns and cities, for people do not generally choose to live in disadvantaged neighbourhoods but are constrained by a range of social and economic factors.

A second difficulty lies in Phillips' suggestion that multiculturalism has failed. Britain has never had an explicit government policy of multiculturalism, such as that practised in Canada, for example. There is no clear UK multicultural policy which we can assess. It is therefore difficult to assert that British multiculturalism has failed. If multiculturalism has failed, it is logical to abandon it. If, however, Britain has experimented with imperfect forms of multiculturalism then these can, theoretically, be revised and adapted. But what has not been tried cannot be said to have failed.

At a local level multiculturalism has been adopted on a piecemeal basis in Britain. Education is one policy area where, until the establishment of a national curriculum for schools in the late 1980s, attempts were made in some English local authorities to introduce multiculturalism into the curriculum (Figueroa 2004; Tomlinson 2005). But these efforts were not uniform or consistent across the country, and were largely restricted to schooling. Multiculturalism cannot be blamed, for example, for a tendency towards segregation in certain parts of the university sector. Universities have been very slow, for example, to meet their obligations under the Race Relations [Amendment] Act 2000 (RRAA), but the sector as a whole has shown little interest in multiculturalism.

The expansion of faith schooling under the Labour government might be interpreted as a multicultural policy. When Labour came to power in 1997 there were over 6,000 faith schools in the state-maintained sector, representing just less than one in three of all state schools. The vast majority are primary schools. The Church of England had (and continues to have) the largest representation, with significant numbers of Roman Catholic and a small number of Jewish schools. In 1998 two Islamic primary schools became publicly funded, with this development being justified in terms of equity, rather than presented as an explicit multicultural policy. Since 2001, there has been a small expansion of publicly funded faith schools. Under the Education and Inspections Act 2006 there are increased opportunities for faith organisations to seek public funding. Interestingly, faith schooling is something which is absent from Phillips's critique of multiculturalism.

A third difficulty in Phillips' critique lies in the appeal to common values, without identifying the basis of those values, and to common traditions such as a common language and the care of children. While Britain has a common language it might equally be characterised as a nation-state comprising many bilingual and multilingual as well as monolingual communities. The evidence does not support a special British tradition of caring for children. The UK has been regularly criticised for its failure to protect and guarantee the rights and well-being of children, and was ranked bottom of an international league of developed countries for children's well-being (UNICEF 2007). An appeal to common values needs to be explicit in the basis and source of those values, as in any society there are likely to be examples of real life situations in which competing claims need to be resolved.

BRITISH SOCIETY, ISLAM AND SHARED VALUES

One year after Phillips asserted that in the UK diverse lifestyles and dress were accepted, a senior British government figure suggested that some Muslim women should consider changing their dress code. Jack Straw, MP for Blackburn, where around 25 per cent of voters are Muslim, claimed that wearing the *niqab* to conceal the face could be seen as a 'visible statement of separation and of difference'. He wrote that 'wearing the full veil was bound to make better, positive relations between the two communities more difficult' and suggested that asking women to consider showing their mouths and noses led to more effective communication (Straw 2006). His remarks were widely reported, attracting extensive national and international debate.[1]

Significantly, there is a link between the new popular discourse around multiculturalism and that which focuses on the choice of dress adopted by some Muslim women. We are asked to consider the implications for community cohesion of both multiculturalism and the *niqab*. In this discourse, both multiculturalism and the *niqab* are associated with 'separation' and with problems of 'communication' between communities. Muslim communities, and especially Muslim *women*, are seen as isolating themselves; multiculturalism and Islam (through specific symbols) are both blamed as causing us to live 'parallel lives'. If women wearing the *niqab*, or indeed the *hijab*, are so isolated and unable to communicate, how do we explain away their presence in the supermarket queue, as university students or working in schools?

As Mondal (2008) argues, the apparent crisis of multiculturalism reflects the fact that Islam itself is seen as a problem. Islam is seen as the limiting case for multiculturalism, testing some citizens' 'duty to integrate' (Blair 2006) and sign up to British values. Gordon Brown argues:

> '...we have to face uncomfortable facts that there were British citizens, British born, apparently integrated into our communities, who were prepared to maim and kill fellow British citizens, irrespective of their religion.' (Brown 2006).

For him, this brings into question British policies on integration and leads him to question the balance between unity and diversity in public policy:

> 'July 7th has rightly led to calls for all of us, including moderates in the Islamic community, to stand up to extremism ... terrorism in our midst means that debates, which sometimes may be seen as dry, about Britishness and our model of integration clearly now have a new urgency.' (Brown *ibid*).

Just as Prime Minister Blair (2006) asserted that the British were 'not going to be taken for a ride' by extremist Muslims who seek to undermine British values, so other European nation-states also see Islam as a threat to their way of life: French republican values are threatened by school girls who wear headscarves (Lorcerie 2005); the Dutch question their model of liberal tolerance, and reveal 'everyday racism' (Essed 2002) which targets Muslim and other visible minority citizens as outsiders; and the Danish media divides Danish citizens into two groups: Danes, who are assumed to adhere to Danish democratic values, and Muslims, who apparently threaten these same values.

SOCIAL COHESION, LEGISLATION AND POLITICAL LEADERSHIP

To contextualise the discourse of senior Labour figures, it is worth reflecting on the achievements of the government on race equality and their leadership in this area. Importantly, the New Labour government introduced the Race Relations [Amendment] Act 2000 (RRAA), which extended existing race relations legislation to cover government and the armed forces and which requires public bodies to promote race equality. This legislation followed the Stephen Lawrence Inquiry report

(Macpherson 1999) which identified institutional racism in British society. The report found institutional racism in all walks of British life, including the police service and education. It proposed 70 recommendations to break down institutionalised racism and it attracted cross-party political support and considerable public goodwill. Unfortunately, the RRAA, the legal vehicle for reform, has not been fully implemented. OfSTED (2005: 26) noted that in 2004/05 more than a quarter of education authorities were failing to comply with race relations legislation.

Before 2005, challenging racism in education was largely seen as a legal or moral issue rather than being a fundamental aspect of democratic practice, as in Sweden (Osler and Starkey 2000). Although education was a stated priority for the Labour government from 1997, questions of racial justice and diversity were entirely absent from the Prime Minister's speeches on education until December 2006.[2] An analysis of speeches on the 10 Downing Street website after 11 September 2001 shows the number of Prime Ministerial words on racial justice increased three-fold, yet he addressed mainstream audiences just twice; the first was his first address to the Welsh Assembly when he discussed military action in Afghanistan and the need to defeat Al Qaeda. He acknowledged and condemned attacks on Muslims in Britain following 11 September and stressed 'Now is a time for people of all races and all faiths in Britain to stand together'. Defeating Al Qaeda, argued the Prime Minister, meant standing up for our values:

> 'We will not fail and we will do it all because we believe in our values of justice, tolerance and respect for all regardless of race, religion or creed just as passionately as they [Al Qaeda] believe in fanatical hatred of Jews, Christians and any Moslems who don't share their perverse view of Islam.' (Blair 2001).

In 2004 he addressed the Confederation of British Industry (CBI) on the subject of immigration, calling for the celebration of 'the major achievements of migrants in this country and the success of our uniquely British model of diversity'. But he reminded his audience of the government's

> '...explicit expectation that rights must be balanced by responsibilities. That there are clear obligations that go alongside British residency and ultimately citizenship – to reject extremism and intolerance and make a positive contribution to UK society' (Blair 2004).

The implication appears to be that immigrants need a special reminder of their obligations and duties, and that they may be less committed to democratic values and more prone to 'extremism and intolerance' than British-born citizens. On the subject of racism the Prime Minister added: 'The vast bulk of the British people are not racist. It is in their nature to be moderate'. As in his 2006 speech on multiculturalism and integration, Blair seems to imply that racism is simply an interpersonal issue. He observes:

'Racism has, for the most part, been kicked out of sport. Offensive remarks and stupid stereotypes have been driven out of public conversation. The basic courtesies, in other words, have been extended to all people.' (Blair 2006)

The institutional racism acknowledged just a few years earlier at the time of the report of the Stephen Lawrence Inquiry report appears forgotten, as does the electoral success of the extreme right British National Party (BNP) in local elections and (since his speech) in the 2009 European Parliamentary elections. Gordon Brown, in a speech on developing an inclusive concept of Britishness, acknowledges the need 'to tackle prejudice, bigotry and the incitement to hatred and to do far more to tackle discrimination and promote inclusion'. He adds:

'there should now be greater focus on tackling inequalities in job and educational opportunities, driving up the educational attainment of pupils from ethnic minorities and a more comprehensive new deal effort to tackle unacceptably high unemployment in areas of high ethnic minority populations.' (Brown 2006)

From the year 2000, with the passing of the RRAA, until after the July 2005 attacks, we see little evidence of leadership in promoting race equality in the discourse of senior politicians. After July 2005 there is a new concern. It is not just immigrants, but British born Muslim citizens who are then identified as being vulnerable to 'extremism and intolerance'. From 2005, concerns about 'home grown' terrorists lead to a greater focus on the school curriculum.

There is no real understanding of structural racism or its impact in undermining efforts to promote unity and integration in these speeches. Policies which aim to strengthen a sense of belonging, either to the local community or to the nation but which fail to address deprivation, racism and inequality are likely to be met, at best, with scepticism. At worst they may further alienate those they seek to include, as acknowledged by the government appointed Commission on Integration and Cohesion (COIC), which observes:

'Integration and cohesion policies cannot be a substitute for national policies to reduce deprivation and provide people with more opportunities: tackling inequality is an absolute precondition for integration and cohesion.' (COIC, 2007: 21)

In contrast to government ministers, Trevor Phillips makes proposals for new strategies to tackle institutional racism, acknowledging, for example, racial inequalities and discrimination facing Travellers and Gypsies (Phillips 2005).

Issues of diversity, democracy, patriotism and citizenship are given a new emphasis in response to the threat of global terrorism and to a perceived need to integrate Muslim citizens in particular. The tension between policy initiatives which promote unity (cohesion) and those which support diversity is not confined to Britain, as Blair acknowledges: 'we are not on our own in trying to find the right balance between integration and diversity. There is a global agonising on the subject'. (Blair, 8 Dec, 2006)

PATRIOTISM, NATIONALISM AND THE CURRICULUM

Gordon Brown invokes the concept of patriotism in his proposals to promote citizenship and British values through the teaching of national history. Generally, talk of patriotism is avoided in Britain and other western European countries, where it is too readily associated with fascism and ethno-nationalism of the 1930s and with the extreme right today. Brown argues for a new kind of patriotism based on shared values, rather than on race or ethnicity:

> 'And just as in war time a sense of common patriotic purpose inspired people to do what is necessary, so in peace time a strong modern sense of patriotism and patriotic purpose which binds people together can motivate and inspire. And this British patriotism is, in my view, founded not on ethnicity nor race, not just on institutions we share and respect, but on enduring ideals which shape our view of ourselves and our communities – values which in turn influence the way our institutions evolve.' (Brown, 14 January, 2006)

This is a call for an explicit new vision of Britain's future, something which itself might be judged somewhat un-British, given that so much in British society is implicit. Brown calls for a range of symbols to promote patriotism, including a national day and the union flag, which he argues must be reclaimed from far right and racist political parties, and adopted as a symbol of unity, tolerance and inclusion. He criticises those on the left who have eschewed patriotism and allowed it to be defined by conservatives as reactionary, individualistic, a defence of backward looking institutions, and xenophobic. He assumes participation and civic engagement will grow from feelings of patriotism.

Some seven months after the London attacks, Gordon Brown (2006) gave a widely reported speech to the Fabian Society on 'The future of Britishness' in which he listed shared British values as 'liberty, responsibility, fairness'. In December that year Prime Minister Blair (2006) identified British values as 'belief in democracy, the rule of law, tolerance, equal treatment for all'. It is not clear what is peculiarly British about these values, which are in keeping with international human rights principles and might be the expressed values of any modern democracy. Indeed, this was recognised by Jack Straw MP, in an article in which he argues that British nationality is based on common civic values:

> 'The values I have talked about are not exclusively British or indeed western: they are common human values reflected in the charter of the United Nations. What is uniquely British is the process by which these principles and ideals were gradually applied here.' (Straw 2007)

Straw argues that to strengthen citizenship and properly understand those values within the context of the UK, we need to tell the 'British story' of democracy so that we understand, through history, how democracy has developed in the UK context. Nevertheless, these democratic civic values are those of the international community, as expressed in the UN Charter and expounded in the Universal Declaration of Human Rights 1948 and in subsequent human rights instruments ratified by Britain. Straw, like Brown, argues that civic values are contextualised through history. Thus an understanding of contemporary citizenship implies a degree of historical knowledge. If we accept this argument and apply it to the school curriculum then education for citizenship and history education are inextricably linked.

Political leaders have generally been less inclined to comment freely on religious education, although Blair (2006) made an exception to this, while in office, and has since leaving office supported RE through his Faith Foundation. As Prime Minister he emphasised the role that RE can play in promoting 'integration':

> 'The 1988 Education Reform Act states that religious education in all community schools should be broadly Christian in character but that it should include study of the other major religions. There is currently a voluntary agreement with faith schools on this basis.
>
> Faith schools also naturally give religious instruction in their own faith. It is important that in doing so, they teach tolerance and respect for other faiths and the Education Department will discuss with the faith groups how this is

achieved and implemented, according to new national guidelines. ... [These guidelines will] marginalize those very small numbers who want to teach religious education in a way which misleads and misrepresents other faiths.' (Blair 2006)

Yet there is no clear evidence that all faith schools are adhering to this 'voluntary agreement' to teach a multi-faith RE syllabus and school inspectors argue that current arrangements for RE curricula need reform if the subject is to contribute to community cohesion (OfSTED 2007).

An equally problematic issue is whether those faith schools where the student population is drawn predominantly or exclusively from one faith community can educate effectively for community cohesion by twinning with a school of a different faith, as Blair proposed. Twinning is now expected of schools with homogeneous student populations as a means of fulfilling obligations under the Education and Inspections Act 2006, to promote community cohesion.

Article 29 of the UN Convention on the Rights of the Child (1989) (CRC), specifies that all children have a right to education in human rights, which prepares them for democratic participation, and for tolerant co-existence with people of different experiences, cultures, ethnic and religious backgrounds from their own. Additionally, each child also has the right to an education which promotes:

'Respect for ... his or her own cultural identity, language and values, for the national values of the country in which the child is living, the country from which he or she may originate, and for civilisations different from his or her own.' (CRC, 1989)

In other words, children have the right to be educated for all forms of diversity, including religious diversity, but also to be supported in their own cultural heritage and that of their families' country of origin. Grover (2007) argues that education for tolerance and diversity, in keeping with the requirements of the CRC, cannot be fostered where there is complete educational segregation. Twinning arrangements are unlikely to be adequate to overcome the disadvantage generated by such segregation or enable effective education for diversity and tolerance, in keeping with agreed international minimum standards.

Those, who like Prime Minister Gordon Brown, advocate teaching for a new post-imperial Britishness, see history as the vehicle for fostering unity, but do not explain how education for diversity will also be fostered. Brown states:

'When we take time to stand back and reflect, it becomes clear that to address almost every one of the major challenges facing our country – our relationships with Europe, America and the rest of the world; how we equip ourselves for globalisation; the future direction of constitutional change; a modern view of citizenship; the future of local government, ideas of localism; and, of course, our community relations and multiculturalism and, since July 7th, the balance between diversity and integration; even the shape of our public services – you must have a clear view of what being British means, what you value about being British and what gives us purpose as a nation.' (Brown 14 January 2006)

Brown's concept of Britishness is rooted in a vision of a nation-state which takes a leading role in world politics and in the global economy. It is a 'both/and' rather than an 'either/or' vision: Britain can be conceived both as a successful individual nation-state and as a member of the European Union; the nation can defend its own interests and be a member of NATO. Essentially, he presents a cosmopolitan vision; he does not present cosmopolitanism and patriotism as mutually incompatible positions. He gives considerable attention to local and global concerns as well as to national identity and interests. He acknowledges Britain's responsibilities in global development and poverty alleviation, while at the same time celebrating national identity and local, community action.

Yet when Brown addresses the role of history and citizenship in schools the local and global pictures largely disappear. We are to 'discover and build from our history'. Brown asserts:

'..we should not recoil from our national history – rather we should make it more central to our education. I propose that British history should be given much more prominence in the curriculum – not just dates places and names, nor just a set of unconnected facts, but a narrative that encompasses our history.' (Brown, Fabian New Year Conference, 16 January, 2006)

We learn that history is, in fact, in Brown's eyes, a grand narrative representing progress towards greater liberty and, eventually, towards democracy.

There is, however, a narrowing of focus when we move from the grand vision to proposals for the school curriculum. The overall political discourse is about a cosmopolitan nation, with a commitment to humanity, and an important role in the world. Yet schools are expected to focus on British history rather than world history. The argument is that Britain needs to look inwards in order to regain its confidence and place among leading nations. Britain needs to gain security and British children need to know more about the nation's roots before they can contribute to the project of enabling Britain to claim its rightful place in the world. These roots are to be found within territorial boundaries. History is presented as an onward march towards democracy, but past struggles for rights are overlooked. The story of the women's suffrage, for example, or the liberation movements of colonial people are excluded. These aspects of the British story are missing, and are not even mentioned as aberrations in the uniquely British progression along the path to democratic freedom.

PATRIOTISM, NATIONALISM AND RACISM

In order to understand the implications for education we need to consider the meaning of patriotism and its possible role in schools. Patriotism and nationalism are sometimes confused. A number of writers have traced the ways in which nationalisms are implicated in racism, with Gilroy (1987) tracing ways in which racism and nationalism have routinely been articulated in Britain in the 1970s and 1980s. Culture can be used to essentialise specific groups, when culture is, in fact, constantly negotiated and re-made (Gilroy 1990). By focusing on the religious and ethnic dimensions of culture, but largely failing to address racism, the Ajegbo report runs the risk of encouraging schools to do likewise, thereby promoting (despite an acknowledgement of multiple identities) an essentialist view of race, ethnicity and religion in teaching and learning in schools.

Parekh (2000: 341-2) defines patriotism as a commitment to a political community:

> 'It does not involve sharing common substantive goals, ... nor a common view of history which they may read differently, nor a particular economic or social system. ... commitment to the political community involves commitment to its continuing existence and well-being ... and *implies that one cares enough for it not to harm its interests and undermine its integrity.*' (2000: 341-2 my emphasis).

This political commitment, according to Parekh, will be felt differently by different individuals and may range from 'quiet concern' to 'intense love'. The role of schools in fostering such political commitment is complex, since any attempt to foster emotional attachment in learners is not a one-sided process in which the student (and the teacher) is passively accepting a feeling of concern or love for the nation. Each individual is negotiating and interpreting the curriculum. As Parekh points out, political loyalty and criticism (of prevailing forms of government, institutions, policies, values, and so on) are compatible, so long as individuals do not undermine the integrity of the political entity and remain open to dialogue.

An international group of scholars highlights positive elements of patriotism which might be fostered through education:

'When patriotism engenders collective solidarity with fellow citizens and loyalty to the law and democratic constitutions, it is positive and useful. This patriotism fosters the social responsibility and civic courage essential for defending the rights and freedoms that a democratic political culture guarantees.' (Banks *et al.* 2003: 23)

They urge caution in promoting an unthinking patriotism though schools, warning that:

'Patriotism is a double-edged sword. ... In the name of patriotism, intolerance towards dissent has been propagated, freedom of speech restricted, and an arbitrary consensus imposed. The accusation of 'unpatriotic behaviour' can intimidate teachers and students into self-censorship. They may bow to conformist pressure that emanates from powerful media, clergy, and the government as to what is legitimate and what is out of bounds.' (Banks et al. *ibid*, 23).

This warning has particular resonance in post 2005 Britain, in which the loyalty of Muslim citizens has been questioned by sections of the media and in which some political leaders have given out mixed messages about both immigrants and minority communities. The government's *Prevent* programme, designed to support educational activities which seek to prevent violent extremism, has targeted, almost exclusively, young people from Muslim communities. It has not targeted those vulnerable to engaging in racist violence promoted, covertly or overtly, by members of far right extremist groups. Its ostensible goal of promoting community cohesion is likely to be undermined by growing evidence of a perception within targeted communities that it forms part of a wider agenda of surveillance and control (Akram and Richardson 2009; Osler 2007 and 2009).

The Banks panel (2003: 23-24) proposes that teachers emphasise *critical* patriotism, which 'encourages reasoned loyalty: pride in the "rights" of the nation alongside a commitment to correct its "wrongs"'. The processes of securing political loyalty or patriotism depend on a sense of belonging, for, as Parekh puts it: 'Citizens cannot be committed to their political community unless it is also committed to them, and they cannot belong to it unless it accepts them as belonging to it.' (2000: 342)

WAYS FORWARD

Policy-makers and schools need to develop curricular approaches appropriate for a multicultural democracy which respect young people's freedom of belief, conscience, and religion. This implies that there is not one story or one vision of the past or present which can be taught. It is only authoritarian states which have pursued this approach with rigour, and they have met with mixed success. No single story of history can be told, and young people, whether they are educated in faith-based schools or non-faith-based schools, need to be exposed to multiple perspectives, which include a critical examination of different belief systems, both religious and secular. It is only through exposure to different visions that young people will have an opportunity to contribute to a shared vision of society which is cohesive and forward-thinking, and which seeks to accommodate difference within a framework of mutual respect and dignity, guaranteeing the human rights of all.

The curriculum for both religious education and history needs to be framed in a way which recognises that students are not only citizens of a nation-state but are also emergent cosmopolitan citizens living in an age of globalization and universal human rights. Education for citizenship in a multicultural democracy also implies knowledge and skills for political participation and political literacy. Citizenship education and religious education are not alternatives; each has its role to play in learning to live together. In non-faith-based schools, it is important to ensure that young people's faiths and belief systems are recognised, rather than denied. Similarly, faith-based education needs to acknowledge that students have multiple identities beyond faith identities, which should be respected in school. These are not simply basic standards for a cohesive multicultural democracy, they are also an entitlement which all young people hold, under the Convention on the Rights of the Child, to an education which not only respects their own cultures and backgrounds, but which prepares them to address the challenges of living together in a multicultural, multi-faith yet secular society and wider global community.[3]

NOTES

1. At the time of writing, French and Belgian legislators are considering banning the *niqab* in public places.

2. A review of speeches on the 10 Downing Street website, from January 1999 to April 2001 identified just five that refer to racial equality or the multicultural nature of Britain.

3. This chapter draws on and develops, in relation to RE, work previously published in Osler, A., (2009) 'Patriotism, multiculturalism and belonging: political discourse and the teaching of history' *Educational Review* Vol. 61, Issue 1, February 2009, 85-100. It is printed here with permission from the copyright holder.

REFERENCES

Akram, J. and Richardson, R. (2009) Citizenship education for all or preventing violent extremism for some? Choices and challenges for schools. *Race Equality Teaching* 27 (3): 49-55.

Banks, J.A., C. A. McGee Banks, C.Cortes, C.L. Hahn, M. Merryfield, K. Moodley, S. Murphy-Shigematsu, A. Osler, C. Park, W.C. Parker (2005) *Democracy and diversity: principles and concepts for educating citizens in a global age*. Seattle, WA: Center for Multicultural Education, University of Washington.

Berkeley, R. (2007) *Right to Divide? Faith Schools and Community Cohesion*. London: Runnymede Trust.

Blair, T. (2001) *Speech by Prime Minister Tony Blair to the Welsh Assembly*. 30 October 2001.
http://www.number-10.gov.uk/output/Page1636.asp
Accessed 24 August 2007.

Blair, T. (2004) Speech by Prime Minister Tony Blair to the Confederation of British Industry. 27 April.
http://www.pm.gov.uk/output/page5708.asp
Accessed 24 August 2007.

Blair, T. (2006) Our nation's future: multiculturalism and integration. Speech given at 10 Downing Street. 8 December.
http://www.number10.gov.uk/output/Page10563.asp
Accessed 3 August 2007.

Brown, G. (2006) Who do we want to be? The future of Britishness. Speech given to the Fabian Society, 16 January.
http://fabians.org.uk/events/new-year-conference-06/brown-britishness/speech
Accessed 3 August 2007.

Claire, H. (2005) 'You did the best you can': history, citizenship and moral dilemmas, in A. Osler (ed.) *Teachers, human rights and diversity: educating citizens in multicultural societies*, Stoke-on-Trent: Sterling VA and Trentham Books.

Commission for Racial Equality (CRE) (2003) *Towards racial equality: an evaluation of the public duty to promote racial equality and good race relations in England and Wales* (2002). Report for the CRE by Schneider-Ross. London: CRE. Available at: http://www.cre.gov.uk/duty/survey.html

Commission on Integration and Cohesion (COIC). (2007) *Interim Statement from the Commission on Integration and Cohesion*. London: Department for Communities and Local Government.
Available at: www.integrationandcohesion.org.uk

Department for Education and Skills (DfES) (2007a) *Curriculum review: diversity and citizenship* (Ajegbo report) PPSLS/D35/0107/14. London: DfES.

Department for Education and Skills (DfES) (2007b) Johnson says pupils need to learn our history to understand British values in citizenship classes. Press notice 2007/0012. 25 January.
http://www.dfes.gov.uk/pns/DisplayPN.cgi?pn_id=2007_0012
Accessed 29 June 2007

Essed, P. (2002) Reflections on 'everyday racism' (P. Essed) in: P. Essed and D. Goldberg (eds.) *Race Critical Theories*. Oxford: Blackwell.

Figueroa, P. (2004) Multicultural education in the United Kingdom: historical development and current status, in J.A. Banks and C. A. McGee Banks (eds.) *Handbook of research on multicultural education*. 2nd edition. San Francisco: Jossey Bass.

Fryer, P. (1989) *Black People and the British Empire: an introduction*. London and Sydney: Pluto Press.

Gilroy, P. (1987) *There Ain't No Black in the Union Jack: the cultural politics of race and nation*. London: Hutchinson.

Gilroy, P. (1990) The end of anti-racism. *New Community* 17 (1): 71-83.

Grover, S. (2007) Children's right to be educated for tolerance: minority rights and inclusion. *Education and the Law* 19 (1): 59-70.

Jawad, H. and T. Benn, T. (2003) (eds) *Muslim Women in the United Kingdom and Beyond: Experiences and Images*. Leiden: Brill.

Kelly, R. (2006) Speech given at launch of the Commission on Integration and Cohesion, 24 August 2006.
http://www.communities.gov.uk/speeches/corporate/commission-integration-cohesion
Accessed 7 September 2007

Lorcerie, F. (2005) (ed.) *La Politisation du Voile en France, en Europe et dans le monde arabe*. Paris: L'Harmattan.

Macpherson, W. (1999) *The Stephen Lawrence Inquiry*. London: Stationery Office.

Mondal, A. (2008) Islam and multiculturalism: some thoughts on a difficult relationship. *Moving Worlds* 8 (1): 77-94.

Office for Standards in Education (OfSTED) (2005) *Race equality in education: good practice in schools and local education authorities*. HMI 589. London: OfSTED.

Office for Standards in Education (OfSTED) (2007) *Making Sense of Religion: a report on religious education in schools and the impact of locally agreed syllabuses*. London: OfSTED.

Osler, A. and Vincent, K. (2002) *Not a problem? Girls and school exclusion*, London, National Children's Bureau.

Osler, A. (2007) *Faith Schools and Community Cohesion*. London: Runnymede Trust.

Osler, A. (2008) Citizenship education and the Ajegbo report: re-imagining a cosmopolitan nation. *London Review of Education* 6 (1): 11-25.

Osler, A. (2009) Citizenship education, democracy and racial justice 10 years on. *Race Equality Teaching* 27 (3): 21-27.

Osler, A. and Starkey. H. (2000) Education for citizenship: mainstreaming the fight against racism? *European Journal of Education* 37 (2): 143-159.

Osler, A. and Starkey. H (2005) *Changing Citizenship: democracy and inclusion in education*. Maidenhead: Open University Press.

Parekh, B. (2000) *Rethinking Multiculturalism: cultural diversity and political theory*. London: Macmillan.

Phillips, T. (2005) After 7/7: sleepwalking to segregation. Speech to the Manchester Council for Community Relations. 22 September. http://www.cre.gov.uk/Default.aspx.LocID-0hgnew07s.RefLocID-0hg00900c002.Lang-EN.htm#top Accessed 24 August 2007

Qualifications and Curriculum Development Agency (QCDA) (2009) *National Non-Statutory Framework for Religious Education*. London: QDCA.

Reid, A., Gill, J. and Sears, A. (2010) *Globalisation, the Nation-State and the Citizen*. New York: Routledge.

Richardson, R. (2004) (ed.) *Islamophobia: issues, challenges and action*. Stoke-on-Trent: Trentham with the Uniting Britain Trust.

Straw, J. (2006) Article in the Lancashire Evening Telegraph. Quoted in BBC World News on-line 5 October 2006.

http://news.bbc.co.uk/2/hi/uk_news/politics/5410472.stm
Accessed 24 August 2007

Straw, J. (2007) We need a British story. *The Sunday Times*. 29 April 2007.
http://www.timesonline.co.uk/tol/comment/columnists/guest_contribu
tors/article1720349.ece
Accessed 28 August 2007

Tomlinson, S. (2005) Race, ethnicity and education under New Labour.
Oxford Review of Education 31 (1): 153-171.

United Nations Children's Fund (UNICEF) (2007) *Child Poverty in
Perspective: an overview of child well-being in rich countries. A comprehensive
assessment of the lives and well-being of children and adolescents in the
economically advanced nations*. Innocenti report card 7. Florence: UNICEF
Innocenti Research Centre.

CHAPTER 5

TOWARDS A JUST SOCIETY:
What is the role of education and schooling?

Clyde Chitty

SUMMARY

IT IS ARGUED THAT SCHOOLS can do much to assist towards the creation of a fair and just society. But this can be especially difficult when the Government itself is the main obstacle to progress – and here the example given is that of sexuality and sexual diversity where many teachers have sought to provide a humane and caring programme of sex education, despite the common misapprehension that much of the relevant discussion in this area has been forbidden by the provisions of Section 28 of the Thatcher Government's 1998 Local Government Act. It is also argued in this chapter that a just society has to believe in the limitless potential of all children and that this means jettisoning atavistic eugenic theories about fixed innate ability and the futility of educating large groups of black and working-class youngsters.

INTRODUCTION

It might appear to be beyond dispute that one of the essential functions of education in a civilised democratic state is the promotion of the accepted values of a just and fair society – a society that, by its very nature, is dedicated to the eradication of prejudice, discrimination and exploitation. Yet the practical reality is by no means as straightforward as this. Concern for issues of social justice as an integral part of the primary and secondary school curriculum is of comparatively recent origin in Britain; and even today, there are many head teachers and classroom teachers who would prefer to adopt a fairly narrow and utilitarian view of the chief functions of schooling. At the same time, there are many politicians who argue that schooling is all about the teaching of traditional subjects and should not concern itself with wider issues of equality and inclusion.

This chapter will begin by exploring the Right's traditional attitude towards the introduction of the treatment of minority groups and human rights issues in general as an essential part of the school curriculum, concentrating particularly on issues raised by the classroom discussion of human sexuality and sexual diversity. It will then move on to examine how schools and teachers have been encouraged to adopt more enlightened and progressive policies by the New Labour administrations of Tony Blair and Gordon Brown, with due acknowledgement of government attempts over the past decade to remove the existing climate of fear and paranoia around the teaching of sex education. Consideration will be given to the need to (re)assert the promotion of human educability as a fundamental principle underpinning everything that goes on in the classroom, accepting that this could represent a clear shift in our treatment of black and working-class pupils. The chapter ends by looking at recent developments in the media's treatment of issues concerning human behaviour and children's welfare, highlighting one or two interventions that give considerable cause for concern.

THE RIGHT'S VIEW OF SCHOOLING

It surely cannot be denied that there are certain groups of people in British society who face prejudice and discrimination, and who suffer disproportionately in relation to others, simply because they happen to be different in some way from the majority. Many campaigners have argued that the classroom discussion of unfairness and injustice has to be seen as an essential step on the road to achieving the steady eradication of prejudice and exploitation; but this so-called 'reconstructionist' view of the purpose of schooling has not gone unchallenged. Over the last thirty years, a number of leading politicians and pressure groups, particularly on the Right of the political spectrum, have argued against the explicit use of the school curriculum to combat prejudice and injustice.

In her triumphalist address to the 1987 Conservative Party Conference, following a third massive electoral victory, Prime Minister Margaret Thatcher sought to ridicule and condemn all those on the 'Hard Left' who were said to be using education to tackle issues of discrimination and social injustice:

> 'It's the plight of individual boys and girls which worries me most. Too often, our children don't get the education they need – the education they *deserve*. And in the inner cities – where youngsters must have a decent education if they are to have a better future – that opportunity to succeed is all too often snatched from them by hard-left education authorities and extremist teachers. Children who need to be able to count and multiply are learning anti-racist mathematics whatever that may be. Children who need to be able to express themselves in clear English are being taught political slogans. Children who need to be taught to respect traditional moral values are being taught that they have an inalienable right to be gay.' (Thatcher 1987)

The previous year (1986), one of Margaret Thatcher's favourite right-wing pressure groups, the Hillgate Group, had published a hard-hitting pamphlet with the title *Whose Schools? A Radical Manifesto* in which it was argued that 'schoolchildren had to be rescued from indoctrination in all the fashionable causes of the Radical Left'. These apparently included: 'anti-racism', 'anti-sexism', 'peace education' (which usually meant Campaign for Nuclear Disarmament propaganda) and even 'anti-heterosexism' (meaning the promotion of homosexuality, combined with an attack on the belief that heterosexuality was 'normal'). According to the Pamphlet, there was evidence of 'an increasing assault on traditional values, whether Christian, Jewish or Muslim, with overt preaching on behalf of homosexuality, sexual licence and social indiscipline, together with a growing failure to abide by the provisions of the 1944 Education Act regarding religious worship and instruction.' If things were to change, all our schools should be 'released from the control of local government', thereby 'depriving the politicised local education authorities of their standing ability to corrupt the minds and souls of the young.' (Hillgate Group 1986, 4, 13, 18)

Margaret Thatcher's successor as Prime Minister, John Major (1990-97), shared the Right's clear contempt for 'fashionable causes' and 'politically correct thinking'. In his keynote address to the 1992 Conservative Party Conference, he was keen to stress his respect for traditional educational values and his rejection of the idea that schools should ever concern themselves with issues of equal opportunity and social justice:

> 'When it comes to education, my critics say I'm 'old-fashioned'. Old-fashioned? Reading and writing? Spelling and sums? Great literature – and standard English grammar? Old-fashioned? Tests and tables? British history? A proper grounding in science? Discipline and self-respect? Old-fashioned? ... Well if I am old-fashioned, so be it.

72

So are the vast majority of Britain's parents. … Because I'm old-fashioned, I want reform of teacher training in this country.

Let us return to basic subject teaching and get rid of all the courses in the theory of education. … Our primary teachers should learn how to teach children to read; not waste their time on the politics of gender, race and class. Our schools are failing our children … because they are worrying about equality and justice. … I think it is quite intolerable that children should spend years in school and then leave unable to read or add up. It is a terrible waste of all those young lives. … We want high standards, sound learning and diversity and choice in all our schools. But in some of the ones we have now – particularly in those inner cities – Isaac Newton would not have learned to count and William Wordsworth would never have learned to write.' (Quoted in Chitty and Simon 1993, 144)

CAN SCHOOLS CHANGE SOCIETY?

It helps the Right to make its case that there are those on the Left who maintain that schools simply reflect society and its dominant culture and can do very little to change it.

This mood of 'educational fatalism', where it still exists, can be said to have its origins in a school of thought popular in Britain and America in the 1970s which argued that the education system was part of the 'ideological state apparatus' and that teachers were simply the helpless 'puppets' of the state. It was the French Marxist philosopher Louis Althusser who argued in 1971 in his influential essay 'Ideology and Ideological State Apparatuses', which was actually used as a set reading text by the Open University in England, that the education system had in modern times taken the place of the Church as the chief means by which the dominant ideology of a capitalist class society was perpetuated, and so also that society itself (Althusser 1971, 123-173). Teachers and other workers within the field of education were inevitably subsumed as agents of ideological domination, and nothing they could do could have any discernible effect. Those who took a radical and oppositional stance in any area of the curriculum, believing that their actions as teachers could bring about social or political change, were, according to Althusser, 'a kind of hero', but one could only pity 'the futility of their efforts' (ibid, 148).

A similar line was taken by the sociologist Basil Bernstein in a paper entitled 'Education cannot compensate for society', published in New

Society in February 1970, referring specifically to issues of ability and linguistic achievement (Bernstein 1970a). Bernstein later claimed that his 'deterministic' theories had been wilfully misinterpreted (see, for example, Bernstein 1970b); but it cannot be denied that they contributed to a general view of schools which denied teachers any real autonomy in matters relating to the curriculum.

HISTORICAL BACKGROUND

Trying to promote issues relating to equality and human dignity is, of course, especially difficult for schools and teachers when the Government itself constitutes the main obstacle to change. Nowhere is this more true than in the case of sexuality and sexual diversity, where successive governments in the 1980s and 1990s attempted to prevent schools from initiating any sort of enlightened discussion of the subject. But even here many teachers refused to be intimidated by the forces of moral authoritarianism and insisted on adopting an emancipatory approach.

It was in 1986 that the Government of Margaret Thatcher found a convenient pretext for launching a major assault on what were regarded as offensive and indeed dangerous teaching practices. This came in the form of a whipped-up controversy over the alleged use by primary school teachers of an innocuous little picture-book from Denmark called *Jenny Lives with Eric and Martin* (Bosche and Mackay 1983). This had been published in Copenhagen in 1981 and first appeared in the United Kingdom in an English translation in December 1983. It attempted to present a positive image of two young gay men bringing up a five-year-old girl, the daughter of Martin. The manufactured 'outcry' over this perfectly harmless and well-intentioned book came in the early Summer of 1986 in the run-up to the first local elections to be held since the abolition of the Greater London Council. A story splashed over the front page of *The Islington Gazette* at the beginning of May 1986, claiming that there had been a 'storm of protest' from parents over the use of 'this gay school book', was taken up by sections of the tabloid press. An editorial in *The Sunday Mirror* claimed to be 'outraged' by the report:

> 'The idea that homosexuals form an oppressed minority is of course nonsense. The notion that they are entitled to propagate their peculiar practices at the public expense is preposterous. Yet they are contriving to do so. They are now insinuating their sexist propaganda into some of our schools.' (*The Sunday Mirror*, 4 May 1986)

And this was followed by front-page stories in the daily press with hysterical headlines like 'Vile Book in School' in *The Sun* (6 May 1986) and 'Scandal of Gay Porn Book read in Schools' in *Today* (7 May 1986). All of which conveniently ignored the fact that the book had been 'discovered' in a London Teachers' Centre and not, as was widely reported at the time, in the library or classroom of a London primary school.

At the time of this 'controversy' over the supposed availability of *Jenny Lives with Eric and Martin*, a new Education Bill was in the process of passing through Parliament. In the House of Lords, a number of Conservative peers demanded action on sex education in schools, claiming that the kind of teaching which 'condoned' homosexuality as a valid alternative to heterosexuality was not only undermining traditional family life and encouraging divorce but was also clearly linked with the increase in rapes, sexual attacks on children and sexual crime in general. The fear engendered by the spread of HIV/AIDS was used to justify a right-wing Christian approach to morality that condemned homosexual lifestyles. In the words of the Christian campaigner Baroness Cox, a prominent member of the Hillgate Group:

> 'I cannot imagine how on earth in this age of HIV/AIDS, we can be contemplating promoting gay issues in the school curriculum. I think that it beggars all description.' (Quoted in Jeffery-Poulter ,1991, 208).

Education Secretary Kenneth Baker bowed to the pressure from the Right of his Party, and a new clause was introduced in the Education Bill (Clause 46 in the resulting 1986 Education (No. 2) Act) requiring that:-

> 'The local education authority by whom any county, voluntary or special school is maintained, and the governing body and head teacher of the School, shall take such steps as are reasonably practicable to secure that where sex education is given to any registered pupils at the School, it is given in such a manner as to encourage those pupils to have due regard to moral considerations and the value of family life.'

It was this 1986 (No. 2) Act which gave responsibility for sex education in schools to school governing bodies which were required (in Clause 18) to 'make and keep up to date' a written statement with regard to the School's sex education programme. The whole tone of the Act was welcomed by Conservative newspapers, *The Daily Telegraph* regarding the legislation as 'an integral part' of 'the Government's campaign for moral revival' (*The Daily Telegraph*, 3 June 1986) and *The Daily Express* describing the last-minute amendment as 'a bombshell' which has at last 'shaken the very foundations of the permissive society.' (*The Daily Express*, 4 June 1986)

The new framework for the provision of sex education in schools was then elaborated upon in DES Circular No. 11/87, *Sex Education at School*, published on 25 September 1987 (DES 1987). This argued (in Section 19) that 'pupils should be helped to appreciate the benefits of stable married and family life and the responsibilities of parenthood'. And the wording of Section 22 was particularly strong:

> 'There is no place in any school in any circumstances for teaching which advocates homosexual behaviour, which presents it as the 'norm', or which encourages homosexual experimentation by pupils.
> Indeed, encouraging or procuring homosexual acts by pupils who are under the age of consent is a criminal offence.' (DES 1987, 4)

This Section concluded by emphasising that for many people, including members of various religious faiths, homosexual practice was not 'morally acceptable' and that therefore deep offence could be caused to them if teachers failed to handle the subject with enormous sensitivity *(ibid)*.

The determination of Mrs Thatcher's ministers to appease the forces of moral authoritarianism was further emphasised by the inclusion of what was to become the notorious Clause 28 of the 1988 Local Government Act. This amended the 1986 Local Government Act by laying down that a local authority shall not:-

(a) intentionally promote homosexuality or publish material with the intention of promoting homosexuality

(b) promote the teaching in any maintained school of the acceptability of homosexuality as a pretended family relationship.

As many commentators have pointed out, Clause or Section 28 was a key cultural and symbolic event in the recent history of sexual politics. It was hardly an example of skilful drafting, with the abuse of terminology in part (b) resulting in 'homosexuality' being defined as a 'pretended family *relationship*' and considerable (perhaps deliberate?) confusion being engendered as to the precise definition of 'promote'. It was also soon clear to legislators that its effect on the teaching of sex education in schools *could* be negligible if one looked closely at the content of very recent legislation in this area. What Dame Jill Knight and the other sponsors of the measure had simply overlooked was that the 1986 Education (No 2) Act had already removed sex education from the control of local authorities – a fact which the Government was forced to concede in a Department of the Environment Circular published in May 1988:-

'Responsibility for sex education in schools continues to rest with School Governing Bodies, by virtue of Section 18 of the Education (No 2) Act of 1986. Section 28 of the 1988 Local Government Act does not affect the activities of school governors, nor of teachers. It will not prevent the objective discussion of homosexuality in the classroom, nor the counselling of pupils concerned about their sexuality. (DoE 1988, 5)

Not surprisingly, this Circular was given very little publicity by the Government or in the press; and very few teachers seemed to be aware of its existence. Clause 28, on the other hand, was the subject of enormous media interest and speculation; and what it managed to achieve was the creation of a climate of paranoia around the teaching of sex education. In the view of Rachel Thomson, at that time Information Development Officer for the Sex Education Forum:-

'Clause 28 played an important role in undermining the professionalism of teachers and in policing the politics of teachers. The phrase 'the promotion of homosexuality' had the insidious effect of constructing teachers as the potential corruptors of young people and of frightening teachers from saying what they thought was sensible and right out of fear of losing their jobs.' (Thomson 1993, 225)

Yet, despite all the difficulties, a number of teachers refused to be intimidated by the various government edicts on sex education; and this surely demonstrates the role of schools in upholding the values of a just and caring society, irrespective of the nature of the government in power at Westminster. In the London Borough of Haringey, for example, the majority of head teachers supported the Council in its decision to tackle discrimination in a 103-page report on lesbian and gay issues in education. The recommendations of the Report included: drawing up a code of good conduct for pupils to counter homophobic bullying and anti-homosexual harassment and teaching children about the sexuality of such writers as E.M. Forster and about the Nazi persecution of homosexuals. In the words of Bob Cross, a Haringey education officer at the time:

'This new Report is all about respecting diversity. ... We're trying to help people form a humane approach to what is essentially a human rights issue.' (Quoted in Davies 1988)

Speaking at the World AIDS Day Conference in December 1991, the late Michael Marland, then Head teacher of North Westminster Community School in London, pointed out that Section 1 of the Conservative Government's own 1988 Education Reform Act specifically required the school curriculum to be concerned with 'preparing pupils for the opportunities, responsibilities and experiences of adult life'. How, he asked, could sexuality be left out of such preparation? (reported in *The Times Educational Supplement*, 6 December 1991). And he followed this up by arguing, in a letter published in *The Times Educational Supplement* on 10 January 1992, that a governing body would be failing in its duty if it did not ensure that its school's sex education programme comprehended 'the range of sexual attitudes and behaviours in present-day society'.

Research carried out by Caroline Benn and Clyde Chitty in the academic year 1993-94 for a report on the state of comprehensive education in Britain first published in 1996 found that sex and relationships education, which was often provided within a structured programme of personal and social education (PSE), was rarely given the priority it deserved. Where, as was often the case, little or no use was made of outside specialists, the task of handling a number of controversial issues in the classroom fell to tutors and others who had had no special training for the task. And the vast majority of the 1500 or so comprehensive schools participating in the Survey were reluctant to talk about sexual diversity in their equal opportunities statements. But there were notable exceptions; and it was felt by the authors that the sex education policy outlined in the prospectus of a comprehensive school in the West Midlands was worth quoting in full:

> 'What is taught in school is just one of a range of factors which will influence a young person's decision to become involved in sexual activity. Our policy is to make our pupils aware of the emotional support and long-term security which are necessary to a fulfilling sexual relationship in our society. We do, however, recognise that a number of our pupils – some of whom may be in the younger age groups – are sexually active or will soon become so; and it is therefore most important that our sex education programme equips them with what they need to know to prevent unwanted pregnancies and the spread of sexually transmitted diseases.

> Homosexuality is not dealt with as a free-standing topic in our PSE

> Programme until the Upper School...Pupils' questions about homosexuality are, however, answered informatively ...and one of our aims is to reassure worried pupils by presenting an unprejudiced view of homosexuals in terms of their human qualities.

It is, perhaps, important to note that in both PSE lessons and also Home Economics, emphasis is placed on the need for responsible behaviour at all times. Pupils are helped to appreciate the values of a stable family life, marriage and all the many responsibilities that go with parenthood. We do, however, acknowledge that these days, families come in all shapes and sizes – ranging from the extended family including children, parents, grandparents, aunts, uncles, etc., to the so-called nuclear family of mother, father and children, single-parent families, adoptive families, families which include a step-parent, and the many other caring relationships which are non- parental but still entirely supportive.' (Quoted in Benn and Chitty 1996, 248)

It needs to be pointed out that, over the past ten years, New Labour ministers and politicians have by and large taken a very progressive stance on matters of equality and social justice. Following a number of nail bomb atrocities carried out in April 1999, and designed to bring bloodshed and chaos to various 'marginalised' communities in London – in Brixton, Brick Lane and Soho – Prime Minister Tony Blair spoke eloquently of the need to build 'the tolerant, multiracial Britain the vast majority of us want to see'. In a speech in Birmingham delivered on 2 May 1999 and intended to mark the 300th anniversary of the founding of the Sikh religion, Mr Blair argued powerfully that an attack on any section of the community was an attack on Britain as a whole:

'When one section of our community is under attack, we defend it in the name of all the community. When bombs attack the Black and Asian Community in Britain, they attack the whole of Britain....When the gay community is attacked and innocent people are murdered, all the good people of Britain, whatever their race, their lifestyle or their class, unite in revulsion and in determination to bring the evil people to justice.' (reported in *The Independent*, 3 May, 1999).

The Prime Minister went on to emphasise that education had an important role to play in defeating any form of vicious nationalism that tolerated attacks on minorities and then replacing it with 'a vision for the 21st century based on respect for human diversity'. Schools had to teach that patriotism and national identity should never be defined 'by reference to those excluded from that identity'.

Section 28 was finally repealed, after a long campaign, in November 2003. As we have seen, it had never actually been able to influence what was taught in schools, but, fifteen years after its introduction, very few teachers were aware of this. As late as July 2000, an alliance of Conservative and backbench peers had blocked repeal of the legislation in the House of Lords by 270 votes to 228.

On November 6 2009, a front-page story in *The Times* announced that a new Children, Schools and Family Bill would make sex education mandatory for all pupils aged 5 -16 in state schools, with parents unable to opt their children out of lessons about contraception, sexually transmitted diseases and homosexuality. Previously, every school was supposed to have a sex education policy but there was no statutory requirement for teaching about relationships or the social and emotional side of sexual behaviour; parents who disapproved could chose to opt their children out of such lessons until they were as old as 19. Under the new laws, to be enforced in 2011, schools would be expected to teach about the importance of marriage, civil partnerships and stable relationships in family life. According to Schools Secretary Ed Balls: 'Sex and relationship education is a very important element in the curriculum, and we see it as a crucial drive to reduce teenage pregnancy.' However, In the light of opposition from faith communities, including the Roman Catholic Church, the Schools Secretary was later forced to introduce an amendment on 23 February 2010 which would allow faith schools to teach about issues of contraception, abortion and homosexuality within the tenets of their religion while still being required to teach pupils about these matters 'in a non-judgmental way' (*Daily Mail*, 24 February, 2010). This came as something of a shock to the Accord Coalition, which campaigns against religious discrimination in all schools, and its spokesperson Rabbi Dr Jonathan Romain said: 'It is quite astonishing that the Government plans to allow state-funded schools to teach the subject of sex and relationships education from any one religious standpoint. Ed Balls in implicitly condoning homophobia in our schools, and this looks like a 21st century version of Section 28 (quoted in *The Times*, 19 February, 2010). In the event, these plans have had to be abandoned as one of the causalities of the so-called 'wash-up' period in the first week of April 2010 before Parliament was officially dissolved prior to the holding of the 2010 General Election.

WHAT SCHOOLS STILL HAVE TO DO

Schools could do much to uphold the values of a just and liberal society by revising the promotional literature they send out to prospective parents. Looked at from many points of view, the prospectuses of so many schools, both primary and secondary, are either bland or misleading or both. Where statements of equal opportunities are concerned, many schools are happy to talk about race, ethnicity, gender and perhaps disability, but are markedly reluctant to go further. The campaigning organisation Stonewall found that in 2006, only six per cent of Britain's schools had clearly-formulated policies and procedures with regard to discrimination or harassment based on sexual orientation (Stonewall 2007). Rather late in the day, the Government has come to realise that schools could do far more to deal with homophobic bullying – and indeed bullying in all its forms and manifestations. In his Foreword to the 2007 DCSF Guidance Document *Homophobic Bullying: Safe to Learn: Embedding Anti-Bullying Work in Schools*, which Stonewall itself helped to compile, the Schools Secretary Ed Balls emphasised that the willingness to treat bullying in school as a trivial matter was totally unacceptable:-

> 'Every child in every school has the right to learn free from the fear of bullying, whatever form that bullying may take. Everyone involved in a child's education needs to work together to ensure that this is the case. ... Schools need to take an active approach to tackling all forms of bullying including homophobic bullying. Schools should be taking action to prevent bullying behaviour, as well as responding to incidents when they occur. A preventative approach to bullying means that schools safeguard the welfare of all their pupils. It also means that schools are playing their part in creating a just society in which people treat one another with proper respect.' (DCSF 2007: 4)

ISSUES OF ABILITY AND POTENTIAL

At the same time, many head teachers fail to clarify their school's basic educational philosophy in the policy documents they publish by resorting to the familiar dictum that 'at this school, all the pupils are encouraged to work to their full potential', as if a child's 'potential' were somehow 'fixed' and someone else (a teacher or an inspector?) could determine what it was. This sort of statement is as trite and meaningless as that by Secretary of State for Business, Innovation and Skills Peter (Lord) Mandelson in an article published in *The Guardian* on 12 August 2009 claiming that the New Labour Government believed in could create 'a just and fair society' by 'unlocking individual potential through education and opportunity'.

In truth, many ministers and teachers still cling to the eugenic theory that, despite all the 'remedial help' they may receive, most black and disadvantaged white working-class children are somehow doomed to failure where genuine educational achievement is concerned (Chitty 2007). They refuse to recognise that we can create a just and inclusive society only if we believe that all children, regardless of class or background, have enormous abilities and talents which it is the teacher's task to develop.

81

In an article published in *The Times* on 23 July 2009 and designed as a contribution to the debate on the reasons for the recent decline in rates of social mobility, political commentator Daniel Finkelstein argued that 'even in the most mobile society possible', the effect of genes is such that 'there has to be a relationship between achievement in one generation and achievement in the next'. And in his recently-published bleak analysis of the failings of the British education system, *A Desolation of Learning*, former Chief Inspector of Schools Chris Woodhead quotes with approval D.H. Lawrence's view that 'it is worse than useless trying to educate at least 50 per cent of our pupils.' (Woodhead 2009, 41). Woodhead points out that in his 1918 essay *The Education of the People*, Lawrence argued that 'we can't make a highly intelligent being' out of a working-class lad like Jimmy Shepherd. 'Why should we', said Lawrence, 'if the Lord created him only moderately intelligent? Why do we want always to go one better than the Creator?' (see Williams 1973, 133). All of which would seem to echo the view of Professor John White that the powerful eugenic vision, and particularly with regard to concepts of human intelligence, has its ideological roots in the more 'radical' and atavistic forms of Protestantism which underpinned the thinking of the puritan and dissenting communities in both Britain and America in the 17th century. In White's view:

> '...predestination is as much a key feature of intelligence testing as it has been of Calvinism and its various puritan offshoots. In both systems, where one will end up in life – or indeed after life – is wholly or largely fixed at birth, whether by God or by nature. There is no way a person destined for "damnation" can come to be "saved", just as there is no way a child of very low IQ at some point in its life can hope to become a doctor or a lawyer.' (White 2006, 2).

This obsession with ability, 'fixed' or otherwise, might help to explain why so many politicians seem wedded to the idea that pupils at both primary and secondary schools have to be 'streamed' or 'setted' for most academic subjects. The 2005 DfES White Paper *Higher Standards, Better Schools for All* argued that schools must take account of the fact that children can be divided into three main categories: 'the gifted and talented, the struggling and the just average' (DfES 2005, 20). With this in mind, New Labour has always argued (see, for example, DfEE 1997, 38) that setting should be 'the norm in secondary schools' and that it was also worth considering as the main form of pupil grouping in primary schools. And this idea has been taken up with enthusiasm by David Cameron and his education advisers. The Conservative Party Policy Green Paper *Raising the*

Bar, Closing the Gap, published in November 2007, argued that evidence had clearly shown that 'mixed-ability teaching did not work' – and that it led to 'disruption, truancy and disengagement' (Conservative Party 2007, 32). And in an interview with *The Daily Telegraph,* published as a front-page story on 7 February 2009, the Conservative Leader promised that a new Conservative government would introduce a new generation of 'super comprehensive schools' or 'Academies', run by charities and entrepreneurs. The Heads of these new 'super schools' – schools to which Mr Cameron would be prepared to send his own children – would have considerable autonomy in most operational matters, but would be required to impose a policy of 'rigorous setting and streaming for all academic subjects'.

Even if most schools lack the willingness or inclination to challenge the main political parties in matters related to pupil grouping, there are at least steps they can take to further the cause of equal opportunities. For one thing, they can carry out a small-scale research project to discover who exactly are the pupils who seem to find themselves in all the 'bottom' sets. They can then make sure that some of their most experienced and committed teachers are the ones who are allocated to these groups at the bottom of the so-called ability range.

Research carried out by David Gillborn and Deborah Youdell has shown that, because the performance tables based on school GCSE results have always concentrated on the percentage of 16-year-old students achieving the 'top' A* to C grades, there has always been enormous pressure on secondary schools to concentrate their efforts on those students at the 'borderline' between grades C and D, while neglecting those unfortunate youngsters thought incapable of gaining at least five of those all-important 'top' grades (Gillborn and Youdell 2000). If schools care about equity and educational opportunities for all, they have to stop being complicit in this blatant 'rationing' of education.

At the beginning of August 2009, a report published by the Sutton Trust, a charity devoted largely to improving social mobility through the education system, argued that schools themselves were largely to blame for the relatively small number of state school pupils at Oxford and Cambridge. Speaking on the BBC Radio Four *Today* programme on the day that the Report was published (10 August 2009), the Trust's Research Director Dr Lee Elliot Major said:-

'The problem lies with the schools themselves: teachers at state schools, and particularly at non-selective schools, are much less likely than those at the independent schools to recommend that their brightest pupils apply to Oxford and Cambridge. There is a confusion between excellence and elitism among teachers in the state sector.' (reported in *The Independent*, 11 August 2009)

A front-page story which appeared in *The Guardian* on 21st August 2009, the day after the 2009 A level results were published, revealed that more than 50 per cent of the A levels taken by students educated in independent schools scored an A grade, compared with only 20 per cent of those taken by state school students. In the words of *The Guardian's* Education Editor, this appeared to demonstrate the failure of schools and ministers to 'break the middle-class stranglehold on entry to higher education'. It was then reported in *The Guardian* on 23rd March 2010 that some 53.9 per cent of the UK undergraduates who started their degree course at Oxford in the Autumn of 2009 were from state schools and colleges, 1.5 percentage points fewer than the previous year. This means that the proportion of privately-educated students had risen from 44.6 per cent in 2008 to 46.1 per cent in 2009.

RECENT DEVELOPMENTS

It was perhaps inevitable that the media frenzy in February 2009 over the case of a thirteen-year-old teenager who, apparently, had fathered a child with his fifteen-year-old girlfriend, should embrace a whole series of ugly and ill-informed attacks on our secondary schools for helping to create the 'decadent moral climate' in which this sort of thing could all too easily.

The Sun's columnist Jane Moore found the story 'a damning indictment of Britain's hugely expensive and ill-advised sex education programme in schools' (16 February 2009); while an editorial in *The Daily Mail* (16 February 2009) blamed all this permissiveness on the so-called 'liberal establishment' in Britain which had 'betrayed our young'.

The Daily Mail's right-wing columnist Melanie Phillips went even further, arguing that the mess we were in was the result of an approach to sex education and contraception by schools and public health professionals that involved treating children as 'quasi-adults capable of making their own life choices'. In her view, sex education programmes in schools were underpinned by a number of 'destructive and nihilistic ideas' which were intended to 'restructure family life around a sexual free-for-all'. She claimed that 'sex education and contraceptive advice in schools simply encouraged teenage girls to fall pregnant whenever they wanted to'. And she concluded that the clear result of this reckless and irresponsible teaching was that 'basic codes of decorum had gone out of the window' and 'children were having sex openly in the streets like rutting animals.' (*The Daily Mail* 16 February 2009)

On 2 January 2010 a front-page story in *The Daily Telegraph* revealed with some alarm that schools risked being branded as 'inadequate' by government inspectors if they failed to promote good race relations, gender equality and human rights. Even those schools with good educational records could be placed in 'special measures' by OfSTED under new rules that gave equality equal weight with examination results and child safety. New official guidance would force inspectors to be aware of 'gender imbalances' in 'upper-ability' sets and to check that after-school sport was not dominated by pupils from just one ethnic group. According to Nick Gibb the Shadow Schools Minister, schools were increasingly expected to tackle 'social problems' at the expense of providing a decent education for their children.

At the beginning of February 2010, *The Daily Mail* endorsed an extraordinary attack by Pope Benedict XVI on the Government's Equality Bill making its way through Parliament. In a speech delivered to 35 Roman Catholic bishops from England and Wales visiting Rome, the Pope argued that the new equality legislation would 'impose unjust limitations on the freedom of religious communities to act in accordance with their beliefs'. Indeed, he went further by declaring that, in many respects, the new Bill actually 'violated the natural law upon which the equality of human beings is grounded and by which it is guaranteed'. This rejection of 'natural law' was regarded by the Pope as 'sinful'. The House of Lords had, in fact, already rejected clauses in the Bill which Catholics feared would have forced them to hire actively homosexual priests and staff or force them to allow women to become priests. But this did not prevent the Pope from urging the bishops to fight against the Bill's underlying principles. And in this he received the strong support of the Anglican Archbishop of York, Dr John Sentamu, who said of the Bill 'this way lies ruin'. (*The Daily Mail*, 2 February, 2010)

CONCLUSION

A just society is obviously one which erects no barriers to its young people on grounds of 'race', gender, sexual orientation and physical disability. But it is also about class and its effect on human achievement – a subject few of our politicians are comfortable talking about because they know that, despite all the reforms of the last two hundred years, Britain, or more specifically

England, is still one of the most class-ridden societies in the so-called civilised world. For this reason, it is sometimes easier to discuss 'race' or gender or sexual diversity where the issues are more clear-cut.

That said, it is still not totally clear where the Conservative Party stands in relation to issues of sexuality and sexual diversity. In recent years, David Cameron has been anxious to persuade lesbian and gay voters that his is no longer the Party of Section 28 or opposition to same-sex civil partnerships. But the Conservative Party has recently found itself embroiled in a furious and very public row over lesbian and gay rights when *The Observer* reported the Shadow Home Secretary Chris Grayling arguing that people who ran bed-and breakfasts in their own homes should 'have the right to turn away homosexual couples' (*The Observer*, 4 April, 2010). This suggests that Cameron's views do not enjoy the support of all the members of his senior shadow ministerial team, let alone his party members.

By and large, New Labour and the Liberal Democrats have a proud record of opposition to all forms of discrimination. But, even here, support for faith schools may have the effect of sanctioning bigotry and prejudice. It is also a sad comment on divisions within our society that when a Labour Government tries to promote an Equalities Bill in Parliament, a large part of the opposition comes from representatives of the Christian Church.

REFERENCES

Althusser, L. (1971) 'Ideology and Ideological State Apparatuses', in *Lenin and Philosophy and Other Essays*, London: New Left Books, 123-73.

Benn, C. and Chitty, C. (1996) *Thirty Years On: Is Comprehensive Education Alive and Well or Struggling to Survive?*, London: David Fulton.

Bernstein, B. (1970a) 'Education cannot compensate for society', *New Society*, 26 February, 344-7.

Bernstein, B. (1970b) 'A critique of the concept of "compensatory education"' in Rubinstein, D. and Stoneman, C. (eds) *Education for Democracy*, Harmondsworth: Penguin Books, 110-121.

Bosche, S. and Mackay, L. (1983) *Jenny Lives with Eric and Martin*, London: Gay Mens Press.

Chitty, C. (2007) *Eugenics, Race and Intelligence in Education*, London: Continuum.

Chitty, C. and Simon, B. (eds) (1993) *Education Answers Back: Critical Responses to Government Policy*, London: Lawrence and Wishart.

Conservative Party (2007) *Raising the Bar, Closing the Gap*, Policy Green Paper No. 1, London: Conservative Party.

DCSF (DEPARTMENT FOR CHILDREN, SCHOOLS AND FAMILIES) (2007) *Homophobic Bullying: Safe to Learn: Embedding Anti-Bullying Work in Schools*, London: the Stationery Office.

DES (DEPARTMENT OF EDUCATION AND SCIENCE) (1987) *Sex Education at School* (Circular No. 11/87), London: DES.

DfEE (DEPARTMENT FOR EDUCATION AND EMPLOYMENT) (1997) *Excellence in Schools*, Cmnd. 3681, London: HMSO

DfES (DEPARTMENT FOR EDUCATION AND SKILLS) (2005) *Higher Standards, Better Schools For All: More Choice for Parents and Pupils*, Cmnd. 6677, London: HMSO.

DoE (DEPARTMENT OF THE ENVIRONMENT) (1988) *Local Government Act 1988* (Circular No. 12/88), London: DoE.

Finkelstein, D. (2009) 'Can you change sides in the class war?', *The Times*, 23 July.

Gillborn, D. and Youdell, D. (2000) *Rationing Education: Policy, Practice, Reform and Equity*, Buckingham: Open University Press.

Hillgate Group (1986) *Whose Schools? A Radical Manifesto*, London: the Hillgate Group.

Jeffery-Poulter, S. (1991) *Peers, Queers and Commons: the Struggle for Gay Law Reform from 1950 to the Present*, London: Routledge.

STONEWALL (2007) *The School Report: the Experience of Young Gay People in Britain's Schools*, London: Stonewall.

Thatcher, M. (1987) Speech to the 1987 Conservative Party Conference.

Thomson, R. (1993) 'Unholy alliances: the recent politics of sex education' in Bristow J.and Wilson A.R. (eds) *Activity Theory: Lesbian, Gay, Bisexual Politics*, London: Lawrence and Wishart.

White, J. (2006) *Intelligence, Destiny and Education: the Ideological Roots of Intelligence Testing*, London: Routledge.

Williams, J. and Williams, R. (eds.) (1973) *Lawrence on Education*, Harmondsworth: Penguin Books.

Woodhead, C. (2009) *A Desolation of Learning: Is this the Education our Children Deserve?*, London: Pencil-Sharp Publishing.

CHAPTER 6

FAITH SCHOOLS AND COMMUNITY COHESION

Geoffrey Walford

SUMMARY

D URING TONY BLAIR'S TEN YEARS IN OFFICE as Prime Minister, there was clear support for the expansion of faith-based schools which was partly linked to his personal Christian faith and to the role that he believed faith should have in society (Blair 2008). However, during that same period of office, there was a growing concern with social and community cohesion and the roles that schooling might have in encouraging or discouraging such cohesion. Many commentators have seen these two aspects as being in conflict with one another.

This chapter uses the concept of community cohesion as a framework within which to set out some of the arguments that have been used by both supporters and detractors of faith schools. It sees community cohesion as a broad concept that is not simply a fixed goal, but is a set of processes with which all involved with schooling need to be engaged.

FAITH SCHOOLS IN THE SYSTEM

In order to understand the present situation it is necessary to give an overview of the past. Faith schools have always been at the centre of the English educational system, as the current system was built upon the pre-existing network of faith-based schools. It was only following the 1870 *Education Act* that the state became involved in the provision, maintenance and organisation of its own elementary schools, when there developed a national system where responsibility for provision was still shared with several different faith-based providers. The 1944 *Education Act* for England and Wales built upon this existing understanding. In order to provide 'secondary education for all' it was essential to include as many of the existing religious secondary schools as possible. These schools constituted the vast majority of the so-called voluntary schools where buildings were owned by the religious group but current expenditure was provided by the state. This sector was divided into two parts with most Roman Catholic schools becoming voluntary aided and most Church of England schools being voluntary controlled, the major differences being that voluntary aided schools had a majority of church-appointed school governors on their Boards, and paid a larger part of any new building costs.

From the 1960s onwards there was both a growth of secularism amongst the indigenous population and a considerable increase in the number of children from ethnic and religious minorities. By the mid-1990s there were about a million Muslims in England, with about 75 per cent having origins in the Indian subcontinent (Vertovec 2002), and about 400,000 children of Muslim parents of school age in England (Sarwar 1994). Most of these children found places in schools provided by the local education authorities. But some parents valued a religious ethos, so a considerable number of Muslim, Sikh and Hindu children attended Church of England schools (where some urban schools even had Muslim majorities), while some were in Roman Catholic schools. What is important to recognise is that, during most of the post-war period, declining interest in Christianity and greater liberalism within the Christian churches themselves, had led to a de-emphasis on Christian religious teaching and large scale abandonment of the theoretically compulsory daily act of worship in all schools. At the same time the liberal thinking of the time had led to a form of multiculturalism where all faiths were treated as valid (Thompson 2004; Barnes 2009). Rather than taking the differences between faiths seriously, all faiths were seen to be different ways to God, and equally worthy. The result was that, within areas of high ethnic minority concentration – such as parts of London, Bradford, and Birmingham – the Anglican schools, in particular, had often accommodated many of the religious needs of all children and, while a broad Christian ethos remained, there was positive acceptance of other faiths. In brief, these Anglican schools (and to a lesser extent the Roman Catholic schools) no longer took their historic faith-base seriously, so it was possible for families and children of a variety of faiths and none to co-exist in the same schools.

TAKING FAITH SERIOUSLY

One reaction to the decreased Christian emphasis in nominally Christian schools was that those who held more traditional beliefs began to establish their own small private schools where they could ensure that their own Christian beliefs were fully reflected in the teaching and ethos (Walford 2000a). Similarly, this perception of growing secularism, alongside a growing confidence within ethnic minority communities, also led to concern amongst various other religious minority parents – in particular Muslim parents who believed that their children were likely to be drawn away from their Islamic belief and practices. As a result, in the late 1980s, various groups established small private Muslim schools for their children.

Following the Conservative government's decision to allow schools to 'opt-out' of Local Education Authority control and become grant-maintained schools (which received funding from central rather than local government), political pressure led to the possibility that existing private schools or new schools could 'opt-in' and become a new type of grant-maintained school (Walford 2000b; Parker-Jenkins 2002). From April 1994, groups of sponsors could propose either the establishment of an entirely new school or that an existing faith-based or other private school should be re-established as a grant-maintained school. When Labour came to power in 1997 it quickly introduced a White Paper *Excellence in Schools* (DFEE 1997) which proposed a new organizational structure for schools and the abolition of grant-maintained status. But before this was implemented the government accepted seven schools into the state-maintained sector as voluntary aided schools including, significantly, two Muslim primary schools and one Seventh Day Adventist secondary school. It was thus Blair's government that made the final decision to fund a greater range of schools for religious minorities.

By January 2007, there were 37 Jewish schools, 2 Sikh, 7 Muslim, one Seventh Day Adventist, one Greek Orthodox, along with 26 Methodist, 4642 Church of England, 2038 Roman Catholic, and 86 other Christian schools. The first Hindu school was opened in September 2008. As there were 20,704 maintained schools, this means that 33.0 per cent of maintained schools were faith-based.

In addition to voluntary schools, there are faith-based City Technology Colleges and Academies. Both of these types of school are technically within the independent sector, but they receive all of their current expenditure and the vast majority of their capital costs from the government. The City Technology Colleges were an invention of Margaret Thatcher's government (Walford and Miller 1991, Whitty *et al.* 1993) which stalled at just 15 schools because it became evident that major industrial and technological companies were reluctant to be involved. Thus a different range of sponsors had to be persuaded to take part, which included sponsors with religious links. For example, the Southwark Diocesan Board of Education of the Church of England had a school in urgent need for new accommodation. The DES had twice refused to approve the necessary capital expenditure, but welcomed the idea that it should become a new CTC in London Docklands (Whitty *et al.* 1993: 47). In Gateshead, a group of evangelical Christians approached Peter Vardy, a local Christian entrepreneur who ran a chain of car dealerships, to sponsor a new CTC. The resulting Emmanuel CTC, has been the site of continual controversy for issues such as the teaching of creationism, homophobia, and its discipline policies. While not selecting students or parents on faith, Emmanuel CTC puts forward a Biblically-based evangelical Christianity.

Given the difficulties that the Conservative government had experienced in trying to obtain sponsorship for CTCs, it is strange that Blair's Labour government should eventually resurrect the policy in the form of Academies. Academies have sponsors who give about £2million towards the capital costs and who henceforth have a controlling interest in the school. They can specialise in modern foreign languages, visual arts, performing arts or media arts, sport or 'any subject specified by order of the Secretary of State'. Their close similarity with the CTCs was emphasised by the fact that the legislation in the *Learning and Skills Act* 2000 simply amended the CTC legislation as it was in the *Education Act* 1996. Various difficulties with the policy led to further changes in the *Education Act* 2002. Schedule 7 to that Act made special provisions for Academies where the premises was originally linked to the Church of England or where a member of the governing body of an Academy is appointed to represent the interests of the Church of England. Such Academies became officially 'church schools'.

In many ways the story of the Academies echoes that of the CTCs, but Blair's government was far more generous in its financial support and other assistance. Sponsors have been able to donate 'in kind' to an extraordinary extent, and the average cost of the first 12 Academies was £23 million (Beckett 2007, 13). Faith groups have seen this as an economical way of building their own schools, and the Blair government was active in trying to attract faith groups to become sponsors.

In early 2009 there were 113 Academies in operation, with several more due to open in future years and a plan for 400 by 2010 (DCSF, 2008). Five of this total are re-named City Technology Colleges, and it is likely that more will make the change. Of these 113, 38 can be defined as having a religious character. At 34 per cent, this number gives a similar percentage of faith schools to national figures for all schools. Two of the Academies – The King's Academy and Trinity Academy are sponsored by the Emmanuel Schools Foundation which is the sponsoring body for Sir Peter Vardy's Emmanuel School (Green 2009). The Foundation has said that it would be prepared to sponsor another ten academies within the North of England. Critics have expresses similar concerns about these two Academies as they have about Emmanuel CTC (Beckett 2007, 68-85; Gillard 2007, 218). Another nine of these Academies are sponsored by the United Learning Trust which is a Christian educational charity created specifically to sponsor academies and a subsidiary of the United Church Schools Trust, which was formerly the Church Schools Company founded in 1883 and currently controlling ten private schools in England. It is worth noting that none of the Academies is sponsored by a non-Christian faith group.

Faith schools are also to be found in the independent or private sector of schooling. While no official record is kept of the religious orientation of these schools, the *Faith in the System* report (DCSF 2007b) claimed that around 900 (nearly 40 per cent) private schools in England had a religious character. This includes a diverse array of faiths from Jewish, Methodist, Moravian or Quaker, to Anglican, Christian Science, Seventh Day Adventist, or Unitarian. Over 500 are linked to the Church of England, and 145 are Roman Catholic. Many of these schools are well-known, highly academic and charge high fees to their elite clientele. Their religious orientation may be seen in little more than their weekly Chapel service. But others include the 80 or so evangelical Christian (Walford 2001), over 100 Muslim (Walford 2003, 2004), and a few other Buddhist and Hindu schools.

The evangelical Christian schools share an ideology of Biblically-based evangelical Christianity which seeks to relate the message of the Bible to all aspects of present-day life whether personal, spiritual or educational. The facilities are usually poor as most of the schools run on very low fees. Teachers are often not paid on national salary scales, but see their teaching as a Christian obligation of service to others. There are currently some 45 schools with membership of the major group – Christian Schools Trust – with an unsteady trend in membership (see Walford 2001; Poyntz and Walford 1994). Tighter government regulations and inspection requirements have led to a sharp decline in the number of Brethren schools, organized in the Focus on Learning Trust. In 2004 there were 64, but this had declined to just 12 in 2007.

Since the 1970s there has been a steady increase in the number of Muslim private schools, linked to a growing dissatisfaction with the state-maintained schools that their children attended. Some parents felt that their children were not achieving academically as well as they might. The inner-city schools that many Muslim children attended did badly on test scores and parents became more concerned that these schools might be failing their children. They were also concerned that the standards of discipline and respect for adults found in these schools were often lower than they wished. But the main reasons for the growth in these schools was related directly to religious beliefs. Most British Muslims are descendants of Indian, Pakistani and Bangladeshi immigrants who came to Britain in the 1950s and 1960s. As they became more established and developed a variety of distinct Muslim communities, they became more religious in their outlook. As they became more religious, their concerns about both the structure and content of the state-maintained educational system grew.

In 2008 there were about 120 private Muslim schools in England. These vary considerably from one high-fee London school designed for the children of diplomats, to several poorly resourced schools in limited accommodation. Most are small with about 150 students. About a dozen are Darul Uloom institutions designed primarily to provide formal training for Imams and Islamic teachers (Open Society 2004, 126). In the past many of these schools have received critical reports from the Office for Standards in Education (OfSTED), particularly because of poor buildings, inadequate resources, poor health and safety standards and the low level of education provided. Changes within the 2002 *Education Act* meant that all new schools were no longer able to obtain 'provisional registration', a state which allowed lower standards on a temporary basis. However, in spite of numerous closures due to poor OfSTED inspections, new schools continue to open. Overall, there appears to be a levelling-off in the number of private Muslim schools rather than a decline. It is difficult to determine exact numbers but from a handful in the 1980s, and about 40 in the mid 1990s, Hewer (2001) estimated that by 2000 there were about 70 Muslim schools, and this has risen to about 120 in 2007. The number of private Jewish schools has increased from 34 in 1997 to 51 in 2007, with corresponding increase in students from 7625 to 10976.

SOCIAL AND COMMUNITY COHESION

I have outlined elsewhere the extent and nature of Tony Blair's support for faith schools that was evident throughout his Premiership (Walford 2008). He believed that faith schools have a particular 'ethos' that is distinct and that encourages moral development as well as academic success. This belief was then supplemented by the additional one – that faith schools could be inclusive and encourage community cohesion.

The concept of community cohesion is complex, changing and contested. It has developed over time, and is now much more wide-ranging and inclusive than originally. An early definition of the concept provided by the Home Office was:

> 'A shared sense of belonging based on common goals and core social values, respect for difference (ethnic, cultural and religious), and acceptance of the reciprocal rights and obligations of community members working together for the common good.' (Home Office 2001).

But this emphasis on 'sense of belonging' and 'respect', while important in themselves, was soon recognised to be too limited and had to be linked to active policy concerns with deprivation, inequality and racism. As the Commission on Integration and Cohesion recognised:

> 'Integration and cohesion policies cannot be a substitute for national policies to reduce deprivation and provide people with more opportunities: tackling inequality is an absolute precondition for integration and cohesion.' (COIC 2007: 21).

Rather than community cohesion being a diversion from the key concerns of inequality within society, it can be used to explore the elements within society and within schooling practices that support and encourage greater equity and support equal opportunity. The report from the Runnymede Trust, *Right to Divide? Faith schools and community cohesion* (Berkeley 2008) does just this, and uses a definition from the Local Government Association (2002), which was developed in cooperation with the Home Office and the Commission for Racial Equality, as a framework for its discussion. Strong cohesion is seen where:

- A common vision and a sense of belonging exists for all communities;

- The diversity of people's different backgrounds and circumstances is appreciated and positively valued;

- Those from different backgrounds have similar life opportunities;

- Strong and positive relationships are being developed between people from different backgrounds in the workplace, in schools and within neighbourhoods.

The Runnymede Report is based upon a series of consultations and workshops with those involved with faith schools – both protagonists and supporters. The various data generating strategies involved a series of consultations with those who were perceived to be experts in the field, six community consultation workshops in different parts of the country (Osler 2007), school consultations, and an online survey of parents and teachers. The report is open about the limitations of the data generated, in particular the difficulty of hearing the diversity of representative minority faith views, but combines this data with that from published sources to present a very thoughtful analysis of how faith schools might contribute to community cohesion. This four-fold framework used by the Runnymede Trust report will be used in the second part of this chapter to structure some of the arguments put forward by supporters and critics of faith schools.

Encouraging pupils towards a shared sense of belonging.

There is an obvious potential tension between the mission of faith schools to promote and pass on their own particular religious identities, and the government's aim that all schools should contribute to a shared sense of belonging that crosses faith boundaries. This is less of a problem for Church of England schools which have traditionally seen their role as serving all of the students in a Parish whatever their faith may be or none. The liberal interpretations of Christianity that grew from the 1960s onwards meant that students of any faith could be reasonably easily accommodated without challenging the ethos of the school. But the potential tension is certainly stronger in Jewish, Muslim or Sikh schools where the whole purpose behind their establishment was to pass on a particular faith to the children of the community.

Those promoting such minority faith schools argue that it is essential that children develop their own faith identity before they encounter and can appreciate the faith identities of others. Faith is seen as imparting moral standards and the obligation to treat others well. But opponents argue that such separation of faith groups from each other can lead to segregation and distrust between groups.

It is well known that the English educational system is strongly differentiated by social class and ethnicity, but the objective of most recent educational policy has been to reduce this differentiation rather than to enforce it. But levels of ethnic segregation remain high in English secondary schools (Burgess and Wilson 2005; Weekes-Bernard 2007), and the increase in school choice has done little to improve the matter as many parents opt for self-segregation. Ethnic segregation is higher for pupils of Indian, Pakistani or Bangladeshi origin than for those of with Black Caribbean or Black African heritage. Dench *et al.* (2006) show how life has changed in the East End of London since the famous account given in *Family and Kinship in East London* (Young and Willmott 1957). The authors argue that many white working-class families have taken refuge in local Christian schools rather than use the non-denominational community schools. According to the 2001 census, in the London Borough of Tower Hamlets 58 per cent of those aged 0-17 were of Bangladeshi origins yet, in 2002, 17 primary schools had over 90 per cent Bangladeshi children, while nine (all denominational) had fewer than 10 per cent. Out of 16 secondary schools, four denominational schools each had three per cent or fewer Bangladeshi children while three nearby non-denominational schools had over 80 per cent. This represents severe ethnic segregation of the local population. The creation of separate schools for religious minorities (which are strongly related to ethic minorities) does nothing to improve the levels of ethnic segregation.

The Runnymede Report (Berkeley 2008) suggests that all faith schools should broaden their intakes to include pupils from different faiths or none, and should act as hubs for interfaith dialogue. This was proposed in the belief that ethnic segregation was in itself undesirable, and that co-presence would ensure that effective policies were developed to ensure mutual respect. It is worth noting that an amendment was proposed to the Education and Inspections Bill in 2006 which would have required new faith schools to accept 25 per cent of their students from outside the sponsoring faith. Even though some 45 Labour MPs defied the party whip, the amendment was rejected. The final *Education and Inspections Act* did, however, introduce the explicit duty to 'promote community cohesion' on all state-maintained schools. The new subject of citizenship was also introduced in 2002. However, neither of these changes applies to the independent sector.

Helping pupils develop a positive appreciation of diversity.

The historic compromises between religious providers and past governments led to Religious Education having an anomalous position in the curriculum – being part of the Basic Curriculum but not part of the National Curriculum. For non-faith schools Religious Education is the responsibility of local SACREs and these schools always teach about several faiths, but faith schools can have their own syllabuses and there is no obligation for them to teach anything about other religions. While many of faith schools do teach about other faiths, a few do so only to show how other faiths are actually wrong. A recent OfSTED report on the teaching of RE (2007) found that there was inconsistency in the quality of teaching of RE and argued that, as currently taught, RE did not promote community cohesion effectively. It is difficult to believe that schools that only teach about their own religion, or teach about the 'errors' in other faiths, are able to promote a positive appreciation of religious diversity.

Of equal concern are the views that some schools may be putting forward about other forms of diversity. A recent Gallup poll of Muslims in the Capital cities of England, Germany and France found that Muslims in London held the most conservative views on several moral issues. Only four per cent of the Muslims interviewed in London thought that homosexual acts were morally acceptable, ten per cent thought abortion was morally acceptable and 11 per cent thought that sex between an unmarried man and woman was morally acceptable (Gallup 2009). These figures are for the general Muslim public, and it is to be expected that those involved in Muslim schools (especially those in the private sector) are likely to have even more conservative views as they have deliberately established their own schools to support their faith. It is worth noting that rather similar conservative views are probably to be found amongst those involved in the New Christian Schools. In addition, some Muslim schools have restrictions on listening or performing most types of music and restrict art practices to images on non-sentient beings (Walford 2003). Strong gender roles are also a feature of some of these schools. It is difficult to see how such schools help pupils develop a positive appreciation of diversity.

However, some Muslim schools can act to challenge traditional gender roles. Some Muslim single-sex girls' schools, in particular, have encouraged academic involvement and success, and considerable numbers of girls have proceeded to higher education in contrast to traditional expectations.

Single-sex schools do still have their own problems, of course, for the boys' schools are usually much less successful, and parents who want a coeducational school for their children are sometimes disadvantaged.

The Runnymede report (Berkeley 2008) suggests that there should be a newly established National Curriculum in RE and that this should include teaching about several major world faiths. It also recommends that all schools should challenge discrimination on all legally defined issues of diversity – including those of gender and sexual orientation.

Removing barriers to equality.

One of the government's major reasons for supporting faith schools is the belief that they have a special ethos that encourages academic success as well as developing moral values. It is certainly true that, on average, students at faith schools obtain better educational qualifications than those at non-faith schools, but it is widely argued that this is due to selection of more able higher social class students and parents. A survey by the Institute for Research in Integrated Strategies (IRIS) of 17,000 children in Church of England and Catholic primary schools in 2006 showed that there is a social class bias in their intakes. 14 per cent of children were eligible for free school meals as opposed to 20 per cent in the catchment areas (Gillard 2007: 222). West (2008) examined the situation for religious schools in London by using data from the National Pupil Database for 2005. She found that, while there were considerable differences between individual schools, overall, just 17 per cent of children in religious schools were eligible for free school meals compared with 25 per cent in non-religious schools. They also educated a smaller proportion of the lowest ability pupils (19% versus 31%). Pupils from all South Asian minority ethnic groups were under-represented, with just one per cent of Pakistani and Bangladeshi students in religious schools, while Black African and Caribbean ethnic groups were over-represented. However, within this group of Black ethnicity students, those who attended religious schools were less likely to be eligible for free school meals (24% versus 37%) (see also West and Hind 2007, Chamberlain et al. 2006).

With such intakes, it is to be expected that faith-based schools would achieve higher educational results. But, in value added terms, their success is much less clear. Schagen and Schagen (2005) examined national value-added datasets to evaluate the school effects at primary and secondary levels. They found that Jewish schools did perform better than other schools in value added terms, but that on balance Roman Catholic schools did not perform any better or worse than other schools. Church of England schools had some significant positive achievements, but the differences were slight. In contrast, a self-published report by Arthur and Godfrey (2006) of more restricted value-added data sets found that secondary school students in Catholic maintained schools in Birmingham performed, on average, better than those attending non-Catholic schools at Key Stages 3 and 4, even when prior attainment and socio-economic status were taken into account. Similarly, Arthur and Godfrey (2005) found a small advantage to students in Church of England schools. Yeshanew *et al* (2008) used data from the National Pupil Database from 2000 to 2004 to examine progress at primary school. Through an analysis of variance and multilevel modelling, they found that, overall, attending a faith school was related to a small but significantly higher key stage 2 performance. Children with special educational needs also did better at faith schools. However, it is worth noting that in all cases the percentages of children eligible for free school meals, having SEN (school action plan), SEN (statement), or having English as a second language were lower in Church of England, Roman Catholic, or Jewish schools than in non-faith schools. The percentage having SEN statements or having English as a second language, for example, was in each case approximately half of the percentage in non-faith schools. It may well be that these other factors are more closely related to any small differences in achievement than school ethos.

While any academic advantage may be actually small, there remains a perception that faith schools provide a better academic environment as well as a more moral one. If so, critics argue that all families should be able to obtain access to these schools if they wish to do so. In practice, there are considerable differences between faith and non-faith schools in their class and ethnic composition. While the historic purpose of most of the Church of England and Roman Catholic schools was to serve the poor, faith schools now have fewer students who are eligible for free school meals than non-faith schools. This is partly due to the geographic location of the schools, but researchers such as Diane Reay (2008) have found that faith schools have allowed middle class parents to achieve 'white flight' and ensure that their children do not share multi-ethnic classrooms. Selection procedures that are based on demonstrable adherence to a particular faith tend to favour the more privileged, so greater community cohesion would probably result from a restriction on selection on the basis of faith. It is worth remembering that, while it is now illegal to interview prospective students or families during the process of selection, those families still have to make a specific application for a place at a faith school. They remain selective in the sense that families have to be prepared to accept the religious teaching of the school and make an application.

Building strong partnerships between people from different groups.

In the non-statutory Guidance (DCSF 2007a) on the duty to promote community cohesion, schools are required to show how they provide 'reasonable means for children, young people, their friends and families to interact with people from different backgrounds'. The Guidance refers to a discussion from the Commission on Integration and Cohesion (2007a):

> 'Meaningful contact between people from different groups has been shown to break down stereotypes and prejudice. Contact is meaningful when: conversations go beyond surface friendliness; in which people exchange personal information or talk about each other's differences and identities; people share a common goal or share an interest; and they are sustained long-term (so one-off or chance meetings are unlikely to make much difference).'

There has long been a concern that separate faith schools for families with differing beliefs could reproduce sectarianism. This is particularly true in Northern Ireland (Gallagher 2005) and Scotland (McKinney 2008) where many critics have identified the divided school systems of Catholic and Protestant schools as potentially contributing to 'the troubles'. Similar dangers have been seen in having separate schools for Muslims, Sikhs, and Hindus where there is a strong correlation between visible ethnic minority status and faith. The racial disturbances in Bradford, Burnley and Oldham in 2001, along with the destruction of the World Trade Centre twin towers in 2001 and the later terror attacks in London in 2005, brought a new focus in government on this issue of potential segregation within communities on faith and ethnic lines.

Faith schools often find it particularly difficult to bring together people from different backgrounds. Indeed, part of the reason for separate faith schools is that parents believe that their children could be 'contaminated' by contact with children of other faiths or social classes. Contact with a range of other adults and students is exactly what some parents do not want for their children, for they fear that such contact will lead to a loss of faith or bad influences from people with differing views and aspirations.

The Runnymede Report (Berkeley 2008) concludes that the government's guidance on creating strong partnerships between schools and communities has been interpreted in a variety of ways. While non-faith and inter-faith organizations have largely tried to bring together people from a range of different backgrounds as intended, faith schools are more likely to have interpreted it as extending ties with their own communities in an inter-generational way rather than developing cross-cultural links. Berkeley (2008: 62) argues for greater priority being given to bringing together people from a variety of backgrounds beyond the faith and the direct challenging of parents who do not wish their children to have contact with those of other faiths.

CONCLUSION

The arguments used by detractors of faith schools are several and varied, and it is worth noting that rather different arguments are used according to what type of school is being considered. Where faith schools are perceived to be strong academically, concern is usually about faith acting as a restriction to accessing those schools. Where faith schools are perceived to be highly traditional in their teaching, concern may be more that they may encourage intolerance of homosexuality or may portray strongly differentiated gender roles. However, in both cases issues of community cohesion are prominent.

The concept of community cohesion is broad, and includes concern for equity among groups from different backgrounds. It has been shown that many faith schools still have some way to go before they can be seen as promoting community cohesion as they are obliged by law to do. While it is possible that separate schooling need not lead to a fragmentation of society and increased racism (Short, 2003), there need to be changes such that they are more likely to increase community cohesion than at present. Necessary changes probably include the need to ensure that faith schools accept a mix of children from different social classes, ethnicities and religions. The last of these requirements would be the most controversial, but it would seem reasonable to expect faith school funded by the state to accept a minimum of, say, 25 per cent of their intake from other faiths without this changing the ethos of the school. The nature and content of Religious Education also needs to be reconsidered such that all schools are required to teach about a variety of religions beyond their own. Religious differences need to be taken seriously (Barnes, 2009) rather than ignored. It is worth considering the extent to which changes should also be required in the independent sector.

Faith schools are an important ingredient of the British educational system and are likely to remain so. But that does not mean that they should remain unchanged. Enhancing community cohesion is vital in our ever-changing world, and schools should play their part in such a process. But it is also worth recognising that schools cannot work alone. Inequalities between people of differing classes, faiths and ethnicities need to be tacked by government at a wider level than just schooling. Community cohesion needs to be enhanced through a range of social and economic policies. But faith schools need to play their part, and that may involve changes to the current position.

REFERENCES

Arthur, J. and Godfrey, R. (2005) *Statistical survey of the attainment and achievement of pupils in Church of England schools*, Canterbury: National Institute for Christian Education Research.

Arthur, J. and Godfrey, R. (2006) *A statistical survey of attainment in Catholic schools in England with particular reference to secondary schools operating under the trust deed of the archdiocese of Birmingham*, Canterbury: National Institute for Christian Education Research.

Barnes L. P. (2009) *Religious Education: Taking Religious Difference Seriously*, No 17, Impact Series, Philosophy of Education Society of Great Britain

Beckett, F. (2007) *The Great City Academy Fraud*, London: Continuum.

Berkeley, R. (2008) *Right to Divide? Faith schools and community cohesion*, London: The Runnymede Trust.

Blair, T. (2008) 'Faith and globalisation.' Speech given at the Cardinal Lectures, Westminster Cathedral, London, 3 April. http://tonyblairoffice/speeches/

Burgess, S. and Wilson, D. (2005) 'Ethnic segregation in England's schools', *Transactions of the Institute of British Geographers*, 30, 1, 20-36.

Chamberlain, T., Rutt, S. and Fletcher-Campbell, F. (2006) *Admissions: Who goes where? Messages from the statistics*. LGA Research Report 4/06. Slough: NFER.

COIC (2007) *Interim Statement from the Commission on Integration and Cohesion*, London: Department for Communities and Local Government.

Dench, G., Gavron, K. and Young, M. (2006) *The New East End: kinship, race and conflict*, London: Profile Books.

DEPARTMENT FOR CHILDREN, SCHOOLS AND FAMILIES (2007a) *Guidance on the Duty to Promote Community Cohesion*, London: DCSF.

DEPARTMENT FOR CHILDREN, SCHOOLS AND FAMILIES (2007b) *Faith in the System*, London: DCSF.

DEPARTMENT FOR CHILDREN, SCHOOLS AND FAMILIES (2008) http://wwwedubase.gov.uk/EstablishmentFindDownload.aspx?type=CS V, (Accessed 14/02/2008.)

DEPARTMENT FOR EDUCATION AND EMPLOYMENT (1997) *Excellence in schools*, London, The Stationery Office.

Gallagher, T. (2005) 'Faith schools and Northern Ireland: a review of the evidence' in Gardner, R., Cairns, J. and Lawton, D. (eds) *Faith Schools. Consensus or conflict?* London: RoutledgeFalmer.

Gallup (2009) 'Poll on Muslim values in England, France and Germany'. www.gallup.com/poll/107512/Moral-Issues-Divide-Westerners-From-Muslims-West.aspx. (Accessed 9/5/09.)

Gillard, D. (2007) 'Never mind the evidence: Blair's obsession with faith schools' *Forum*, 49, 3, 213-228.

Green, B. (2009) 'Discipline and school ethos: exploring students' reflections upon values, rules and the Bible in a Christian City Technology College', *Ethnography and Education*, 4, 2, 197-209.

Hewer, C. (2001) 'Schools for Muslims', *Oxford Review of Education*, 27, 4, 515-527.

HOME OFFICE (2001) *Building cohesive communities: a report of the Ministerial Group on Public Order and Community Cohesion*, London: Home Office.

LOCAL GOVERNMENT ASSOCIATION (2002) *Guidance on Community Cohesion*, London, Local Government Association.

McKinney, S.J. (2008) 'Do Catholic schools in Scotland cause or promote sectarianism?' in S.J. McKinney (ed) *Faith Schools in the Twenty-First Century*, Edinburgh: Dunedin.

OfSTED (2007) *Making Sense of Religion: a report on Religious Education in schools and the impact of locally agreed syllabuses*, London: Ofsted

Open Society (2004) *Muslims in the UK: Policies for engaged citizens*, Open Society Institute, EUMAP.

Osler, A. (2007) *Faith Schools and Community Cohesion*, London: The Runnymede Trust

Parker-Jenkins, M. (2002) 'Equal access to state finding: the case of muslim schools in Britain', *Race, Ethnicity and Education*, 5,3,273-289

Poyntz, C. and Walford, G. (1994) 'The new Christian schools: A survey', *Educational Studies*, 20,1, 127-143

Reay, D. (2008) 'Class out of place: the white middle classes and intersectionalities of class and "race" in urban schooling in England', in L. Weis (ed) *The Way Class Works*, New York: Routledge.

Sarwar, G. (1994) *British Muslims and Schools*, London: Muslim Education Trust.

Schagen, I. and Schagen, S. (2005) 'The impact of faith schools on pupil performance', in Gardner, R., Cairns, J. and Lawton, D. (eds) *Faith Schools. Consensus or conflict?* London: RoutledgeFalmer.

Short, G. (2003) 'Faith schools and social cohesion: Opening up the debate', *British Journal of Religious Education*, 25, 2, 129-141.

Thompson, P. (2004) 'Whose confession? Which tradition?' *British Journal of Religious Education*, 26, 1, 61-67.

Vertovec, S. (2002) 'Islamophobia and Muslim recognition in Britain', in Haddad. Y. (ed) *Muslims in the West: From sojourners to citizens*, Oxford: Oxford University Press.

Walford, G. (2000a) *Policy and Politics in Education. Sponsored grant-maintained schools and religious diversity*, Aldershot: Ashgate.

Walford, G. (2000b) 'From City Technology College to sponsored grant-maintained schools', *Oxford Review of Education*, 26, 2, 145-158.

Walford, G. (2001) 'The fate of the new Christian schools: from growth to decline?' *Educational Studies*, 27, 4, 465-477.

Walford, G. (2003) 'Muslim schools in Britain', in G. Walford (ed) *British Private Schools: research on policy and practice*, London: Woburn Press.

Walford, G. (2004) 'Muslims and their educational strategies in England', in Daun, H and Walford, G. (eds) *Educational Strategies among Muslims in the Context of Globalization. Some National Case Studies*, Leiden: Brill.

Walford, G. (2008) 'Faith-based schools in England after 10 years of Tony Blair' *Oxford Review of Education*, 34, 6, 689-699.

Walford, G. and Miller, H. (1991) *City Technology College*, Buckingham: Open University Press.

Weekes-Burnham, D. (2007) *School Choice and Ethnic Segregation – Educational decision-making among Black and minority parents*, London: Runnymede Trust.

West, A. (2008) 'Religious schools in London: School admissions, religious composition and selectivity' *Oxford Review of Education* (forthcoming).

West, A. and Hind, A. (2007) 'School choice in London, England: Characteristics of students in different types of secondary school.' *Peabody Journal of Education*, 82, 2-3, 498-529.

Whitty, G., Edwards, T. and Gewirtz, S. (1993) *Specialisation and Choice in Urban Education. The City Technology College experiment*, London: Routledge.

Yeshanew, T., Schagen, I. and Evans, S. (2008) 'Faith schools and pupils' progress through primary education', *Educational Studies*, 34, 5, 511-526.

Young, M. and Willmott, P. (1957) *Family and Kinship in East London*, London: Routledge and Kegan Paul.

CHAPTER 7

WHICH COMMUNITY? WHOSE COHESION?
COMMUNITY COHESION, CITIZENSHIP
AND RELIGIOUS EDUCATION:
From revolutionary democracy
to liberal autocracy

Liam Gearon

SUMMARY

SOME OF THE CONTENTIOUS contemporary inter-relationships between community cohesion, citizenship and religious education are addressed and traced to a complex historical lineage of philosophical, political and theological change originating in eighteenth century revolutionary democracy. Analysing the often overlooked legacy of eighteenth century revolutionary democracy in twentieth century totalitarianism, the chapter argues that – difficulties of historical causality aside – the repressive heritage of both eighteenth century revolutionary democracy and twentieth century totalitarianism is evident in community cohesion initiatives through an emergent 'liberal autocracy'.

INTRODUCTION

Arising from the European Enlightenment, I argue that eighteenth century revolutionary democracy has helped shape our notions of social and community cohesion in the twenty-first century: explicitly through the political discourse of human rights and democratic citizenship, and covertly through historically entrenched and trenchant attitudes to religion.

However, those proponents of this tradition who educationally and politically laud a supposedly utopian legacy too often neglect the dystopian aspects of eighteenth century revolutionary democracy, the violent and repressive implantation of Enlightenment ideals (autonomy, citizenship, democracy, human rights); neglecting too the influences of such revolutionary democracy upon twentieth century totalitarianism.

Further, I argue that the issues at stake here are more than of historical interest: that in a twenty-first century context religious education specifically here risks state manipulation by serving the interests of a particular political community, and specific form of coherence, one whose rationalist and political traditions are identified through their scepticism and even antagonism to religion, finding articulation in the four features of what I define as a newly emergent 'liberal autocracy'.

COMMUNITY COHESION, CITIZENSHIP AND RELIGIOUS EDUCATION

The European Enlightenment radically altered thinking about the legal and political status of religion, philosophically marking the intellectual ascendancy of human reason over theology and divine revelation, the contemporary manifestations of which I have traced elsewhere.[1]

The door to the weakening of Christianity's political authority in Europe was opened through the sixteenth century Reformation and the wars of religion that followed, and with the secular determination of political peace of the 1648 Treaty of Westphalia, all of which laid the foundation for the philosophical Enlightenment revolution in the eighteenth century (Gearon, 2006; 2007; 2008; 2009; 2010). Revolutionary democracies which followed fast from the Enlightenment further and drastically reduced the scope of ecclesiastical influence on society, accentuated by formal separations of religious authority from political power.

Here scepticism of religion and faith in human reason grounded the revolutionary democracy where faith in heaven would gradually – over the next two centuries – seek the often violent imposition of man-made political utopias (Arthur, Gearon and Sears, 2010; Burleigh, 2006; 2007). The post-Enlightenment period thus initiated marginalization of religion from the arts and humanities, from philosophy as much as public life but also the increasing presumptions of a liberal secularism within social and political life (Gearon, 2008; 2009; 2010).

The origins and inclinations of this modern polity, linking human rights to citizenship under nation-states, is nowhere better encapsulated than in Thomas Paine's (1985; [1791/2]) *Rights of Man* where he defends revolutionary democracy, and reiterates its attack on religion:

> 'In casting our eyes over the world, it is extremely easy to distinguish the governments which have arisen out of society or out of the social compact, from those which have not; but to place this in a clearer light than what a single glance may afford, it will be proper to take a review of the several sources from which governments have arisen, and on which they have been founded. They may be all comprehended under three heads. First, Superstition. Secondly, Power. Thirdly, The common interest of society, and the common rights of man.' (Paine, 1791: 69).

Thus by superstition Paine means religion, by power he means tyranny, and by the common rights of man he means democracy.

When the New Labour Government came to power in 1997 it initiated a reforming legislative programme firmly and incontestably based within this historical context, most explicitly evident upon a legislative framework based on a human rights agenda and democratic citizenship – the 1998 Human Rights Act, the 1950 European Convention on Human Rights, the 1948 Universal Declaration of Human Rights, the 1945 foundation of the United Nations itself all modelled on eighteenth century revolutionary democracy and reflecting the 1789 French constitutional *Rights of Man and of the Citizen* (Paine, 1791/2).

Thus if the 1998 Human Rights Act was the defining moment upon which the majority of all subsequent (post-1997 New Labour) legislation was based, a distinctive, contemporaneous *educational* development was the commissioning of a report on the feasibility of a new national curriculum subject of *citizenship*. The publication and influence of the Advisory Group on Citizenship, the 'Crick Report' (Crick, 1998) on the subsequent formation of national curriculum citizenship is well documented (Keast and Craft, 2010).

The role of religion in relation to these essentially secular principles was always going to be sensitive. Although provision for the right to freedom of religion or belief is embedded in the 1998 Human Rights Act, national curriculum citizenship gave little attention to religion. Indeed, many theorists see citizenship as thoroughly secular in origins, history and contemporary orientation (Heater, 2004). Crick, militantly humanist and anti-religious, followed this line strongly in a highly secular report which considerably underplays not only the role of religion but wider issues of cultural diversity within liberal democracies.

Two and three years after Crick, however, events prompted more urgent initiatives in relation to cultural diversity. Government thinking on cohesion was thus initiated in the aftermath of riots in English northern cities in November 2001. In a world still stunned by the 9/11 bombings, a sense of sudden dismay settled upon the political establishment that religion was the cause not of meek compliance but violent disorder, that – with wide differences between religions in relation to democratic principles accepted (see Gearon, 2003) – religion was not only resurgent in public life and global governance but potentially a major source of disruption of those principles of liberal (rights-based) democratic citizenship. It took the bombings of 7/7 in London 2005 to reinvigorate the urgency of political debate in this area. Thus the Commission on Integration and Cohesion was established in 2006 to consider issues of diversity following, amongst other factors, the shock that the 7/7 bombers were British born, and the 2006 Education and Inspections Act made it a legal requirement for schools in England to promote community cohesion and for OfSTED to report on this aspect of educational provision (DCSF, 2007, 2008).

Drawing on a wide consultation and a number of 'thinkpieces', the Commission on Integration and Cohesion (CIC) established a working notion of community cohesion defining a society in which:

'there is a common vision and sense of belonging by all communities; the diversity of people's backgrounds is appreciated and valued; similar life opportunities are available to all; strong and positive relationships exist and are developed in the workplace, schools and the wider community'.[2]

The Commission's final report, *Our Shared Future* (CIC, 2007) characterised community cohesion (again) as a 'sense of belonging' where people understand 'their rights and responsibilities in relation to the place where they live' and trust that 'local institutions act fairly in arbitrating between different interests'. Here we see the human rights framework within community cohesion, overseen at present by the Equalities and Human Rights Commission.

Such initiatives have in turn been coordinated with attempts to enhance community cohesion through specific curriculum areas, notably citizenship.

Arguably this was a second effort, since Crick and the introduction of national curriculum citizenship (from 1999) was supposed to enhance community and political participation, but had a manifestly limited effect in transforming the socio-political climate of Britain as initially hoped for (Keast and Craft, 2010; Kerr, 2010). Thus the *Diversity and Citizenship Curriculum Review* (DCSF 2007), authored by Sir Keith Ajegbo, a former secondary head teacher, was commissioned to 'review the teaching specifically of ethnic, religious and cultural diversity across the curriculum, exploring particularly whether or not "modern British social and cultural history" should be a fourth pillar of the Citizenship curriculum'.

The Diversity and Citizenship Curriculum Review became – much as the Crick Report (1998) had a decade earlier – an important milestone in providing the Government and schools with principles and practical guidelines for facilitating community cohesion, especially in respect to diversity and difference, within citizenship. In its own terms, the *Diversity and Citizenship Curriculum Review* was 'commissioned in response to a growing debate about whether UK society engages with issues around race, religion, culture, identity and values in the UK today, in a way that meets the needs of all pupils'. The rhetoric of the Report reflects this:

> 'Do we, as individuals and as a nation, respect each other's differences and build on commonalities? Do we appreciate our own and others' distinct identities? Do we really have an understanding of what it is to be a citizen, of how it is to live in the UK? And, most importantly, are we ensuring that all our children and young people have the education they need to embrace issues of diversity and citizenship, both for them to thrive and for the future of our society? This 'education for diversity' is fundamental if the UK is to have a cohesive society in the 21st century.
>
> UK society is made up of many ethnicities, cultures, languages and religions, and it is constantly evolving. The UK has a rich heritage of cultural and ethnic diversity, stretching back over many centuries. However, so many of the people we talked to discussed the complexity of the world we live in and the many identities that children inhabit. There is a moral imperative to address issues of disparity and commonality and how we live together. It is crucial that all children and young people, through both the formal and informal curricula in schools, have a real understanding of who lives in the UK today, of why they are here, and of what they can contribute.' (Ajegbo, 2007, 16)

Elaborating on diversity in international context – from the economy and migration to globalisation and technological change – the *Review* acknowledges the:

'changing nature of the UK and potential for tension to arise now makes it ever more pressing for us to work towards community cohesion, fostering mutual understanding within schools so that valuing difference and understanding what binds us together become part of the way pupils think and behave'. (*ibid*, 16)

In relating national life to international politics, the *Review* links the needs of community cohesion to recent conflicts around cultural and religious difference:

'In 2001 the inter-ethnic disturbances in Bradford, Burnley and Oldham led to the Home Office Cantle Report on Community Cohesion, which argues that the teaching ethos of schools should reflect the different cultures within the school and within the wider community, and that Citizenship education should address these issues ... Major international events, such as 11 September 2001 and the London bombings in July 2005, have contributed to the debate on community cohesion and shared values, particularly because the latter were perpetrated by British-born Muslims. In the wake of these events, community cohesion is a key focus for the Government.' (*ibid*, 18)

As with the CIC's (2007) *Our Shared Future, the Diversity and Citizenship Curriculum Review* underlines the obligations from the 2006 Education and Inspections Act to promote social and community cohesion in law, explicitly linking national and international developments in the re-emergence of religion as a force in global governance. Both Reports are clearly political doctrine as much as educational policy.

A key recommendation of the *Diversity and Citizenship Curriculum Review* is that a fourth strand be added to national curriculum citizenship, entitled *Identity and Diversity: Living Together in the UK*, bringing together three conceptual components:

- Critical thinking about ethnicity, religion and 'race'
- An explicit link to political issues and values
- The use of contemporary history in teachers' pedagogy to illuminate thinking about contemporary issues relating to citizenship

It is recommended that the following areas should be included:

- Contextualised understanding that the UK is a 'multinational' state, made up of England, Northern Ireland, Scotland and Wales
- Immigration
- Commonwealth and the legacy of Empire

- European Union
- Extending the franchise (e.g. the legacy of slavery, universal suffrage, equal opportunities legislation)

These recommendations were included in the new citizenship order, a strong incursion into territory formerly that of religious educators (Gearon, 2009; 2010).

These extant citations make a link between community cohesion, citizenship and religious education clear and unambiguous. Yet religion – reduced to 'living together in the UK' – risks being delimited to social and community cohesion. Religion is politically sanitised. Serving to cohere rather than critique the state, religion is not seen as true but useful. This notion that religious education is in service of an agenda to prevent extremism has been made profoundly evident in the involvement of the Religious Education Council of England and Wales in a major and unprecedented Government initiative enlisting religious educators in the war against extremism.[3]

Further, any notion that there is a wider history associated with the formation of British national identity from Christian origins is woefully absent. If the *Review's* analysis of English and indeed British history went back further than 1945 his report might be less worrying. However, any sense of the historic and continuing contribution of Christian religious tradition to the national, political and indeed religious identity of the British Isles is implicitly suspect, potentially divisive, 'anti-cohesive', and liable to be tarnished with the soubriquet of extremism.

This position is arguably contrary to the legal position of religious education in England. In *Making sense of religion*, OfSTED (2007) summarises the relationship between religious education and the law:

> 'The legal requirements governing religious education (RE) were set out in the Education Reform Act of 1988 and confirmed by the Education Acts of 1996 and 1998. ... RE must be provided in accordance with the local agreed syllabus. Uniquely, although RE is a statutory subject, it is not part of the National Curriculum. The content of RE is determined at the level of the local authority (LA) and each LA must review its agreed syllabus every five years. An agreed syllabus should 'reflect the fact that the religious traditions in Great Britain are in the main Christian whilst taking account of the teachings and practices of the other principal religions represented in Great Britain' (Education Reform Act (ERA) 1988 Section 8 (3)).' (OfSTED 2007, 4)

In English law Christianity thus still retains a situation of historical prominence which dates back for almost two thousand years.[4] As a former head of religious education in a community school in Glastonbury, Somerset, the site of the ancient and rich history was evident, dating back by tradition to the earliest centuries of Christianity; and the small town was witness too of course to the worst, murderous excess and cultural vandalism of the Protestant Reformation, including the destruction of one the finest medieval abbeys in Europe, and the murder of its Abbot Whiting. If England is a nation which supports diversity and freedom of religion, not only of belief in private but worship in public, the country still has a monarch who is Head of the Church of England. Protestant Christianity in England remains the state religion. England, a constitutional monarchy and parliamentary democracy has its historical foundations as yet resting firmly within Christian history.

Notably epitomised by the culturally myopic *Diversity and Citizenship Curriculum Review*, current New Labour Government policy on social and community cohesion is radically, if subtly altering the historical, integrally Christian religious identity of the country for ideological motives, which originate within a specific, easily identifiable tradition of revolutionary democracy variously indifferent to, sceptical of, and historically antagonistic to religion.

FROM REVOLUTIONARY DEMOCRACY TO LIBERAL AUTOCRACY

As I have shown elsewhere (see again note 1), the precedent for a close relationship between politics and education is not new. Indeed, from its inception, the United Nations' integrally related political transformation through human rights with their promotion through teaching and education. This was part of a concerted international response to the defeated political extremism we know as 'totalitarianism'. Examine the preamble to the UN's Universal Declaration of Human Rights and you will find there not only the instigation of the Declaration as a response to and defence against the barbarism of such regimes but also the role of education as an integral partner with international law and politics in effecting and maintaining socio-political change through these human rights principles.

This correlation between politics and pedagogy is perhaps self-evident but historical understanding of its origins in the era of mass, that is, democratic politics is less understood (Gearon, 2010). Most notably there are surprising nuances in the historical relationship between Enlightenment political values of citizenship, democracy and human rights in the eighteenth century and totalitarianism in the twentieth. As had occurred during the French Revolution in particular, ironies abound here in how totalitarianism itself modelled itself largely upon the autocratic imposition of a general will upon whole populations.

The use of educational means to achieve political ends in social and community cohesion in response to religious extremism (Home Office, 2005) shows, however, a *new* development in the relationship between religion, politics and education (Arthur, Gearon and Sears, 2010). It shows political-educational responses to totalitarianism in the UN-era in the late twentieth century developed to another dimension in dealing with religious extremism in the twenty-first.

We have, however, immediate difficulty in sustaining such an analysis in the space of a short chapter, but whatever the space the difficulty is perennial: questions of cause and effect are notoriously problematic in political history, no less than they are within the abstractions of philosophical discourse. However, a great deal of writing on political extremism of the twentieth century attempted precisely this with respect to conceptualisations of totalitarianism. Why and from where did Nazism arise? Why did Fascism arise? What accounts for the repressions of the Soviet Union or Communist China? Are there common characteristics of each of these historical/ political phenomena? What was it in the twentieth century that meant so many of these regimes were associated with individual men: Hitler, Mussolini, Stalin, Mao? The literature on any single one of these is vast and pre-empts even a sensible list of citations (see, for example, Friedrich and Brzezinski, 1967; Friedrich, Curtis, and Barber, 1979; Gleason, 1995; Roberts, 2006; Zizek, 2001).

The term 'totalitarianism' itself arose within Mussolini's Italy, when, in 1924, Gentile coined the expression 'uno stato totalitario' *positively and not pejoratively* to define Mussolini's efforts at statecraft within Fascist Italy (for a wider terminological discussion, see Schapiro, 1972). Whether Fascist Italy was totalitarian or simply autocratic raises a multitude of other related questions in political philosophy. To what extent does totalitarianism differ from autocracy? Is totalitarianism or autocracy different from more ancient forms of repressive 'governance' such as 'tyranny' (Strauss, 2000)? And if tyranny is often unfavourably compared to, in contradistinction with 'democratic' Greek city states or the citizenship

114

ideals of Aristotle's Politics or Plato's *Republic*, what of the autocratic, tyrannical, inequitable, 'totalitarian' aspects of life in Plato's *Republic* (Popper, 1946?). Schapiro's (1972) Cold War discussion extends the fascinating history of the term, its origins, uses and misuses, with a literature showing just how powerfully self-sustaining the term totalitarian seems to be (again, see Friedrich and Brzezinski, 1967; Friedrich, Curtis, and Barber, 1979; Gleason, 1995; Roberts, 2006; Zizek, 2001).

I contend here that the examination of totalitarianism remains peculiarly important: for in the manifold and worldwide philosophical debates and policy initiatives in citizenship, democracy and human rights, historical antecedence is often forgotten – from eighteenth century revolutionary democracy, the origins in contemporary times of this dominant liberal democratic model for a collective, global politics mirrored in a global educational philosophy lie in the immediate post-Second World War years with the 1945 formation of the United Nations (UN) and its aspirational 1948 Universal Declaration of Human Rights.

The UN-era might here be defined as an era seeking political moderation in an age of ideological extremism (Gearon, 2009). In parallel, twentieth century political theory defined and analysed this extremism under the nomenclature of totalitarianism, seeking greater understanding of its origins, its parameters, and its future: from Popper's (1946) *The Open Society and Its Enemies*; Arendt's (1951) *The Origins of Totalitarianism*; Talmon's (1952) *The Origins of Totalitarian Democracy*; to Friedrich and Brzezinski's (1956) *Totalitarianism and Dictatorial Autocracy*. Popper's (1946) two volume work – a critique of the totalitarian impulses of Plato, in the first, and of Marxist historical materialism in the second – is well known. Also well known is Arendt's classic (1951) study linking totalitarianism with antecedents in anti-Semitism, colonialism and imperialism, and her notion that totalitarianism is necessarily a modern phenomenon since only with technological prowess can government truly aspire to a 'totalitarian' control. In an increasingly 'surveillance society' this has an even prophetic ring, but we should also recall the most influential political theorists of the time wrote their works as dystopian *fictions*. George Orwell's *Nineteen Eighty-Four* has arguably had more political impact than any formal tract in political theory.

Acknowledged widely as the most influential thinkers on totalitarianism (Schapiro, 1972), Friedrich and Brzezinski (1956) based their theoretical considerations upon (then) contemporary political observation, asserting their well-known, and at the time pivotal six-fold typology of totalitarianism.[5] They also do much to elaborate how totalitarian ideology often replicates the explanatory possibilities of theology in which the 'totalitarian ideology consists of an official doctrine which radically rejects the pre-existing society in terms of a chiliastic proposal for a new one' and as such 'contains utopian elements, some kind of notion of paradise on earth', giving totalitarian ideologies 'a pseudo religious quality. In fact, they often elicit in the less critical followers a depth of conviction and a fervour of devotion usually found only among persons inspired by a transcendent faith.'

Friedrich and Brzezinski are important for being amongst the most prominent theorists of totalitarianism to suggest a totalizing replication of the theological in political form. But they are not alone. Talmon's *The Origins of Totalitarian Democracy* similarly considers French revolutionary politics as:

> '..."political Messianism" or the 'postulate of some ultimate, logical, exclusively valid social order' as 'a matter of faith ... Its significance to the believer, and the power it has to move men and mountains, can hardly be exaggerated. Now, in Europe and elsewhere, for the last century and a half, there have always been men and movements animated by such a faith, preparing for the Day, referring all their ideas and acts to some all-embracing system, sure of some pre-ordained and final denouement of the historic drama with all its conflicts into an absolute harmony. Jacobins may have differed from the Babouvists, the Blanquists from many of the secret societies of the first half of the nineteenth century, the Communists from the Socialists, the Anarchists from all others, yet they all belong to one religion. This religion emerged in the second half of the eighteenth century ... The most difficult problem of the secular religion was to be the antinomy of freedom and the exclusive Messianic pattern' (Talmon, 1952, 12).

However, unlike other pro-Western, pro-democratic theorists, Talmon more radically questions the very origins, the totalitarian features of liberal democracy in the very nature of revolution, in particular its violent, dictatorial and terroristic imposition. Talmon thereby challenges many of the presuppositions about citizenship, democracy and human rights shared by contemporary commentators on totalitarianism.

Talmon's theoretical orientation has thus become, I would argue, one of the most pertinent in today's politicised educational discourse over social and community cohesion. His erudite thesis is a remarkably simple one.

Examining in scholarly detail the key features of the French Revolution, its origins, its emergence, and above all the violent *imposition* of its Enlightenment ideals (of autonomy, democracy, government by the people, liberty from 'oppressive' power of Church and aristocracy), he charts its catastrophic decline into the systematic barbarism and systemic violence against dissent. Drawing upon a critique of key Enlightenment thinkers such as Rousseau, Talmon uses those facets of revolutionary democracy to remind readers of those features shared by (then mid-) twentieth century totalitarianism regimes.

Talmon's analysis of the respective classical (philosophical, Greek and Roman, notably pre-Christian) influences on eighteenth century revolutionary democracy are critical – and present day religious and citizenship educators cannot help but see parallels in the secular debates when Talmon writes that the

> 'strongest influence on the fathers of totalitarian democracy was that of antiquity, interpreted in their own way. Their myth of antiquity was the image of liberty equated with virtue. The citizen of Sparta or Rome was proudly free, yet a marvel of ascetic discipline. He was an equal member of the sovereign nation, and at the same time had no life or interests outside the collective tissue' (Talmon, 1952: 13).

In characterising the key sources of modern-day citizenship pertinent to education, it is precisely the same (philosophical, Greek and Roman, notably pre-Christian) lineage which we are told is so significant by key narrators of citizenship education today (Crick, 1998; 2000; Heater, 2004).

In dealing with an analysis of social and community cohesion in England – and by extension the political and policy involvement of the international community in matters of culture and religion (see again note (1)) – we are not likely to get very far by trying to fit these within the framework of a revolutionary democracy or totalitarianism. England in the early twenty-first century is not a revolutionary democracy or a totalitarian regime. That said, there might be some religious communities in Iraq and Afghanistan who would argue this, who would say that western aggression in their countries is precisely the assertion of democracy by force of violence, and the imposition of liberal cultural and political norms, even those of democracy, citizenship, and equality. A number of western theorists such Chomsky (2003; 2006; 2007) might share such a view. As radical secularists themselves, however, such theorists always have difficulty with the *religious* aspects of such dissent. In Schapiro's (1972) analysis of contemporaneous totalitarian regimes a similar debate ensured about whether the America of Vietnam, and an American foreign policy supporting Latin American dictatorships, made the USA a totalitarian regime, a view which Schapiro disavowed.

Undeniable, however, is the fact that internationally the resurgent significance of religion in public life and global governance marks a reversal of religion's marginalization from the philosophically and politically revolutionary contexts of the eighteenth century (see again note (1)). In England this is evident where religious education is placed in service of social and community cohesion, part of a wider enlisting of educators in the war against extremism. The question to ask here, then, somewhat ironically, is whether religion is in danger of becoming no longer *marginalized* by politics and public life but *subsumed* by it, *over*-politicized and *over*-integrated into secular public-political life? Are politicians and educators in danger of not now ignoring or overlooking but *manipulating* religion, what Milbank (2006) in *Theology and Social Theory* called 'policing the sublime'.

The notion of a liberal autocracy is a term of limited *political* currency (see, for example, Zakaria, 2003) – reflected in the espousal of democracy by (illiberal, rights-neglecting) regimes which claim democratic status but patently lack the characteristics of democracy understood by many western nations. As Held (2003) in his contemporary classic has argued, there are many models of democracy, and here I am arguing for a new and wider usage of liberal autocracy to reflect new patterns, especially the political use of *culture*, and in regard to our present discussions, the political applications of religion and education to social and community cohesion. I argue, there are four key features pertinent to the definition of an emergent 'liberal autocracy'.

FEATURES OF AN EMERGENT 'LIBERAL AUTONOMY'

One, through mass democracies in the nineteenth and totalitarianism in the twentieth, its origins are traceable back to the European Enlightenment and eighteenth century revolutionary democracies, historical contexts skeptical of and often antagonistic to religion. In historical antecedence, however, twentieth century secular liberal democracies are inheritors of a tradition based upon the violent, repressive forces not only of eighteenth century revolutionary democracies but totalitarian regimes of the twentieth – Italy under Mussolini, Germany under Hitler, the Soviet Union under Stalin. This historical causality between Enlightenment and totalitarianism is now gaining ground. Baumann's (2000) reflections on modernity and the holocaust are notable.

Two, liberal autocracy is characterized by the formation of alternative overarching ('totalizing') frameworks which are *secular* and *political*, emphasizing (in varying degrees) citizenship, democracy and human rights. Here, only exceptional theorists such as Wolin (2008) have given much attention to this 'totalising' influence in liberal *democracies*. In historical context, the age of revolutionary democracy and its aftermath was increasingly skeptical of religion. If separation of Church from State limited the political influence of religion, its philosophical power was weakened by the intellectual triumphs of the Enlightenment, the 'Age of Reason' ushered in an era of more militant attacks upon religion *per se*: from Feuerbach and Nietzsche to Freud, from Marx to Durkheim, the truths of religion and theology were deemed illusory, a human projection of unfulfilled desires upon an indifferent universe, the work of a primitive stage in the human imagination, and the surpassing of which was the mark of all things progressive. Simply put, it was envisaged that the mind of man could replace the mind of God. These philosophical and political developments provided the ground for the totalitarian experiments unleashed upon the twentieth century. Studies relevant here are those which highlight the rise of the 'political religion' – from French Revolution through the Soviet era to the rise of Nazism (Burleigh, 2006; 2007). Like Talmon's 'Political Messianism', Gray's (2007) consideration of *Apocalyptic Religion and the Death of Utopia* details how even avowedly secular, militantly atheistic, revolutionary movements replicate the structures of the theological systems they seek to replace (Gearon, 2010a).

Three, liberal autocracy is characterized by the development of ideological replication through cultural and educational means, and the autocratic disavowal of discourse beyond the foundational terms of (for example) citizenship, democracy and human rights. One historical and one contemporary example shall here suffice.

In historical terms, in *Democracy and Education*, Dewey (1916) presents a three-fold history of education in relation to politics: *first*, he presents a sympathetic, rather generous reading of Plato's *Republic*, suggesting that Plato's democratic ideals would have gone further but for the anti-democratic forces of his time. Though today this is an unsustainable reading of Plato, it is insightful for establishing as ancient the link between politics and pedagogy – if Plato's *Republic* is in large part and obviously a work of political theory it is also in large degree a work of *educational* practice. *Second*, Dewey leaps from Plato to the Enlightenment, reading Rousseau – *Emile* as much as *The Social Contract* – to suggest the eighteenth century as a model of cosmopolitan citizenship, in other words, a citizenship bound by a positive, noble understanding of human nature itself. *Third*, Dewey outlines the parallel emergence of democracy and rights with strong nation-states. Dewey argues that the nineteenth century educational implications are first evident in Germany's introduction of compulsory schooling to inculcate national sentiment and further the goals of the State (see the innovative early work of West 1979; 1991; 1994; Gearon 2010b). However, Dewey's analysis is entirely secular, and in this regard, entirely partial. Like so many other post-Enlightenment thinkers any contribution of religious tradition to democratic polity is almost wilfully neglected. We only have to see the way that Dewey historically leaps from Plato to the eighteenth and nineteenth centuries to see this. The future role for education in this context is secular and religion is conceived as nothing more than the common concerns of this earth, as the pragmatist concerns of democratic politics. In educational terms, Dewey represents the sacralisation of secular politics through the educational deification of democracy (for a wider discussion, see Gearon 2010).

In contemporary times, optimism about the prospects of democracy often conceals, closes, and seals up the very openness which it espouses. In the immediate aftermath of the Cold War, the hubris of Fukuyama's (1992) 'end of history' thesis encapsulated this, as he confidently charted what he perceived as an unstoppable rise of liberal democracies in the late twentieth century since those democratic revolutions in the eighteenth. Huntington's (1992) *Clash of Civilizations* was a retort to this ideological complacency. In brief, Huntington suggested that tensions between civilizations will in the future be based not upon political ideology but on culture, and especially religion. Huntington's crude carving up of the world into conflicting civilizations has been rightly criticized for its naïve geo-political and historical generalizations. He has also been criticized as irresponsible for bringing to the post-Cold War world a lexicon of conflict. Yet for many, 11 September 2001 seemed to confirm Huntington's thesis. The United Nations (2008) '*Alliance of Civilizations*' remains a rearguard action to counter Huntington with a more conciliatory view of the relations between cultures. In all of this, the persistence of *religion* in the public sphere presents a challenge to the secularizing assumptions of modernity embedded in them all.

Four, liberal autocracy advances cultural and educational strategies for dealing with *challenges* to these totalizing democratic and secular frameworks, especially through unexpected socio-political patterns of renewal in the influence of religion in public life. Such developments appear inherently benevolent: who could be against an UN agency which promotes freedom of religion and belief? Yet the more the states and inter-governmental agencies like the United Nations begin to intervene in and breakdown the barriers between public and private the more that the United Nations and its nation-state agencies begin to replicate the very totalitarian structures they were constructed to combat. If totalitarianism has a lineage worryingly close to revolutionary democracy, the more contemporary democracies seek control of cultural and especially religious life the more they resemble the tyranny they claim to defend against.

CONCLUSION

A society which requires law to ensure that different cultural groups cohere is entering dangerous political territory, and one which struggles over its identity may be at risk of losing it. A society which seeks to ensure community cohesion through force of law may already have weakened beyond repair the core of social meaning which its collective history once provided. A society which looks only to contemporary history for its roots is in grave danger of dissociating itself from more ancient foundations, and those societies built on shallow ground rarely contain the material for constructing the future. In this regard, short-term political emphasis upon social and community cohesion is here symptomatic of a wider crisis of identity in British society. The political-educational use of religion and religious education conceal the *symptoms* of a mounting socio-cultural crisis while wilfully ignoring the *cause*, while at the same covertly manipulating the religious traditions they claim they to defend.

If a number of religious education theorists have recognised that there are subtle ideological forces at work to impose even to 'indoctrinate' children and young people with a mindset sceptical or at least neutral to religion, often associated with Enlightenment reason and resultant educational ideals of autonomy (see for example to range of contributions to Felderhof, Torevell and Thompson, 2007; notable amongst these are Barnes, 2007 and Wright, 2007), there is limited recognition of the full autocratic extent and political precedence of such developments. The most recent coercion of the subject into the agenda of social and community cohesion simply accentuates this.

In posing the questions which constitute the main title of this chapter, I argue that religious education is being used in the service of social and community cohesion to serve the interests of a particular political community, and a *particular* form of coherence, one whose rational and political traditions – historical but alive in contemporary context – are easily identified through their antagonism to and or (belatedly) the manipulation of religion.

Thus, if the most effective forms of totalitarian governance are those which make thinking outside of the system barely conceivable, often in subtle moves to break down the distinction between public and private, then it can be argued that the use of religion and education to engender community cohesion brings similar risks. The ultimate danger is the subjugation of both religion and education to secular politics, making both an adjunct of what Wolin (2008) has called the 'specter [sic] of managed democracy and inverted totalitarianism', what I term an emergent liberal autocracy.

NOTES

1. Four critical contexts (see, for example, Gearon, 2007; 2008; 2009)

    Critical Context 1: Religion and Politics

    > If the role of religion in public and political life has been historically underplayed since the European Enlightenment, there is now increasing evidence of the importance of religion in post-Cold War public and political life. Often, though not exclusively, this centres on issues of human rights, including freedom of religion or belief. This trend has been highlighted by a number of theorists of religion: Burleigh (2006; 2007); Casanova (1994); Davis, Milbank and Zizek (2005); de Vries and Sullivan (2006); Fox and Sandler (2006); Gearon (2002; 2006; 2007; 2009); Hanson (2006); Haynes (2006); Harpviken and Rioslien (2005); Himmelfarb (2004); Hoelzl and Ward (2006); Jackson (2002; 2004); Jackson, Miedema, Weisse and Willaime (2007); James (2006); Juergensmeyer (2005); Runzo, Martin and Sharma (2004); Rushton (2004); Smart (1969; 1989); Swaine (2006); Trigg (2007); Ward (2003); Woodhead (2002).

    Critical Context 2: Religion and the United Nations (UN)

    > The UN system incorporated and defined freedom of religion or belief since the 1948 Universal Declaration of Human Rights but the early history of the UN tended to downplay religious and ideological diversity. After a long neglect (or low

level treatment) of religion explicitly, the UN system from the late 1970s and with the Declaration on the Elimination of All Forms of Intolerance and Discrimination Based on Religion or Belief (1981) began to recognise the international significance of religion for a stable world order: Ayton-Shenker (1995); Bennett and Finnemore (2004); Bowles (2004); Boulden and Weiss (2004); Forsythe (2000); Jackson, Miedema, Weisse and Willaime, (2007); Harpviken and Rioslien (2005); Krasno (2004); Lerner (2000); Marshall (2000); Scott and Cavanaugh, 2007; Shattuck, (2003); Trigg (2007); UNESCO (2006); UNESCO (2006a).

Critical Context 3: Religion in Citizenship Education

The role of religion in citizenship education (and related curricula areas such as civics and human rights education) has been underplayed (Audigier, 1998; Crick, 1998; 2004; Davis, 2007; Heater, 2004; Huddlestone and Kerr, 2006; Kerr, 2003). Reflecting broader global trends there is now increasing recognition of the importance of religion in citizenship and human rights education, although the recognition of the importance of teaching about religion remains arguably less strong in civic or citizenship education than in religious education: Ajegbo (2007); Arthur, Davies and Hahn, 2008; EPPI (2005); Gearon (2004); Lindholm et al. (2003); McLaughlin (1992; 2000); NFER (2007); Osler and Starkey (2006).

Critical Context 4: Citizenship in Religious Education

The political has been underplayed in religious education, and contentious historical contexts sidestepped, including notions of citizenship (Grimmitt, 2000). Yet the exponential growth of civic or citizenship education around the world has forced religious education to consider the political and historical, a matter itself forced upon education by manifold changes in the world in which we live: Ajegbo (2007); de Souza, Engebretson, Jackson, McGrady (2006); Gearon (2006; 2007; 2008; 2009); Jackson, Miedema, Weisse and Willaime (2007); Lindholm, Durham and Tahzib-Lies (2003); Osmer (2003); Sterne (2007).

2.   The Commission on Integration and Cohesion (CIC) produced a wealth of supporting documentation, including 'thinkpieces' to help the Commission form its conclusions (visit www.integrationandcohesion.org.uk/).

Downloads from:
http://collections.europarchive.org/tna/20080726153624/http://www.int egrationandcohesion.org.uk/Research_documents.aspx (accessed 22 March, 2010)

3.   From the Religious Education Council of England and Wales: 'The RE Council of England and Wales has successfully bid for funding from the DCSF to develop a training programme for religious education teachers on community cohesion and preventing violent extremism. This is known as the REsilience project. The project is scheduled to last until 31 March 2011 and will be managed by the RE Council in conjunction with Penzer Allen Ltd.' http://www.religiouseducationcouncil.org/content/blogcategory/48/77/

4.   For a conservative source, see Winston Churchill's *History of the English-Speaking People* (Churchill, 1999) and – as the only leader of the conflict to write a major history of a defence of the islands the Romans called Britannia – see Churchill's several volume history, *The Second World War* (Churchill 1985).

5.   Friedrich and Brzezinski's six-fold typology of totalitarianism:

1. an official ideology, consisting of an official body of doctrine covering all aspects of man's existence to which everyone living in that society is supposed to adhere, at least passively; this ideology characteristically focused and projected toward a final state of mankind (sic), that is to say, it contains a chiliastic claim, based upon a radical rejection of the existing society and conquest of the world for the new one;

2. a single mass party led typically by one man (sic), the 'dictator,' and consisting of a relatively small percentage of the total population (up to 10 per cent) of men and women, a hard core of them passionately and unquestioningly dedicated to the ideology and prepared to assist in every way in promoting its general acceptance, such a party being hierarchically, oligarchically organized, and typically either superior to, or completely intertwined with the bureaucratic organization;

3. a system of terroristic police control, supporting but also supervising the party for its leaders, and characteristically directed not only against demonstrable 'enemies' of the regime, but against arbitrarily selected classes of the population; the terror of the secret police systematically exploiting modern science, and more especially scientific psychology;

4. a technologically conditioned near-complete monopoly of control, in the hands of the party and its subservient cadres, of all means of effective mass communication, such as the press, radio, motion pictures

5. a similarly technologically conditioned near-complete monopoly of control (in the same hands) of all means of effective armed combat;

6. a central control and direction of the entire economy through the bureaucratic co-ordination of its formerly independent corporate entities, typically including most other associations and group activities. (Friedrich and Brzezinski, 1956: 88; cf. Schapiro's 1972 critique)

REFERENCES

Ajegbo, K. (2007) *Diversity and Citizenship*, London: DfES.

Amor, A. (2001) 'The Role of Religious Education in the Pursuit of Tolerance and Non-Discrimination', study prepared under the guidance of Prof. Abdelfattah Amor, Special Rapporteur on Freedom of Religion of Belief, for the International Consultative Conference on School Education in Relation with Freedom of Religion and Belief, Tolerance and Non-Discrimination, Madrid, 23-25 November 2001). Retrieved 1 August 2005 from the UN website:www.un.org and links through to http://ap.ohchr.org/documents/dpage_e.aspx?m=86

Arendt, H. (2004) [1951] *The Origins of Totalitarianism*, New York: Schocken Books.

Arthur, J. and Davies, I. (eds.) (2010) The Routledge *Education Studies Textbook*, London: Routledge.

Arthur, J. Gearon, L. and Sears, A. (2010, forthcoming) *Education, Politics and Religion: Reconciling the Civic and the Sacred in Education*, London and New York: Routledge.

Arthur, J. Davies, I. and Hahn, C. (2008) (eds.) *SAGE Handbook of Education for Citizenship and Democracy*, London: SAGE.

Audigier, F. (1998) *Basic Concepts and Core Competencies of Education for Democratic Citizenship*, Strasbourg: Council of Europe.

Ayton-Shenker, D. (1995). 'The Challenge of Human Rights and Cultural Diversity', Geneva: United Nations Department of Public Information.

Bailey, R. (2000) *Education in the Open Society*: Karl Popper and Schooling, Aldershot: Ashgate.

Barnes, P (2007) 'Religious Education and the Misrepresentation of Religion' in Felderhof, Torevell and Thompson (2007).

Barnes, P., Wright, A. and Brandom, A-M. (eds.) (2008) *Learning to Teach RE in the Secondary School*, London: Routledge.

Bauman, Z. (2000) *Modernity and the Holocaust*, Cambridge: Polity Press.

Bennett, M. N. and Finnemore, M. (2004) *Rules for the World: International Organizations in Global Politics*, Ithaca, N.Y: Cornell University Press.

Boulden, J. and Weiss, T. G. (eds.) (2004) *Terrorism and the UN: Before and After September 11*, Bloomington Indiana: Indiana University Press.

Bowles, N. R. (2004). *The Diplomacy of Hope: The United Nations since the Cold War*, London: I.B. Tauris.

Burleigh, M. (2006) *Earthly Powers: Religion and Politics in Europe from the Enlightenment to the Great War*, London: Harper Perennial.

Burleigh, M. (2007) *Sacred Causes: The Clash of Religion and Politics from the Great War to the War on Terror*, New York: HarperCollins.

Casanova, J. (1994) *Religion and Public Governance*, Chicago: Chicago University Press.

Chomsky, N. (2003) *Power and Terror: Post-9/11 Talks and Interviews*, edited by John Junkerman and Takei Masakazu, New York: Seven Stories Press, Tokyo, Little More.

Chomsky, N. (2006) *Failed States: The Abuse of Power and the Assault on Democracy*, New York: Metropolitan Books / Henry Holt.

Chomsky, N. (2007) *What We Say Goes: Conversations on U.S. Power in a Changing World*: Interviews with David Barsamian, New York: Metropolitan Books.

Churchill, W. (1985) *The Second World War*, six volumes, London: Penguin.

Churchill, W. (1999) *A History of the English-Speaking Peoples*, London: Cassell.

CIC (2007) *Our Shared Future*, London, Commission on Integration and Cohesion. www.integrationandcohesion.org.uk/Our_final_report.aspx

Crick, B. (1998) *Education for Citizenship and the Teaching of Democracy in Schools: Final Report of the Advisory Group on Citizenship*, London: QCA.

Crick, B. (2004) Introduction, Heater (2004) *Citizenship: The Civic Ideal in World History, Politics and Education*, Manchester: Manchester University Press.

Davies, I. (2007) 'What is Citizenship?' in Gearon (2007), 1-8.

Davis, C., Milbank, J. and Zizek, S. (eds.) (2005) *Theology and the Political: The New Debate*, Durham: Duke University Press.

De Souza, M., Engebretson, K. Jackson, R. and McGrady, A. (eds.) (2006) *International Handbook of the Religious, Spiritual and Moral Dimensions of Education*, Netherlands: Springer Academic Publishers.

De Vries, H. and Sullivan L.E. (eds.) (2006) *Political Theologies: Public Religions in a Post-secular World*, New York: Fordham.

De Tocqueville, A. (2003) [1836] *Democracy in America*, translated G. E. Bevan, introduction and notes I. Kramnick, London: Penguin.

Dewey, J. (1916) *Democracy and Education*, online http://www.ilt.columbia.edu/Publications/Projects/digitexts/dewy/, accessed 9 November 2008.

EPPI (2005) *An International Review of Citizenship Education Research*. The Evidence for Policy and Practice Information and Co- ordinating Centre. London: EPPI.

Equalities and Human Rights Commission (www.ehrc.gov.uk)

Felderhof, M., Torevell D., and Thompson, P. (2007) *Inspiring faith in schools; studies in religious education*, London: Ashgate Publishing Co.

Forsythe, D. P. (2000) *Human Rights in International Relations*, 3rd edition, Cambridge: Cambridge University Press.

Fox, J. and Sandler, S. (eds.) (2006) *Religion in World Conflict*, London: Routledge.

Friedrich, C.J. and Brzezinski, Z. (1967) *Totalitarian Dictatorship and Autocracy*, 2nd edition, New York: Praeger.

Friedrich, C.J., Curtis, M., and Barber, B.R. (1979) *Totalitarianism in Perspective: Three Views*, New York: Praeger.

Fukuyama, F. (2006) *The End of History and the Last Man*, New York: Free Press.

Fukuyama, F. (2007) *After the Neocons: America at the Crossroads*, London: Profile.

Gearon, L. (ed.) (2002) *Religion and Human Rights: A Reader*, Brighton and Portland: Sussex Academic Press.

Gearon, L. (2003) *How Do We Learn to Become Good Citizens?: A Professional User Review of UK Research*, London: British Educational Research Association.

Gearon, L. (2004) *Citizenship through Religious Education*, London and New York: Routledge.

Gearon, L. (Guest Editor) (2006) *Children's Spirituality and Children's Rights*, Special Issue, *International Journal of Children's Spirituality*, 11 (2).

Gearon, L. (2006a) *Freedom of Expression and Human Rights: Historical, Literary and Political Contexts*, Brighton and Portland: Sussex Academic Press.

Gearon, L. (2007) *A Practical Guide to Teaching Citizenship in the Secondary School*, London and New York: Routledge.

Gearon, L. (Guest Editor) (2007) *Religion, Human Rights and Citizenship*, Special Issue, *British Journal of Religious Education*, 30 (2).

Gearon, L. (2008) in Barnes, P., Wright, A. and Brandom, A-M. (eds.) 'Religious Education and Citizenship', *Learning to Teach Religious Education in the Secondary School*. London and New York: Routledge.

Gearon, L. (2009) *Citizenship and Religious Education*, Oxford: St Gabriel's Trust.

Gearon, L. (ed.) (2010) *Learning to Teach Citizenship in the Secondary School*, second edition. London: Routledge.

Gearon, L. (2010a) The Totalitarian Imagination: Religion, Politics and Education in De Souza, Durka, Engebretson and Gearon.

Gearon, L. (2010b) 'Professional Learning' in Arthur and Davies (eds.) *Introduction to Education Studies*. London: Routledge.

Gleason, A. (1998) *Totalitarianism: The Inner History of the Cold War*, Oxford: Oxford University Press.

Gray, J. (2007) *Black Mass*, London: Penguin.

Grimmitt, M.H.(ed.) (2000) *Pedagogies of Religious Education*, Great Wakering: McCrimmons.

Hanson, E.O. (2006) *Religion and Politics in the International System Today*, Cambridge: Cambridge University Press.

Harlow, B. and Carter, M. (eds.) (1999) *Imperialism and Orientalism: A Documentary Sourcebook*, Oxford: Blackwell.

Harpviken, K. B. and Roislien, H. E. (2005) *Mapping the Terrain: The Role of Religion in Peacemaking*, Oslo: International Peace Research Institute, for the Norwegian Ministry of Foreign Affairs.

Haynes, J. (ed.) (2006) *The Politics of Religion: A Survey*, London and New York: Routledge.

Heater, D. (2004) *Citizenship: The Civic Ideal in World History, Politics and Education*. Manchester: Manchester University Press.

Himmelfarb. G. (2004) *The Roads to Modernity: The British, French and American Enlightenments*, New York: Alfred A. Knopf.

Hoelzl, M. and Ward, G. (eds.) (2006) *Religion and Political Thought*, London: Continuum.

Home Office (2005) *Preventing Extremism Together*, http://www.aml.org.uk/pdf_files/PET_Report.pdf

Huddlestone, T. and Kerr, D. (2006) *Making Sense of Citizenship: A Continuing Professional Development Handbook*, London: Hodder.

Huntington, S. (2002) *The Clash of Civilizations*, London and New York: Free.

Institute for Community Cohesion, www.coventry.ac.uk/researchnet/icoco

Jackson, R. (2002) *International Perspectives on Citizenship, Education and Religious Diversity*, London: Routledge.

Jackson, R. (2004) *Rethinking Religious Education and Plurality: Issues in Diversity and Pedagogy*, London: Routledge.

Jackson, R., Miedema, S., Weisse, W., and Willaime, J-F (2007) (eds.) *Religion and Education in Europe: Developments, Contexts and Debates*, Munster: Waxmann.

James, H. (ed.) (2006) *Civil Society, Religion and Global Governance: Paradigms of Power and Persuasion*, London: Routledge.

Juergensmeyer, M. (ed.) (2005) *Religion in Global Civil Society*, Oxford and New York: Oxford University Press.

Keast, J and Craft, L. (2010) in Gearon (2010).

Kerr, D. (2003) 'Citizenship Education Research', in Gearon, L. (ed.) (2010).

Krasno, J. E. (ed.) (2004) *The United Nations: Confronting the Challenges of a Global Society*, Boulder Colorado, London: Lynne Rienner Publishers.

Lerner, N. (2000) *Religion, Beliefs, and Human Rights*, Maryknoll, New York: Orbis.

Lindholm, T., Durham, W.C. and Tahzib-Lies, B. G. (eds.) (2003), *Facilitating Freedom of Religion or Belief*. The Hague: Kluwer.

Marshall, P. (ed.) (2000) *Religious Freedom in the World: A Global Report on Freedom and Persecution*, London: Broadman and Holman.

McLaughlin, T. (1992) 'Citizenship, diversity and education: a philosophical perspective', *Journal of Moral Education*, 21 (3): 235-50.

McLaughlin, T. (2000) 'Citizenship Education in England: The Crick Report and Beyond' *Journal of Philosophy of Education*, 34(4): 541-570.

Milbank, J. (2006) *Theology and Social Theory*, 2nd edition. Oxford: Blackwell.

Mill, J.S. (2008) [1859] *On Liberty*, with related documents, edited by A.. Kahan. Boston: Bedford/ St. Martins.

NFER (2007) Vision versus *Pragmatism: Citizenship in the Secondary School*, Slough, National Foundation for Educational Research).

OfSTED (1997) *Making Sense of Religion*. London: OfSTED.

Osler, A. and Starkey, H. (2006) *Education and Democratic Citizenship* 1995-2005, London: British Educational Research Association.

Osmer, R. R. (2003). *Religious Education between Modernization and Globalization: New Perspectives on the United States and Germany*, Grand Rapids, Michigan: W.B. Eerdmans.

Paine, T. 1985 [1791/2] *Rights of Man*. Harmondsworth: Penguin.

Popper, K. (1946) *The Open Society and Its Enemies*, London: Routledge.

Roberts, D. D. (2006) *The Totalitarian Experiment in the Twentieth Century: Understanding the Poverty of the Great Politics*, London: Routledge.

Rousseau, J.J. (2007) [1762] *Emile, or On Education*, Sioux Falls: NuVision.

Rousseau, J.J. (1968) [1762] *The Social Contract*, translated by Maurice Cranston, London: Penguin.

Runzo, J., Martin, N.M. and Sharma, A. (eds.) (2004) *Human Rights and Responsibilities in the World's Religions*, Oxford: Oneworld.

Rushton, R. (2004). *Human Rights and the Image of God*, London: SCM.

Schlesinger, S. C. (2003) *Act of Creation: The Founding of the United Nations*, Boulder, Colorado: Westview Press.

Shattuck, J. (2003) 'Religion, Rights and Terrorism', Harvard University conference on Religion, Democracy and Human Rights, www.law.harvard.edu (and follow links).

Smart, N. (1969) *The Religious Experience of Mankind*, Toronto: Collier Macmillan.

Smart, N. (1999) *The World's Religions*, 2nd edition, Cambridge: Cambridge University Press.

Smith, A. (2008) [1776] *An Inquiry into the Nature and Causes of the Wealth of Nations*, edited by K. Sutherland. Oxford: Oxford World's Classics.

Sterne, J. (2006) *Teaching Religious Education*, London and New York: Continuum.

Strauss, L. (2000) [1961] *On Tyranny*, revised edition, edited V. Gourevitch and M.S. Roth. Chicago: Chicago University Press.

Schapiro, L. (1972) *Totalitarianism*, London: Pall Mall Press.

Swaine, L. (2006) *The Liberal Conscience: Politics and Principle in a World of Religious Pluralism*, New York: Columbia University Press.

Talmon, J.L. 1961 [1952] *History of Totalitarian Democracy*, Mercury Books.

Trigg, R. (2007) *Religion in Public Life: Must Faith Be Privatized?* Oxford: Oxford University Press.

Ward, G. (2003) *True Religion*, Oxford: Blackwell.

Woodhead, L. et. al. (eds.) (2002). *Religions in the Modern World*, London: Routledge.

UN (2008) Alliance of Civilizations, www.unaoc.org/content/view/39/187/lang,english/ accessed 29 May 2008.

UNESCO (2006) *Guidelines on Intercultural Education*, Paris: UNESCO.

UNESCO (2006a) Expert Meeting on Intercultural Education Report, Paris: UNESCO.

United Nations (2008) Alliance of Civilizations.

West, E.G. (1979) 'Literacy and the Industrial Revolution', *Economic History Review* 31 (3), http://www.ncl.ac.uk/egwest/pdfs/Literacy%20and%20the%20Industrial%20Rev.pdf, accessed 8 December 2008.

West, E.G. (1991) 'The Rise of the State in Education', *Policy: A Journal of Policy and Ideas* http://www.ncl.ac.uk/egwest/pdfs/independent1.pdf, accessed 8 December 2008.

West, E.G. (1994) 'Education without the State', Economic Affairs 14 (5), 12-15.

Wolin, S.S. (2008) *Democracy Inc: Managed Democracy and the Specter of Inverted Totalitarianism*, Princeton: Princeton University Press.

Wright, A (2007) 'Religious Education and Liberal Nurture', in Felderhof, Torevell and Thompson (2007).

Zakaria, F. (2003) *The Future of Freedom: Illiberal Democracy at Home and Abroad*, New York: Norton, 2003

Zizek, S. (2004) *Did Somebody Say Totalitarianism?* London and New York: Verso.

CHAPTER 8

COMMUNITY, DIVERSITY AND TRUTH:
What might local faith communities reasonably expect of Religious Education in the state schools of a secular democracy?

Andrew Wright

SUMMARY

WHAT MIGHT LOCAL FAITH COMMUNITIES reasonably expect of religious education in the state schools of a secular democracy? It is important to recognise from the outset the rich diversity of secular democracies, each offering different forms of state education to varying demographic constituencies. Given such diversity, it will be necessary to restrict the scope of the following discussion; hence, the first section will unpack the notions of 'secularism', 'democracy', and 'education' in order to establish viable boundaries for the chapter. State schools in secular democracies are not ideologically neutral: the vast majority are rooted in the tradition of western liberalism, and the second section will establish a distinction between 'political' and 'comprehensive' liberalism, and suggest that local faith communities may reasonably expect that the provision of state education be grounded in the former. The following three sections explore political liberalism's core principles of tolerance, freedom and reason, and identify what faith communities may reasonably expect, and concomitantly reasonably not expect, in a state education system grounded in a liberal polity.

SECULARISM, DEMOCRACY AND EDUCATION

The term 'secular' may be used to describe, explain, or express aspirations about society. Auguste Comte's claim that accounts of reality have proceeded from the theological-fictitious, through the metaphysical-abstract, to the scientific-positive combines an explanation of the supposed decline of religion in society with the aspiration that the remaining vestiges of religious superstition be eradicated (Wernick 2005, 81ff; Wright 2000, 47ff). The success of critical realists and others in undermining positivism and rehabilitating metaphysics and theology as legitimate spheres of intellectual investigation has produced a situation in which questions of explanation and aspiration are now fundamentally contested (Archer *et al.* 2004). This carries with it an important pedagogic imperative: in a plural environment in which questions of ultimate truth and human flourishing are disputed, a primary role of public education should be to equip students to engage intelligently with such questions, rather than prescribe particular partisan answers to them. An 'authoritarian method of teaching... to which the most desirable form of response on the part of the learner is the unquestioning acceptance of doctrines' should be replaced by a critical pedagogy in which, for example, the transmission of 'scientific laws and facts' gives way to the cultivation of 'the critical attitudes and ways of thinking of a scientist' (Hirst and Peters 1970, 29f). It follows that the curriculum should leave questions of explanation and aspiration open: they are the lifeblood of education itself, rather than problems to be (prematurely) resolved prior to the start of the learning process. Hence our immediate task is not to explain secularism, nor to offer a vision of how society ought to develop, but merely to establish a descriptive understanding of the phenomenon.

Charles Taylor, in his ground-breaking *A Secular Age* (2007), identifies three interconnected yet distinctive accounts of secularism: first, an emergent secular society is one in which the political apparatus of the state is progressively disconnected from religious beliefs and commitments; second, an emergent secular society is one in which the impact of religious communities on public life is progressively diminishing; third, an emergent secular society is one moving 'from a society where belief in God is unchallenged and indeed unproblematic to one in which it is understood to be one option among others, and frequently not the easiest to embrace' (Taylor 2007, 3). On the first account, the USA is a more secular society than the UK because its separation of church from state contrasts sharply with the formal place of the Church of England in the British political establishment. On the second account, France is a more secular society than the Irish Republic because the influence of Roman Catholicism on Irish culture continues to have greater impact than the combined influence of Catholicism and Protestantism on French culture. On the third account, the USA, UK, France and Ireland are all more secular than Pakistan: whereas the citizens of the former four states generally experience religious commitment as a challenging and often problematic departure from an apparent non-religious norm, the citizens of Pakistan generally experience basic commitment to Islam – as opposed to their response to tensions between different traditions within Islam – as normative and, as such, not in itself particularly challenging or problematic in itself. Throughout this chapter 'secular' is used in a way which conforms to Taylor's third account: a secular society is one in which – regardless of either the relationship between the state and religious institutions, or the extent to which religious communities impact on public life – religious commitment, in the face of alternative options, is experienced as challenging and often problematic.

If a democratic state is one governed by its citizens, normally via their elected representatives, how might we understand the notion of a 'secular' democracy? There are, of course, many religious democracies, each embracing a particular state religion, though, as the contrast between Islamic Pakistan and Christian Britain makes clear, the significance of such a formal relationship varies enormously. On Taylor's first account of secularism, a secular democracy is one in which there is no formal relationship between religious communities and the state apparatus. Here the state is officially neutral with regard to religious belief, though this does not preclude religious communities impacting on government policy, as evidenced, for example, by the political influence of the Christian Right in the USA. On Taylor's second account, a secular democracy is one in which religious communities have relatively little impact on the political process, regardless of the presence or absence of a formal relationship between the state and a given religious community. Though citizens might be guided by religious principles in their voting practices, the collective will of religious communities as such is not sufficiently strong to be of any lasting concern to politicians: thus, for example, British political parties do not, generally, seek political capital by addressing religious issues or aligning themselves with specific religious constituencies. On Taylor's third account, a secular democracy is a plural democracy, one in which some citizens embrace a plurality of different religious positions, whilst others embrace as (apparently) normative various non-religious options. Such a plural society may or may not enjoy a formal relationship between the state and a specific religious community, and religious communities may or may not have a significant impact on public policy. Further, citizens of plural democracies will engage with the democratic process on different ideological grounds: pragmatic, liberal, humanistic, religious etc. Thus Muslims committed to the principle of a theocratic Islamic state may engage with the political process not because of any ideological commitment towards democracy per se, but because the Qur'an requires them, whenever possible, to work for the wellbeing of the wider community when residing in a non-Muslim country.

The provision of state schooling in secular democracies is a particularly complicated issue. On Taylor's first account of secularism, the division of religious community and state means that religious education is, for the most part, notable for its absence from the curriculum. On Taylor's second account, the lack of religious influence in the public sphere, whilst not precluding religious education from the curriculum, nevertheless tends towards the progressive diminishment of the subject and its replacement by a variety of alternatives – social, personal, moral, spiritual and citizenship education etc. On Taylor's third account, the rich variety of religious and non-religious worldviews present in society suggests the possibility of a vibrant religious education concerned to engage with deeply controversial issues in a spirit of mutual understanding, orientated towards the common pursuit of ultimate truth and truthful living, and driven by a concern to cultivate public religious literacy. Such a possibility is far from being a reality, though the system of religious education in England and Wales perhaps comes closest to achieving this ideal. Significantly, education in England and Wales embraces a structural pluralism in which the state sponsors both local community (non-religious) and faith community schools. I have argued elsewhere, on liberal grounds, that whenever practically possible a secular democracy ought to sponsor faith community schools (Wright 2003). Our concern in this chapter will be restricted to multi-faith religious education delivered in plural schools without a specific religious foundation.

POLITICAL AND COMPREHENSIVE LIBERALISM

A secular democracy hosting a range of different religious and non-religious faith communities cannot be ideologically neutral. In refusing to privilege any particular faith community it will, in effect embrace an agnostic stance, and agnosticism is not neutral: to affirm 'Christians *believe* Jesus was God incarnate' is to adopt a position significantly different from the Christian claim that 'Jesus was God incarnate' and the atheistic claim that 'Jesus *was not* God incarnate'. Such agnosticism is grounded in the tradition of western liberalism. Faced with the possibility of a further descent into social anarchy in the aftermath of the English Civil War, John Locke advocated the principles of freedom of belief, tolerance of the beliefs of others and a commitment to reason as means of avoiding further violent conflict between different political and religious factions. In doing so he sought to establish an open, charitable and judicious environment in which all parties could work together to explore their differences and pursue questions of truth and truthful living. Locke's original vision was of a 'political' liberalism that sought to act merely as mediator between conflicting worldviews. In sharp contrast, the 'comprehensive' liberalism that grew out of political liberalism advocated an all-embracing liberal worldview: the principles of freedom, tolerance and reason were presented as ends in themselves, rather than as a pragmatic path to the greater end of empowering different groups to explore contrasting accounts of the ultimate nature of reality and the ultimate human good (Wright 2004, 20ff; Wright 2007, 29ff).

A plural secular democracy must give space for adherents of the faith tradition of comprehensive liberalism; however, to adopt comprehensive liberalism as *the* default ideology would constitute a distinctly illiberal strategy (Kekes 1999). In effect, the state's response to cultural pluralism would be to impose a monolithic comprehensive liberalism: autonomy would be presented as the highest good, and alternative religious and non-religious visions of the *summa bonum* relegated to the private sphere of optional beliefs not worthy of public debate. Paradoxically, comprehensive liberals can be tolerant only if they are themselves intolerant of the intolerant – racists, sexists, homophobes etc. In distinguishing between what ought and ought not to be tolerated, comprehensive liberals draw on the principle of freedom of belief: individuals are free to act as they choose provided they cause no harm to others, and the principal harm done to others is to restrict their own autonomy. This leads to the adoption of ethical stances rigorously opposed by many religious communities, whose moral judgements are based on theological resources rather than liberal principles: thus, for example, the freedom of a woman to terminate a pregnancy by an abortion stands opposed to the Roman Catholic advocacy of the sanctity of the life of the unborn infant. Further, the principle of freedom is significantly underdetermined: the assumption that we will always exercise our freedom in responsible and appropriate ways cannot necessarily be taken for granted: we may be free to spend our lives on a feeding-frenzy of sex, drugs and rock-n-roll, but in doing so we will almost certainly be making choices that are not conducive to our moral and spiritual wellbeing. The freedom of self-determination, understood as emancipation from all external constraints, is very different from the freedom to make informed and reflective judgements about our beliefs, commitments, relationships and responsibilities. The function of education must pass beyond the cultivation of autonomy and empower pupils to exercise their freedom wisely. The issue here is not the rights and wrongs of contested moral, spiritual and worldview stances per se, but rather the educative process through which such issues are addressed in a plural secular democracy. To embrace comprehensive liberalism as the default position in schools is to affirm the principles of freedom and tolerance as absolute non-negotiable values that are not open to rational scrutiny. As a result, such schools will become advocates of a particular, fundamentally contested, worldview. A school committed to political liberalism, on the other hand, will embrace the principles of freedom and tolerance as a non-absolute interim ethic designed to enable all faith traditions, including the faith tradition of comprehensive liberalism, to engage in conversations designed to pursue truth and cultivate truthful living. This being the case, local faith communities may reasonably expect religious education in the state schools of a secular democracy to embrace a political liberalism designed to cultivate appropriate levels of public religious literacy, rather than induct pupils uncritically into the norms of a comprehensive liberal worldview.

TOLERANCE

The liberal commitment to tolerance means that members of religious and non-religious faith communities should reasonably expect to be afforded a warm welcome in schools. Tolerance here translates as hospitality, and good hosts will afford their guests a warm welcome regardless of any personal misgivings they might have about their beliefs and lifestyles. The offer of hospitality demands a reciprocal response on the part of guests: a generous willingness to show respect towards their host by recognizing the norms and expectations regarding conduct in the host's home. Such mutual goodwill, or basic civility, constitutes the necessary basis for the educational enterprise, and is one of the greatest contributions of the liberal tradition to the wellbeing of humankind.

There is, however, a danger of the cultivation of reciprocal goodwill becoming an end in itself, rather than providing the necessary springboard into effective education. This is especially so in areas of social tension in which mutual respect, because it cannot be taken for granted, needs to be pro-actively cultivated. An underlying problem here is that comprehensive liberalism's vision of human flourishing, limited as it is to the exercise of personal autonomy in a tolerant environment, identifies the establishment of basic civility as one of the ultimate ends of education rather than its necessary prerequisite. Political liberalism, in sharp contrast, embraces the virtues of freedom and tolerance not as ends in themselves, but as the means to the greater end of developing a plural society capable of pursuing truth and truthful living in an informed and literate manner. Though members of all faith communities may reasonably expect that the liberal welcome extended to them should provide the basis of a rich educational provision, it is appropriate that they remain cautious of the possibility that their children will be offered little more than a confessional induction into a liberal lifeworld and ideology. If hospitality is the necessary foundation for multi-faith education, it must never be allowed to act as a substitute for effective learning: the teacher's role cannot be reduced to that of cultural host whose task is merely to welcome all parties to the education banquet; rather, such hosting should constitute no more than the necessary prelude to the feast itself.

Hospitality that remains at the superficial level of polite conversation is in constant danger of becoming patronizing: hosts who celebrate the presence of strangers in their home without taking the trouble to engage with them in any depth risk utilizing their guests for their own self-aggrandizement. To celebrate the external cultural trappings of Islam whilst avoiding engaging in its core theological claims at a level that recognises the possibility that they could actually be true is, ultimately, profoundly disrespectful – especially in an educational context. Genuine respect demands both honesty about fundamental and potentially irreconcilable differences, and a willingness to explore them in an educative manner. A rich understanding of the weather requires pupils to move beyond surface level descriptions of different weather systems and seek to explain the weather by accounting for the various causal mechanisms – both natural, and, at least since the industrial revolution, manmade – which generate and sustain particular weather systems. Similarly, an effective religious education will require pupils to move beyond surface level descriptions of different faith traditions and identify the various causal mechanisms – historical, psychological, sociological, moral, aesthetic, spiritual etc. – that will enable them to begin to explain and evaluate various religious and non-religious accounts of the ultimate nature of reality. In seeking such deep understanding account needs to be taken of specifically theological explanations: for example, that Islam constitutes a human response to divine revelation contained in the Qur'an. To acknowledge that faith traditions make truth claims about the ultimate order-of-things that are fundamentally contested is to introduce a cognitive dissonance into the classroom that constitutes the very heart of the learning process. A local faith community may reasonably expect that the welcome afforded them translates into a commitment to explore critically their specific truth claims alongside the truth claims of alternative faith traditions.

Such critical engagement will inevitably introduce cognitive, emotional and spiritual tensions into the classroom. A liberal school is likely to operate with an anti-homophobic policy, whereas Roman Catholic pupils, insofar as they are faithful to the teachings of their church, will simultaneously condemn homophobia, embrace homosexuals as children of God, and reject some homosexual practices. The former will ground their commitments on the twin principles of freedom and tolerance, whilst the latter will ground their commitments on the twin principles of Biblical teaching and the Aristotelian tradition of natural law. These differences are not detrimental to the learning process, but rather a necessary part of it: effective education requires pupils to listen to the voices of those from faith traditions other than their own, and to begin to discern and respond intelligently to similarities and differences between them.

It is not reasonable to expect that hospitality be extended to the formal explicit recognition of all local faith communities within the curriculum. In an ideal world this would be the case, but the planning and management of an education system has no option but to observe practical restrictions. To insist that the worldviews of all local faith communities are made the subject of in-depth systematic study would reduce learning to an encyclopaedic assimilation of basic facts. To sacrifice pedagogic depth for breadth in this way is detrimental to religious literacy: pupils would leave school with a quantitively rich but qualitatively impoverished understand of religion, and as such be ill equipped to engage wisely – in thought, feeling, word and deed – with religious issues in adult life. History cannot reasonably expect to cover the history of every culture, or geography every geographic region, across the globe. Curriculum development requires an informed selection of curricular content that takes into account both the global significance of the subject and specific local concerns. The absence of a particular faith tradition from the explicit curriculum does not preclude welcoming pupils from that tradition in the classroom, nor the celebrating of their beliefs and commitments, nor empowering them to respond to the curriculum from their perspective of their received traditions.

FREEDOM

The concept of 'freedom' plays an important role in most religious and non-religious faith traditions: Buddhists advocate freedom from illusion and desire; Christians seek freedom from sin; atheists strive for freedom from irrational superstition. Such freedom has a positive dimension, since freedom *from* something is necessarily freedom *for* something else: Buddhists advocate freedom for the bliss of Nirvana; Christians seek freedom for a sanctifying relationship with God; atheists strive for rational self-determination. Political liberalism's concern for the freedom to hold fast to a particular worldview in an informed and intelligent manner contrasts strongly with comprehensive liberalism's advocacy of the ideal of personal autonomy as an end in itself. The former is epistemically open, willing to entertain the possibility that one amongst many contested worldviews may be true; the latter is epistemically closed, convinced that self-determination constitutes the highest human good. This brings comprehensive liberalism into direct conflict with most religious traditions: where Muslims strive to submit themselves to the will of Allah and Jews strive to obey the Torah, comprehensive liberals seek freedom from all such allegiances. Ironically, in so doing comprehensive liberals actually submit themselves to the truth of a particular cultural tradition that can be traced back from the Enlightenment through the Renaissance to certain aspects of ancient Greek philosophy.

A local faith community may reasonably expect that their children will be free to hold fast to their beliefs, and, within reasonable limits, to express and celebrate the cultural accoutrements of their particular worldview. To ban the hijab or yarmulke in classrooms is not a neutral act: it expresses the humanistic belief that we are first of all human beings and only secondarily (and optionally) children of God. Contrary to appearances, this is not a minor issue about dress codes: it privileges comprehensive liberalism as the normative default position, and carries the implication that religions play a negative and divisive role in society – if this were not the case, there would be no reason for them to disguise their faith commitments. If children are to be free to express their worldviews, then they must be free from any coercive induction, whether covert or explicit, into the worldview of comprehensive liberalism. At the same time, it is reasonable to expect them to engage with alternative faith traditions: not only is it impossible to insulate them from such contacts in a secular society, it is also an educational imperative that such engagement takes place, and that it is conducted in a manner conducive to the growth of religious literacy.

Almost all our knowledge is mediated, transmitted to us via various authorities: scientists, artists, journalists, teachers etc. (Lackey and Sosa 2006). We learn to be scientists not by suspending our prior knowledge and conducting experiments from scratch, but through induction into the normative traditions and practices of the scientific community via the testimony of teachers and textbooks. Such induction operates at both an explicit and implicit level: explicit lessons are conducted in the context of a range of implicit assumptions about the nature of science and scientific activity. Thus much of our learning takes place through osmosis: we are nurtured into the habits of the scientist. Such implicit learning is unavoidable, since the prior assumptions on which a learning community is based will have an inevitable effect on learners, whether they accommodate themselves to these underlying assumptions or choose to resist them. Whether a school has a religious or non-religious foundation, whether it organises its life around political or comprehensive liberalism, it will still present certain set assumptions to pupils as normative. In this context it is *not* reasonable for a local faith community to expect that a plural school in a secular society will nurture their children within their faith tradition. Such nurture requires the existence of a learning community that subscribes, both tacitly and explicitly, to the underlying assumptions and beliefs of the faith community and organises its life around them. It is, however, as noted earlier, a reasonable expectation that the liberal state sponsored faith community schools meet these requirements whenever this proves practicable on educational, economic and other similar grounds.

REASON

Political liberalism's commitment to tolerance and freedom are means to the greater end of enabling different communities within a plural society to pursue contested questions of ultimate truth and truthful living in a hospitable and open environment. In order to achieve this goal, the primary task of religious education must be to cultivate appropriate levels of public religious literacy, understood as the capacity to think, feel, speak and act wisely in relation to the contested question of the ultimate order-of-things and of human flourishing in relation to ultimate reality.

Contemporary religious education cannot avoid the impact of a particular, positivistic story about the relation between reason and religion, namely that religious belief is essentially an irrational leap of faith that, at best, may be tolerated as a private activity provided it neither harms others nor intrudes on the public sphere. It is precisely reasoning of this kind that leads some secular democracies to reject religious education in state schools. The first and most important response to this story is to note that it is fundamentally disputed: many religious adherents *are* highly intelligent people, more than capable of giving a rational defence and justification of their faith commitments. If this were not so, there would be no place for the study of theology alongside religious studies, in the modern university. It is highly significant here that Richard Dawkins and his fellow 'New Atheists', in advocating this positivistic story, fail consistently to engage with academic theology: as a result, and in direct contradiction of their own commitment to reason, they draw conclusions on a *priori* grounds without any sustained attempt to consider the available evidence (McGrath 2004, 82ff). At the same time, however, they acknowledge their position is contested and seek proactively to defend it by providing their children with a supplementary confessional atheistic education modelled on the longstanding Christian model of youth camps (BBC News 2009; Urban Saints 2009). In so far as it apparently excludes a commitment to listening attentively and critically to the very best formulations of those who oppose its particular faith commitments, it constitutes an indoctrinatory form of confessionalism. This, clearly, is contested territory, and according to political liberalism the only appropriate response is to debate the issues openly and intelligently. The very fact that the rationality of religious belief is contested by intelligent people on both sides of the argument demands the cultivation of religious literacy in the classroom.

Although the positivistic story continues to hold certain, albeit increasingly limited, authority in the public sphere, its influence in academic circles is now virtually non-existent. The story was based on two premises that are now no longer viable. The first was that knowledge must be based on secure foundations: either of direct empirical observation and/or of the rational coherence of propositional truth claims; the second was that legitimate claims to knowledge require a high degree of epistemic certainty. With regard to the former, it is clear that we know much more about the world than raw empirical sense data: we know that water consists of hydrogen and oxygen even though we cannot taste either chemical, and we recognise evil acts even though we have no empirical means of weighing or measuring them. Further, we now recognise that it is a fallacy to insist that the world conform to our prior epistemic assumptions: Newton assumed, on the basis of Aristotelian logic, that time and space are absolute categories; Einstein, in the process of struggling to make sense of his observations of the natural world, was forced to conclude that Newton's logic was wrong – time and space are relative to one another. To understand the world rationally is not to force it to conform to raw empirical observation or some a *priori* logical system: on the contrary, the pursuit of truth consists not in transforming the world to make it fit with our experiences and assumptions, but allowing reality itself to transform our minds in line with Aquinas' maxim *adequatio intellectus et rei* – the intellect (of the knower) must be adequate to the thing (known). The second premise, that the only valid knowledge is certain knowledge, is also inadequate: in pre-modern times most human beings were absolutely certain that the world was flat, but were wrong to be so. Certainty is not a criterion for truth: throughout our lives we make informed judgements about situations we find ourselves in – the honesty and integrity of another person for example – without the luxury of any certainty that our judgements are correct. This is precisely the kind of judgement we draw on in answering questions about the ultimate nature of reality: the atheist who believes that there is no reality transcending the natural order of things makes a judgement call that conflicts with the judgement call of religious adherents. Both atheism and religious belief entail faith commitments: it is not true that atheism is a normative position that religious adherents supplement with an irrational leap of faith – if there is no direct proof that God exists, neither is there direct proof that the natural order is self-generating. All knowledge, in every sphere of intellectual activity, takes the form of 'faith seeking understanding': faced with a complex reality that transcends our limited capacity to comprehend it, we have no option other than to strive to give the best possible account of it, a process that demands that we attend sympathetically and critically to alternative accounts.

There is no space here to unpack these epistemic issues in greater depth. Nevertheless, the fact that the epistemology of religious and non-religious worldviews is the subject of debate, both amongst the general public and in the highest academic circles is itself justification for the reasonable assumption that religious education in a secular democracy should empower pupils to participate in the debate by cultivating and enhancing their religious literacy.

CONCLUSION

Local faith communities in a secular democracy must recognize that multi-faith schools with no religious foundation operate within the tradition of western liberalism: thus it is unreasonable to expect that they will provide a confessional education designed to nurture the faith of their children; at the same time, it is reasonable for them to expect that such schools will avoiding inducting them into the worldview of comprehensive liberalism. They may expect liberal schools to offer their children a hospitable and tolerant welcome, whether or not there is space for the explicit study of their faith tradition within the explicit curriculum. They may expect their children to be free to express their faith openly, and to explore alternative faith traditions in a sympathetic and critical manner – especially by addressing questions of ultimate truth and truthful living in relation to the ultimate order-of-things. Above all, they may expect liberal schools to cultivate their children's religious literacy, not as a replacement for their education and nurture within their faith tradition, but as a supplement to it – a supplement attentive to the fact that in a secular society in which any faith commitment, whether religious or secular, is experienced as challenging and often problematic, the cultivation of religious literacy is an urgent and necessary task.

REFERENCES

Archer, M. S., Collier, A. and Porpora, D. V. (2004) *Transcendence: Critical Realism and God*, London: Routledge.

BBC News (2009) Camp Offers 'Godless Alternative', http://news.bbc.co.uk/2/hi/uk_news/8172844.stm (accessed 21 August 2009).

Hirst, P. H. and Peters, R. S. (1970) *The Logic of Education*, London: Routledge and Kegan Paul.

Kekes, J. (1999) *Against Liberalism*, New York: Cornell University Press.

Lackey, J. and Sosa, E. (ed.) (2006) *The Epistemology of Testimony*, London: Clarendon Press.

McGrath, A. E. (2004) *Dawkin's God: Genes, Memes, and the Meaning of Life*, Oxford: Blackwell.

Taylor, C. (2007) *A Secular Age*, Cambridge, MA: Belknap Press.

Urban Saints (2009) Urban Saints, http://www.urbansaints.org/pages/100/Home.htm (accessed 21 August 2009).

Wernick, A. (2005) *Auguste Comte and the Religion of Humanity: The Post-theistic Program of French Social Theory*, Cambridge: Cambridge University Press.

Wright, A. (2000) *Spirituality and Education*, London: RoutledgeFalmer.

Wright, A. (2003) 'Freedom, Equality, Fraternity? Towards a Liberal Defence of Faith Community Schools', *British Journal of Religious Education*, 25 (2), 142-152.

Wright, A. (2004) *Religion, Education and Post-modernity*, London: RoutledgeFalmer.

Wright, A. (2007) *Critical Religious Education, Multiculturalism and the Pursuit of Truth*, Cardiff: University of Wales Press.

CHAPTER 9

REFLECTING HONESTLY:

Ideological conflict, religious education and community cohesion

Matthew G Thompson

SUMMARY

THIS CHAPTER WILL EXAMINE the secular humanist foundation on which the UK Government's social and educational strategy is constructed. That foundation will be shown to be inadequate, unable to comprehend the nature of religion and prone to fuelling the Islamophobia it intended to address. The chapter concludes by suggesting a pedagogical framework for RE grounded in a spirit of humility, which facilitates the reflective honesty and heart-opening necessary to embrace the challenges of a multi-cultural and multi-faith society, especially those presented by the global renaissance of Islam as a powerful and dynamic influence upon secularised Western societies, such as the UK.

THE LIMITATIONS OF THE SECULAR UNDERSTANDING OF COMMUNITY COHESION

The global renaissance of Islam as an assertive, powerful and dynamic force pervading every sphere of life causes fear and confusion in secularised Western societies such as the UK. Governments and their education systems have been rudely awoken from dreamy liberal secular slumbers that neatly confined religion to private spheres in which Islam, like Christianity before it, could be reduced to just another tame cultural life-style option. Fear and confusion are apparent in two interrelated spheres. First, the teaching of Religious Education (particularly Islam) in schools which is thrust into the front line of central government's strategy to promote 'community cohesion', and 'the Prevention of Violent Extremism', which comprises the second sphere. Following the imposition of mandatory Citizenship Education and the duty on all schools to promote community cohesion (Education Act 2006), all teachers become agents of these ideological agendas, yet are provided with confusing guidance for understanding and implementing them. RE teachers are expected to understand and address the realities and dangers of Islamophobia, yet avoid promoting Islamic dawa (mission) and thereby returning their subject to Religious Instruction.

Following the 7/7 (2005) bombings awareness of faith came to the fore as a key factor in the Government's analysis of community cohesion. Funding was targeted at trying to promote better inter-faith understanding, conceived primarily, in both theory and practice, as the promotion of a positive understanding of Islam intended to combat widespread Islamophobia. The framework for this Government analysis is dominated by secular, social-scientific categories, which, in their inability to fully comprehend religions, open the door for uncritical promotion of Islam which can exacerbate rather than address Islamophobia.

Two examples illustrate this:

In 2006 the Government established its *Commission on Integration and Social Cohesion*, which, in 2007, published its report *Our Shared Future* (Singh 2007). The report is firmly grounded in a secular, social scientific framework that understands and responds to social issues, including faiths, in terms of narrow, purely secular categories of social justice and recent theories about the emergence of 'fluid, multiple, trans-national identities' (*ibid*). There is no attempt to understand the nature of identity, meaning and purpose that lies at the heart of the Islamic (or any other) faith community in their own terms. Not surprisingly therefore its solutions are vague recommendations focusing on a purely secular, narrowly conceived 'equalities' (of opportunity) and 'rights' agendas. All this is grounded in the central policy of promoting a nebulous sense of a 'shared future' which, it is claimed, can bind together diverse communities (*op. cit.* 45).

With respect to education, the Government commissioned the Ajegbo report (Ajegbo 2007) which recommended imposing a more prescriptive, centrally devised Citizenship Education curriculum with a new, 'fourth strand' on 'Identity and diversity'. Unfortunately, as with the original conception and implementation of Citizenship Education (The Crick Report QCA, 1998), the framework in which identity, citizenship, meaning, value and purpose are all conceived, once again, is a narrow, secular, social scientific one which, whilst claiming to promote critical thinking and enquiry skills, in reality shows scant understanding of faiths. So, although the report rightly urges that there needs to be a development of resources to help 'mainstream' faith and inter-faith dimensions into that new fourth strand of Citizenship Education, it then boldly advocates that 'an understanding of issues of identity and diversity in the context of citizenship is best approached through a political and historical lens.' (*op. cit.* 95).

The Government's narrow secular framework draws heavily upon a secular human rights agenda, grounded in the United Nations' Universal Declaration of Human Rights (UDHR), which they assume provides a secure bedrock of common values and vision on which to build a cohesive, yet diverse society and an education system to nurture and promote it. This is a pattern repeated in the writings of many of the 'experts' driving policy and practice with respect to Citizenship Education and community cohesion. For example, Audrey Osler (Osler 2008), in her critique of Ajegbo's *Citizenship Education Review*, agrees with that Review's assumption that a secular programme of political literacy (which underpins Citizenship Education) is the correct framework for understanding and addressing issues of identity and diversity. However, she argues for a more radical, political framework which, she claims, allows for dissent and more critical thinking on race, ethnicity and religion. She then urges that this alternative framework should be grounded in the UN Convention on the Rights of the Child (1989), the UDHR (1948) and the European Convention on Human Rights (1950) (ECHR) incorporated into UK domestic law through the Human Rights Act, (1998) (HRA). She admits that some people may draw their values from their faith, but then boldly asserts that, 'within the broad human rights framework to which nations and non-governmental organisations have subscribed and achieved consensus, a dialogue is possible. These principles can be applied within the community of the school and in the wider community of the nation' (Osler 2008, 13). She does not appear to recognise that the UDHR is neither cross-cultural, nor cross faiths. Nor does she appear to recognise that both her demand for a 'fundamental shift in our understanding of childhood' and 'a cultural change in our schools' (*op. cit.*12) and also the fact that she favours the ECHR because it represents a legal framework that can be legally enforced in schools, all constitute the imposition of a narrow secular political framework that, through legal enforcement, literally would forbid any dissent and therefore allow for far less critical thinking on race, ethnicity and, in particular, religion. In other words, her initial call for political literacy ends up being a call to impose a very particular and restrictive secular political vision which is reductionist in its understanding of faiths.

The pattern is repeated by Lynn Davies in her attempt to understand and tackle the issue of what, to refer to the title of her book, she calls *Educating Against Extremism* (Davies 2008). Davies asserts that her issue is with 'those who cannot accept other belief systems or lifestyles and who seek to impose their own' (*op.cit.* 19) and declares that part of her solution to this 'extremism' is to be, 'opening up, presenting *alternatives* to understandings and…the notion that there can be different versions of events' (op. cit. 60 her emphasis). Davies' ideal teacher is 'a respected authority who, crucially, is not dogmatic, but is warm and sympathetic and just asks questions' (*op. cit.* 61). However, these admirable sentiments sit uncomfortably alongside the following aspects of Davies' thesis. First, her recourse to Richard Dawkin's reductionist and philosophically naïve and confused framework for understanding religion. Secondly, her bold and unreasoned assertion of what (following Dawkins), with respect to religious belief, she deems to be 'the very *fact* that there is no evidence and that unquestioning belief is therefore necessary' (*op. cit.* 16, my emphasis). Finally, her dismissive and condescending talk (hardly 'warm and sympathetic') of 'Jesus and his followers' as her prime example of a 'type of cognitive dissonance in which normal links between perception and reality have broken down' (*op.cit.* 17) and her (unreasoned) assertion that 'the reasons for religious adherence' as being, 'in the end no different from any other expression of a market preference' (*op. cit.* 96).

Davies, like Osler, wishes to impose her own narrow, secular political framework (with its reductionist and distorting approach to religion) of 'political education for diversity' (*op.cit.* 155) on all our schools. Her 'counter-terror education' is a 'political' or 'peace' education based, as with Osler, on the UDHR and seen as exemplified in UNESCO's Associated Schools and their 'Fun to be Nice' programmes (*ibid*). According to Davies, the foundation of values upon which this framework is to be built cannot be religion. Her distaste of religion is so vehement that the mere suggestion that it could provide such a foundation, is dismissed as a case of a 'breathtaking intolerance and superior attitude' (*op. cit.* 160).

However, according to Davies, it is, apparently, neither intolerant nor an example of 'superiority' for her to propose that all our schools should impose her 'humanist and earthed alternative' to a morality based on religion, namely 'human rights' which, she says, 'is made by people, and therefore can be scrutinised as man-made and the best bet for that historical era' (op. cit. 162). Apart from hypocrisy with respect to claims of 'superiority', Davies fails to elucidate the philosophical nature of the proposed human rights framework which underpins her thesis (and the Government's *Citizenship Education, Community Cohesion* and *Prevent* strategies).

Davies shows no awareness of the normative, prescriptive nature of Human Rights claims and their logical dependence upon theories of human nature (for John Locke, a father figure of Human Rights, this theory was grounded in Biblical revelation). She appears to have little grasp of vital philosophical distinctions between relative and absolute moral value judgements, between statements of fact and statements of value, and the logical difficulty of deriving the latter from the former. Her unexamined and unexplained assertions that human rights are 'based not on ideals but on entitlements' and that 'Rights is not a belief system, it is an ethical system' (*op. cit.* 163) belie a philosophical confusion that does little to convince the reader that her proposed alternative framework for morality is truly 'earthed'.[1]

Like Osler, Davies ends up seeking (under the guise of the tolerant language of respect and rights) to impose her own very particular and narrow secular political education built upon a philosophically unstable, shifting foundation of secular humanist relativism. At its heart, this foundation elevates and upholds the individual human self as sovereign, sole authority with respect to values and vision.

The secular humanist origins of the United Nations and UNESCO in the American Humanist Association and works of Julian Huxley and their vision to create a transnational, secular new world order grounded in unity and peace, appears noble, but is very much grounded in Huxley's assertion that, 'the general philosophy of UNESCO should... be a scientific world humanism, global in extent and evolutionary in background. Evolution in the broad sense denotes all the historical processes of change and development at work in the universe.' (Huxley 1976).

Secular humanism is a very particular philosophical world view that, whilst claiming to uphold the value and dignity of the human individual, also denies the revelatory foundations of religious truth, limits the conception of the reality of humanity (and our world) to purely natural forms and then elevates man above God to be the ultimate source and measure of all value and supreme sovereign master of his own destiny. The measure of that value and shared vision is most commonly conceived in terms of the utilitarian pursuit of worldly 'happiness'. Traditional religions, with their traditional moralities grounded in divine revelation, are to be contained within categories such as 'personal life-style choices'. If they dare reveal their true nature as making absolute epistemological, moral and spiritual claims of universal and eternal consequence, then they must be seen ultimately as oppressive, denigrating and irrational powers that restrict the freedom, dignity and pleasure of the individual and which the 'truly enlightened' individual must liberate themselves from in order to achieve their true potential for happiness and enlightenment.

The limitations and dangers of the secular humanist worldview are evident through history. Wherever human beings have sought to elevate the individual self in the secular humanistic spirit of unity, enlightenment, liberation, justice and equality, they have been as equally susceptible to the dangers of pride, arrogance and oppression as their religious counterparts. Therefore, they also invariably sink into oppressive forms of totalitarianism and imposition of rule by the 'enlightened' elite who have convinced themselves that they have been freed from the violent extremism and superstition that so oppresses the poor enslaved ignorant masses. The reigns of terror following the French and Russian revolutions, brought untold evil and suffering and established the most inflexible, illiberal and intolerant totalitarian regimes, all in the name of human rights, peace, freedom and liberation.

According to Davies, extremism is defined as 'the inability to see and break down one's own and other's complex pieces of belief and behaviour in its different parts, complexities and contradiction.' (Davies 2008, 129). Regrettably, Davies and Osler both clearly demonstrate in their writing this inability. In seeking to impose the particularity and limitations of their narrow, secular humanist frameworks, they are as equally vulnerable to extremism as their religious counterparts.

SECULAR REDUCTIONISM:
LIMITING THE UNDERSTANDING OF FAITHS IN RE

The same narrow, secular humanist world-view, with its distorting, reductionist approach to understanding religion increasingly is the controlling influence amongst the establishment policy makers with respect to R.E. The introduction of a *Non-Statutory National Framework for Religious Education* (QCA 2004), the OfSTED report *Making Sense of Religion* (OfSTED 2007) and the recently published *Religious Education in English Schools: Non-Statutory Guidance* (D CSF2010) all represent increasingly centralised (secular dominated) government control over curriculum content and delivery.

This secular world-view is prevalent in the work of Robert Jackson and the Warwick Religions and Education Research Unit (WRERU). Jackson was one of the declared 'experts on freedom of religion or belief' who helped draw up the *Toledo Guiding Principles on Teaching About Religions and Beliefs in Public Schools* (ODIHR 2007), which strongly urges RE to be conceived and delivered within a human rights framework. WRERU have been funded by the UN to help develop the *Oslo Coalition Project* and the promotion of 'Teaching for Tolerance', related to UNESCO's *Interreligious Dialogue Programme* (Jackson 2004). Recently WRERU have also been commissioned by DCFS to undertake a comprehensive review of all Religious Education resources with reference to their potential to contribute to community cohesion (Jackson 2).

Jackson's team developed 'ethnographic approaches' to understanding religion, which are firmly rooted in secular, social, scientific, anthropological frameworks.[2] Concepts of culture and faith identity are seen as varied and fluid and therefore the individual is to be understood as equally creator as well as receptor of identity. What this amounts to in pedagogical practice is an emphasis on understanding the diversity within as well as between faiths, but also a stress on enabling pupils to become 'active interpreters of religious meaning making' and encouraging them to engage in 'hermeneutical activity' (Grimmitt 2000, 39). According to Jackson, there is a resulting 'oscillating movement between the learner's concepts and those of what he calls the religious "insider"' (*op.cit.* 133-134). There is an underlying assumption in this approach (shared with secular humanism and gnostic, universalist approaches to truth, religion and spirituality, including their Islamic manifestations) that faith and spirituality are universal human phenomena (as perceived by those thereby implicitly claiming an enlightened understanding that transcends the historically and culturally induced partiality of the masses) and of which religions are culturally varied, fluid and interchangeable manifestations. Accordingly, the individual self should be viewed and nurtured, even within faiths, as a much more autonomous, self-enlightened source of value and meaning.

Jackson's approach receives disproportionately large establishment support and exercises disproportionately wide establishment influence partly because it is so compatible with and appealing to the establishment secularists who control education policy and funding. Seeking to domesticate religions, reducing them to cultural phenomena, confining them through obfuscating discourse about boundaries/definitions of religion, is an approach which over-emphasises the diversity, individuality and complexity of religions so that the wood cannot be seen for the trees and one can close one's eyes when it comes to religions' powerful, uniform undercurrents. These latter include absolutist and all-pervasive claims with respect to their truth and their application to all spheres of life. Though working outside Jackson's 'interpretive' framework, Philip Barnes recently took the reductionist, domesticating approach to understanding religions even further in calling for a 'new non-theological model of religious education' which can 'equip pupils with the skills and abilities to assess and evaluate religion and religious phenomena' (Barnes 2009).

This is the approach upon which many of those with responsibility for the RE curriculum and inspection (and also many across Europe, UNESCO and Japan) are pinning their hopes in tackling urgent issues of how to teach Islam and, in the UK, how to conform to the government's ideological programmes. Sarah Smalley (2005), as Chair of the Association of RE Inspectors, Advisors and Consultants drew on Jackson's work to urge teachers to bring pupils' attention to the diversity within Islam so as to combat media stereotypes of Muslims as suicide bombers. In order to encourage teachers to be 'positive but realistic' about Islam, she uses Jackson's anthropological approach to urge RE teachers to focus on 'the people' rather than the religion or beliefs of Islam (*op. cit.* 5). This, she thinks, enables teaching about Islam to focus on 'the ordinary decency of Muslim lives' (*op.cit.* 7). However, this approach, which effectively drives a divide between a belief and the believer, although valuable in some respects, when confronted with any aspect of Islamic belief and practice that appears awkward, difficult or controversial, amounts in practice to burying one's head in the sand.[3]

Contra to the wishful thinking of secular experts, in reality, religions are powerful forces making ultimate claims on us all. No amount of urging heads to be turned away to focus on 'ordinary lives of decent people' can make the more challenging manifestations of this reality go away.

RESTRICTING UNDERSTANDINGS OF INTER-FAITH DIALOGUE AND ISLAMOPHOBIA

The weaknesses of the secular humanist, social scientific, human rights framework for understanding and addressing Islamic (and any other form of religious) extremism are further evident with respect to the government's *'Prevent'* strategy. This follows the recommendations of the social scientist Tufyal Choudhury to pursue a policy of providing large scale funding for comprehensive programmes promoting positive perceptions of Islam across all education sectors. This strategy is grounded in the premise that the prime cause of Islamic extremism is Islamophobia fuelled by ignorance concerning the true nature of Islam. According to Choudhury, media bias against Islam, linked to general hostility towards the faith, drives Muslims to extremism (Choudhury 2007, 23). The Government follows his view (based on Appleton 2005) that part of the solution is to fund the promotion of a British Islam 'which is "receptive, integrationist and dynamic"' (*op. cit.* 30). Hence the public funding of organisations such as The Quilliam Foundation and The Radical Middle Way.

Maurice Coles adopts a similar approach, demanding that all education agencies, schools and institutions must deepen their understanding of Islam and the needs of Muslim pupils. This, he asserts, 'must lead to effective strategies and real action in all areas of educational life, so that Muslims and non-Muslims can begin to understand the contributions of Islam to our shared histories and the major issues that face British Muslims today' (Coles 2008, 37).

Choudhury and Coles are correct in pointing out a key cause of Islamophobia. However, it is clear from the writings of Coles, Choudhury and (as we shall see) Ataullah Siddiqui, that the understanding of Islam which they wish to see imposed throughout the education system, is conceived within an Islamic framework which permits little substantial critical thought or analysis. The danger of publicly funding uncritical propagation of Islamic thought and understanding is that it all too easily appears as privileging Islam and state-funding *dawa* (consequently fuelling rather than addressing Islamophobia).[4]

Siddiqui's report on *Islam at Universities in England* (Siddiqui 2007) recommended funding for Islamic Studies departments (and for them to be more Islamic, less secular in their approach) and for training programmes promoting positive understanding of Islam. Siddiqui has written a number of articles on inter-faith (particularly Islamic-Christian) dialogue and understanding (Siddiqui 1 and 2005), in which his evaluation of Christian theologians appears to make any Christian challenge to the authenticity of the prophecy of Muhammad and the Qur'an as inherently contra the spirit of inter-faith dialogue and understanding.[5] A theologically illiterate, secular government falls easy prey to such appearances and, thereby, to the remedies subsequently proposed, which inevitably imply repressing critique of Islam for fear of fuelling Islamophobia.

Siddiqui is influenced by Isma'il Al-Faruqi's (1921-1986) understanding of inter-faith dialogue (Siddiqui 1999). Al-Faruqi held Islam (and its ummah) to be not merely an infallible faith, but a potentially perfect new world community, state and 'international order' for all humanity. Islam and its shariah law is said to be true for all times, peoples and places, transcending all boundaries of ethnicity, blood, tribe, nationality, priestly hierarchies, etc. Sounding like Sayyid Qutb (1906-1966) in this respect, Al-Faruqi asserted that, 'the ummah's greatest asset is its Islamic vision of world-order and inter-human relations' (Al-Faruqi 1, 27) and subsequently demanded that the West (and East) 'must ...stop their falsification of Islam and misrepresentation of its views' (*op. cit.* 28). When the ummah, embodying Islam, becomes the world-community, it will, said Al-Faruqi, '...move the hearts of humans towards enlightenment and guidance, and consequently, towards peace and felicity' (*ibid*).

Al-Faruqi therefore called for an 'Islamisation of knowledge' (Siddiqui 1999), a process philosophically analogous (though contrasting in its socio-political manifestation) to Qutb's belief that Islam 'does not force people to accept its belief, but it wants to provide a free environment in which they will have the choice of beliefs. What it wants is to abolish those oppressive political systems under which people are prevented from expressing their freedom to choose whatever beliefs they want, and after that it gives them complete freedom to decide whether they will accept Islam or not' (Qutb 2005, .56). The danger of this approach is that it can justify both the silencing of any critique of Islam (making it appear as irrational Islamophobia) and also the wide-scale public promotion of exclusively positive images of Islam as (in Orwellian fashion) the 'promotion of freedom'. As Qutb says, 'No political system or material power should put hindrances in the way of preaching Islam. It should leave every individual free to accept or reject it, and if someone wants to accept it, it should not prevent him or fight against him.' (*op. cit.* 58).

The problem is that the choice can hardly be considered free when critique of Islam, its central Prophet and revelation are suppressed. In Qutb's Orwellian world, freedom means freedom from corrupting *jahilia* influences which include any open critique of Islam, the Prophet Muhammad and the Qur'an. Hence his declaration that 'Islam has a right to remove all ...obstacles which are in its path so that it may address human reason and intuition with no interference and opposition from political systems' (*op. cit.* 74).

The Government's secular humanist framework also shares with Islam a potential for utopianism. For Islam, like Rousseau (1712-1778), in holding that human nature essentially is good (awaiting completion rather than re-creation), can encourage belief in the possibility of a perfectible (through following shari'ah) political and social system on earth.[6] Furthermore, Islamic utopianism is manifested in unrealistic approaches within much Muslim scholarship (and society) to the social and political manifestations of shari'ah law in Muslim societies. This is particularly evident for example in the propagation of romanticised exaggerations of a purported golden age of inter-faith tolerance under Islamic rule in Cordoba (e.g. Sheikh Hamsa Yusuf 2007). This strengthens belief that Islam provides the eminently suitable framework to establish fruitful inter-faith dialogue and community cohesion. It is also found in the equally unrealistic claims that Islam provides the answer for how to teach Religious Education in a multi-faith/cultural society (e.g. Ibrahim 1993).

In removing critique of Islam from the arena of honest, rational dialogue guided by informed and empowered teachers and undertaken in the spirit of good faith and trust between people with a common concern for the collective welfare of all, it thereby, all too easily, is handed over to those whose motives and methods are suspect (further fuelling Islamophobia). Within the Muslim community, it increases an important additional cause of Islamic violent extremism, namely, the victim mentality with its concomitant Western/ Christian/Jewish phobia, in which Muslims view themselves as innocent victims of a campaign of oppression and humiliation by the satanic powers of a Christian crusading West, ultimately controlled by manipulating Jewish conspirators.

Revision of history was needed, in former times, to combat the irrational prejudice and bigotry that characterised much understanding of Islam and Muhammad in Western Christian communities. However, the solution, no matter how well ideologically motivated, is not to swing to the opposite extreme (e.g. Armstrong 1991) and fail to acknowledge the injustices and sufferings experienced by non-Muslims under Muslim rule (see for example Jenkins 2008, Chapter 4). The cries of those multitudes who have suffered (and today still suffer) under Muslim rule, will come back to haunt such apologists, just as surely as the cries of those who suffered at the hands of Crusaders, European Slavers, Conquistadors, Inquisitors and colonialists have haunted Christians who sought to idealise and spiritualise Western, worldly imperialist systems.

So where can educators turn to allow for reasonable, rational critique of Islam that avoids any return to Islamophobia? If there is no truly neutral, objective, overarching framework for inter-faith dialogue and for promoting the faith dimensions of community cohesion in our schools and wider society, what then are the pedagogical consequences for RE?

CONCLUSION

Reflecting honestly: a pedagogical framework to help religious education address community cohesion

First, it is necessary to raise awareness that the secular humanism of the Government/UN/UNESCO's human rights agendas and, in the field of RE, Jackson's Warwick team's ethnographic approach to religion, do not present a neutral, objective perspective. They contain underlying assumptions that religions are just culturally variable and fluid expressions of a universal spirituality which the enlightened elite perceive. Similar tendencies towards such universalism (and gnosticism), with its claim to provide an epistemologically neutral panacea for embracing diversity, is inherent in much Islamic thought.

The presumptuousness in claiming such epistemological objectivity and moral, religious and spiritual neutrality is symptomatic of the self-deception illustrated in the telling of the Indian story of the blind men and the elephant brought before the all-wise King. Each blind man grasps onto a different part of the elephant and falsely assumes he has understood the whole. The story is presented as a critique of any attempt on behalf of any particular faith or philosophy to lay claim to the Truth. But, of course the deeper arrogance lies in those who identify with the all-seeing King who presumes to know, with imperial, absolute certainty, that what each man grasps is just a different part of the entire picture which only he, the mighty King, can see.[7]

Religions cannot (without serious distortion) be confined within secular containers of social and cultural categories and the human rights agenda. Religions make full and absolute claims about truth, reality and morality which impact directly on all our lives. To be truly encountered and understood they need to be seen in that fullness. Jabal Buaben provides a Muslim response to the question of whether a non-Muslim can teach about Islam, demanding that Islam be taught within its own paradigm, allowing the Qur'an and the Sunnah of Muhammad 'to speak for themselves' (Buaben 1999, 26) and therefore ensuring both that all resources are cleansed of anything that could be perceived of as prejudice or bias and that all teachers be trained to respect Islam and avoid Islamophobia (*ibid.*). He is surely correct in his initial demand. It is essential that each of us brings the fullness of our own tradition and its understanding of truth, human nature and society to the table. Part of that fullness in Islam is the welcome acceptance of plurality and difference which A. Siddiqui, along with universalists such as F. Schuon (Schuon 1989) and S. H. Nasr (Nasr 1993) have sought to elucidate as an essential part of Qur'anic revelation. However, to avoid elevating ourselves beyond fellow guests to host at the table, the respect and training demanded must allow if acceptance of the other be sincere for a process of critical reflection and humble acceptance that there is no religiously nor epistemologically neutral framework available to facilitate this.

My tentative suggestion is that Religious Education would benefit from pedagogical strategies that enabled a faith (once presented in its own terms) to be seen as mirrored in the experience of others of different faiths and none, who also have encountered the impact (not always positive) of its lived out reality. This provides important, humbling perspectives for practitioners of faiths and useful means for combating inherent tendencies within every faith (including secular humanism) to slide into destructive spiritual pride and self-righteousness. Within the Christian tradition, the mirror of the experiences of our Jewish neighbours reflects the blood-stained distortions of a faith whose origin is supreme love and humility, yet which all too often has impacted on others with bitter hatred, violence and pride. It has been a sobering lesson for Christians to understand how their central focus, the cross of Christ, can appear as a symbol of terrifying victimisation as well as awesome divine Grace.

The God of Abraham, Isaac and Jacob is no respecter of persons, yet in Christian tradition God gives a powerful, paradoxical example of holding up a mirror to Himself through the person of the Syro-Phoenician woman (Matthew 15: 21-28). That mirror reflects a potent combination of upholding the infinitely unique, costly and exclusive claim of Divine Grace (which cannot, without cheapening, be distributed at any price) together with its humble, vulnerable, self-giving heart. This provides exemplary guidance for approaches to inter-faith dialogue and RE.

It is of equal value for the Islamic faith to see the fullness of its lived-out reality mirrored in the experiences of non-Muslims living under Muslim rule. So long as this is done sensitively, in a spirit of humility and truth (not in bitterness, hatred or revenge), such honest reflection could provide additional means for combating Islamophobia fuelled by both resentment from non-Muslims (to whom Islam appears increasingly to receive privileged treatment), and also Islamic extremists exploiting a sense of victimhood.

It is vital to ensure that the mirror is held up only *after* the faith has been fairly and fully presented in its own terms. If the risk of this process multiplying phobias/victimhood is deemed too high, then lower level, less immediately productive, but nevertheless long-term trust building forms of mirroring could examine how non-negotiable foundational beliefs (such as the authenticity of the prophethood of Muhammad in Islam, or the crucifixion and resurrection in Christianity) are understood, impact upon and questioned by our neighbours.

An important perspective that traditional Christianity can bring to the table of inter-faith dialogue and RE is realism about human nature and society. This is a powerful anti-dote to the proliferation of potentially destructive secular or Islamic utopianism. It provides a realistic perspective on the role of the intellect, which is a helpful counter-balance to the gnostic, universalist tendencies of both secular and Islamic philosophies.

In traditional Christianity, the intellect plays a key yet necessarily secondary role to the heart in the quest for truth, goodness and righteousness. It is in the heart, the locus of human identity, where each of us has to reflect and make the ultimate choice between the fundamental alternatives of elevating the individual self to the ultimate source of all meaning and value, where 'man is measure', or harkening to the Word of God (the blessed Hebrew command 'Shema') in which 'the fear of the Lord is the beginning of wisdom'.

NOTES

1. Even UNESCO in the first edition of its *International Journal on Multicultural Societies* (IJMS Vol. 1, No. 1, 1999) published an article which, although lacking in philosophical depth, was able partly to understand and acknowledge the severe limitations of the UN/UNESCO concept of Human Rights and its inability to provide a substantial foundation of universal ideals and norms of human behaviour and values which its idealistic, secular Western conceivers dreamed of (Spickard 1999).

2. The prime influences on this framework according to Jackson (Jackson 1), were the Canadian universalist Wilfred Cantwell Smith (1916-2000), the anti-Western polemic of Edward Said (Said 1991) and the American ethnographer Clifford Geertz (1926-2006).

3. In an article on pedagogies and Islam featured on the popular RE-net website for R.E. practitioners (www.re-net.ac.uk), Revell (2008) appeals to Gearon's claim (Gearon 2001) that Human Rights agenda can provide a neutral framework for the critique of obnoxious political aspects of faiths. Gearon refers to a process in which he 'tried to raise questions for an enhanced political awareness for religious education through human rights' (Gearon 2001, 148) and claims that, 'the best models...for such a political religious education are those which look at the place of religion in the context of an international values consensus' (ibid) which for him, following and quoting Ayton-Shenker (1995), means the UN and its UDHR, Convention On the Rights of the Child, etc. and operating within the context of 'postcolonial criticism' of Edward Said. For Gearon, 'human rights have the scope to bring real and enduring relevance to religious education' (*ibid*).

4. The term *Islamophobia*, popularised by the Runnymede Trust Report of 1997 (Runnymede 1997), had potential to help understand, identify and address irrational prejudice, discrimination and hatred towards Muslims. Yet, through incoherent, often superficial (Allen 2007) formulation (including logically flawed attempts to parallel it to racism) it can be hijacked as a tool to censor any reasoned and rational critique of Islam. A recent example can be found in Van Driel (2004), where Richardson represents a critique of Islam through stereotypical bigotry of the right-wing press and follows the 1997 Commission on British Muslims and Islamophobia report's (Runnymede 1997) attempt to impose a dualistic, bi-polar criteria for distinguishing between legitimate disagreement/criticism and phobic dread/hatred. This criterion enforces a labelling system categorising everyone according to whether they are 'open-minded' or closed-minded' through imposing false dichotomies in which you have to decide between Richardson's exclusive and very narrow options. These include deciding between, for example, viewing Islam as, either 'monolithic, static and

authoritarian', or as 'diverse and dynamic with substantial internal debates'; as either, 'inferior, backward and primitive compared with the so-called West', or as 'different but equal'; as either, 'an aggressive enemy to be feared, opposed and defeated', or as 'a cooperative partner with whom to work on shared problems'. In relation to Muslims, similarly narrow and extreme dualistic categories are imposed. For example, Muslims must be seen as either 'manipulative, devious and self-righteous in their religious beliefs', or as 'sincere and genuine' (Richardson quoting Runnymede 1997 in Van Driel 2004, 27).

Imposing such restrictive criteria beyond the narrow contexts of extreme Islamophobia in which they were conceived, surely constitutes a closed-minded categorising and stereotyping. Allen (2004) goes part way to exposing this stereotyping by using the term 'mediatising' to describe it and also indicating that part of the cause may be the strong influence of journalists (as opposed to sound academic scholarship) in determining the discourse and presentation of the issue of Islamophobia (Allen 2007, 23-24). The potential of using the term *Islamophobia* to help understand and address widespread ignorance and prejudice towards Muslims and to promote better understanding, respect and friendship between Muslims and non-Muslims has been substantially reduced.

5. For example, Hans Kuhn is criticised for implying a human authorship for the Qur'an and for seeking 'to explain borrowings from the Judaeo-Christian tradition' (Siddiqui 1). Other theologians are praised for what Siddiqui regards as 'recognizing the *fact* that the Islamic concept of God is not something other than their own' (*ibid*, my emphasis) and also for what he deems to be their 'growing realisation' that, in accordance with his (Siddiqui's) own demand, 'they *have to* see the Prophet of Islam in a new and more positive light (*ibid*. my emphasis)

6. Davies, following Gray, points out the dangers of such utopianism, but also follows his secular, reductionist analysis of Christianity with its theologically inept assertion that the Kingdom Jesus taught did not arrive, and that consequently, 'the history of Christianity is a series of attempts to cope with this founding experience of eschatological disappointment' (Gray 2007) quoted in Davies 2008, 17). Gray (showing no awareness, let alone understanding of key Christian texts such as 2 Peter 3), misrepresents Christianity as an essentially utopian faith, responsible for secular forms of utopianism that dominated the 20th and the 21st centuries. The doctrine of the Fall, so integral to Christian belief, mitigates against any form of utopianism.

7. This point has been made in a different context by Zacharias (2000)

REFERENCES

Ajegbo, Keith (2007) Chair, *Diversity and Citizenship: Curriculum Review* London: DfES.

Allen, C. (2007) *The 'First' Decade of Islamophobia*. Stourbridge: Obtainable from Chris Allen, PO Box 4029, Stourbridge, West Midlands, DY9 9WZ.

Allen C. and Nielsen.J. (2002) *Summary Report on Islamophobia in the EU after 11 September 2001*. Download from http://wallscometumblingdown.wordpress.com/ (accessed 25.3.2010).

Al-Faruqi, Isma'il (1) (No date given) *Islam: Movement for World-Order*. Found online at International Institute of Islamic Thought: www.iiit.org/Resources/IsmailalFaruqi/tabid/94/Default.aspx (accessed 30.03.09.)

Appleton, M. (2005) *The Political Attitudes of Muslims Studying at British Universities in the Post 9/11 World (Part 1)*, 2005, Journal Of Muslim Minority Affairs, Vol 25 (2).

Armstrong, Karen. (1991) Muhammad: A Western Attempt to Understand Islam, London: Victor Gallanz.

Armstrong, Karen (2006) *Muhammad: Prophet for our Time*, London: Harper Collins.

Barnes, Philip. 'The question: Is multifaith religious education a failure?' in guardian.co.uk. First published at 10.51 GMT Monday 16 March 2009 www.guardian.co.uk/commentisfree/2009/mar/11religious-education-religion Accessed 21.03.09.

Baumann, G. (1996) *Contesting Culture: Discourses of Identity in Multi-Ethnic*, London, New York and Cambridge: Cambridge University Press.

Buaben, J. (1999) 'Can I Teach Your religion? – A Muslim Response' in Brown, E. et al (eds.) (1999) *World Religions in Education: Can I Teach Your Religion?* London: The Shap Working Party

Choudhury, T.l. (2007) *The Role of Muslim Identity Politics in Radicalisation (a study in progress)* London: Dept. CLG April 2007

Coles, M. I. (2008) *Every Muslim Child Matters Practical Guidance for schools and children's services*. Stoke on Trent: Trentham Books.

Commission on British Muslims and Islamophobia (2004) *Islamophobia: issues, challenges and action*. Stoke on Trent: Uniting Britain Trust and Trentham Books.

Commission on Integration and Cohesion (chaired by Darra Singh) (2007) *Our Shared Future* London, Crown Copyright.

Davies, L. (2008) *Educating Against Extremism*. Stoke on Trent: Trentham Books.

Department for Communities and Local Government: *Preventing Violent Extremism: Next Steps for Communities*. published by Dept CLG July 08 ISBN 978-14098-0311-9

DfES) (2007) *Curriculum review: diversity and citizenship* (Ajegbo report) PPSLS/D35/0107/14. London: DfES.

DCSF (2007) *Guidance on the duty to promote community cohesion*, London: DCSF

DCSF (2010) *Religious Education in English Schools: Non-statutory guidance – 2010* Download from www.teachernet.gov.uk/

DCSF (2010) *Materials used to Teach about World Religions in English Schools* – Research Report DCSF – RR197 by WRERU. Download report from www.dcsf.gov.uk/research

Education and Inspections Act 2006 http://www.opsi.gov.uk/acts/acts2006/20060040.htm

Gearon, L. (2002) 'Human Rights and Religious Education: Some Postcolonial Perspectives', *British Journal of Religious Education*, 24:2, 140-150.

Huff, T. E. (2003) *The Rise of Early Modern Science: Islam, China, and the West*. 2nd Edition Cambridge: Cambridge University Press.

Fadl, K. A. (2007) *The Great Theft. Wrestling Islam from the Extremists*, New York: Harper Collins.

Geaves, R. A. (1998) 'The Boarders between Religions: A Challenge to the World Religions Approach to Religious Education', *British Journal of Religious Education* 21:1

Geaves, R. A. (2005) *Aspects of Islam*. London: Darton, Longman and Todd Ltd.

Geaves, R. A. (2005) 'Islam and Christianity: Competing media of Orientalism and Occidentalism' (paper given on May 24th 2005) *Islam and the Media*, Elwes Park Campus, University of Gloucestershire

Geaves, R. A. (2007) *Twenty years of Fieldwork: Reflections on Reflexivity in the study of British Muslims*. Chester: Chester Academic Press.

Gray, J. (2007) *Black Mass: Apocalyptic Religion and the death of Utopia*, London: Penguin Books.

Grimmitt, M.H (ed.) (2000) *Pedagogies of Religious Education*. Great Wakering: McCrimmon Publishing Co. Ltd.

Home Office (2001) *Community Cohesion: A Report of the Independent Review Team Chaired by Ted Cantle*, December 2001 (The Cantle Report)

Home Office (2002) *Building cohesive communities, report of the ministerial group on public order and community cohesion*, Chaired by John Denham, 2001 (The Denham Report).

Huxley, J. 1976. A philosophy for UNESCO, *The UNESCO Courier* (Paris) No 29 (March)

Ibrahim, M. (1993) 'Islam and the Teaching of World Religions' in Erricker, C. (ed.) (1993) *Teaching World Religions*, Oxford: Heinemann Educational.

Jackson, R (1997) *Religious Education: An Interpretive Approach*, London: Hodder and Stoughton

Jackson, R (1) (1997) *The Interpretative Approach* webcast at www.re-net.ac.uk (accessed 12.02.09.)

Jackson, R (2) (2010) *Materials Used in Schools to Teach World Religions Project*
http://www2.warwick.ac.uk/fac/soc/wie/research/wreru/research/current/dcsf/ (accessed 10.03. 2009)

Jackson, R. (3) (2009) Religion in Education. A contribution to dialogue or a factor of conflict in transforming societies of European countries. (REDCo)
http://www2warickac.uk/fac/soc/wie/research/wreru/research/current/redco/ (accessed 10.03. 2009)

Jackson, R. (2004) *Intercultural Education and Religious Diversity: Interpretive and Dialogical Approaches from England*, Oslo Coalition Project
http://folk.uio.no/leirvik/OsloCoalition/Jackson0904.htm (accessed 09.03.09.)

Jenkins, P. (2008) *The Lost History of Christianity*, Oxford: Lion Hudson.

Manji, I. (2004) *The Trouble with Islam, PLACE?* Mainstream Publishing Company.

Maududi, A. A. (1939) *Jihad in Islam* (Address originally delivered on Iqbal Day, April 13, 1939, at the Town Hall, Lahore) Beirut: Holy Koran Publishing House.

Moran, P. (2000) 'Let me teach RE, not someone's ideology! Reflections on How Multicultural Concerns have been Shaping Religious Education', Online at:
www.islamatschool.org.uk/GC/GCSETopicsPages/Articles.htm (accessed 20.04.08.)

Nasr, S. H. (1993) *The Need for a Sacred Science*, Richmond: Curzon Press Ltd.

ODIHR (Office for Democratic Institutions and Human Rights) (2007) *Toledo Guiding Principles on Teaching About Religions and Beliefs in Public Schools*. Warsaw: Organisation for Security and Co-operation in Europe Office for Democratic Institutions and Human Rights.

OfSTED (1997) *The impact of new agreed syllabuses on the teaching and learning of religious education*, London: Her Majesty's Stationery Office

OfSTED (2007) *Making sense of religion: a report on religious education in schools and the impact of locally agreed syllabuses*, download from www.ofsted.gov.uk

Osler, A. (2008) 'Citizenship education and the Ajegbo report: re-imagining a cosmopolitan nation, *London Review of Education*, Vol 6, No 1, March 2008, 11-25

Oslo Coalition Project (www.oslocoalition.org)

QCA (2004) *Religious Education: The Non-Statutory National Framework*, download from www.qcda.gov.uk/

Qutb, S. (2005) *Milestones*. New Dehli: Islamic Book Service

Smalley, S. (2005) 'Teaching about Islam and Learning about Muslims: Islamophobia in the Classrooom' in *Resource* 27:2, Spring 2005 (published By PCfRE)

Revell, Lynn (with help from Simon Hughes) (2008) *Pedagogies and Islam (draft paper)*. At Re-net: http://www.re-net.ac.uk/

Richardson, R, et al. (eds.) (2007) *The search for common ground. Muslims, non-Muslims and the UK media*. A report commissioned by the Mayor of London. London: Greater London Authority.

Runnymede Trust, (1997) *Islamophobia: a challenge for us all*. London: Runnymede Trust.

Said, E. (1991) *Orientalism*. London: Penguin.

Schuon, Frithjof (1989) *Understanding Islam London*: Unwin Hyman Ltd.

Siddiqui, A. (1) 'The Changing Perception of Islam. Christian theology and theologians' in *Creative Encounters, Journal of interreligious insight*, http://www.islamic-foundation.org.uk/islam-interfaith.htm (accessed 01.03.09.)

Siddiqui, A. (1999) (ed.) *Islam and Other Faiths* by Isma'il Raji Al-Faruqi. Leicester: The Islamic Foundation and IIIT

Siddiqui, A. (2005) 'Islam and Christian Theology', In Ford, D. (2005) (ed) *An introduction to Christian Theology since 1918* (3rd Edition) Oxford: Blackwell Publishing.

Siddiqui, A. (2007) Islam at Universities in England. Meeting the needs and investing in the future. (The Siddiqui Report), London: DCSF (online at http://www.dcsf.gov.uk/hegateway/uploads/DrSiddiquiReport.pdf)

Singh, D. (Chair) (2007) *Our Shared Future. Report by the Commission on Integration and Cohesion*. London:

Spickard, J. V. (1999) 'Human Rights, Religious Conflict, and Globalisation. Ultimate Values in a New World Order', *International Journal on Multicultural Societies* (IJMS) Vol. 1, No. 1

Stark, R. (2003) *For the Glory of God*. Woodstock: Princeton University Press

Van Driel, B. (2004) Ed. *Confronting Islamophobia in Educational Practice*. Stoke on Trent: Trentham Books

Zacharias, R (2000) *Jesus Among Other Gods*, Nashville: Thomas Nelson.

CHAPTER 10

THE CONTRIBUTION OF RELIGIOUS EDUCATION TO SOCIAL AND COMMUNITY COHESION:
an Islamic educational perspective

Abdullah Sahin

SUMMARY

THIS CHAPTER DEVELOPS an Islamic education response to the question of RE's contribution to social and community cohesion in Britain. The central dilemmas facing British Muslim communities and the wider Muslim diaspora in Europe are identified. These dilemmas are mainly framed by how Muslims interact and position themselves within a secular, culturally and religiously diverse public space. If British Muslims come from diverse ethnic and cultural backgrounds, their faith constitutes an important component of the core values that define their individual and communal identities. Their religiosity plays a crucial role too in the emerging self understandings of young British Muslims and the way they interpret the diversity around them. Religious extremism and radicalisation pose important challenges to community cohesion that cannot be adequately addressed unless issues around the character of Muslim religiosity within the context of secular and multicultural British society are properly explored.

The broad educational rationale of mainstream RE in England and Wales in many ways represents a unique model of teaching religion in secular multicultural societies. A distinctive feature of RE is that it treats faith traditions as well as other value systems as educational resources to facilitate 'learning about and learning from religion' in the hope that this leads to the personal, social and, indeed, faith development of the learner. This chapter argues, contrary to popular claim, that this broad 'secular' educational rationale should not be seen as incompatible with the core educational values of Islam. Muslim educational thought contains a strong tradition of critical education, based on the central Qur'anic educational concepts such as *taaruf*, or 'knowing and learning from one another', which certainly supports this broad educational vision.

INTRODUCTION

In today's globalised world we are increasingly witnessing that contemporary Islam and the secular humanism of late modernity are in need of revising and rethinking their overall horizon of meaning in order to interact with each other more intelligently. As we enter the twenty-first century the ground beneath their meta-narratives has already been shaking; while the West has begun to pay attention to the destructive exclusivism contained within its rhetoric of 'rational enlightenment', the Muslim world is beginning to come to terms with the fact that the meaning of being *Islamically faithful* should be reconsidered in the light of contemporary world conditions.

It is unfortunate that the role of faith among Muslims living in the European diaspora is only just being recognized. It is 9/11 and the July 7th 2005 bombings in London that have forcefully brought religion and Islam to the centre of discussions of the policy makers in the UK. Unfortunately, since the debate has been largely framed within the context of national security concerns, we still do not have a long term educational strategy to address religious extremism. There is now a flood of literature (e.g., Roy, 2004; Lincoln, 2006) on political Islam, terrorism, the deterritorialised imagined *umma*, etc. All of these compete to best describe or classify 'the enemy within' by the degree of extremism Muslims reflect in their way of being Muslim.

The scale of the challenge we face is beyond depicting the problem as a matter of 'them and us'. Modern British/European Islam is an undeniable cultural reality but what is at stake is the future of its subjectivity and communal identity. If we, both Muslims and the wider policy makers, cannot offer an authoritative educational vision for young generations of British Muslims, we should not be surprised that their agency will be

166

forged by the extremism of radical Islam and isolationism expressed as rejection of an exclusivist wider secular society.

To prioritize religiosity and faith development, however, is not to deny that there are other factors at play here such as the historic legacy of colonial trauma, grievances over 'Western' foreign policy in the Middle East, socio-economic exclusion or Islamophobia that are among the contributory factors to extremism. Moreover, there is the reality of non-religious forms of extremist violence associated for example with the far right. This chapter emphasizes the need for investing in a long term educational policy in order to address serious issues of community cohesion and extremism.

MODERN MULTICULTURAL SOCIETIES AND LIMITS OF IDENTITY POLITICS

Complex historical factors, market driven globalisation and mass migration have brought diverse cultures closer to the extent that a specific tradition–based self definition is no longer a possibility. As members of diverse ethnic, religious and cultural communities positioned within the larger European societies we are now living *in the face of each other*. This reality has tremendous consequences for how we, people of both majority and minority groups, construct our identities. If we consider the case of Muslim communities in the European diaspora we can observe the uncomfortable consequences of this encounter more clearly. We can talk about many commonalities among the diverse communities that make up the totality of society; however, when we attend to differences, the difficulties and challenges of living in culturally and religiously diverse secular societies become acutely clear. One thing is hard to deny: living *in the face of each other* requires reconsidering one's world-view and recognizing, with humility, the limits of one's identity and the presence of the other in one's self understanding.

This challenging contextual reality could also facilitate a positive outcome: the gift of openness to one another. Openness does not mean an unconditional subscription to a different life style for that would actually mean assimilation; openness means, rather, a critical awareness about one's core values and the felt need to be in a continuous dialogue with the other. The alternatives to critical openness are either the emergence of minority ghettos or the dominant group's expectation of assimilation. Unfortunately, in Europe, including Britain, due to complex political and economic reasons, ghettoisation and assimilation are increasingly becoming the overall policy trend. The values of critical openness, vital to the emergence of an overall sense of belonging in a multicultural society and achieving a degree of social cohesion, need to be nurtured by both the wider society and the so called minority groups.

Modes of religiosity, RE and community cohesion

The fear of being assimilated can be clearly discerned within the traditional reactionary perception of Islamic education. As practised in the mosques and *madrasas* in Britain, for example, Islamic education generally reflects an authoritarian and rigid process of knowledge transmission centred round the authority of the teacher and the text. Hence, most educationalists think that the educational legacy of Islam and Western modernity remain inherently oppositional as Islamic education aims to inculcate specific faith-based values while Western education aims to contribute to the overall development of an autonomous subject. Thus multi-faith RE has been perceived by Muslims with suspicion as it is taken to be promoting secular values that are deemed to be contradictory to Islam.

Perhaps this depiction has some truth in it but it fails to engage with the broad educational rationale underpinning non-confessional RE and most importantly ignores the plurality within the Muslim educational legacy and the possibility that both paradigms can share some central educational ideals. Can nurturing values of critical openness be a shared educational goal for both Muslim education and 'secular' RE?

I have argued elsewhere (Sahin 2010a) that *secularity*, unlike the narrower and more ideological concept of *secularism*, can be interpreted as a crucial inclusive principle informing modern democratic political order and should not be seen as inherently in conflict with or a threat to religion. I have further suggested that an Islamic socio-political theology, based on the Islamic social principles such as *maslaha* (common good) encourages a *critically faithful* Muslim presence, which entails active engagement within the framework of secular democratic politics that is committed to preserving human dignity, and upholding values of socio-economic justice and the common good (*op. cit.*).

I am aware that increasingly the phenomenon of secular *extremism* has also become prevalent. Often secular policy makers and educationalists, who not only lack religious literacy but also fail to appreciate the importance of faith to many communities, do not take seriously the positive role of faith in community cohesion and conflict resolution. A recent example of such a naïve secular educational position is discernible in the work of L. Davies (2008) who attempts to analyze the nature of extremism and offer what she claims to be a pedagogic model to educate against extremism. As a typical secular educationalist she automatically equates concepts like critical and openness with Western modernity while implicitly equating unquestioning submission and absolutism with being religious. Such secularist perspectives appear to show no appreciation that main stream RE can play a significant role in building competence in combating extremism by contributing to pupils' critical openness and encouraging ideological self-criticism. It is unfortunate to note that in such a secularist approach the so called counter terror educational strategy in schools can easily be reduced to a check list/tool kit level of simplicity (*op.cit.*).

When, as a Muslim researcher and educator, I began to listen to the life stories of British Muslim youth in the late 1990s, I began to realize the limits of a teacher/ text-centred and transmission-orientated Islamic education taking place in the mosques, madrasas and faith based Muslim schools. The life-world of these young people was informed by a multiplicity of cultures: at home they were socialized into traditional Islamic values interpreted within parental cultural backgrounds and at the school they were exposed to a wider secular culture. Gradually I became interested in understanding how they managed the presence of cultural multiplicity around them and how they developed their sense of loyalty and the sense of who they are in the face of demands made by different authorities in their lives.

The literature on minority youth studies I reviewed was largely confined to visible marks of identity such as race, ethnicity and language. The possibility of religiosity as an important factor in the lives of 'Asian children and young people' was rarely given consideration. The literature indicated presence of 'hybrid, hyphenated' identities particularly among black people and pointed to the curious phenomenon of 'living between two cultures'. However, the specific role of faith appeared to have been grossly underestimated or overlooked. The overall anticipation in this literature was that as the new generations got a better education and better jobs they would move up the social ladder and gradually become secularized or assimilated into the norms of wider society. There were clear signs of secular bias within the social science research community as well as in the discourse of educational and social policy makers. It is regrettable to observe that more recent empirical research on diverse Muslim societies still shows signs of this secular shortcoming in properly acknowledging and adequately attending to the faith dynamic within these communities (Sahin 2010b).

However, the transnational identities observed among migrant Muslim communities contained a strong faith presence that was linked with political developments in the Middle East and Indian sub-continent. This reality of being part of the world-wide Muslim community, *Umma*, had a tremendous impact on the identity formation of Muslim youth. A cursory look at the larger scene would have made clear that faith had been emerging as a dominant factor in their lives. However, the real question for me was how and in what direction faith was taking most of these young people. I became interested in exploring the construction of their religious subjectivity where loyalty to authority and the desire for autonomy are negotiated.

I used a psycho-social identity research model that is based on a semi-structured interview schedule to explore religious identity. It was developed out of the theoretical insights of Erik Erikson (1968) and the empirical research of developmental psychologist James Marcia on identity status (1993). The model assumes that identity gets constructed within a commitment/exploration continuum. As such there are several possible identity resolutions or modes: a *diffused* mode where neither commitment nor exploration is present; a *foreclosed* mode where there is a strong commitment that is not informed by the exploration process; an *achieved* mode which is observed when commitment has undergone a process of exploration and finally, if there is a strong exploration but no real commitment, the identity mode is classified as *exploratory*. The model is not fixed – while an individual's personality could exhibit several aspects of these modes, regression and progression on the continuum are also possibilities. As such the identity is studied through a 'post-foundational phenomenological framework' (Sahin, 2005).

The findings, in brief, showed that male participants reflected a predominantly *foreclosed* mode of religious subjectivity while female participants fell largely under the *exploratory* mode. There were also a significant number of young people in the *diffused* mode who were losing interest in religious issues. On the whole, while Islam was perceived as a source of inspiration, increasingly a rigid appropriation of faith was also emerging. Most of the participants raised the concern that Islam presented to them at home and the mosque was mixed with the culture of their parents' country of origin. They wanted 'pure Islam' instated. Male participants often mentioned that they intended to take a year out to study Arabic in an Arab country. It was becoming clear that as these young people grappled with a sense of who they were, a process triggered most intensely in multicultural societies, faith was becoming an important centre of authority in their lives.

However, when closely investigated, the dominant characteristics of the religious authority acknowledged by the youth indicated a strong literal perception of Islamic sources: the Qur'an and the *Sunna*. A key source behind this literalist religiosity has been the increasing impact of Muslim transnational revivalist movements that originated in different parts of the Muslim world. Most of the young people preferred to be identified with the radical discourse of transnational Muslim movements than with the traditional religious discourse they found at their parents' home or in their local mosques. Young people needed this sense of difference, particularly when faced with the demands of a secular multicultural society, and the radical groups were meeting their needs by providing them with a sense of difference and confidence. As a result, a large intra-faith conversion was taking place, towards the *foreclosed* end of the identity continuum. This is one of the least desirable religiosity modes in a multicultural society as it indicates having a strong vulnerability to extremism.

It is significant that this work was originally undertaken well before 9/11 when policy makers were showing no serious interest in the growing Muslim question in multicultural British society. In fact multiculturalism, an inclusive policy principle, itself appeared to be perceived as an uncritical toleration of difference that simply ignored engaging with the 'sensitive' faith related issues. However, I was fortunate enough to have the support and guidance of a well respected RE specialist, Professor John M Hull, whose insight had already penetrated the heart of the educational challenge facing Muslim children in multicultural Britain. He had deep awareness of the special case of Islam, not only due to the reality of Muslim demographics, but also because of the implications that the historical power competition between *Islam* and *Christianity* has for the interfaith relations and community cohesion of modern Britain. He was anxious that Muslims, alongside other faiths, should be part of the open and critical educational dialogue facilitated by RE so that, while respecting differences, a sense of shared purpose and solidarity could also be fostered. Treating the religious heritage of humanity as an educational resource for all could help avoid the destructive consequences of 'religionism', i.e., reifying faith into a rigid ideological structure.

The educational rationale for RE in the schools of England and Wales is not based on any particular *religious* tradition, although, of course, the subject has a Christian antecedence. However, this does not mean that it is necessarily in conflict with the religious and educational values of other faith traditions. Unlike the countries (such as France and the USA) where secular is strictly interpreted to mean confining religion to the private sphere of life, RE in the schools of England and Wales, in many ways, symbolizes a progressive way of accommodating religion within the public space of a secular democracy. It should be noted that even in France there are now calls for finding a way of facilitating the public teaching of religion (Pépin, 2009).

I do not, however, want to claim perfection for the form of RE that has evolved in the UK but rather that its strengths outweigh its weaknesses. Looked at from the perspective of minority faiths, the system, including its legislative provision, does still reflect the strong presence of Christianity. This is a natural consequence of the subject's roots being found in a tradition of Christian education and, more arguably, in recognition of the continuing influence of Christianity on the country's cultural identity. However, as expressed in *Religious Education: The Non-Statutory National Framework* (DfES/QCA 2004), notwithstanding the predominance of the study of Christianity as a consequence of the religious clauses of the 1988 Education Act, it is important that Local Authorities make sure that 'the religious education curriculum is broad and balanced'. Local Authority Agreed Syllabus Conferences have the legal responsibility for the 'the specificity of content, both in terms of the religions and beliefs studied.' (*op.cit.*,12) As local faith communities are represented on both the Agreed Syllabus Conference and the legally required SACRE (Standing Advisory Committee for RE) the subject is both enriched and safeguarded by their active involvement. If, as a last resort, some parents are unhappy with the RE provision on faith or religious grounds they have the right to withdraw their child. The question of the RE teacher's faith is not relevant so long as she/he approaches the teaching of the subject in a professional manner and avoids being religiously confessional. That said, there are still insufficient numbers of RE teachers from minority faith communities who can offset the often simplistic representation of their faith traditions which does continue to be a concern among them.

RE has well established pedagogies (Grimmitt, 2000) that avoid religious confessionalism and aim to achieve its main attainment targets; learning about and learning from religion. The initially dominating phenomenological method in RE that is perceived to be centred upon providing factual descriptions has attracted criticism. There is no space to discuss this here except to point out that there have been many developments within the field of phenomenology and in its application in social science including education and RE. Even the writings of Edmund Husserl, the founder of modern phenomenology, carefully read, reflect a move away from studying the way consciousness directs and represents objects so that knowledge is founded on secure grounds to the exploration of human experience (the life-world) in its historical/temporal conditions and inter-subjective character. Thus, in a phenomenologically grounded pedagogy, description incorporates a strong moral awareness while attempting to grasp personal/collective interpretations that are articulated in the believer's life world.

RE in the UK, despite the criticisms, remains a well established interdisciplinary field that has created a learning/teaching platform which enables religion and faith to be studied in a way which is appropriate within a plural society in which belief is diverse. Questions about whether RE relativises and domesticates the religious traditions, imposing an alien and secularist structure upon them will no doubt continue to be raised. However none of the criticisms or objections is persuasive enough to declare the model so flawed as to be unacceptable or unusable. They certainly do not constitute justification for opting for the confessional model whereby students are segregated into separate classrooms according to their faith affiliation. More subtle demands for a 'neo-confessional' approach to RE are also unconvincing and unrealistic. When it comes to building capacity and so called resilience against religious extremism RE's role, together with citizenship education, is crucial. This constructive role of RE is yet to be fully invested in and effectively utilized and some continue to have moral and professional misgivings about whether RE should play this role. (i.e. reactions to the government-supported programme 'REsilience' are mixed.) But without a readiness on the part of all faith communities to explore together the common ground upon which reasoned faith and understanding can be encouraged through RE, a crucial community resource for peace, reconciliation and cooperation will be neglected, possibly even lost.

The reminder of the chapter, by exploring the core of educational theology in Islam, aims to demonstrate that the broad educational rationale underpinning RE does not necessarily contradict Muslim educational self understanding and stresses the need for close cooperation between Muslim educators and the wider RE practitioners.

THE CRITICAL/DIALOGICAL ROOTS OF ISLAMIC EDUCATION

The phrase "Islamic education" is a modern expression. With the establishment of nation states in the Muslim world at the turn of the nineteenth century, Western style secular education was also imported. This has inevitably led to the emergence of a dichotomy between secular education and the traditional forms of education as the systems have produced different and mainly conflicting mind sets. Islamic education in the wider political discourse of late nineteenth-twentieth century revivalist, transnational Muslim movements has come to be used as a faith-based (Islamic) educational model alternative to the Western secular conception of education that is centred round the humanist ideals of Western modernity. In this sense, Islamic education though including religious education is not limited by it. Islamic education is used as an overarching title containing all teaching and learning activities that takes place within the family, mosque and the school. In short it is perceived to be a total educational system that is an alternative to the Western educational model.

Today's general perception of Islamic education within the European Muslim diaspora including Britain overwhelmingly reflects this ideological motive which strongly emphasizes a categorical difference between Muslim and secular conceptions of education. It is not surprising to observe that the authority of tradition is used to legitimize this fundamentally reactionary definition. This modern and ideological construct (Islamic education) is often *read into* the tradition.[1] Thus because modern Western education is perceived to be materialistic Islamic education is largely defined appositionally as an overwhelmingly esoteric, spiritual framework in which the educational process is mostly identified with the term *ta'dib*, a set of coercive moral practices (Nasr, 1989; Al Attas, 1980).

The empirical findings of my work with British Muslim youth (Sahin, 2005) indicate that there is an urgent need to rethink the theory and practice of Islamic education in Britain. Under current circumstances, while extremism and rigid faith construction have become a significant threat to

Muslim young people, most of the Islamic education provision is still preoccupied with transmission and forging the identity of young people in an authoritarian fashion. It appears that the study of Islam carried out in contemporary Muslim educational settings is unable to develop an intelligent mature faith among Muslim youth. As such it is important to reconsider how education is imagined within the Islamic self-understanding. An obvious place to start reconsidering the meaning of *being Islamically educated* is in the Qur'an and the Prophetic model (*Sunna*). Listening to the experience of young Muslims is also an integral part of this reconsideration.

The 'cloud-grass theory of education' in Islam

The Arabic word *tarbiya* is the most often used concept to express the educational process in Muslim culture. *Talim/tadris* (teaching), *ta'dib* (moral disciplining), *talqin* (instructing) are also used to describe different aspects of the educational process. The word *tarbiya* in Arabic is directly linked with two interrelated verbs *rabba/rababa* (to cater for and be in control of one's upbringing, to guide, reform and administer) and *rabaa*, to increase and nurture, (Ibn Manzur, 1989). As such *tarbiya* includes all processes that are active in one's upbringing, e.g. physical/spiritual nourishment, care and guidance. A close etymological analysis of *tarbiya* related words will reveal what can be called the 'cloud-grass theory of education' in Islam: Nature itself has the capacity to educate e.g. clouds, by bringing down water necessary for the growth of vegetation, possess an educational function; hence they are called *rabab*. Incidentally *educare*, the Latin origin of the English word education in its etymology also has the meanings of springing up to existence, nurture and to lead.

Al-Rabb, one of the names that God chooses to describe himself in the Qur'an comes from the root *rabba*. *Al-Rabb* conventionally translated as 'the Lord' carries the original etymological meanings of looking after, caring for and leading. As such in his classical Qur'an dictionary al-Raghib al-Esfahani (d.502/1108) observes that *al-Rabb* is directly linked with *tarbiya* (education) which he defines as 'the gradual, stage by stage developmental process informing an organism's growth until the complete actualization of its potentials'.

The authority of the Lord (Al-Rabb) rests on being able to provide physical, spiritual sustenance and guidance that are essential to facilitate the personal development of individuals and communities. Thus the

Qur'an declares that the Lord is worthy of worship precisely because He not only created humanity but constantly attends to, listens to, nurtures and guides them. As such God expects that humanity will be grateful to Him in recognizing 'His favours unto them' and express this gratitude by worshipping Him alone (*ubudiyya*). God is not in competition with humanity or desires to exercise His power arbitrarily but owns His creation by being mindful of their needs in the hope that they may develop mature self-awareness. Above all humanity is entrusted with the stewardship of the earth (*khalifa/khalaif*, 35:39; 38:26)[2] Thus, in the Qur'an the fundamental mode of communication between God and humanity is essentially articulated in an educational framework which is technically expressed by the theological concepts of *rububiyya* and *ubudiyya* in Muslim tradition. The opening chapter of the Qur'an declares God to be the educator *par excellence–rabb al-alamin* (the educator of all worlds). However like in any genuine educational process, as distinct from indoctrination or mere training, there is a mutual balance and respect between the authority of the educator and the autonomy of the learner. Facilitating a growth process by looking after, nurturing and guiding those who are to be educated is central to the meaning of *tarbiya*. Based on this it can be easily deduced that an important feature of Islamic education is that it should facilitate growth by guiding and attending to the needs of the learner in the hope of bringing about a balanced, faithful personality. As such, according to the Qur'an, possessing knowledge is not sufficient to be called a genuine educator (9:31, 3:79, 62:5-6).

Divine curriculum in the service of humanity: the Qur'an and purpose of education

Considered educationally the Qur'an, therefore, becomes God's curriculum to educate humanity in His knowledge and wisdom (3:48; 12: 3-7). As such, apart from recognizing God as educator, the Qur'an exhibits several educational qualities. The Qur'an introduces itself as a guide (2:185) and aims to assist people to realize their humanity in all aspects of life. The initial appeal is to human reasoning capacity thus we observe that frequently the Qur'anic passages end with a thought provoking statement such as "Don't you reflect" etc. (3:190 – 191; 10:5; 29:20; 39:28: 89:5).

Without taking the dynamic characteristics of the Qur'anic revelation seriously, its cohesive vision cannot be grasped. A piecemeal reading of the Qur'an can easily reveal textually justifiable accounts that are totally in contradiction to its wider vision. Most of the discussions on human freedom/responsibility vis-à-vis God's power and majesty in the Qur'an by the classical Muslim scholars reflect such a one-dimensional hermeneutic strategy (Rahman 1989; van Ess 1972; Watt 1948). The content, composition and delivery strategy of revelation (*wahy*) in Islam has an explicit educative purpose to engage the listener (reader) and to bring about a transformation in him/her. Thus most of the Qur'an was revealed as short passages in response to a felt concern, difficulty or a disputation experienced by the Prophet and the early Muslim community in order to provide guidance for them. As Gwynne's interesting study (2004) aptly discovers, 'the Qur'an does not present its content as self-evidently significant but frames it in patterns of discussion to demonstrate how that material engages the hearer'.

In fact, much of the Qur'an is in the form of arguments. This shows clearly that the Qur'an recognizes the human need to reason and have explanations in order to make up their minds or to follow a particular advice. For example, central to Qur'anic rationality is its emphasis that God does not act in arbitrary ways. He has a clear pattern of behaviour (*sunnat Allah*) (17:77). Reasoning and argument are integral to the content of the Qur'an and inseparable from its structure. As such, the Qur'an, by using a rhetorical logical style, becomes a critical discourse that is not only sanctioned by divine authority but is also justified according to the authority discerned by human reasoning. S. El-Sheikh (2003) while closely exploring structures/styles of practical reasoning and dialectical critique in the Qur'an gets closer to grasping the critical pedagogy informing the Qur'anic dialogues

The Islamic perception of revelation reflects strong contextual elements: it responds to the specific needs of the first historical audience (12:2) and puts forward a gradual principle to solve their social problems (2:219). It is not the specific historical solution formulated but the wider ethical value framework guiding the solution which preserves the relevance of faith in diverse historical circumstances (13:38, 5:48).

The Qur'an recognizes the change–bound nature of human life hence, without hesitation, when necessary it abrogates parts of the revelation and replaces them with a better or more fitting one (2:106, 16:101). Most importantly, it emphasizes the developmental processes active in both the physical and psycho-spiritual aspects of human nature. Humans possess the capacity of both good and bad. Subjectivity is shaped by these forces but not limited to them – a continual growth as well as regression is a strong possibility (95:4-6, 91:7-11). As a consequence, like human cognitive capacity (*'ilm*) the human capacity for faith (*iman*) is also developmental as it is a part of the human condition (58:11).

Within the Qur'anic worldview God is the absolute sovereign of the universe but this does not mean that He acts arbitrarily. As mentioned previously His conduct follows principles; He uses His authority authoritatively: He possesses knowledge, wisdom, acts justly and, above all, He is prepared to listen. The Qur'anic dialogues containing prophet Abraham's *methodic skepticism* (6:74-80, 2:260) while discovering monotheism and questioning the bodily resurrection in the Hereafter vividly illustrates a listening, conversing God. The relationship between God (the educator) and the learner takes a dialogical process in which both parties take seriously each other's autonomy and authority.

The case of prophet Abraham shows that being faithful does not mean a mere submission or surrender (49:14) but a critical, intelligent awareness and qualified acceptance. Last but not least the Qur'an teaches through stories.[3] As such the Qur'an becomes an educational book to guide and inspire humanity rather than a book of instructions that should be literally perceived and applied to life.

The Qur'anic outlook described above provides solid ground to develop a progressive Islamic educational philosophy. In short, the Qur'an firmly recognizes the historical/contextual contingency informing human existence by providing a radical educational response to the gender, ethnic, religious and linguistic diversity of humanity. The *difference*, as such, is perceived as an opportunity and reason for engaging with the dialogic process of 'knowing one another and learning from each other (*taaruf*)' (30:19-26, 49:13) in the hope of developing a holistic perspective (*tawhid*) on life.

The character of religious and educational authority in Islam

The Prophetic model (*Sunna*) and the Companions' appropriation of it gradually led to the emergence of a living tradition centred around the Qur'an and increasingly the prophetic *Sunna* as it symbolised the practical application of the Qur'anic teachings in real life conditions.[4] However there was an open attitude to both the Qur'an and *Sunna* as the caliphs, particularly Umar (d.644), radically reinterpreted the Qur'anic legal injunctions. This showed the existence of an early dynamic hermeneutics of the Muslim core sources.

Within classical Muslim heritage both progressive and literal conservative attitudes toward education can be observed.[5] However the early Muslim attitude towards central authority sources, the Qur'an and the *Sunna*, indicate a strongly open educational approach. It should be noted that during the early period of Islam, perhaps due to its situation in a largely oral culture, religious authority did not lie in the written word as such but between the text and its reader/commentator. Hence the scholar, *alim* (reader/commentator) held a crucial position and is also seen as the inheritor of the prophetic role and legacy (Abbot 1957; Madigan 2001). (6)

The shift of authority from the reader/commentator to the 'authoritative text' emerged during the post-formative period of Islam. Prophetic authority, originally embodied in the form of a living tradition, *Sunna*, gradually came to be seen as textual, preserved in the collections of Prophetic reports, Hadith. Despite this shift it is the *authoritative knowing and acting* at individual and communal levels that constitute the centre of religious authority and not a body of instructions or the assumed infallibility of a particular person. As such religious authority in Islam has a strong *interpretative and communal* character. This necessary hermeneutic component which is recognized by the tradition as *ijtihad*, independent thinking, has important pedagogic implications: there is an interactive process between the sacred address and the hearer/commentator whose reflections discern guidance from the message to be emulated by the society. The whole hermeneutic process remains open to scrutiny by the wider faithful community and is incomplete as God's knowledge and wisdom is unbounded (18:109) and thus requires a constant reflection which is taken to be a duty and an act of worship. Examined closely, the centre of educational authority in Islam, contrary to some appealing suggestions by Messick (1996) and Makdisi (1989) is neither really textual as such nor resides within law-centred so-called professional guilds (*madhahib*) which emerged out of the politically-manipulated organizational forms of *waqf* and *madrasa*.

The dominant epistemological framework developed within classical Muslim thought suggests such an open-ended process. Based on the guidance of the Qur'an and authentic *Sunna*, Muslim scholars managed to establish the cultural and intellectual institution of *ijtihad*, independent thinking, by making use of analogy (*qiyas*), arguments concerning public interest (*maslaha*), consultation (*shura*) and consensus (*ijma*) to help the community to lead an *Islamically meaningful* life within the conditions of a rapidly changing world.

The emergence of such a practical and, in many ways, flexible system of Islamic rationality in which the authority of faith and reason are balanced is not accidental but reflects the principles, values and practical strategies suggested by the Qur'an in resolving both individual and social problems experienced by the early Muslim community. For example, we observe that the Qur'an in matters related to public security, even within the challenging circumstances of war, invites the faithful to *think through* the issues so that the decisions are based on convincing evidence and critical reflection (4:83; 49:6). Most importantly this rational capacity of discernment (*istinbat*) is expected to be exercised by the prophet and 'those who are in charge' of the affairs of the community. Thus, in Islam the authority of the prophet, and community leadership in general, is strongly linked with knowledge acquisition and competence to reflect and discern (4:83).

The humanist aspect of the educational philosophy of Islam – despite the prevalence of later conservative forces – has never completely been lost. The *adab* literature (Rosenthal, 2007) which gradually came to contain the bulk of classical Islamic humanism and which flourished largely under the influence of Persian converts to Islam, has retained the critical educational spirit of the Qur'an. The *sufi* legacy of Islam can be seen as another response aimed at curtailing the increasingly literalist mindset that had come to dominate classical Muslim legal thought. It should be stated that legal interpretation of the core Muslim sources (the Qur'an and *Sunna*) exhibited a considerably degree of open critical attitude that is generally symbolized with the concept of *ra'y* (independent/discretionary reasoning). Thus nearly all distinct hermeneutic strategies developed within the classical Muslim intellectual genres – legal, exegetical, philosophical, theological, educational etc. – exhibit critical engagement with both the tradition as well as with the challenges of the changing contextual reality.

I hope this brief exposition of educational theology in the Qur'an demonstrates clearly the critical and dialogical aspects of education in Islam. Islamic education, like Islam itself, is not monolithic. I am convinced that there are ample reasons why both Muslim educators and RE practitioners working in a secular setting can and should engage in an open dialogue. This remains crucial in addressing the pressing issues of community cohesion that are a concern to us all.

NOTES

1. For details of the gradual historical reification process active in the traditional Muslim understanding of Islam as a 'religious system' see Smith W.C. (1991) whose work, despite the fact it was undertaken decades ago, is still exceptionally relevant to contemporary discussions on Islam.

2. In the Qur'an quotations the chapter number is indicated first.

3. For an interesting work on the story structure of the Qur'an see Dundes, A. (2003).

4. The Prophet's role as educator is a crucial aspect of Islamic Education that requires a separate study. It is suffice to stress that the pedagogic practice of the Prophet is the Qur'anic educational model put into practice thus the Prophet is a role model (33:21) for Muslims to emulate. The Qur'an is keen on stressing the human qualities of the Prophet (3:159; 68:4; 41:6) rather than presenting him with a 'charismatic authority' that is usually taught to be an important element of prophecy in Judeo-Christian tradition. See, Blenkinsopp, J. (1996) ; Weber, M. (1952) and Chilton, B. and Neusner, J. (1999).

5. For a recent survey of classical Muslim educational thought see Günther, S. (2006)

6. For an interesting study on the nature of writing, orality and authority see Carr, D.M. (2005)

REFERENCES

Abbot, N. (1957) *Studies in Arabic Literary Papyri, I Historical Texts*, Chicago: Chicago University Press

Al-Attas, N.M. (1991) *The Concept of Islamic Education*, Kuala Lumpur, ISTAC.

Blenkinsopp, J. (1996) *A History of Prophecy in Israel*, Louisville, Kentucky: Westminster/John Knox Press

Al-Esfahani, R. (2003) *Mujam Mufradat Alfaz Al-Qur'an*, Damascus: Dar Al-Qalam.

Davies, L. (2008) *Educating Against Extremism*, Stoke on Trent: Trentham Books

DCSF (2008) Preventing violent extremism; tool kit for schools, http://www.dcsf.gov.uk/violentextremism/toolkitforschools/indexs.html

DfES/QCA (2004) *Religious education: The non-statutory national framework* QCA (2004) Download from:
http://www.qcda.gov.uk/libraryAssets/media/9817_re_national_framework_04.pdf

Carr, D.M. (2005) *Writing in the Tablet of the Heart: Origins of Writing and Scripture*, Oxford: Oxford University Press.

Chilton, B. and Neusner, J, (1999) *Types of Authority in Formative Christianity and Judaism*, London: Routledge.

Dundes, A. (2003) *Fables of the Ancients? Folklore in the Qur'an*, Lanham, Maryland: Rowman & Littlefield Publishers.

El-Sheikh, S. (2003) *'Al-Mujadalah and Al-Mujadilah Then and Now: Kalam, Dialectical Argument, and Practical Reason in the Qur'an'*, The Muslim World, Vol 93 No 1, 1-50

Erikson, E. (1968) *Identity: Youth and Crisis*, New York: W.W. Norton & Co

Grimmitt, M.H. (ed) (2000) *Pedagogies of Religious Education*, Great Wakering: McCrimmon Publishing Co. Ltd.

Günther, S. (2006) *'Be masters in that you teach and continue to learn': Medieval Muslim Thinkers on Educational Theory, in: Comparative Education Review*, 50 (3), 367-388.

Gwynne, R.W. (2004) *Logic, Rhetoric, and Legal Reasoning in the Qur'an*, London: RoutledgeCurzon.

Hallaq, W. (2001) *Authority, Continuity and Change in Islamic Law*, Cambridge: Cambridge University Press.

Hefner, R.W. and Zaman, M.Q. (eds) (2006) *Schooling Islam: The Culture and Politics of Modern Muslim Education*, Princeton: Princeton University Press.

Ibn Manzur, M (1989) *Lisan alArab*, (Edited by Abdullah Ali al-Kabir *et al*), Cairo: Dar al-Maarif.

Lincoln, B. (2006) *Holy Terrors: Thinking about Religion after September 11*, Chicago: Chicago University Press.

Madigan, D.A. (2001) *The Qur'an's self-image: Writing and Authority in Islam's Scripture*, Princeton: Princeton University Press.

Makdisi, G. (1981) *The Rise of Colleges: Institutions of Learning in Islam and the West*, Edinburgh: Edinburgh University Press.

Marcia, J. et al (eds) (1993) *Ego Identity: A Handbook for Psychological Research*, New York: Springer Verlag.

Messick, B. (1996) *The Calligraphic State: Textual Domination and a History in a Muslim Society*, London: University of California Press,

Nasr, S.H. (1989) *Knowledge and the Sacred*, New York: State University of New York Press

Pépin, Luce (2009) *Teaching about Religions in European School Systems: Policy issue and trends*, London: Alliance Publishing Trust

Rahman, F. (1968) *Islamic Methodology in History*, Karachi: Islamic Research Institute.

Rahman, F. (1989) *Major Themes of the Qur'an*, Chicago: Chicago University Press.

Robinson, C. F (2003) *Reconstructing Early Islam: Truth and Consequences*, in Berg H. (ed), Method and Theory in the Study of Islamic Origin, Leiden: Brill. 101-137.

Rosenthal, F. *Knowledge Triumphant; the Concept of Knowledge in Medieval Islam*, Leiden: Brill.

Roy, Oliver (2004) *Globalized Islam: The Search for a New Ummah*, New York: Columbia University Press.

Sahin, A. (2010a) 'Islam, Secularity and the Culture of Critical Openness: A Muslim Theological Reflection' in Birt, Y. et al. (eds) *British Muslims and Secular State*, Leicester: *Kube Publications (forthcoming)*.

Sahin, A. (2010b) 'The Dynamics of Muslims' Sense of Belonging: Reflections on Recent Empirical Research', *The Muslim World Book Review*, 30:3, 6-17

Sahin, A. (2005) 'Exploring the Religious Life-World and Attitude toward Islam among British Muslim Adolescents', in, Francis, L. *et al.* (eds.), *Religion, Education and Adolescence: International Empirical Perspectives*, Cardiff: University of Wales Press, 164-184.

Smith, W.C (1991) *The Meaning and End of Religion*, Minneapolis: Augsburg Fortress. (First published in 1962)

van Ess, J. (1972) 'Scepticism in Islamic Religious Thought', in Malik.C. (ed) *God and Man in Contemporary Islamic Thought*, Beirut, American University of Beirut: Centennial Publications.

Watt, M. (1948) *Free-Will and Predestination in Early Islam*, London: Luzac and Company Ltd.

Weber, M. (1952) *Ancient Judaism*, (Translated and edited by Gerth, H.H. and Martindale, D), New York: Free Press.

CHAPTER 11

PEDAGOGIES OF RELIGIOUS EDUCATION FOR INTER-COMMUNICATION AND INTER-CULTURAL UNDERSTANDING:
What are they? Do they work?

Vivienne Baumfield

SUMMARY

JUSTIFICATION OF THE PLACE of Religious Education in the curriculum on the grounds of its contribution to inter-cultural understanding is not new. However, dialogic approaches to teaching and learning in Religious Education in which an explicit connection between inter-communication and inter-cultural understanding is made are gaining in popularity. In particular, the use of ICT in the classroom to support dialogue between pupils from different cultural and religious backgrounds is currently receiving attention in both the research and practice communities within Religious Education. This chapter reviews how current policy on the promotion of community cohesion in the school curriculum is being translated into pedagogies for inter-communication and inter-cultural understanding in the Religious Education classroom.

GOVERNMENT-RELATED INITIATIVES AND INTER-CULTURAL UNDERSTANDING

Teacher educators responsible for the preparation of new teachers of Religious Education are familiar with the tendency for candidates at interview to link the teaching of the subject with the promotion of respect for other cultures. This perception of Religious Education's role in the promotion of inter-cultural understanding as axiomatic can also be found in justifications for the subject in curriculum policy. Charles Clarke, when Secretary of State for Education, gave a speech to launch the *Non-Statutory Framework for Religious Education* (2004) in which he asserted that:

> 'Children have a right, and indeed, should expect to be told about what is important to their friends who may hold different beliefs to their own.'

> (http://www.qcda.gov.uk)

The QCA (now QCDA) fact-sheet to disseminate information regarding this most recent attempt to justify the place of Religious Education in the school curriculum has a photograph of a 'jigsaw of faiths' made by school pupils and summarises the rationale for the subject as follows:

> '(the framework) emphasises the contribution of Religious Education to pupils' Spiritual, Moral, Social and Cultural development and highlights how Religious Education supports inclusion, particularly in combating prejudice and promoting respect for others' beliefs and values.' (QCA, 2004)

General statements on Religious Education such as these ignore evidence that suggests that simply being exposed to the beliefs of others could actually increase prejudice by highlighting differences (Carrington and Short, 1992). Policy documents, such as QCDA's introduction to Religious Education in the curriculum, are more specific about classroom practice in their promotion of an interaction whereby pupils learn about how others view the world '…whilst exploring and communicating their own (beliefs and values)' (http://www.qcda.gov.uk.). Continuity can be seen here with the aspirations of the *Schools Council Working Paper 36* (HMSO, 1971) to establish a reflective process in Religious Education in which pupils engage in dialogue with their own experience and bring this to bear in a dialogue with living religions. However, we can also see evidence of the dilution Grimmitt (2000) identified in the formulation of attainment targets for Religious Education; where this evaluation of self in religious terms and religion in personal terms as originally envisaged is reduced to 'learning about' and 'learning from' religion.

In England, the Education and Inspections Act (2006) introduced the requirement for all schools to promote community cohesion. Evidence from the OfSTED (Office for Standards in Education, Children Services and Skills) subject survey for 2007/08 suggests that Religious Education is making a 'good' or 'outstanding' contribution through lessons that offer a rare opportunity in schools for pupils to express opinions and explore ideas and matters relevant to community cohesion (http://news.reonline.org.uk /article.php?28). One of the examples of good practice highlighted by OfSTED is the exploration of controversial issues related to religion and belief in the modern world through dialogue; this aspect of Religious Education's contribution to community cohesion is taken up in the DCSF (Department for Children, Schools and Families) funded project, *Religious Education and Community Cohesion in Secondary Schools and Colleges (2010).* The project provides funding for the creation of a programme to extend the subject knowledge and skills of those teaching Religious Education in a fifth of maintained secondary schools in England to develop confidence and competence in three areas:

- Handling controversial theological and social/ethical issues.
- Promoting understanding and respect for difference through exploring key concepts such as identity and community, faith and belief.
- Enabling dialogue.

Guidelines on Religious Education in schools circulated by Standing Advisory Councils for Religious Education (SACREs) since the 2006 Act also provide suggestions for classroom practice. For example, in Cornwall the guidance on the role of Religious Education in the promotion of community cohesion (http://www.cornwall.gov.uk) refers to the importance of teaching pupils the skill of 'disagreeing respectfully' promoted by Lat Blaylock from the professional service 'RE Today' (Blaylock, 2002). Reference to this concept can also be found in many Agreed Syllabuses for Religious Education. In addition to the DCSF funded project, the Institute of Community Cohesion linked with the School Development Support Agency leads a *Faith and Cohesion Project.* The outcome of consultation with young people as part of this project, 'What Young People Want' (http://www.faithandcohesion.org), includes a request that more time should be devoted to religion and multi faith teaching in schools and that there should be activities that can lead to 'meaningful sharing'. Creating the right conditions for dialogue is prominent in the project's 25 criteria for assessing inter-faith activities that involve young people. The principles are in accordance with the procedural values identified in the *Parekh Report* on the future of multi-ethnic Britain (Runnymede Trust, 2000), which are:

- Willingness to give reasons for views
- Readiness to be influenced by better arguments
- Tolerance
- Mutual respect
- Aspiration to peaceful resolution of differences
- Willingness to abide by collectively binding decisions.

The DCSF advocate dialogic teaching across the curriculum in their national strategy guidelines where they list five principles drawn from the work of Robin Alexander (2006):

1. *Collective*: teachers and children address learning tasks together, whether as a group or as a class, rather than in isolation;

2. *Reciprocal*: teachers and children listen to each other, share ideas and consider alternative viewpoints;

3. *Supportive*: children articulate their ideas freely, without fear of embarrassment over 'wrong' answers; and they help each other to reach common understandings;

4. *Cumulative*: teachers and children build on their own and each others' ideas and chain them into coherent lines of thinking and enquiry;

5. *Purposeful*: teachers plan and facilitate dialogic teaching with particular educational goals in view.

(http://nationalstrategies.standards.dcsf.gov.uk/node/84633)

Dialogic teaching is seen as the antidote to the dominant tendency for teachers to manage classroom talk through recitation; a pattern of discourse controlled by the teacher through a pattern of teacher Initiation, pupil Response, teacher Evaluation (IRE). Research has shown that by inhibiting pupils' active participation in the construction of meaning through genuine inquiry recitation has a negative impact on attainment (Bakhtin (1986), Mercer (1995) Wells (1999) and Alexander, (2006).

As we can see, support for approaches to teaching and learning based on the encouragement of dialogue is evident in recent policy statements regarding the role of Religious Education in promoting inter-cultural understanding and more widely across the curriculum as a significant pedagogical strategy. In the following section, examples of dialogic teaching in the Religious Education classroom in primary and secondary schools are examined.

WHAT PEDAGOGIES CONTRIBUTE TO INTER-COMMUNICATION AND INTER-CULTURAL UNDERSTANDING?

Dialogic approaches in religious education

> 'Of all the tools for cultural and pedagogical intervention in human development and learning, talk is the most pervasive in its use and powerful in its possibilities.' (Alexander, 2008, 93)

Communication as an active, co-operative process in which participants are changed and new understanding emerges is fundamental to pedagogies promoting dialogue. Such pedagogies are indebted to the philosophy of John Dewey for whom education is a practice involving the interplay between psychological and social factors (Biesta, 2006). According to this view, teaching is not a process whereby the teacher instructs but rather one in which s/he constructs a social situation in which communication, and so learning, can take place:

> 'We never educate directly, but indirectly by means of the environment.' (Dewey,1916, 23)

Dewey's philosophy of education is sometimes described as 'child-centred' but this is a misrepresentation. It is communication that is at the centre of a dynamic in which experience is invested with meaning and becomes knowledge through the conjoint action of dialogue. Suissa (2008) recognises the importance of this pragmatist shift from truth to meaning for the development of a more robust approach to the question of relevance in education. Relevance is achieved through the recognition of the way in which meanings grow out of the interactions and transactions of human beings with one another and with their environment; it is not a question of the reduction of one to the other but rather an 'intermingling' through dialogue:

> 'It is out of this intermingling that communal meanings are constructed and continually reassessed in an attempt to improve the conditions of life and society.' (Suissa, 2008, 138).

This emphasis on the active engagement of learners in the practice of meaning making, as opposed to being the passive recipients of knowledge as an end in itself, has important implications for the role of education in promoting democracy. Whilst Dewey can be absolved of some of the excesses associated with child-centred learning in the Black Papers (Cox and Dyson, 1971), he is undoubtedly optimistic regarding the extent to which his participative theory of communication can promote social harmony.

Dialogic approaches in Religious Education take the pupil as the starting point and are reflexive, engaging them in the re-examination of their opinions through dialogue with others. They are dependent on the pupil having the scope to select and review topics and are, therefore, not compatible with a restricted approach to curriculum design or pedagogy. If the classroom is to be conducive to dialogue then pupils need to have the opportunity to encounter different opinions and to be free to respond in the light of his or her own views. If the school is to be a forum for such debate then there must be an ethos conducive to democratic dialogue; one that will exhibit the characteristics of what Cush (1999) has termed 'positive pluralism' in so far as;

> 'It takes the differences and incommensurability of world views seriously, but approaches them from a viewpoint of 'epistemological humility' or 'methodological agnosticism'.

> (http:www.uni-marburg.de/religionswissenschaft/journal/diskus)

Constructivist Pedagogies of Religious Education Project

Grimmitt (2000) has developed an approach to teaching Religious Education that acknowledges a constructivist view of knowledge in which what is known in any discipline is the result of multiple interpretations, constructed, and therefore controversial or problematic. Language plays a key role in this process and the role of the teacher in managing the context for dialogue so that pupils' active construction of understanding is made explicit takes precedence over the imparting of knowledge through instruction. He proposes a three stage pedagogical strategy as follows:

1. *Preparatory Pedagogical Constructivism*

   Pupils are engaged in an enquiry into their own experience as a preparation for an encounter with the item of religious content.

2. *Direct Pedagogical Constructivism*

   Exposure to the religious content without explanation and instruction, so that it becomes the stimulus for active construction of meaning.

3. *Supplementary Pedagogical Constructivism*

   The provision of supplementary information about the item of religious content to enable the elaboration of their emerging constructs and the consideration of alternative perspectives.

Grimmitt outlines the constructivist principles of learning embodied in this pedagogical strategy:

> '...religious content is *always* brought into a dynamic relationship with critical and reflective thought ...is *always* related to the constructions that pupils are using...the sequence of learning is *always* from encouraging egocentric interpretations of experience within *situated thought, through alternative contextualised interpretations* (as represented by interventions from pupils or the teacher), to *evaluative judgements* about the interests which each interpretation serves and expresses.' (Grimmitt, 2000, 217).

The benefits for Religious Education of this approach is that, unlike instruction through recitation, it enables pupils to develop the inter-subjective and intra-subjective understanding required to engage sensitively with the positive and negative effects of religion upon human life. Grimmitt describes how using this approach has improved the motivation of pupils in Religious Education lessons and resulted in more sophisticated engagement with religious ideas. He also points out the demands that this approach makes on the teacher who cannot rely on transmission of received 'facts' but must be ready to deconstruct and reconstruct their own understanding as they guide the pupils.

The Building E-Bridges Project

The *Building E-Bridges project* (2008, McKenna *et al*) forms part of '*Religion in Education: a contribution to dialogue or a factor of conflict in transforming societies of European countries*' (REDCo), the first major research programme for Religious Education funded by the European Commission. *Building E-Bridges* used email to facilitate dialogue between pupils in primary schools in Leicester and East Sussex based on a model of three dimensions of dialogue derived from Bakhtin (1986):

- *Primary dialogue* in which the broader context of the partner schools acknowledges diversity;

- *Secondary dialogue* where attitudes conducive to positive engagement with others are promoted through email exchanges with dialogue partners from different schools;

- *Tertiary dialogue* involving the active exchange of views on relevant topics drawn from the RE and citizenship curriculum.

The project built on previous work on promoting dialogue in the Religious Education classroom (Ipgrave, 2001), which had found that the approach raised self-esteem and enabled pupils, including under-achievers, to express their views and engage in the discussion of fundamental human questions.

Whilst the evaluation of the impact of *Building E-Bridges* is positive, some of the reservations expressed have implications for the use of dialogic approaches in Religious Education. The pupils emphasised the building of friendship through the email exchanges and were more interested in exchanging information that demonstrated membership of a shared youth culture than in exploring any areas of religious or ethnic difference. Consequently, the discussion featured what the researchers term 'social chit chat' (McKenna *et al*, 2008: 107) and there was a lack of cognitive challenge. When pupils were prompted by the teachers to ask questions linked to the topics being studied in Religious Education, they remained at the level of external features, such as how a festival was celebrated, with little reference to personal beliefs or convictions. The researchers conclude that the disappointing tenor of the discourse in the email exchanges is partly the result of the limitations of the Religious Education syllabus and the fact that the teachers were not subject specialists. They also suggest that, unsurprisingly, the pupils did not think of themselves as representatives of a faith group and preferred to respond to each other as individuals. They conclude that the teachers needed more support in providing a framework for the email exchanges so that more challenging issues could be discussed. They concede that they had, perhaps, overestimated the extent to which pupils with apparently diverse backgrounds would in fact view the contact as an encounter with 'difference' and that this would provide a sufficient basis for dialogue.

Face to Faith

The Tony Blair Faith Foundation has developed a programme, *Face to Faith*, designed to support schools in the fulfilment of the 2007 Toledo *Guiding Principles on Teaching About Religions and Beliefs in public schools*. The values underpinning the programme include the following statement about education:

> 'Good learning creates understanding, overcomes prejudice and opens the gates of dialogue. We are here to teach and to learn, not to convince or convert.' (www.tonyblairfaithfoundation.org)

The programme is designed to promote religious literacy and involves a series of facilitated video-conferences between schools and the establishing of an online community to provide sustained engagement between students. Teachers participating in the programme are provided with module outlines and detailed lesson plans building up to and following on from each video-conference. *Face to Faith* builds upon the work of the *Building E-Bridges* project and both Julia Ipgrave and Robert Jackson from the Warwick Religious Education Research Unit (WRERU) are on the advisory board. The programme will also be evaluated by WRERU although at the time of writing there are no reported outcomes.

Philosophy for Children (P4C)

P4C was developed by the American philosopher Matthew Lipman as an approach to teaching philosophy to children through a sequence of specially written stories (Lipman, 2003). The central pedagogical strategy of the programme is the community of enquiry; a concept derived from the pragmatist epistemology of Charles Sanders Peirce who first used the term to describe the way in which scientists create knowledge through collaborative problem solving. Essentially, the community of enquiry involves the elicitation of pupils' questions arising from a common stimulus, usually a narrative, which then form the structure of a whole class discussion. The role of the teacher is to mediate the discussion by establishing a climate conducive to the expression of opinions and ensuring that the basic rules of taking turns to speak and showing how your contribution builds on what has already been said are followed. The aim of the community of enquiry is to build understanding through the testing of assumptions and clarification rather than through an adversarial model of argument. It is designed to overcome the constraints of the normative social dynamics of the classroom by privileging dialogue between pupils above the standard patterns of recitation or pseudo-enquiry.

Devon County Council recommend *P4C* in their Agreed Syllabus and teachers in primary and secondary schools across the UK have found this approach to be conducive to the promotion of dialogue in the Religious Education classroom. SAPERE (the Society for Advancing Philosophical Enquiry and Reflection in Education) is the UK charity that promotes *P4C* and they provide courses on using the approach to teach RE (see http://www.thinkingeducation.co.uk). The Institute for the Advancement of Philosophy for Children (IAPC) founded by Matthew Lipman at Montclair State University has tended to emphasise the secular nature of philosophical enquiry but one of its associate members, Jen Glaser from the School of Education at Tel Aviv University has developed *P4C* in the context of Religious Education in a Jewish School (njjewishnews.com/njn.com/071207/njInquiringMinds.html).

Recommendations of *P4C* as an approach to be used in Religious Education tend to rely on evaluations of its impact when used as a free-standing programme. Trickey and Topping (2004) conducted a systematic review of the evidence of the impact of *P4C* and concluded that pupils, in primary and secondary school contexts, were:

- more willing to speak out in front of the class, offer more reasons when expressing their opinions and more ready to accept alternative ideas (Campbell, 2002)

- listened more carefully to the views of others, were less likely to react negatively to contributions and were more supportive to each other in group interactions (Williams, 1993).

For teachers, there is evidence that they:

- show respect for each pupil, accept individual differences, are non-threatening in their interventions and allow more active participation from pupils (Cotton, 2002)

- contribute to the success of *P4C*, which is highly teacher sensitive (Sternberg and Bhana, 1996).

Thinking through Religious Education

'Overall there has developed an ethos of respect in the classroom during these activities. This has been cultivated by the pupils themselves. One pupil wrote in her log (diary): 'Just because someone has a different idea doesn't make either of us wrong.' This mature reflection surprised me but this was not an isolated example of this type of response.' (Baumfield, 2002: 2)

Thinking through Religious Education (Baumfield, 2002) features exemplars of lessons produced by secondary school teachers in the North East of England. The project was developed with a subject network of Religious Education teachers interested in evaluating the impact of using the thinking skills approaches being developed by the University of Newcastle's *Thinking Skills Research Centre* on their pupils. The impetus for the project came from the decision to include thinking skills in the revision of the National Curriculum (DfEE, 1999) and the need to address the issue of standards in Religious Education following a series of OfSTED subject reports highlighting a number of deficiencies including the need to shift the focus from what is being taught to what is being learned, to develop understanding rather than the recall of facts and promote a language of respect and inclusion in order to enable the evaluation of ideas. The generic thinking skills approaches used in the project were based on the ideas of Dewey in terms of the importance of the mediation of experience and Vygotsky's emphasis on the role of language in concept development. Articulation was identified as an important aspect of learning through the use of thinking skills strategies:

'Pupils talk about their work and are encouraged to describe and articulate their thinking. This has several benefits. From the teacher's point of view, you get a chance to see how the pupils are thinking as they explain their reasoning. This is an opportunity to address any misconceptions and to develop their thinking. For the pupils, talking is seen as 'easy', but they get the chance to change their minds in the light of what others say.' (Baumfield, 2002: 5).

Some of the teachers in the network used the opportunity provided by funding from the Teacher Development Agency (TDA) to conduct a more sustained investigation into the impact of the use of thinking skills on pupils' extended writing in GCSE Religious Studies lessons. They had found that their pupils, particularly the boys, were more engaged in the lessons and demonstrated increased social and emotional maturity in their contributions to group discussions. The comments recorded in interviews with pupils endorse the value of thinking skills in promoting productive dialogue in Religious Education:

'I was able to listen to different opinions'.

'I could not have thought of some of the things on my own'.

'Other people's opinions sometimes make sense. Sometimes you haven't thought of that opinion before'. (Baumfield, 2002, 109)

The teachers now wanted to see if this improvement in oral responses could be transferred to the extended writing required by the examination. Written work completed during the twelve week period of the research project was marked in the usual way against GCSE level descriptors and comparisons were made with previous work and with the pupils' predicted grades. The written work took account of a wider range of opinions and ideas were developed and extended more than had previously been the case. As a consequence, the levels achieved matched at least a grade above what was predicted in most cases. In one school the pupils were tracked into their final year; the class exceeded the target of 25% of pupils achieving grades A-C in the examination by 30%, so that 55% gained grades A-C. Comparable Religious Education classes in the school who had not participated in the project did not make such an improvement.

Hermeneutical tasks

O'Grady (2008) in his exploration of pupil motivation in Religious Education, found that opportunities to enter into 'dialogue with difference' was a key factor. In order to facilitate the participation of pupils in such dialogue, O'Grady developed a series of hermeneutical tasks designed to promote dialogue with an aspect of a religious tradition as well as the more immediate dialogue with their peers in the classroom. One of the examples he gives is a unit on Islam:

'CYCLE 1: Islam, peace and surrender.

The pupils used a variety of sources to study the life of Muhammad. Then they imagined that they could interview him, listed their questions and discussed the answers he might offer and their own thoughts on the relevant matters. They considered Qur'anic verses that express the belief in *tawhid* (the oneness of Allah, the God) and interpreted the concepts of oneness and uniqueness in art compositions of their own issues over the prohibition of representational art in Islam were discussed. The students raised their own questions about the practice of *zakat* (almsgiving) and developed these into drama sketches. They watched a film about prayer in Islam and held discussions comparing their own values to those shown. The participant observation notes recorded highest apparent motivation when ideas could be explored through drama and pupils could consider values of their own in relation to Islam. For those pupils who were Muslims it was a first experience of conversation about Islam with non-Muslims'. (O'Grady, 2008, 367)

Investigation through a series of action research cycles, found these hermeneutical tasks to be effective in establishing,

> '...an equal relationship between religious education content and pupils' responses and reflections'. (O'Grady, 2008, 368)

O'Grady draws upon the interpretive approach to Religious Education (Jackson, 1997) and a recent systematic review of citizenship education in schools in which the transformational potential of dialogical learning to empower pupils to relate strongly to their life experiences is highlighted (Deakin Crick et al, 2004).

DO THE PEDAGOGIES WORK?

The pedagogies for Religious Education reviewed in this chapter provide evidence that dialogic approaches can be beneficial in the promotion of attitudes and skills conducive to inter-communication and inter-cultural understanding.

Impact on learners

For the pupils, dialogic approaches enable them to bring their own experiences to bear in the encounter with new, and possibly strange, ideas and beliefs. Dialogue encourages them to voice their opinions but also to be tentative and willing to accommodate alternative perspectives. The shift in the pattern of classroom discourse provides more space for pupil talk with less overt teacher direction and this is beneficial in the building of confidence and widening participation in lessons. In fact, the dialogue in the classroom resembles more closely the type of talk that is common in informal learning contexts and this benefits pupils with learning difficulties (Baumfield and Devlin, 2005). The evidence for increased pupil participation in lessons and their enjoyment of the opportunity to express their ideas is strong. Engagement in learning through dialogue also has a positive impact on attainment and there is some evidence to show that talking can develop extended writing in Religious Education, for example. Evidence of the transfer of positive attitudes in the classroom to contexts outside of the school is, understandably, less robust and this is an area requiring further research.

Implications for teachers

Dialogic approaches require the teacher to shift their practice away from instruction to facilitation and whilst many Religious Education teachers may feel comfortable with engaging pupils in discussion, meeting the need to ensure that the talking is purposeful is demanding. In order to fulfil the role of the 'curious facilitator' the teacher needs to have a sophisticated understanding of the content of the syllabus so that s/he can enable the pupils the freedom to explore ideas whilst always being able to see how they can be linked to key religious concepts. Self-discipline is also required so that the excitement of seeing the pupils enjoying discussion does not pre-empt the need to introduce cognitive challenge. The teacher may need to steer pupils away from focusing on developing friendships through talk towards the less comfortable aspects of dialogue in which difference and disagreement is acknowledged. The *Building E-Bridges* project highlights the need to consider carefully how to encourage encounters with different perspectives as sometimes the assumptions made by adults are not shared by pupils. Where 'difference' may be self-evident to a teacher it can be unimportant to the pupils (or vice versa). Dialogic teaching approaches such as the community of enquiry are valuable as they can provide useful 'scaffolds' for teachers as well as for learners. Also, the quality of the feedback, as pupils articulate their ideas, is a powerful incentive; it is innately interesting to teachers and useful in the diagnosis of gaps in knowledge or understanding.

Unintended outcomes

Dialogic teaching is being encouraged across the curriculum but there can be problems when this approach is adopted in some subject areas or in some classes and not in others in a school. Whilst it may be seen by some as not necessarily a disadvantage for Religious Education to be associated with subversion by empowering pupils to question and be confident in expressing their views, dialogic teaching could have unintended outcomes. It is important to emphasise that dialogue is also a means of learning the skills of social interaction and an opportunity to exercise judgement. Lipman (2003) draws upon Dewey's emphasis on the importance of dialogue for democracy and emphasises the need to foster being reasonable in its fullest sense as an affective as well as a cognitive disposition.

Stephen Law (in Hand and Winstanley, 2008) considers two popular objections to the use of dialogic approaches, with their privileging of questioning in the process of meaning making, in Religious Education. One is that encouraging young people to be critical and think independently about moral and religious questions promotes relativism. He suggests that the opposite could be true in so far as avoiding critical thinking is more likely, in today's society, to undermine religious belief by trivialising it or implying that faith is irrational. Another objection is that parents have the right to send their children to school confident that they will not be subjected to teaching that undermines their faith. Again, Law emphasises that encountering alternative viewpoints and being open to questions can strengthen faith and that to do anything else in a school context would not be educational. Fancourt (2007) has investigated the question of whether a teacher of Religious Education who is adopting a dialogic approach should express their personal views. He carried out an action research project in his own classroom and found that pupils appreciated the fact that the teacher not only encouraged them to be able to discuss differences in belief but was also willing to be equally open themselves. He suggests that in the context of a broadly dialogical approach the teacher can be a participant in discussion without exercising undue influence on individual beliefs.

Any attempt to answer the question of 'What works?' requires careful consideration of intentions, enactment and impact and the interactions that can and do take place between these aspects in different contexts. Current interest in pedagogy is encouraging given its neglect in the past. With the exception of the work of Michael Grimmitt (2000), the attention of researchers and policy makers has focused on the aims and content of Religious Education rather than on how it can or should be taught. We should, however, be wary of a tendency to speak of 'pedagogy' as teaching methods, which excludes the broader sense of the relationship between teaching and learning within a particular socio-cultural context. If 'pedagogy' were to become a surrogate for effective teaching it could increase the demands on the Religious Education teacher to solve society's problems through their individual prowess as a classroom practitioner.

REFERENCES

Alexander, R.J. (2006) *Towards Dialogic Teaching: rethinking classroom talk*, York: Dialogos

Alexander, R.J. (2008) *Essays on Pedagogy*, Abingdon: Routledge

Bakhtin, M.N. (1986) *Speech Genres and other late essays*, (Y. McGee, Trans) Austin: University of Texas Press

Baumfield, V.M. (2002) *Thinking Through Religious Education*, Cambridge: Chris Kington Publishing

Baumfield, V.M. and Devlin, N (2005) 'Staying on task: can a thinking skills approach support productive pedagogy for inclusion?' *Journal of Research in Special Educational Needs* 5 (1), 37-42

Biesta, G (2006) '"Of all affairs, communication is the most wonderful": the communicative turn in Dewey's Democracy and Education' in D.T Hansen (ed) *John Dewey and Our Educational Prospect*, Albany, NY: State University Press, 23-37

Blaylock, L. (2002) 'RE in Practice 11-16: is it true?' *RE Today*: 13

Campbell, J. (2002) 'An evaluation of a pilot intervention involving teaching philosophy to upper primary school children in two primary schools using Philosophy for Children methodology', University of Dundee, unpublished M.Sc. thesis.

Carrington, B. and Short, G. (1992) 'The Development of Children's Understanding of Jewish Identity and Culture', *School Psychology International* 13(1), 73-89

Cotton, K. (2002) *Teaching Thinking Skills: School Research Series*,. Portland, Oregon: North West Regional Educational Laboratory

Cox, C.B. and Dyson, A.E. (1971) *The Black Papers on Education*, London: Davis-Poynter Ltd.

Cush, D. (1999) 'Potential pioneers of pluralism: the contribution of RE to intercultural education in multi-cultural societies', Diskus Vol 5 (online journal) http:www.uni-marburg.de/religionswissenschaft/journal/diskus

Deakin Crick R., Coates, M., Taylor. M., Ritchie, S (2004) 'A systematic review of the impact of citizenship education on the provision of schooling' in *Research Evidence in Education Library*, London: EPPI-Centre, Social Science Research Unit, Institute of Education, University of London

Dewey, J. (1916) 'Democracy and education', in Boydston J.A. (ed) *John Dewey the middle works, 1899-1924: Vol.9*, Carbondale: Southern Illinois University Press

DfEE (1999) *Revised National Curriculum*. London: HMSO

DCSF (2010) *Religious Education and Community Cohesion in Secondary Schools and Colleges* (http://www.religiouseducationcouncil.org)

Grimmitt, M. H. (ed) (2000) *Pedagogies of Religious Education*, Great Wakering: McCrimmon Publishing Co. Ltd.

Fancourt, N. (2007) 'The 'Dialogical' Teacher: should teachers express their commitments in the classroom?' In Bakker C. and Heimbrock H-G., *Researching RE Teachers. RE Teachers as Researchers*, Munster: Waxmann

Hand, M. and Winstanley, C. (2008) *Philosophy in Schools*, London: Continuum

HMSO (1971) *Schools Council Working Paper 36* London: HMSO

Lipman, M. (2003) *Thinking in Education*, 2nd edition, Cambridge: Cambridge University Press

Ipgrave, J. (2001) 'Pupil-to-pupil dialogue in the classroom as a tool for religious education', Warwick Religious and Education Research Unit (WRERU) Occasional Papers 2, Coventry: University of Warwick

Jackson, R. (1997) *Religious Education. An Interpretive Approach*, London: Hodder and Stoughton

McKenna, U., Ipgrave, J. and Jackson, R. (2008) 'Inter Faith Dialogue by Email in Primary Schools: An Evaluation of the Building E-Bridges Project', Münster: Waxmann

Mercer, N. (1995) *The Guided Construction of Knowledge: talk amongst teachers and learners*, Clevedon: Multilingual Matters

O'Grady, K. (2008) 'How far can you go? Can you get reincarnated as a floorboard?' *Religious Education pedagogy, pupil motivation and teacher intelligence*, Educational Action Research 16:3, 361-376

QCA (2004) *The Non-Statutory National Framework for Religious Education* QCA/04/1371 London: QCA

Runnymede Trust (2000) *The Future of Multi-ethnic Britain: Parekh Report*, London: Profile Books

Sternberg, R. and Bhana, K. (1996) 'Synthesis of research on the effectiveness of intellectual skills programs: snake oil remedies or miracle cures?', *Educational Leadership* 44:2, 60-67

Suissa, J. (2008) 'Philosophy in the Secondary School – a Deweyan Perspective' in Hand, M. and Winstanley, C. *Philosophy in Schools*, London: Continuum

Trickey, S. and Topping, K.J. (2004) 'Philosophy for Children: a systematic review', *Research Papers in Education* 19:3, 365-376

Wells, G. (1999) *Dialogic Inquiry: towards a sociocultural practice and theory of education*, Cambridge: Cambridge University Press

Williams, S. (1993) *Evaluating the effects of Philosophical Enquiry in a secondary school*, Derby, UK: Derbyshire County Council

http://www.qcda.gov.uk accessed 11/09/09.

http://news.reonline.org.uk/article.php?28 accessed 11/09/09

http://www.cornwall.gov.uk accessed 14/09/09

http://www.faithandcohesion.org accessed 14/09/09

http:// www.tonyblairfaithfoundation.org accessed 15/10/09

http://nationalstrategies.standards.dcsf.gov.uk/node/84633 accessed 15/10/09

http://www.thinkingeducation.co.uk accessed 02.11.09

njjewishnews.com/njjn.com/071207/njInquiringMinds.html accessed 02.11.09

CHAPTER 12

THE 2007 BIRMINGHAM AGREED SYLLABUS:
Educating pupils and the community

Marius C. Felderhof and Simone Whitehouse

SUMMARY

MARIUS FELDERHOF and Simone Whitehouse set out their experience of the development of the Agreed Syllabus for Religious Education in Birmingham (2007) which has taken RE in a radically new direction.

INTRODUCTION

When in 2005 Birmingham SACRE advised the City that its 1995 Religious Education Agreed Syllabus was required to be reviewed, it also signalled the syllabus would need to be significantly revised. This necessitated an Agreed Syllabus Conference; a body to be set up according to legal statute and on a basis that was more than a mere formality – as may sometimes happen when no significant change in the curriculum is envisaged. The situation in Birmingham demanded a more deep-rooted revision. This perception was based on two developments. The first was the publication in September, 2004 by the Qualification and Curriculum Authority (QCA), (together with the Department for Children, Schools and Families), of a *Non-Statutory National Framework for Religious Education*. The second was the increasing use of computers and the internet within schools. Any modern religious education syllabus must now consider the opportunities and challenges this offered.

THE PROCESS OF REVIEW AND REVISION
DESCRIBED AND EXPLAINED

In considering a more serious review, steps had to be taken to ensure the proper resourcing of a strictly legal process.[1] This was done through backing from the City's School Effectiveness Division – but only after political approval. The Division supported the process financially from its budget and contributed the expertise of the RE adviser, S. Whitehouse, an advisory teacher, R. Hack and a computer programmer, J. McAdam. A consciousness that the revision process needed to conform scrupulously to the requirements of the law arose from previous experience in the City in 1970-75. The draft 1975 Agreed Syllabus had stirred public controversy with the proposal to include Marxism and Secular Humanism, and a legal challenge was mounted to resist it.[2] There was a clear desire to avoid a similar fate.

To oversee and direct the Agreed Syllabus Conference, the City appointed Mr Guy Hordern as chair. Mr Hordern was already chair of SACRE and had a long standing interest in Religious Education. More importantly, he also had close ties with the City's Conservative Party, which together with the Liberal Democrats, controlled the City Council. His political experience and connections proved invaluable in securing political support and funding for the revision of the Syllabus and its web-based resources.

Finally, the City appointed Marius Felderhof as the drafting secretary. Dr. Felderhof was a senior lecturer in Systematic Theology at the University of Birmingham Department of Theology and Religion.[3] He had been the chair of Committee A for many years and was perceived to have the confidence of the many religious traditions represented there. He also had an ongoing theological interest in Religious Education. Some anticipated that through his advice the new Syllabus would gain in academic substance and rigour. Whether this is indeed the case is for the reader to decide. What cannot be doubted was the ambition of the City to maintain its reputation to be leaders in RE by making significant resources available.

In his letter of appointment to Dr. Felderhof, Cllr. Les Lawrence, the Cabinet member for Children, Young People and Families, stressed the importance of having an RE Syllabus that conformed to law, was educationally viable and made religious sense. In emphasising these three considerations of legality, educational viability and religious sense, he was signalling some long standing concerns with Religious Education as it was being delivered in schools in England and Wales generally and which Birmingham would now seek to address. These concerns we shall discuss below, following some further observations about the process.

As is well known, the 1944 Education Act set out the main elements of the process for devising a Syllabus for Religious Education, and in effect identified four specific interests that were required to be reconciled. Each of the four groups has one vote and an effective veto since unanimity is a legal necessity. What was different in the current process was a growing consciousness that each group had different responsibilities and interests. The Local Authority clearly has a duty to represent the community as a whole and was expected to champion principles of inclusion and social cohesion. The teacher's group was expected to consider issues to do with pedagogy and the principles and practicalities of schooling. The Church of England, as the established church, was expected to defend the moral and spiritual well-being of the nation and as a consequence to ensure that RE played its role in that endeavour. The C of E committee was therefore expected to stand up for the main stream of religious life. The fourth committee (of dissenting churches and other faiths), by far the largest with some 24 members, was also expected to reflect on religious life and, in addition, to ensure the accuracy of any information provided on less familiar faiths. They also clearly had a responsibility to see that minority interests were safeguarded, and thus like the local authority group, to ensure inclusion.

It has been said that RE in community schools should rise above sectional interests, and that everyone should see themselves committed to one common, secular enterprise. But as Philip Barnes has argued so elegantly, before you can cultivate tolerance it is vital to acknowledge real differences.[4] The real work of the Agreed Syllabus Conference is precisely to tease out the differences and democratically to negotiate, to argue and to persuade, perhaps even to cajole, in order to overcome the gap that separates the different interests. Practically this was done at the level of the Conference, but often addressed in detail at the level of a smaller scrutiny committee that examined every word and line. Those who argue for the seamless unity in RE often do so from positions of power and their presumption is that everyone will conform. If differences are taken seriously then when agreement does finally come, there is much greater ownership, solidarity and backing for the product.

The recognition of genuine religious interests may also come as a surprise to those who have strongly argued for a secular form of RE in community schools.[5] It is often supposed that in a secular society, the secular state should support a secular understanding of the religious world. However, the law requires the school curriculum as a whole to be broadly based and balanced. It is difficult to see how this is achieved if the religious form of life is not adequately represented in *religious* terms. In a secular society it is precisely the religious voice which is absent and which should be heard in an educational context if young people are not to acquire a distorted view of religious faith and of people of faith. There is no available neutrality that is somehow the sole privilege of a secular state versus the commitments of religious communities. Secularity is itself a position. The best that can be hoped for is fairness, openness and accuracy in any accounts one happens to provide. These values are realised most fully when in any descriptions of the other, the other concurs and endorses the information and the discourse in which it is offered.

From the outset the Anglican Bishop, the Roman Catholic Archbishop and all the members of the Faith Leaders' group in Birmingham were approached in face to face discussion and encouraged to nominate their most able representatives. The condition was explicitly stated that these representatives should have a deep knowledge and appreciation of their particular faith tradition. If, incidentally, they had a knowledge of schooling as well, this would be regarded as a bonus rather than a prerequisite since the Conference would look to the teachers' committee for the essential educational in-put. This step was taken consciously to strengthen the link between schooling and the wider community and to avoid treating the curriculum as a wholly specialist preserve or as a privileged domain of an educational community.

The reasons for this approach is that it may well be the case that the very traditions and practices of current schooling, (together with current RE theory), blind one to the constraints on the expression of religious life or to the many ways in which people are authorised to discriminate against the use of religious conceptions.[6] In order to test and communicate the religious sense of an RE curriculum, one may in fact need people who are wholly fresh to the task and see the enterprise with new eyes. There is, for example, a widely held prejudice, especially prevalent amongst intellectuals that religion is fundamentally about subscribing to a set of cognitive beliefs. In contrast, many religious people themselves see religion as a practice and direction in life. From a religious perspective the key challenge in life is to the human will rather than to the human mind, to what one chooses to do rather than to what one thinks. A curriculum that focuses on the latter (on beliefs) rather than the former subtly introduces a distortion. Admittedly, thought and will are not unrelated but primacy matters here.

Teachers, of course, have their concerns. For example, what can one possibly do in the finite time available? What scope is there for creativity in teaching? How can one engage pupils who, as persons, have their own history, integrity and freedom, which entitles them to the fundamental respect that prohibits bullying? How does one assess development, specifically, moral and spiritual development? What does moral and spiritual development look like?[7] How does one incorporate progression in one's teaching? How does RE fit in with the other curricular demands on the school? These are important questions, and there are many more! Sometimes the religious demands and the educational demands appeared to be wholly irreconcilable; assessment being a case in point. There are religious demands that openly state, 'judge not', but teachers must make judgements about their pupils and about their own teaching. Moral theory makes inner motivations a key to any moral valuations but inner motivations are not normally accessible to public inspection, thus making any moral assessment on that score impossible. If one is nevertheless constrained to assess everything one does at the behest of the school authorities, what should the teacher do? Should s/he only teach what is assessable?

AN ATTEMPTED SOLUTION TO RECONCILING THE REQUIREMENTS OF LEGALITY, EDUCATIONAL VIABILITY AND RELIGIOUS SENSE:

Reconciling the requirements of legality, educational viability and religious sense would not prove easy. But the outcome was a serious attempt to do so and that in itself was significant. It was in fact the legal requirements that provided the clue to a solution. Educational statute sets the overarching goal of education as the spiritual, moral, social and cultural (SMSC) development of children and society. This was an influential reminder that the primary focus of the curriculum should be children and society and their development, not religion(s) per se. The dominant focus could, therefore, never be religion or religions because there was always the requirement that whatever is studied must contribute to a spiritual, moral, social and cultural development.

The Conference welcomed the by now traditional attainment targets for RE, learning about and learning from religion, but reversed them. There were two good reasons for this. The first was to ensure that 'learning from faith' would be the driving force of SMSC development. The second was that 'learning from faith' proved helpful as an important principle in determining the selection of material. Given the vast range of what might be 'learned about religion' and the finite time available to teach it, one needs good, public reasons for selecting 'x' rather than 'y'. Effectively the answer was: what does the character development of the whole child and of society require?

Firstly, the whole child was considered on the basis of a handy device, namely, the traditional description of persons as consisting of three faculties: cognitive, affective and conative (to do with willing). To these were added the considerations of (a) key skills and (b) social needs and relationships. The latter also naturally led to the considerations of the needs of society e.g. cohesion, functioning institutions. This holistic view of a pupil embedded in a social setting and of education as the development of the whole child (or young person) required some definition of the kind of qualities we hoped such a person and such a society would exhibit. The conference finally settled on its list of 24 dispositions[8] after considering and rejecting whether 'Being Playful' should be one of them.[9]

An obvious question is whether anyone is justified in seeking to influence a young person's and society's character in this way? But as Wolterstorff observed in his book, *Educating for Responsible Action* (1980):

> 'It is virtually impossible for a teacher to avoid seeking to shape students' tendencies – to strengthen some and weaken others – and it is certainly impossible for a teacher to act in such a way that he or she will in *fact* not alter the students' tendencies. ... *Which* tendencies to seek to inculcate, and *how*, are the relevant questions – not *whether*.'[10]

In England and Wales, answering the *Which* and the *How* questions comes by way of negotiation, following a legal process, and, as a democratic society, the Agreed Syllabus is then adopted by elected representatives. The legitimacy comes precisely from adhering to law and engaging the wider community as fully as possible.

That the development of the young person and society should be the dominant concerns led to two challenges. First, it was necessary in an RE curriculum to show how diverse religious traditions might conceivably contribute to such development. Second, it was necessary to consider how does one engage the whole community in the same SMSC agenda as the schools? In addressing the first challenge the website was devised as a key teaching tool showing where in the judgement of the religious traditions concerned their resources might contribute to the dispositions at which the Conference was aiming – an enquiry which involved moving from a religious tradition to a disposition.[11] Alternatively the website made it equally possible to move in the opposite direction: from a disposition to the religious material. In addition to the website, SACRE soon commissioned TV Junction, a production firm, to make a number of films, one for each of the dispositions and show how a particular disposition was being exhibited in the life of one or more of the religious communities in the City. The films were pitched at two different levels, initial and advanced, to be used with different age groups or ability levels. The films were put on a DVD, *Faith makes a difference*, together with a primary and a secondary CPD film to acquaint teachers with the substance and possibilities of the new Agreed Syllabus and distributed to schools.

In addressing the second challenge of engaging the wider community in the same SMSC agenda as the schools, the website was again a useful tool. Firstly, it made all the information widely available but as will be seen below, invited participation from teachers and others in devising schemes of work and lesson plans and in offering material to be considered for inclusion. So in addition to teacher training days where head teachers and classroom teachers were told about the thinking behind the syllabus and shown how this might work in the classroom, – as well as how to navigate the website – further meetings were held for senior City officers and in the wider community. Out of this experience a further DVD, *Religious Education in Birmingham*, was made to inform faith communities about the ambitions of the RE syllabus and in this DVD the Faith Leaders played a full role alongside the Cabinet member for Children, Young People and Families. One outcome of this endeavour was the inclusion of religious education in the strategic planning partnership of *Be Birmingham*.[12] Now the dispositions would be seen to be fit for the whole community as well as schools and RE is itself perceived to be a part of a much larger agenda.[13] Schools cannot succeed in cultivating dispositions that are not already ideals embraced by the wider community.

It is the ownership of the Agreed Syllabus in Birmingham and the City's commitment to the cultivation of dispositions which have brought all the religious traditions together. This in turn has led to a growing solidarity in the City, manifested in part in a staunch resistance to the centralising work of the QCA and its *Non-Statutory National Framework for Religious Education* (2004) (NSNFRE). The draft guidance prepared by the government which sought to embed the NSNFRE in an official directive to local authorities and schools was taken to be misconceived in constraining the freedom Local Authorities have in law. Even this might have been tolerated had the content of the NSNFRE been more to the City's liking. The NSNFRE's emphasis on a growing list of religions about which pupils are expected to learn alongside secular philosophies does not recognise the limits on teaching time. Nor does it recognise the limits set by law on the inclusion of secular philosophies within RE. And finally, it does not fully recognise the primacy religious life gives to human wellbeing that goes far beyond the acquisition of mere information. Where the NSNFRE sees the need to encourage certain attitudes, it fails to link these to the specific learning about religions.

MAKING IT ALL WORK IN PRACTICE

In order to support schools further it was thought exemplar teaching materials needed to be produced for both primary and secondary schools. Teachers could then see the dispositions in place and either take the exemplars and use them (the majority of primary schools have) or adopt the principles outlined in the schemes of work and adapt them for their own settings. In introducing the new syllabus many sessions were held in different parts of the city for primary and secondary colleagues to understand the change in focus; the reversal of the attainment targets; through the teaching of dispositions almost as 'filters' through which learning from and about will take place; wanting to use ICT to the fullest and to give the teachers of the city more flexibility.

This was a major re-focusing for teachers and they needed to be guided through the thought process of the Agreed Syllabus Conference. During the training days, teachers were asked to reflect on the teaching of RE. They were asked to put their thoughts about RE on post-it notes and to think about positive and negative aspects of the subject. Many teachers commented on the perceived lack of resources, negative parental support, their lack of subject knowledge (in terms of fear of getting things wrong) as some of the stumbling blocks that they encounter whilst teaching Religious Education. Some of the positive aspects stated were the opportunities that the subject can offer, the resources that the city has in terms of people of faith as visitors to schools and of places to visit, the support of parents and cross curricular opportunities. This picture was painted repeatedly by teachers across the different types of schools and contexts within the city.

It was then explained that Birmingham SACRE is trying to address these obstacles and is supporting teachers by producing a DVD to use in classrooms and with the generation of exemplar schemes of work – this seemed to provide the support which was needed at the time. In particular, teachers saw the value in developing lessons communicating from the pupils' perspective first – in terms of the learning from faith – then moving into the religious content. Importantly teachers were able to see more clearly the benefit of the subject to pupils when they were able to teach in this way; at least they could now do so in terms which they had not done earlier. This impact of a renewed valuing of the subject has been seen throughout the city with both primary and secondary colleagues.

Teachers are encouraged by the Agreed Syllabus to take professional responsibility, and within statutory limits, are freed to select and make use of the material from the various religious traditions. Whilst they must communicate the Christian tradition they can select other material on the basis of certain principles, namely, to reflect the family backgrounds of the children, their ages, aptitudes, interests and whatever will both deepen and broaden the children's moral and spiritual horizons.

To this end of adapting the syllabus to the pupils and schools, different models of the schemes of work were produced. For secondary schools exemplar six-week units were produced by the RE adviser working in conjunction with teachers – adapting their already existing schemes of work through the filter of the dispositions. For example in the unit 'Who wants to be a Millionaire?', Christian Aid, the Sikh concept of Kirat Karni and the Muslim practice of Zakat are to be taught through the dispositions of Being Fair and Just; Being Accountable and Living with Integrity and Living by Rules.

For primary teachers who do not necessarily have an RE background, full schemes of work have been produced. As the exemplar material could not be written for each unique school situation three models were constructed. Model One represents a scheme of work deemed appropriate for a school in which the majority of pupils come from a Christian or nominal Christian background. Model Two represents a scheme of work that might be used in a school where the majority of pupils come from a Muslim faith tradition. Model Three has imagined a school in which there is a significant percentage of children from each of the four largest faith groups in Birmingham. All of the models include teaching from a wide variety of religious traditions. When creating the exemplar material, due note was taken of the need to teach the statutory elements of the syllabus.

Also the pedagogical view that very young children benefit most from first being introduced to just one or two faith traditions was accepted. Therefore the number of faith traditions to be taught increases only gradually across the primary age range. Within each exemplar, progression has been ensured by the use of key questions. The syllabus employs key questions in the place of learning objectives to reflect the explorative nature of each disposition at each Key Stage. The key questions are there also to ensure progress throughout the spiral syllabus as the dispositions are covered from different angles and through the filter of different faith traditions.

In designing the exemplar material a variety of teaching approaches were deliberately used. This is reflected in the activities that are suggested, but also in the planning. The majority of dispositions have been addressed in a three lesson model. In these cases often the first lesson will have a 'PSHE' flavour as the intention is to begin with what the children already know. The second lesson will often introduce a religious way of looking at the topic without giving specific teaching from any one religious tradition. The third lesson will then address the topic using the teaching of one or more religious traditions as support and source material. Whilst many of the dispositions have been addressed as three lesson modules; others have been combined (i.e. two dispositions taught together); or given a shorter or longer treatment.

It is anticipated that over time each school will devise a scheme of work to reflect their own pupil composition. Teachers are encouraged to compare the detail of a lesson series across the three models provided as in some instances differences are minor, whereas in others they are significant. There is an emphasis on the freedom for primary teachers to write their own activities, lessons or schemes. All teachers are encouraged to submit activities, lessons and units of work to the website for the curriculum committee of SACRE to approve – so that the sharing of good practice is furthered. Faith communities have the same opportunity. Already many primary schools are devising curriculum maps to link the 'new RE' with citizenship, PSHE and the SEAL (Social and Emotional Aspects of

Learning) curriculum. Whilst secondary colleagues are finding more opportunities to 'promote' RE within the KS 3 Strategy as developing pupils' skills as independent enquirers, creative thinkers, reflective learners, team workers, self managers and effective participators.

Claire Finkel at Glenmead Primary School has the responsibility for Humanities and MFL and was one of the first co-ordinators to teach the new syllabus. Glenmead is in the north of the city; a mainly white populated school in a multi-faith city. Claire welcomes the new changes, in her words, 'It's learning about what faith means to individuals, what religious life means and how it affects their life. It's about helping children to understand different people's beliefs and where they are coming from. How we sometimes might not agree with those beliefs but they are important to the people that hold them and that we can still get along even if it is not the same thought'. Claire is hoping that the new Syllabus will bring a more relevant dimension to RE: 'I know within our school, RE had gone a bit stale over the last few years, teachers were finding it a little bit irrelevant and they are not sure why they were teaching it. They were finding that a lot of children haven't got a faith themselves so they don't really understand what it means. We are really hoping that through the new approach we can teach children about things that are happening in the media and bring a global dimension into the classroom through RE as a subject.'

Claire thinks that RE is now more relevant for teachers and for pupils. 'The focus has changed and therefore the style of the lessons had to change. It's more practical and it's got to be latched onto the children's life; it can't just be an abstract thing. They have to understand what it could mean to them and how religious belief affects a person.'

With the DVD *Faith makes a difference* teachers can show within their classrooms the dynamic faiths in Birmingham living out the dispositions. Clips include members of the Muslim faith sorting clothes at an Islamic Relief depot and talking about their motives for getting involved; Rastafari peace officers talking about living out their faith in Handsworth and Street Pastors working on the streets with members of rival gangs. Teachers in Birmingham are beginning to see that the syllabus is making a difference within their classrooms.

The most significant change is the manner in which teachers are focusing and teaching the subject – making it more dynamic and relevant to the pupils in their classroom – the 'learning from' aspect has enabled this to happen where it was less of a focus before. Pupils are beginning to see an answer to the question 'what's the relevance?' Hopefully in the next few years we will be able to see more of this development and be able to reflect on how the syllabus is developing the conative dimension of the children and young people within the city, active and keen to change the world.

Claire Finkel is beginning to see this change developing and states, 'My RE lessons have changed and we are doing less worksheet based, what is this? And what does this do? And we've really started to develop a conversation. I have found that by developing our lessons in this way you are really listening to the children. It's about how it fits into life. The children are really excited about the lesson because it has got a new format to it, they really want to be there and they want to have their say.'

We are still continuing to work with faith communities on developing further lesson plans for their faith traditions. The website is also receiving exemplars from the teaching community within Birmingham. All in all, RE in Birmingham is caught up in a very dynamic process that should remain active until the next formal syllabus revision.

NOTES

1. Throughout the process the City's solicitor's office was consulted.

2. For details see Copley, T. (2008) *Teaching religion : sixty years of religious education in England and Wales*, Exeter: University of Exeter, 107-110

3. This involved a substantial financial transaction between the City and the University of Birmingham whereby Dr Felderhof was seconded to the City from the University for a period of two years.

4. Barnes L. P. (2009) *Religious Education: Taking Religious Difference Seriously*, No 17, Impact Series, Philosophy of Education Society of Great Britain

5. Alberts, W. (2007) *Integrative Religious Education in Europe, A Study of Religions Approach*, Berlin: Walter de Gruyter

6. I was once told by a student teacher that one could not use the word 'God' in the classroom on the grounds that this would be to indoctrinate children.

7. Perhaps in religious life one starts each day again at the beginning.

8. 'A disposition is a prevailing quality of character marked by an inclination, or will, to act in a particular way or by a tendency to a certain kind of action.' (as defined in the Birmingham Agreed Syllabus of 2007). The Syllabus can be downloaded from www.birmingham-asc.org.uk

9. Being Imaginative and Explorative; Appreciating Beauty; Expressing Joy; Being Thankful; Caring for Others, Animals and the Environment; Sharing and Being Generous; Being Regardful of Suffering; Being Merciful and Forgiving; Being Fair and Just; Living by Rules; Being Accountable and Living with Integrity; Being Temperate, Exercising Self-Discipline and Cultivating Serene Contentment; Being Modest and Listening to Others; Cultivating Inclusion, Identity and Belonging; Creating Unity and Harmony; Participating and Willing to Lead; Remembering Roots; Being Loyal and Steadfast; Being Hopeful and Visionary; Being Courageous and Confident; Being Curious and Valuing Knowledge; Being Open, Honest and Truthful; Being Reflective and Self-Critical; Being Silent and Attentive to, and Cultivating a Sense for, the Sacred and Transcendence.

10. Wolterstorff, N. (1980) *Educating for Responsible Action*, Grand Rapids: Wm. B. Eerdmans, Publishing Co., 6.

11. The website is www.birmingham-asc.org.uk

12. See Birmingham City Council (2008) *Birmingham 2026, Our Vision for the Future*, 54

13. SACRE was asked by the City's scrutiny committee to contribute to its Relationships and Sexual Health education policies in the light of its RE contribution. SACRE has also developed a DVD to advise Early Years practitioners with some relevant guidance although strictly speaking they do not have to deliver RE.

CHAPTER 13

DIVISION, DIVERSITY AND VISION:
Religious education and community cohesion in Northern Ireland

Norman Richardson

SUMMARY

I N ANY DISCUSSION OF CONCERNS about social and community cohesion in Northern Ireland the topics of religion and education are never far from the surface. Much has been written about the potential problems of a society in which the majority of the school-going population is educated separately on the basis of traditional perceptions of religious/cultural identity, though relatively little of this has focused on the role of Religious Education as a factor, positively or negatively. This chapter will examine some of the ways in which these traditional concerns, together with the more recent incidence of racist attitudes and behaviour, have been tackled through education, with a particular focus on Religious Education. A case is made, borne out by reference to research, that the retention of a Churches-dominated 'essentially Christian' approach in Northern Ireland inhibits a more inclusive and constructive contribution by RE to dealing with issues of diversity and division. Citing a number of positive examples the chapter concludes with suggestions for development that might enable schools and teachers to strengthen the future vision and role of Religious Education in helping children and young people to learn to live peacefully with their differences.

THE CONTEXT OF DIVISION AND DIVERSITY IN NORTHERN IRELAND

Northern Ireland's divisions are often expressed in religious terms as a conflict between Catholics and Protestants, but while religious observance in the region remains higher than in most other parts of the UK, the use of the denominational terminology does not necessarily indicate actual religious belief or practice. Rather it is for many people a shorthand way of expressing their sense of cultural, national and political identity. Associated with these identities is a complex of volatile issues around perceptions of unresolved mutual antagonisms, injustices and discrimination, often bolstered by long historical memories and sometimes justified by resorting to a religious rhetoric which outside observers may find perplexing. In Northern Ireland the concept of community cohesion has often seemed little more than a very remote ideal.

Despite many striking improvements since the mid–to-late 1990s, this geographically remote corner of the UK remains a divided and significantly separate society. One of the most overt expressions of this is in education where still around 90% of people of perceived Catholic and Protestant identity attend separate schools. This is in part due to a sense of security which some people derive from what might crudely be described as being with 'their own kind' (inevitably reinforced at times of community tension) and partly from the insistence on the part of the Catholic Church hierarchy that Catholic children should be educated within a Catholic ethos where they will receive confessional religious instruction. There have been many challenges to this continuing separateness, not least from those who have, with moderate success, established a shared or Integrated Education system, currently catering for just over 6% of the school-going population. Yet despite opinion polls and research showing that a majority of the population is in favour of greater educational integration, significant change seems unlikely in the foreseeable future. Debate frequently centres on the question of whether separate schooling is a *cause* of division in society or merely a *symptom*. The reality, perhaps, is that both cause and symptom have become entwined and almost inextricably bound together. But as Connolly, Smith and Kelly (2002,) have observed, the outcomes of educational separation can mean that 'schools can too easily become fertile learning grounds for young children where they soon develop awareness of themselves as part of a particular community and develop prejudiced attitudes about others'. (*op.cit.* 51)

As well as educational separateness, many people in the province live in separate communities and even where there is some degree of social mixing or where people from different communities are in employment together, the level of interaction is often governed by a culture of avoidance that prevents more meaningful mutual awareness. There has undoubtedly been progress and change from the raw times of 'the Troubles', and it would be quite inappropriate to paint a wholly negative picture, but many difficult issues remain under the surface, occasionally bubbling up into overt antagonism and sectarianism. Some observers have described this as a form of 'benign apartheid' – no-one is forcing anyone to live apart, but many people seem to have a sense of security in retaining their separateness, while some of the structures of society, including schooling, help to keep this in place. This kind of 'separate development', however, clearly has inherent dangers when individuals and communities grow up with little or no interaction. Connolly, Smith and Kelly (2002) have shown how negative attitudes to difference can be found in Northern Ireland's pre-school children as young as age 3 years, with potential for a hardening of such attitudes towards sectarianism and racism as children grow towards adolescence. The transition from a society in open conflict to one in which there is a greater sense of sharing and cohesion is undoubtedly going to be a process of generational change.

Alongside these traditional fractures in the functioning of Northern Ireland a newer dimension of diversity and potential division has emerged. Both jurisdictions on the island of Ireland have experienced a significant growth in the numbers of incoming minority national, ethnic and religious communities in the past decade and more. Now that it is no longer an obvious trouble-spot to be avoided, Northern Ireland has experienced a level of inward mobility that has raised new issues around cohesion and the capacity of diverse communities to live together in a shared society. One of the more disturbing statistics arising from the period following the paramilitary ceasefires in the mid-1990s indicated a significant increase in the number of reported racist incidents. This trend has continued, leading to newspaper headlines describing Belfast as 'the race-hate capital of Europe' (as reported, for example, in *The Guardian*, 10 January 2004 and *The Belfast Telegraph*, 16 October 2006). Research by Connolly and Keenan (2001) suggests that racial prejudice is, in fact, 'around twice as significant as sectarian prejudice in the initial attitudes of the population of Northern Ireland'. An academic article examining levels of bigotry in western countries also received considerable publicity when it revealed that in terms of attitudes to five minority groups 'the highest proportion of bigoted persons (bigotry count ratio) was in Northern Ireland and Greece' (Borooah & Mangan 2007, 305). (1) It seems very clear that many people in Northern Ireland have a problem when it comes to dealing with difference, and it is not surprising that observers have assumed that the experience of local separation has manifested itself in a broader general difficulty in accepting and respecting 'the other'.

Many organisations, including Non-Governmental Organisations (NGOs) and statutory bodies, have over the years worked to improve cross-community and inter-cultural relationships and legislation has also been set in place to this end. A law prohibiting incitement to hatred 'on grounds of religious belief, colour, race or ethnic or national origins' has been in force in Northern Ireland from 1970 and strengthened at various stages since, though there is a general recognition that while legislation may regulate behaviour it cannot necessarily affect attitudes. Section 75 of the 1998 Northern Ireland Act imposes a statutory duty on public authorities to ensure that they promote equality of opportunity and good relations, including 'between persons of different religious belief, political opinion [and] racial group' (HMSO, 1998). (Schools, however, have so far been exempt from Section 75 legislation, to the intense frustration of some equality and human rights groups.) Consequently much social, educational and community relations policy since the mid-1980s has focused on a 'hearts and minds' approach, reflecting a change in government policy at that time away from seeking a purely military/security solution to the region's problems. The purpose of this chapter is to examine how education in general, and Religious Education in particular, has contributed to this process, and to explore some positive options for future development.

EDUCATING FOR A SHARED FUTURE?

The education system in Northern Ireland, formally and informally, has attempted to play a positive role in addressing many of these issues of social and community conflict. In the spirit of the 1998 Belfast Agreement, which advocated 'the promotion of a culture of tolerance at every level in society' (NIO 1998, Section 6:13), government issued its *A Shared Future* policy in 2005, including the statement that: 'All schools should ensure through their policies, structures and curricula that pupils are consciously prepared for life in a diverse and inter-cultural society' (OFMDFM 2005, 2.4).

For some educators this was a welcome endorsement of what they had been attempting to do since the early 1970s. Educational interventions and initiatives over this period had stemmed from two main concerns: firstly the negative effects of almost total separation of children at a very formative age; secondly the growing belief that schools must actually tackle the issues of cultural difference and division in the curriculum. Strategies enabling children and young people from the different communities to meet and learn about each other, based on the Contact Hypothesis (Allport 1954; Amir 1969, etc.), were employed from the start of the Troubles and were strengthened by significant Department of Education funding from 1987 onwards.[2] In terms of the curriculum some schools participated in pilot schemes, testing out programmes developed by voluntary and academic groups which usually involved considering divisions in Northern Ireland in the context of a broader frame of reference (race relations; the Middle East; South Africa, etc.). With the introduction of the Northern Ireland Curriculum from the early 1990s (following the general pattern of the National Curriculum in England and Wales) six statutory Educational (Cross-Curricular) Themes were introduced, including *Education for Mutual Understanding* (EMU) and *Cultural Heritage*. These focused on self-esteem, relationships, cultural diversity and interdependence and teachers were encouraged to implement these themes through all the other subjects of the curriculum.

Undoubtedly some of these cross-community contact and curriculum initiatives have impacted positively on some young people and their teachers over the years, and work done in some schools has enabled a building up of trust and confidence as a basis for more challenging discussions and strengthened relationships. Contact schemes have, however, regularly been criticised as 'token', superficial or ineffective by others, sometimes justifiably. Research by the schools inspectorate (ETI 1999; 2000) and by academics (Smith & Robinson, 1996; Leitch and Kilpatrick, 2004; O'Connor, Hartop & McCully, 2002) has revealed the main obstacles to progress as being a reluctance on the part of many teachers to deal with the harder-edged, divisive issues, not least in subject areas such as History and RE, and a corresponding over-reliance on low-level contact programmes and 'softer' curriculum topics.[3] There is a clear need for such programmes to go well beyond polite superficialities and to deal with genuine issues in relation to learning to live with difference.

In the Revised Northern Ireland Curriculum (CCEA 2007), however, these issues have been given a more mainstream position. *Education for Mutual Understanding* (EMU) as a cross-curricular theme has given way to *Personal Development and Mutual Understanding* (PDMU) as one of six areas of learning in the primary curriculum, and *Local and Global Citizenship* is now in place for Key Stages 3 and 4. Both these areas deal explicitly and unambiguously with issues of diversity, equality, human rights and relationships in the community and can no longer be easily sidelined.

DIFFICULTIES WITH RELIGION IN EDUCATION

For some people religion in schools (particularly RE and assemblies for worship) is clearly regarded as part of the problem – a major obstacle to community cohesion – and it is not unusual to hear the suggestion that the situation would be considerably improved 'if religion was taken completely out of the schools'. Reporting on a conference on Northern Ireland's cultural traditions in 1989, a group of academics designated religion as 'one of the darkest regions in education' (Crozier 1989, 81). In the observation of Byrne & McKeown:

> 'Any examination of the current education system in Northern Ireland demonstrates that, in spite of the increasing secularization of society generally, the churches have continued to assert an important and continuing influence and authority' (Byrne & McKeown 1998, 322).

This influence has often been highlighted by the fact that the Department of Education and other statutory authorities have traditionally sought to deflect any public discussion of Religious Education on the grounds that this was 'the responsibility of the churches'.

Historically the Churches in Ireland were the educational providers before state provision, as in many other European countries, and a form of dual system has continued right up to the present in Northern Ireland. The Protestant churches transferred their former denominational schools into state control (thus the term 'controlled schools') following the 1930 Education Act, having ensured the retention of certain rights in relation to management and non-denominational Bible instruction. In the 1947 Education Act (which in many ways paralleled the English 1944 Act) these rights were maintained with provision for Religious Instruction 'based upon the Holy Scriptures according to some authoritative version or versions thereof'. This clause remains in force, although Religious Instruction was re-designated as Religious Education in the 1989 Education

Reform Order. Protestant clergy (Presbyterian, Methodist and Church of Ireland) also continue to have inspection rights in relation to RE in controlled schools, though these are now very seldom carried out.

The Catholic Church in Ireland has long maintained a very forthright position in favour of the continuation of a distinctive system to cater for Catholic children. In various documents the Catholic bishops and the Northern Ireland Council for Catholic Maintained Schools have emphasised their commitment to diversity, inclusion and equality (CCMS undated); at the same time, however, they have expressed strong opposition to the idea of integrated education and Catholic families with children attending integrated schools have often felt themselves to be treated unequally by the Church (Macaulay 2009). The Church originally contributed to capital and maintenance costs in exchange for the right to teach confessionally, but since 1993 this sector has been fully publicly funded while yet retaining all its rights in relation to religious teaching.

Since the early 1990s Northern Ireland has had a statutory 'Core Syllabus for Religious Education' prepared, at the request of government, by the four largest Christian denominations (Catholic, Presbyterian, Church of Ireland and Methodist). Many applauded this apparently generous ecumenical co-operation and perceived it as a significant step forward for education and good relationships in the Province. The idea of a 'core' syllabus was that there would be a common body of material taught in all schools, beyond which schools could add additional material if they wished, depending on what was permissible within their school type. While some in the government clearly hoped that this would encourage ongoing co-operation and sharing, leading to better understanding and relationships, the Catholic bishops quickly made it clear that everything in the Core Syllabus was already in their existing catechetical programmes – in other words, that nothing needed to change in the Catholic schools. The only place where the Core Syllabus made any kind of impact was in the controlled schools, which for the first time had to follow a common programme.

The almost unanimous decision of the Churches' Working Group was to produce an exclusively Christian syllabus, a decision which was ultimately endorsed by government despite many representations from minority faith communities and others. The Core Syllabus (DENI/HMSO 1993) included a phrase in one of its attainment targets that 'pupils should develop ... sensitivity towards the beliefs of others', and its proponents acknowledged that schools could teach about 'other religions' if they wished, but schools found that there was more than enough content in the Syllabus itself and with only a few exceptions such possibilities were ignored. For the most part the 1993 syllabus simply sustained a narrow, conservative status quo in relation to RE and failed to respond to the challenges of a divided society and one which, even then, was increasingly diverse.

A decade later government repeated its invitation to the same four Christian denominations to prepare a Revised Core Syllabus, though this time they were pressed to include some teaching of world religions. Once again, however, an exclusively Christian Working Party was established – even in the case of the sub-committee on world religions – and there was no attempt to discuss anything with members of other faith communities until after the revised syllabus had been drawn up. Having agreed to include world religions only at Key Stage 3, the Working Party adopted a defensive tone and emphasised the importance of 'maintaining the essential Christian character of Religious Education' (Churches' Working Party 2003, 4) and dismissively added that the study of other faiths 'will require only a modest amount of teaching time in each year of key stage 3' (*op cit*, 11). More extensive teaching of world religions, including to primary school pupils, was rejected by the Churches on the grounds that it would cause confusion, citing Barnes' critique of the RE system in England (Barnes 2002, 28f) as evidence for such fears.[4] One brief clause in the Key Stage 2 syllabus does actually state that teachers should 'provide opportunities for pupils to ... be aware of and have respect for differing cultures and faiths' (DE 2007, 19), but offers no indication of what this might involve or how it could be done.

This Revised Core Syllabus, which was eventually accepted by government without any amendment to the Churches' proposals, was perhaps an even greater disappointment than the original version. The Minister of Education, in approving the Syllabus, wrote effusively that it 'will help to better prepare [sic] our young people to deal with the challenges of life and work in today's global society' (DE 2006). Despite the (limited) inclusion of world religions and the clause about promoting 'sensitivity towards the beliefs of others', the Syllabus (DE 2007) represents a lost opportunity on the part of the Churches and the Department of Education and a failure to exemplify genuine ecumenical co-operation and the possibility of partnership with other faith communities. Published as an unelaborated listing of predominantly Biblical material, it lacks vision and imagination and appears to have little to offer in respect of helping children and young people to understand and deal creatively with local and global religious diversity.

Observation and research on RE in Northern Ireland, though not extensive, bears out many of these concerns. Student teachers regularly report their dismay with the quality of RE found particularly in controlled primary schools – teachers avoiding the subject or swapping with a colleague perceived to be 'more religious'; using timetabled RE slots for other work; unwillingness to move beyond a small repertoire of very familiar Bible stories; low-level activities such as word searches; lack of any treatment of religious diversity (Richardson 2008c). One student recorded that her placement school: 'was fairly multicultural, but it was clear that the attitude was that this was a Christian-ethos school and if you come here you will simply accept that and be part of it or opt out.' (*op cit*, 7) Another observed that:

> 'Religion was regarded as a subject that was not easy to discuss, and there seemed to be a sense of not talking about or sharing personal experiences. … By neglecting the subject pupils may find it hard to discuss religion and become more open to diversity.' (*op cit*, 5)

The Northern Ireland Education and Training Inspectorate has no right to inspect RE in schools unless requested by a board of governors, which happens only rarely. This means that the controlled schools sector in particular lacks any effective quality control in relation to RE. In the Catholic schools RE is undoubtedly treated with much greater consistency and seriousness, but anecdotal evidence suggests that the predominance of 'faith formation' leaves little time for any significant consideration of religious diversity.

CHALLENGES FOR TEACHERS

Teachers are a crucial element in any educational initiative, though it has been argued that in a divided society like Northern Ireland, teachers are in many ways one of the most disadvantaged groups, having been educated in separate schools, in many cases trained separately and then having returned to teach within a separate system (Richardson 2008a, 42; 2008b, 15f). It is hardly surprising, therefore, that many are reluctant to tackle issues with their pupils that they have never themselves had the opportunity, confidence or skills to discuss with their cross-community peers.

A study of the experiences of minority faith parents (Richardson 2003b) revealed that when approached about the cultural and religious needs of children, many teachers did not know how to respond. Research among student RE teachers from both Catholic and Protestant backgrounds (Richardson 2003a; 2006) evidenced a lack of even basic knowledge of religious traditions other than their own. While there was a definite willingness to engage more with religious and cultural diversity issues, the general feeling of many of the students was that they were thwarted by limited prior experience and the anticipation of continuing limited opportunities. Opportunities to address this within initial teacher education have been improving, though progress is uneven, but the situation in continuing professional development is considerably less certain due to a severe shortage of personnel and an unwillingness to focus any significant training outside of the strict requirements of the RE Core Syllabus. There is clearly still a long way to go in the process of developing teacher competencies appropriate to this crucial area of education.

POSITIVE INITIATIVES IN RELIGIOUS EDUCATION

While the official approaches to Religious Education have been seen to leave much to be desired, the subject has nevertheless played a role in the process of educating for improved community understanding and relationships, thanks particularly to a number of unofficial initiatives. In the 1970s John Greer, a lecturer at the (New) University of Ulster, worked with RE teachers from both communities and Catholic colleagues to develop a programme of studies to enable post-primary pupils to explore similarities and differences in the various Christian denominations, leading to publications for pupils and teachers entitled 'Irish Christianity' (Greer & McElhinney 1985). Greer's work, which later developed into a cross-community training programme for RE teachers focusing on skills in classroom discussion (McElhinney, Harris & Greer 1988), was greatly valued by a small core of progressively-minded RE teachers, but dismissed (and even derided) by some of the professional RE Advisers in the Education and Library Boards (Northern Ireland's local education authorities).

At around the same time an ecumenical peace education initiative established by the (Protestant) Irish Council of Churches and the (Catholic) Irish Commission for Justice and Peace was developing a range of resources for primary school pupils, including 'Looking at Churches and Worship in Ireland' (ICC/ICJP 1985; revised 1992), which also focused on learning from similarities and differences in church traditions. This resource was piloted and later taken up by a much wider range of schools than had been anticipated, including many in the post-primary sector. The limitation of programmes of this kind, however, was that they were ahead of their time and not perceived as being within the mainstream of Religious Education.

Encouragingly the 1993 RE Core Syllabus required pupils at Key Stage 4 to study 'Christian practice and worship in two traditions', presumably with the intention that this would include both Catholic and Protestant traditions (though it was pointed out by some that Key Stage 4 was far too late to be starting such work). Nelson (2004, 254-5) has demonstrated, however, that a significant minority (40%) of controlled schools chose to avoid including the Catholic Church in their study, opting instead for two contrasting Protestant denominations, noting that 'there seems to be an emphasis on choosing what is familiar ... and is considered "safe"'. In fairness it should be pointed out that this 'loophole' was closed by the 2007 Revised Core Syllabus, which (in one of its wiser decisions) specified study of 'the Roman Catholic tradition and at least one Protestant tradition' (DE 2007, 34).

Some individual schools have taken a more adventurous approach to RE in terms of its capacity to develop awareness and mutual respect, notably though not exclusively in the integrated schools sector. A number of post-primary schools acknowledged the importance of teaching topics on both Christian diversity and world religions long before it was required in the 2007 Core Syllabus, and saw this within the context of education for mutual respect and understanding. Some primary schools have similarly adopted a much broader approach, sometimes involving parents, often focusing on diverse festivals and special times and including visits to various places of worship. Yet such examples so far still represent the exceptions to the norm.

RE apart, the opportunities presented by Northern Ireland's Revised Curriculum in relation to exploring cultural diversity and intercultural relationships are steadily helping teachers to move into topics that were previously regarded with discomfort and caution. It is one of the ironies of this situation, however, that particularly for primary schools the issues around religious and cultural diversity that are omitted from the RE Core Syllabus can now be taught quite legitimately through PDMU and other 'non-RE' areas.

TOWARDS A NEW VISION FOR RE

Religious Education is not a panacea for the world's ills, but it nevertheless has an important role to play as a dimension of education for intercultural awareness and inclusion. Connolly, Smith and Kelly (2002, 51) have emphasised that:

'... schools need to ensure that they develop and foster an inclusive ethos. They certainly have a responsibility to encourage meaningful cross-

225

community contact and to create an environment within which difference and cultural diversity are valued and respected'.

This holds true for RE as it does for all other dimensions of education, and to work towards this in Northern Ireland we will need a renewed vision and a commitment to a much more proactive programme which will have particular implications for classroom teachers, for whole school policy and for government and its agencies.

For teachers of RE a key skill is the capacity to speak openly and comfortably about religious and cultural difference. Many people feel awkward about discussing religion for fear that they will 'offend someone'. Teachers who cannot or will not talk about religious difference are passing on a subtle but unhelpful message that perpetuates the culture of avoidance. If children and young people are to learn that it is possible to talk about differences and to be able to disagree while maintaining respect for the person who is different or who thinks differently, they need to see this behaviour modelled by teachers.

At a whole school level awareness of, and openness to, difference must be evident to the entire school community. An ethos of respect for difference will reveal itself in many ways – in the way a school welcomes its members and visitors; in the visual images that are displayed; in inclusive and fair pastoral structures; in school assemblies and community events. Ethos is also emphasised in the *Toledo Guiding Principles on Teaching About Religions and Beliefs in Public Schools*:

> 'Effective teaching about religions and beliefs also benefits from a school ethos that focuses on human rights and democratic principles, intercultural respect and understanding, ... a safe learning environment for all students, and critical thinking' (OSCE/ODIHR 2007, 61)

The skills and practices required for good quality RE teaching are actually important in relation to the whole curriculum and relate closely to the key principles of intercultural learning – what the Council of Europe (2008, 4.3) has termed 'intercultural competences'. These involve teaching and learning strategies in managing conflict creatively and dealing with controversial issues, including the recognition of conflicting truth claims. Religious learning must engage children both intellectually and affectively, helping them to understand that some differences and conflicts cannot be resolved and to learn ways of living peacefully with life's many uncertainties and differences. This process needs to start early in the school years if it is to become a part of natural attitude development, informed by expanding knowledge and experience; it is too important to be left 'until they are older'. All of this needs to be a key dimension of teacher education and professional development, and not just for RE specialists.

The continuing reality of educational separation, while not exclusive to Northern Ireland, remains one of the greatest obstacles to the development of informed mutual respect and community cohesion. This author is persuaded by the evidence that shared or integrated schooling is effective and eminently preferable to separation, but it is clear that this will not change quickly and therefore cannot be the only strategy. So long as schooling continues to be substantially separate there will be a need for processes of purposeful meeting and sharing, based on awareness of the flaws of past practice in cross-community contact programmes. Teachers have sometimes indicated that because their school is not 'mixed' or does not include children from different ethnic backgrounds they do not need to be concerned with diversity issues in RE. But surely such schools are actually *most particularly* in need of diversity awareness and of opportunities for interaction and mutual learning with their peers from a range of other cultural and religious backgrounds. A Religious Education that does no more than reinforce stereotypes, even if only by the exclusion of alternative beliefs and practices, is surely a very dangerous thing.

For such processes to be developed effectively beyond the level of just a few enthusiasts it will be necessary for the Department of Education to show that it takes RE much more seriously as an important player in education for a shared future. As long as RE hovers uncertainly at the edges of the curriculum, somehow belonging more to the care of the Churches than to the mainstream of education, then this will be difficult to achieve. Government must take a proactive role in urging the Churches into a broad and genuine partnership with other faith communities and other interest groups. This was the thinking of the Northern Ireland Inter-Faith Forum when it called for:

> '... all educators, including those from the churches and the other faith communities, to commit themselves enthusiastically in dialogue and partnership to this task of developing an education system which contributes to the establishment of a fair and just society in Northern Ireland for all sections of the community'. (NIIFF, 2001)

To many people outside Northern Ireland the community conflicts of the recent past must have seemed remote and anachronistic, especially when religion was perceived to play a significant role in the situation. More recent global events have perhaps helped to set things in a different light, however, and international agencies have begun to recognise the importance of encouraging informed and reflexive attitudes towards religious diversity at all levels in society, not least education. The argument that religion is too divisive and should thereby be excluded from schools seems much less tenable in such times, as it runs the risk of perpetuating avoidance and unawareness.

In this process Northern Ireland has much to learn from the experience of other parts of the UK and the wider world – but perhaps some of the long and difficult learning processes that RE in Northern Ireland is still going through can help to inform this debate in other places too.

NOTES

1. Borooah and Mangan's five groups were 'people from another race, immigrants or foreign workers, Muslims, Jews, homosexuals' and the responses were based on the question: 'Would you like to have persons from this group as your neighbour?'

2. Now known as the Schools' *Community Relations Programme*, this funding is available to schools who agree to work together on a programme of encounter-based activities according to established criteria.

3. A primary school principal once reported to the author his frustration with the Protestant minister who was the chair of the school governors and who had agreed reluctantly to permit a contact programme to go ahead but with the insistence that the children should not under any circumstances be allowed to talk about religion!

4. Barnes only hinted in this paper at a critique which he developed much more strongly in subsequent articles, but it was clearly enough for the Churches' Working Group to hang onto in their desire to reject anything remotely like the English system.

REFERENCES

Allport, G. W. (1954) *The Nature of Prejudice*, Reading, Mass: Addison-Wesley.

Amir, Y. (1969) 'Contact hypothesis in ethnic relations', *Psychological Bulletin*, 71, 319-342.

Barnes, L. P. (2002) 'World Religions and the Northern Ireland Curriculum', *Journal of Beliefs & Values*, 23(1), 19-32

Borooah, V. K. and Mangan, J. (2007) 'Love Thy Neighbour: How Much Bigotry is there in Western Countries?' in *Kyklos: International Review for Social Sciences*, 60/3, 295-317, Oxford: Blackwell

Byrne, G. and McKeown, P. (1988) 'Schooling, the churches and the state in Northern Ireland: a continuing tension?' in *Research Papers in Education* 13(3), 319-340, London, Routledge

CCEA (2007) *The Northern Ireland Curriculum*, Belfast, Council for Curriculum, Examinations and Assessment

CCMS (undated – 2006) *Diversity and Inclusion in Catholic Maintained Schools*, Holywood, Council for Catholic Maintained Schools

Churches' Working Party (2003) *Proposals for a Revised Core Syllabus in RE in Grant-Aided Schools in Northern Ireland*, The Churches' Religious Education Core Syllabus Review Working Party

Connolly, P. and Keenan, M. (2001) *The Hidden Truth: Racist Harassment in Northern Ireland*, Belfast, Northern Ireland Statistics and Research Agency

Connolly, P. Smith, A. and Kelly, B. (2002) *Too Young to Notice? The Cultural and Political Awareness of 3-6 Year Olds in Northern Ireland*, Belfast, Community Relations Council

Council of Europe (2008) *White Paper on Intercultural Dialogue – Living together as equals in dignity*, Strasbourg, Council of Europe Ministers of Foreign Affairs

Crozier, M. (ed) (1989) *Cultural Traditions in Northern Ireland: Varieties of Irishness*, Belfast: Institute of Irish Studies, Queen's University

DE (2006) *Minister's response to the proposals for a revised core syllabus*, Bangor: Department of Education for Northern Ireland (http://www.deni.gov.uk/minister_s_response-8.pdf – accessed 28/08/2009)

DE (2007) *Core Syllabus for Religious Education*, Bangor: Department of Education

DENI/HMSO (1993) *The Northern Ireland Curriculum: Core Syllabus for Religious Education*, Bangor: Department of Education for Northern Ireland

ETI/DE (1999) *Report on the Educational Themes: Primary Inspections* 1998-99, Crown Copyright 1999, Bangor: Education & Training Inspectorate, Department of Education

ETI/DE (2000) *Report of a Survey of Provision for Education for Mutual Understanding (EMU) in Post-Primary Schools* (Inspected: 1999/2000), Crown Copyright 2000, Bangor: Education & Training Inspectorate, Department of Education

Greer, J. E. and McElhinney, E. P. (1985) *Irish Christianity: Five Units for Secondary Pupils and A Guide for Teachers*, Dublin: Gill & Macmillan

ICC/ICJP (1985; 1992) *Looking at Churches and Worship in Ireland*, Belfast, *Irish Council of Churches* / Dublin: Irish Commission for Justice and Peace – Joint Peace Education Programme

Leitch, R. and Kilpatrick, R. (2004) 'Teachers' and Pupils' Educational Experiences and School-Based Responses to the Conflict in Northern Ireland', *Journal of Social Issues* 60 (3), 563-586

Macaulay, T. (2009) *Churches and Christian Ethos in Integrated Schools*, Macaulay Associates – Report commissioned by the Northern Ireland Council for Integrated Education (web published: http://cain.ulst.ac.uk/issues/education/docs/macaulay270109.pdf – accessed 27/08/2009).

McElhinney, E. P., Harris, J. E. and Greer, J. E. (1987) *Classroom Discussion: New Approaches to Teaching in Religious Education – Final Report of the Project Teaching Religion in Northern Ireland*, Coleraine: University of Ulster.

Nelson, J. (2004) 'Uniformity and Diversity in Religious Education in Northern Ireland', *British Journal of Religious Education*, 26 (3), 249-258

NIIFF (2001) *A Statement on Religious Education*, issued January 2001, Belfast: Northern Ireland Inter-Faith Forum

NIO (1998) *The Belfast Agreement – Section 6: Rights, Safeguards and Equality of Opportunity*, Northern Ireland Office (http://www.nio.gov.uk/agreement.pdf – accessed 26/08/2009)

O'Connor, Hartop, B. and McCully, A. (2002) *The Schools Community Relations Programme: A Review*, Bangor, DENI

OFMDFM (2005) *A Shared Future: Policy and Strategic Framework for Good Relations in Northern Ireland*, Belfast: Office of the First Minister and Deputy First Minister

OSCE/ODIHR (2007) *Toledo Guiding Principles on Teaching About Religions and Beliefs in Public Schools*, Warsaw: OSCE Office for Democratic Institutions and Human Rights

Richardson, N. (2003a) *Religious Diversity in Northern Ireland: Questions and Challenges for Educators* (paper given at the Educational Studies

230

Association Ireland conference: St Mary's University College, Belfast, April 2003)

Richardson, N. (2003b) *Curricular, Faith and Pastoral Issues for Minority Faith Children in Northern Ireland Schools: The Views of Their Parents* (paper given at the Diversity, World Faiths and Education Conference, Belfast, November 2003)

Richardson, N. (2006) *Student Teachers and Religious Education* (paper given at the 2006 AULRE Conference, Stranmillis University College, Belfast)

Richardson, N. (2008a) 'Education for Religious Tolerance: the Impossible Dream?' in Patalon, M. (ed), *Tolerance and Education – Studia Kulturowa* 2/2008: 39-53, Pedagogical Institute, University of Gdansk (web published: http://studia.kulturowe.ug.gda.pl/sk-2.pdf – accessed 28/08/2009)

Richardson, N. (2008b) 'The Challenge of the New: Education, Religion and Citizenship in a Traditional and Conflicted Society – a case study of Northern Ireland', in Lähnemann, J. and Schreiner, P. (eds), *Interreligious and Values Education in Europe*, Münster, Germany: Comenius-Institut & Peace Education Standing Commission of Religions for Peace

Richardson, N. (2008c) *Student Teachers' Perceptions of Primary Religious Education in Northern Ireland Schools* – paper given at the 2008 AULRE Conference, Homerton College, Cambridge (web published: Research Resources for RE, Stranmillis University College – http://www.stran.ac.uk/informationabout/research/researchresourcesfor re/)

Smith, A. and Robinson, A. (1996) *Education for Mutual Understanding: The Initial Statutory Years*, Coleraine: University of Ulster Centre for the Study of Conflict.

CHAPTER 14

THE CONTRIBUTION OF LOCAL AUTHORITIES AND THEIR SACRES TO PROMOTING COMMUNITY COHESION THROUGH RELIGIOUS EDUCATION

Joyce Miller

SUMMARY

I N THIS CHAPTER, a case study is presented of work carried out in Education Bradford from 2000 that brings together religious education, community cohesion, race equality and citizenship. The key concepts of their community cohesion strategy are presented and their reliance upon and congruence with religious education is noted. Four aspects of the situation at the beginning of the decade – riots, reports, RE and race equality – are introduced and compared with the current situation when community cohesion is conflated with preventing violent extremism and the implications of this for RE are discussed. Finally, two main ways forward are suggested: increased emphasis on the social and political dimensions of religion and an identification of and response to the barriers to community cohesion in religious education.

INTRODUCTION

Early in this decade Bradford declared that it was a contender for the 2008 European Capital of Culture and began a high profile campaign under the slogan *'One landscape, many views'*. During the campaign there was an almost palpable sense of community pride and optimism so rarely felt in a District that is in desperate need of economic and social regeneration. Regrettably, the bid failed but the slogan has remained and it neatly encapsulates the extraordinary and varied place that Bradford is – 60% rural with tiny village schools; wealthy towns, such as Ilkley, with correspondingly high house prices; inner city areas suffering from multiple social deprivation largely because of the loss of the wool trade from which Bradford has not yet recovered. It is also a city that is ethnically mixed though the numbers are lower than many realise: the number of its Black, Indian and Bangladeshi residents is relatively small and the total minority ethnic populations of Bradford constituted just over 21% at the 2001 census. The Pakistani-heritage population, which is the largest minority group, is often portrayed as 'fundamentally flawed' and in need of reform (Alam and Husband 2006, 17) and terms such as 'parallel lives' and 'sleepwalking into segregation' are applied too readily by some politicians and community leaders. Bradford is also infamous for its 'affairs' – the 'Honeyford affair' and the 'Rushdie affair' – adding yet more negative perceptions.

Despite – or perhaps because of – these challenges, there is energy to improve Bradford and there is celebration of its religiously and ethnically diverse nature. There is also an increasing number of critiques of policy and public discourse, mainly from local academics, challenging the assumptions from which Bradford's image has suffered for so long.[1]

Community cohesion has been high on the political agenda, both locally and nationally, since the Cantle report of 2001, commissioned in the wake of the riots in Bradford and other northern towns. Local politicians seized the concept eagerly and worked to promote a safer and stronger community, linking it firmly to economic regeneration (Burnett 2008, 45). Cohesion, social or community, remains a complex concept but is here to stay though understanding of its meaning continues to change, as we shall see.

There are aspects of community cohesion with which few would argue in principle, such as the characteristics of a cohesive community as set out by the Local Government Authority (LGA) in 2002, and widely used since:

- a common vision and sense of belonging for all;
- the diversity of people's different backgrounds and circumstances is appreciated and positively valued;
- those from different backgrounds have similar life opportunities;
- strong and positive relationships are being developed between people from different backgrounds in the workplace, in schools and within neighbourhoods.

Clearly these refer to all communities and to all citizens and they are there to be translated into policy and action by all agencies, public and private, corporate and individual. They apply to education and, therefore, to religious education and there is a moral imperative on all schools (as well as an OfSTED duty) to envisage and enable their contribution to a more cohesive and just society. There may be some danger in educationists believing that RE's content is sufficient or that its contribution should be focused on only the second characteristic above when, in fact, it has a broader and deeper role to play. It is also only one part of a whole school and whole curriculum approach, and it cannot be separated out. This is why community cohesion policies have to be created and supported by all members of the school community.

COMMUNITY COHESION STRATEGY

In the development of Education Bradford's community cohesion strategy in 2004, we realised that the process we undertook was at least as important as the product and it took a small team of people several working days to complete the task. Although we were colleagues, this was the first time that we had worked together on a specific project and we realised that we could only make real progress if we shared common understandings. The group was very diverse: three women and one man; two ethnic minority and two white; we came from three different continents with our forebears from at least one other; we were from four religious backgrounds with a fifth through 'conversion'; we spoke eight different languages along with a working knowledge of four 'liturgical' languages. We spent a whole afternoon talking about who we thought we were – our 'identities' and what we understood by 'community' in community cohesion.

'Identity' and 'community'

These last two terms, identity and community, became key concepts in our strategy, more accurately expressed in their plural form, as we articulated an understanding of them as multiple, organic, changing and multi-faceted. Each of us has many aspects to our identity, expressed in a number of cognate terms: 'multiple identity', the government's favoured term (e.g. Home Office 2004, 7; DfES 2007, 29) or 'hyphenated identity' (Cooper & Lodge 2008, 13) or 'hybrid identity' (Davies 2008, 33). Similarly, we all belong to many communities in which different aspects of our identity take precedence. Bradford is not a single community, it is rather a 'community of communities'. The 'Muslim community' is not a homogeneous entity but is multi-ethnic, multi-linguistic and multi-national with different social classes and ages who possess different levels of wealth and education. In other words, it is as divergent as most other communities and any attempt to present it otherwise is fraught with danger and runs counter to the promotion of community cohesion.

'Skilled cultural navigators'

We took each of the four characteristics of a cohesive community from the LGA's descriptors and we developed a vision of what each would look like when applied to an educational setting. Next, we set out an action plan on how they could be achieved. In the process of doing that we identified other key concepts, one of the most significant of which was borrowed from Roger Ballard – 'skilled cultural navigators' (1994) – though it may have been more accurate to use the phrase 'skilled inter-cultural navigators'. It was our aim that:

> 'Everyone involved in education will have the confidence to become 'skilled cultural navigators', aware of their own identities and communities, and willing to engage with openness and empathy with the identity (ies) and community (ies) of others.'

In order to do this, everyone needs to have the opportunity to visit communities, meet community members and engage in conversation to understand what it means to be a member of that community, to identify commonalities and to begin, hopefully, to respect differences. What this means is that rather than religious education being a contributor to cohesion, it lay at the heart of our strategy because one of the main methodologies we drew on is from an approach to the study of religions, ethnography, and its concomitant pedagogy in religious education, the interpretive approach (Jackson 1997, 2000). It was through the methods employed in ethnographic approaches to the study of religion, such as participant observation, that significant parts of our community cohesion strategy could be realised.

The REDCo project

In 2006 Education Bradford was invited to join the REDCo project – 'Religion in Education: A contribution to dialogue or a factor of conflict in transforming societies of European countries' – for which the interpretive approach forms the theoretical basis. One of the reasons for accepting this invitation was that it gave an opportunity to see if the community cohesion strategy we had developed worked in practice. Senior managers at one of our secondary schools indicated willingness for their school to take part, not least because it was in the process of becoming a humanities specialist college and they were keen to improve the school's relationship with its local communities. What followed, over the next year, was a series of continuing professional development experiences for the staff of the humanities faculty when, following the principles of the interpretive approach and using ethnographic-style methods, teachers engaged with their communities through interview and participant observation. In whole days off-site, they went to community centres and places of worship, they talked to community leaders and interviewed representatives of religious communities and shared, among themselves, the issues and questions that were raised. These included the difference between religion and culture, diversity within religious groups and divisions between them, the place of women in Islam and other complex questions. The teachers worked with unfailing interest and enthusiasm, despite their frustration at not receiving uniform answers from their various informants. They did, however, understand more fully the complexity and diversity within their school's communities. As one of them said, she now had 'A bit more clarity and a bit more confusion'. The teachers became, according to senior staff interviewed six months later, far more confident in dealing with controversial issues in the classroom. Although this project was conducted in a mainly Muslim school, it is totally transferable to all schools in all settings where there is a need to develop a deeper understanding of the local communities (Miller 2009).

THE SITUATION IN 2001 – THE FOUR R'S

Although I would argue that all communities need a cohesion strategy, there appeared to be an urgent need for one in Bradford, not least because of the events that occurred in 2001. In the history of community cohesion, that was a highly significant year.

Riots and reports

The riots in northern towns led to two major reports, the 'Cantle Report' (2001) and the 'Denham Report' (2001), the first focusing on local and the second on national government responses to the very serious events that had occurred earlier that year. Coincidentally, the 'Ouseley Report' (2001) was published at the time the riots took place, having been commissioned by the local strategic partnership to review race and community relations. It paints a very dismal picture, highlighting seven different sets of fears within Bradford. There have since been criticisms of the review team's methods and outcomes. Alam and Husband state:

> '... in a study based on consultation rather than systemic research, this dominant paradigm of a city living under a generic mantle of fear was a tendentious contribution to policy development' (Alam and Husband 2006, 3).

In a linked publication, Alam writes of the:

> '...oddly uncontroversial Ouseley report ... [which] focuses on ethnicity as the principle (sic) marker of community, largely neglecting social class, income and even neighbourhood.' (Alam 2006, 18).

This stance, adopted by Ouseley, Cantle and others of self-segregating communities living in fear of each other, has shaped public discourse on community cohesion (and related policy matters) and is now seriously contested. I regret that my own understanding of these issues has only been developed more fully in retirement.

The first of Ouseley's recommendations in his report, *Community Pride not Prejudice*, was that Bradford should develop its own citizenship curriculum, even though it had only just been introduced as a requirement for secondary schools, following the work of Bernard Crick. In response to this, we created our 'Enhanced Citizenship Curriculum' (Education Bradford 2003; Miller 2005, 2006a; Richardson and Wood 2004). Although Crick had quoted the Policy Studies Institute that 'an explicit idea of multi-cultural citizenship needs to be formulated for Britain' (Crick 1998, 17) there is little in his report or in the subsequent National Curriculum 2000 to enable this to happen. There is reference to, for example, 'equality and diversity' (44) but, crucially, the attainment targets make no mention of these or related concepts. One of our first tasks, therefore, was to add to the attainment targets and to include key concepts, skills and knowledge that would help promote race equality and respect for difference. As well as developing our own curriculum, we took some of the existing study units from the National Curriculum and developed them further. For example, from 'Britain a Diverse Society', we prepared three study units:

- Identity and Community in the Bradford District (Year 7)
- Diversity in Great Britain (Year 8)
- A Global Community (Year 9)

In each of these we addressed some of the key issues that the Ouseley report had raised and asked teachers and their students to explore some hard questions about living in Bradford and to develop a vision of society for the future. Where possible, we aimed for congruence between Citizenship and RE and the Standing Advisory Council of RE (SACRE) was used as a consultative body. The first study unit in the RE local agreed syllabus for secondary schools, for example, is 'Religion in the Locality' which fits well with the first Citizenship study unit for Year 7.

Religious Education

In 2001, the local agreed syllabus for RE was reviewed and significant changes made to existing practice. Bradford has a long and distinguished history in promoting multi-faith RE, not least through its Interfaith Education Centre, and there was a tradition of thematic RE. The Agreed Syllabus Conference endorsed this approach believing that in an area such as Bradford this was the best way of creating the balance between emphasising commonality and respecting difference. One of the main changes in the syllabus was to reduce the number of study units to be taught in any year to three to enable pupils and their teachers to engage in religious enquiry in much greater depth. The syllabus requires that all major faiths should be taught during the primary and the secondary phases of education, enabling a developing understanding of religions by pupils. There was a greater emphasis on progression and differentiated expectations were developed for each study unit and each stage (we split key stage 2 into lower and upper). These were carefully framed to enable the achievement of the level descriptors which were set out in two attainment targets, each with three strands. While these are based on national guidance they were carefully rephrased in order to be entirely congruent with the expectations and content of Bradford's syllabus.

We were pleased with the outcome of an OfSTED inspection of SACRE in 2003, when it concluded that the syllabus was of 'a very high quality' and that 'the standards set are challenging'. In the 2006 revision, we went a step further and showed how each of the strands within the levels of both attainment targets could be assessed through the suggested content and the illustrative teaching and learning strategies set out in each of the primary study units. We also demonstrated links across the curriculum in order to support teachers.

The phrase 'broad and balanced curriculum' dominated our thinking in the writing of the 2001 syllabus: it was for us important that all the major religions should be included, that a range of approaches to the study of religions should be employed, along with different ways of learning. Significantly, our aims included key words: conceptual understanding, informed appreciation, richness of religions, commonality, sensitivity, valuing diversity, and creating meaning. All of these are congruent with the characteristics of a cohesive community as set out by the LGA, though we would always insist that RE is more than community cohesion, however rich a contribution it might make to it.

One of our best ideas during the review of the agreed syllabus in 2001 was to involve young people which Ofsted described as 'an exciting innovation'. We were involving teachers and seeking their views: why not ask the same questions of the recipients of the syllabus? We ran a student Agreed Syllabus Conference for a day, which proved so successful that we decided to establish a student SACRE, with the help of an award of £3,000 from the National Association of SACREs and the St Peter's Saltley Trust (Gates 2006). The original idea was to have a 'shadow' SACRE but it proved impossibly difficult to find young people to fill all the roles; nonetheless, we ran the student SACRE successfully for a number of years and facilitated contact between young people from across the District in a safe, neutral environment where they were able to explore questions of religion and belief and aspects of living in a multi-ethnic environment.

> 'Wise words and a commitment to a future full of respect, toleration and working together.' This is what you will hear if you sit down with 'sensible, sane young people', said the then Bishop of Bradford in the House of Lords in April 2002, the week after he had been their guest at an 'Any Questions?' session.

The Student SACRE attracted a good deal of media interest, including a feature on Radio 4 and the request for an article from the *Times Educational Supplement* (Miller 2003). The idea was quickly adopted, and developed, by other SACREs. The conference the students organized for both the adult and students SACREs on refugees and asylum seekers was the highlight of the project and gave further evidence of the Bishop's words.

The Student SACRE was the one of several projects in which Education Bradford brought students together from different schools. One of the most successful was the Schools Linking Project, now an independent national organization, still based in Bradford.[2] Another project brought together pupils from a range of primary schools in the '7,000 hours' project when, with a Westhill/ NASACRE grant, pupils surveyed attitudes to collective worship within their schools.[3] With the Professional Council for RE (PCfRE) we ran a major project called *Respect for All*, with funding, first from the QCA and then the DfES. This brought together eight secondary schools from four different local authorities to work together on joint projects to promote community cohesion, in collaboration with a City Learning Centre whose technical expertise helped us to devise innovative and exciting approaches to learning, including the students making DVDs of themselves as a means of introduction to their partner school. This was one of the ways of initiating dialogue which was one of the key concepts that underpinned this work through exchanging stories, through drama and through joint visits to places of worship. It would be wrong to suggest that the project developed smoothly and according to plan: there were many glitches along the way; we lost some schools and LEAs and we gained new ones; some projects came to fruition and others did not. Nonetheless, the levels of commitment and engagement from staff and students alike were evidence that not only is such work worth doing, there was (and remains) an urgent need for it (Miller 2006b). One of the ways in which this project was supported was a series of DVDs on places of worship in Bradford, linking to the government's current agenda on learning outside the classroom.[4] Bradford's Interfaith Education Centre makes a significant contribution to this with more than 21,000 pupils visiting a place of worship last year.

Race equality

In the Foreword to the edition of *REsource* that was dedicated to the *Respect for All project*, John Keast wrote that the title was created by the QCA in the wake of the Macpherson report following the death of Stephen Lawrence. That report resulted in the Race Relations Amendment Act (RRAA) (2000) – the first change in race equality legislation since 1976 – and required schools to have both a race equality policy and a race equality action plan. This was something that Bradford, along with other local authorities, took very seriously and significant support and challenge went into the promotion of race equality. It is interesting to note that as late as 2004, in his second major report on community cohesion, Ted Cantle stated that community cohesion and race equality are 'synonymous' (2004, 57). In five short years, we seem to have moved a very long way and a different understanding of community cohesion now dominates public discourse. There is apparently little political focus on the elimination of racism, including the institutional racism that was such a dominant theme at the beginning of the decade. Islamophobia and anti-Semitism are increasing and this is not the time to ignore the imperative to challenge all forms of racism.

THE SITUATION IN 2009

In November 2007, in a statement to the House of Commons, the Prime Minister affirmed the importance of religious education and the teaching of world religions. This was not in a speech on education nor even community cohesion but on national security.[5] In January the following year I made a quip at the QCA/NASACRE conference saying that, for the first time, RE had become a form of counter-terrorism. I would not make that quip now, nor would an audience laugh, because that is precisely where RE now finds itself in the national *Prevent* agenda.

In 2008 the DCSF published a 'toolkit' for schools on preventing extremism (2008). In many respects, it is a rather bland document which tries hard not to focus entirely on Islam and which provides whole-school guidance including leadership and curriculum. There is some focus on religious education and its importance in addressing, for example, 'violent extremist narratives' (2008, 28). This is also one of the key requirements in the DCSF's invitation to tender document for a project to prevent violent extremism and promote community cohesion, aimed at RE teachers through a continuing professional development programme. That tender was won by the Religious Education Council of England and Wales (REC), which, despite its reservations about the Prevent agenda, believed (rightly) that it was the best organisation to deliver such training with sensitivity and awareness of its potential dangers.[6] This is now known as the *REsilience project* and is scheduled for completion by March 2011.

There are several issues that arise in relation to the *Prevent agenda*, which is one of four strands in the government's Contest strategy (HMG 2009). The first danger is the way in which the focus on Islamist activities may damage perceptions of the Muslim community as a whole in Britain and therefore run counter to community cohesion. Second, there is a mistaken conflation of 'fundamentalism', 'radicalism', 'extremism' and 'violent extremism' for they are not part of a continuum. Philip Lewis, for example, affirms that 'there is no natural continuum from radical Muslim to militant violence' (2007, 150). However, the government now says that radicalism is a 'key driver of contemporary international terrorism' (HMG, 2009, 42) and it defines radicalism as 'the process by which people come to support terrorism and violent extremism'. This is a dangerous tautology. Radicalism can be defined in a variety of social and political contexts and is not intrinsically connected to violence. Such matters may appear to be outside the realm of RE teachers and SACREs but they are not and the *REsilience project* will have to steer a careful course through these political minefields if it is going to enable RE teachers to address such complex, controversial and sensitive questions in their classrooms.

Despite her antipathy to religion, RE professionals can also learn from the work of Lynn Davies (2008) on preventing extremism through education. She advocates what she calls 'interruptive democracy', 'critical idealism', a stress on commonalities, human rights, media literacy, political education and 'comparative religion'. Her focus on school ethos and her critique of a target-driven curriculum and traditional school discipline are thought provoking and more challenging than the DCSF's 'Toolkit'.

WAYS FORWARD

There are two ways forward for religious education that have not yet received sufficient attention. The first is a detailed response to the suggestion made in the OfSTED report of 2007 *Making Sense of Religion* in which it states:

> 'The curriculum and teaching in RE do not place sufficient emphasis on exploring the changing political and social significance of religion in the modern world. As a result, the subject's potential to contribute to community cohesion, education for diversity and citizenship is not being fully realised.' (*ibid.*, 7)

This links with the importance of media literacy, particularly in secondary schools, and the new curriculum provides ample opportunity for cross-curricular and in-depth study of the issues that are raised daily in the media about religion, politics and society.

The barriers to community cohesion

The second way forward is to ask the question: what constitutes a barrier to the promotion of community cohesion and how can RE begin to address the answers that might be given? The question requires more careful research but tentative answers may well include those set out in the DCSF guidance (2007, 4). They might also include:

- Lack of individual and community confidence in their own community. This may be in areas of economic and social disadvantage and may be particularly evident in some white working class and underachieving Black and Minority ethnic (BME) groups. There is a need here for increased social bonding (Putnam 2000) to enable groups to recognise the strengths and opportunities within their own communities and to have pride and confidence in them. RE has often focused on 'social bridging' and it may be necessary to develop a more balanced approach.

- Resentment at British and western foreign policy, particularly over Iraq, Afghanistan and the Israeli-Palestinian question. This can impact on young Black and ethnic minority pupils, particularly male Muslims, and may promote negative attitudes to society as a whole.

- Misconceptions related to key concepts in religions and communities. These can vary from understandings of terms such as *jihad* or *Kafir*, to understandings of Truth/ truth, and to current terminology with regard to asylum seekers, refugees and migrant workers.

- Issues linked to immigration and a perception of preferential treatment for minorities/some groups. 18% of people believe that immigration is the main issue facing Britain today (DCSF 2007, 4).

- Failure to understand that all identities and communities are multiple, changing and organic and that fixed views will have negative impact

The overcoming of these barriers may lie in:

- An issues-based approach to RE in which children and young people identify the questions to which they want answers

- Personal engagement with communities through ethnographic approaches, as set out, for example, in Bradford's community cohesion strategy

- A media-literacy approach, exploring contemporary issues through media coverage and critical engagement with it

- A human rights approach to fundamental questions of freedom (including freedom of religion and belief), migration, and family life.

CONCLUSION

One of the most interesting phenomena of our times is the rise of religion as a major topic in political discourse. This gives RE teachers opportunities to engage in careful analysis of such issues with their pupils which will not always feel comfortable but which will open up opportunities for real dialogue. If this is what RE teachers must do, then SACREs and local authorities have both a duty and an opportunity to support them. The focus of community cohesion initially, largely because of Ted Cantle who was a local authority officer, was on local answers to local situations and all LAs were required to develop a local strategy. The need for this has not diminished despite increasing national control of the cohesion agenda and its conflation with *Prevent*. Community based approaches to cohesion issues through low-key local work which is both careful and challenging is one of the main ways forward, and RE has a role to play in this. There is a helpful reminder from the Commission on Integration and Cohesion which warns against 'sleepwalking', not into segregation as Trevor Phillips would have it, but into 'simplicity' (2007, 3). The complexities of community cohesion and its translation into policy and practice are legion and a more informed and nuanced debate is urgently needed for all who are engaged in education. RE has long had, and will continue to have, a role to play in the creation of a safer, more equal and less divisive future for all our pupils and their communities but we need to proceed with both urgency and caution.

(Joyce Miller retired from her post as Head of Diversity and Cohesion at Education Bradford in 2007. The views in this article are her own.)

1. See, for example, Alam and Husband (2006) and Findley and Simpson (2009)

2. See www.schoolslinkingnetwork.org.uk

3. The DVD created from this project is available from Education Bradford's Interfaith Education Centre

4. See www.lotc.org.uk and www.reonline/sacredspace

5. See Hansard: 14 Nov 2007 : Column 671

6. Because of my opposition to it I find myself, as the REC's deputy chair, in the role of chair of the executive delivery group.

REFERENCES

Alam, M Y. (ed.) (2006) *Made in Bradford*, Pontefract: Route.

Alam, M. Y. and Husband, C. (2006) *British-Pakistani Men from Bradford*, York: Joseph Rowntree Foundation.

Ballard, R. (1994) *Desh Pardesh: The South Asian Presence in Britain*, London: Hurst.

Burnett, J. (2008) 'Community cohesion in Bradford: neoliberal integrationism' in John Flint and David Robinson (eds) *Community Cohesion in Crisis?* Bristol: The Policy Press, 35-56.

Cantle, T. (2001) *Community Cohesion: A report of the independent review team chaired by Ted Cantle*, London: Home Office.

Cantle, T. (2004) *The End of Parallel Lives? The report of the community cohesion panel*, London: Home Office.

Commission on Integration and Cohesion (2007) *Our Shared Future*, London: Commission on Integration and Cohesion.

Cooper, Z. and Lodge, G. (eds) (2008) *Faith in the Nation*, London: IPPR.

Crick, B. (1998) *Education for Citizenship and the teaching of democracy in schools: Final report of the advisory group of Citizenship*, http://www.qca.org.uk/libraryAssets/media/6123_crick_report_1998.pdf (accessed July 16, 2009)

Davies, L. (2008) *Educating against Extremism*, Stoke on Trent: Trentham Books.

DCSF (2007) *Guidance on the Duty to Promote Community Cohesion*, London: DCSF.

DCSF (2008) *Learning to be safe: A toolkit to help schools contribute to the prevention of violent extremism*, http://www.dcsf.gov.uk/violentextremism/downloads/DCSF-Learning%20Together_bkmk.pdf (accessed July 16, 2009)

Denham, J. (2001) *Building Cohesive Communities, A report of the ministerial group on public order and community cohesion*, 2001, London: Home Office.

DfES (2007) *Curriculum Review Diversity and Citizenship*, London: DfES.

Education Bradford (2003) *The Enhanced Citizenship Curriculum*, www.ngfl.ac.uk/re/citizenship (accessed July 16, 2009)

Finney, N. and Simpson, L. (2009) *Sleepwalking into Segregation? Challenging myths about race and migration*, Bristol: The Policy Press.

Gates, B. E. (2006) 'Religion as cuckoo or crucible: beliefs and believing as vital for citizenship and citizenship education', *Journal of Moral Education*, 35 (4), 571-594.

HMG (2009) *Pursue Prevent Protect Prepare: The United Kingdom's strategy for countering international terrorism*, London: TSO.

Home Office (2004) *Strength in Diversity – towards a community cohesion and race equality strategy*, London: Home Office.

Jackson, R. (1997) *Religious Education: an interpretive approach*, London: Hodder & Stoughton.

Jackson, R. (2000) 'The Warwick religious education project: the interpretive approach to religious education' in Grimmitt, M.H. (ed) *Pedagogies of Religious Education*, Great Wakering: McCrimmons, 130-152

LGA (2002) *Guidance on Community Cohesion*, London: LGA Publications.

Lewis, P. (2007) *Young, British and Muslim*, London: Continuum.

Macpherson, W. (1999) *The Stephen Lawrence Enquiry*, London: The Stationery Office.

Miller, J. (2003) 'Out of the shadows' *TES Magazine*, 28 February http://www.tes.co.uk/article.aspx?storycode=376209, (accessed July 16, 2009)

Miller, J. (2005) 'Building better communities' *TES Magazine*, 1 April http://www.tes.co.uk/article.aspx?storycode=2113564(accessed July 16, 2009)

Miller, J. (2006a) 'Enhanced Citizenship Education in Bradford', http://www.unlockdemocracy.org.uk/?p=238 (accessed July 16, 2009)

Miller, J. (2006b) 'Respect for All: Promoting community cohesion through religious education' *Resource 28(2)*, 4-7

Miller, J. (2009) 'Raising Humanities teachers' understanding of their pupils' religious and cultural backgrounds' in Ipgrave, J., Jackson, R. and O'Grady, K. (eds) *Religious Education Research through a Community of Practice*, Münster: Waxmann, 119-138

OfSTED (2007) *Making Sense of Religion: A report on religious education in schools and the impact of locally agreed syllabuses*, http://www.ofsted.gov.uk/Ofsted-home/Publications-and-research/Browse-all-by/Education/Curriculum/Religious-education/Secondary/Making-sense-of-religion (accessed July 16, 2009)

Ouseley, H. (2001) *Community Pride not Prejudice: making diversity work in Bradford*, Bradford: Bradford Vision.

Putnam, R. D. (2000) *Bowling Alone: the collapse and revival of American community*, New York: Simon and Schuster.

Richardson, R. and Wood, A. (2004) *The Achievement of Pakistani Learners: work in progress*, Stoke on Trent: Trentham.

CHAPTER 15

PUBLIC EXAMINATIONS IN RE AND RS:

Do GCE and GCSE syllabuses adequately address the issues of social and community cohesion?

John Rudge

SUMMARY

THIS CHAPTER EXPLORES how far the range of examination courses for 16 and 18 year olds deal with the theme of community cohesion, and the different ways in which they engage students with this topic. A number of differing approaches are considered, along with the extent to which they are a required or optional element of courses. It draws out some of the contrasts in emphasis between GCSE and A level courses. The chapter concludes with some observations about the relevance of courses dealing with community cohesion to the wider context of religious education.

INTRODUCTION

Firstly, a brief word about nomenclature. Historically, there has been a dispute between advocates of 'Religious Education' (RE) and supporters of 'Religious Studies' (RS) as the title for public examinations in this subject. The conflict was eventually decided in favour of the latter, mainly on the somewhat bizarre grounds that it sounded more academic. This rather pointless debate actually conceals a profound difference of perspective among aficionados of the subject, to which a brief reference is made towards the end of the Chapter. For our purposes, RS will be used in reference specifically to public examinations, and RE to the subject as a whole, including public examinations.

A casual glance at the title of this chapter might understandably lead the reader to the conclusion that there is a serious category mistake here. Public examinations in RS don't do community cohesion. And there is a significant measure of truth in this observation. Certainly at A level, the overwhelming majority of candidates do not go anywhere near the issue of community cohesion, either explicitly or implicitly, and most probably do not come within the orbit of the concept of 'religion in the modern world'. This is, firstly, because they are following courses in which the application of religion to the modern world does not feature as part of their area of study; secondly because A level courses tend to focus on highly traditional approaches to the subject; and thirdly because changes in specifications (syllabuses) at this level seem to take place only at a glacial pace. The pressure from some quarters to maintain the *status quo* is considerable.

The overwhelming, and growing, majority of A level candidates in the subject enter for examinations based on courses in Philosophy of Religion, and Ethics. Most of these courses have a traditional core which goes back over many years and which represents a style of thinking and approach to the issues which have not changed for many decades. Of course, the perception that this approach precludes engagement with the modern world is open to a limited challenge. For example, courses in applied ethics do seriously examine issues within a contemporary context, particularly in the fields of medical and sexual ethics. It could also be said that however traditional the field of study, students will be expected to show their awareness of the latest scholarship in that field. Nonetheless, it remains the pattern, dictated partly by the expectations of some theological faculties in universities, that a broad range of content and style of questioning has, in essence, remained unchanged for many years.

The same cannot be said of the majority of GCSE courses. On the whole, these have been highly responsive to recent thinking in the subject, developments in the pattern of the national curriculum and rapid changes within society. Many of the courses on offer do, it is true, prefigure the philosophy and ethics courses available at AS and A level, and they continue to retain other more traditional approaches, through the study of the Gospels, for example. But they also usually incorporate a wider curriculum perspective through a focus on various aspects of religion under the broad umbrella of 'religion in the modern world' or 'the contemporary study of religion'. Whilst they have not in the past, unsurprisingly, used the precise terminology of 'community cohesion', some of the themes and key concepts of that ideal have been in place for some time.

THE DEVELOPING FRAMEWORK FOR EXAMINATIONS
IN RELIGIOUS STUDIES

The Qualifications and Curriculum Development Agency (QCDA), the regulatory authority for examinations, has been careful to avoid dictating to examination boards the detailed content or programmes of study for examination courses, leaving a reasonable degree of latitude for innovation and enterprise. The emphasis has been on getting the testing regulations right rather than prescribing what students should study in their courses. So, for example, a recent move has been to abandon 'coursework' in many areas, including RS, because of the way in which some candidates and centres have misused this process to their own advantage.

However, the 'field of enquiry' or scope of prescribed content for study remains wide open. And RS is not the only subject where this is the case. However, the situation in this subject is exacerbated by the legal system under which each Local Authority (LA) has responsibility for drawing up a curriculum just for those students who live in the area. Inevitably, a diversity of content has been the result of this system.

Until relatively recently, this has not been seen as too much of a problem, and there has been a tacit acceptance, in any case, that candidates at examination level can show the same skills over a wide range of content. That in itself remains questionable and problematic, given the diversity of courses. But a further net outcome has been a discontinuity between what students have been encouraged to study in Key Stages 1 to 3 and what they might study at examination level. Underlying this has been an additional problem which has to do with a further lack of clear progression in the levels or expectations at which students are working. This is seen most clearly where there has been little correlation between the eight-level scale of attainment used in Key Stages 1 to 3 and the grade descriptors used for GCSE and A level examinations. Continuity and progression are ongoing matters for debate in RE.

However, elements of this free-for-all have begun to change. Firstly, the advent of a *Non-statutory National Framework for RE* (QCA/DfES, 2004), whilst not carrying the force of law, has encouraged those responsible for RE to look more closely at the issues of continuity and progression leading into the curriculum for 14 to 19 year-olds. Secondly, some of these changes are beginning to be included in the criteria set for all examinations by the QCDA.

At GCSE level, there is now both a framework in which religion in contemporary society can be studied as a central element in courses, (and in some cases is a requirement for all), and a process which has been carried forward from developments in the KS1 – 3 curriculum. This in turn reflects a move towards the concept of a national framework for RE. Without entering into the debate about the viability, efficacy or desirability of such a framework, it is certainly possible to acknowledge its growing influence on the examination system in the subject. This is also linked to the current practice of Local Authority Agreed Syllabus Conferences (ASCs) to stipulate that the programmes of study for Key Stage 4 statutory RE can be subsumed under the courses offered at GCSE level by the various examination boards. Whilst ASCs do not attempt to direct centres and students towards the offerings of any one particular board, many do set out limited criteria of their own. The most commonly used criterion is that any course followed by students at this level must involve the study of Christianity and at least one other religion. Independent and private schools are not, however, bound by such criteria.

Furthermore, an emphasis on the study of religion in a contemporary setting has been a feature of GCSE courses for some years, so that new criteria are to a large extent simply a further development of established practice. The language and terminology of the criteria may have changed, but the substance remains largely the same. GCSE courses should now, among other aspirations, 'challenge young people and equip them to lead constructive lives in the modern world' and must enable learners to 'enhance their personal, social and cultural development, their understanding of different cultures locally, nationally and in the wider world, and to contribute to social and community cohesion.' (QCDA subject criteria for GCSE Religious Studies) An even more significant change is to give equal weighting to the two main assessment objectives which reflect broadly the curriculum goals of 'learning about' and 'learning from' religion. This change will be revisited in the wider issues considered at the conclusion of this chapter.

For a number of years, AS and A level candidates have been offered a curriculum in which they are able to choose between content drawn from one or more of the following areas related to the study of religion:

- Philosophy
- Ethics
- Theology
- History

250

- Texts
- Practice
- Anthropology, psychology and sociology.

There has hitherto been no prescription about how these areas should be studied in relation to different religious traditions or in relation to the wider concept of religion. Notable absentees from this traditional, long-standing list are any real acknowledgement of the expanding numbers of university departments now offering courses broadly in the area of the contemporary study of religions, or of any reference to the engagement of religion(s) with issues in the contemporary world. Therefore any focus on such issues as the relationship between religions, the development of religious dialogue or community and religious cohesion has been hitherto almost entirely coincidental.

New criteria have continued to use the above categories for study at AS and A level. This means that there has been a strong emphasis on the perceived need to preserve the past shape of the subject. However, the new criteria have added a further heading as a concession to modernity:

- Religion in contemporary society.

This has had a small but not insignificant impact on new courses on at this level.

At this point, it may be helpful to explore some of these new courses on offer from the examination boards, firstly at GCSE level and then at A level.

GCSE

The GCSE criteria were published in 2007 and provided the basis for the various examination boards to draw up their specifications for first examination in 2010. Most have observed the safety rule that continuity with the past is of paramount importance. Apparently new courses may simply be a reworking of existing courses. Course developers, usually senior examiners, are only too aware of the cry from teachers to change as little of the content as possible because of the logistics of writing new schemes of work and finding appropriate resources. That argument carries rather less weight than was the case in the past because of the relatively easy access teachers now have to pedagogical guidance and resource material, particularly through electronic means of communication. Nevertheless, even GCSE is a field where an innate conservatism has a firm grip on the possible extent of changes.

Perhaps unsurprisingly, we can identify at least three different approaches to the issue of community cohesion for the 2010 examination series.

AQA Examination Board

The approach followed by the AQA examination board, has been to include reference to community cohesion under a heading embracing a cluster of ideas and concepts in one of the optional specifications. The main specification (A), under the heading of *Religious Beliefs and Lifestyles*, represents a traditional, somewhat abstract, approach to each of the world's major religions, focusing on the beliefs and practices of communities. Where religions are studied from an ethical point of view, a number of contemporary issues are included for study, but these do not include directly the area of community cohesion (except in the more general and implicit sense of broad topics dealing with such matters as war and peace and conflict).

The second optional specification (B) is called *Ethics, Philosophy and Religion in Society*. The approach offered here is a response to the need for a 'thematic approach' to the study of religion. Within this specification, students can enter for one unit (short course) or two units (full course), out of a choice of six units. The first unit, *Religion and Citizenship*, is the most pertinent to the present discussion. The title of this unit reflects a perceived need in some schools to deal with much of the Citizenship agenda under the umbrella of Religious Studies. In the current climate, this attempt to amalgamate the two areas of study is unlikely to succeed for a whole host of reasons, though across the examination boards this hybrid still attracts sizeable entries. Also, community cohesion is a seen to be a natural focus of study in both contexts. Within that unit, students answer questions based on a further choice of four out of six topics. Of these topics, the most pertinent is *Religion and the Multicultural Society*, though there are other topics where the implicit element could be relevant, such as *Religion and Identity or Religion and Human Rights*. Other Units such as *Religion and Life Issues* could also be relevant, though not explicitly.

Within *Religion and the Multicultural Society*, candidates are offered a wide range of 10 topics for study, most of which would be relevant to an exploration of the concept of community cohesion. Examples of this would be 'concepts of interdependence and multiple identities' or 'concepts of tolerance, respect, diversity, multiculturalism and political correctness.' Students are invited to study these topics from the perspective of one or more of the world's major religions, hence the association of this route with the so-called 'thematic approach'. However, the concept of community cohesion itself does not appear to feature.

Overall, the approach is to categorise community cohesion as a minor sub-set of the wide range of options available to examination candidates.

Edexcel Examination Board

A different example is found in the specification available through Edexcel. This is rather more straightforward, since community cohesion features in all units, meaning that it is a required area of study for all students taking the examination, whether in its short or long course format. Basically, sixteen courses of study are on offer, the first seven on the broad theme of *Religion and Life*, a thematic study based on one or more religions. These seven all follow a common pattern of four sections each, comprising 'believing in God', 'matters of life and death', 'marriage and the family' and 'community cohesion'. Those who follow a course based on Units 9 to 15 study particular religions under four different sections, and in the fourth of these they study one topic (out of eleven) dealing with 'how and why' the particular religious community they are exploring 'is involved in working for social and community cohesion.' Unit 8 is the only one not to mention community cohesion by name. The overall title of this unit, however, is *Religion and Society* (based on a study of Christianity and at least one other religion), and two of the units deal with the broad areas of 'rights and responsibilities' and 'peace and conflict'. The preamble to this Unit also suggests that students 'should be encouraged to relate their studies to the issues of social and community cohesion.' This Unit represents another approach to the 'RE and Citizenship' theme.

Interestingly, Edexcel has managed to insinuate community cohesion into an unusual host. Unit 16 in a sense stands alone, in that the field of study is St Mark's Gospel, and represents the last remaining area of traditional textual study. It still attracts a sizeable clientele. It could be seen as a hangover from an earlier century when it was regarded as desirable for young adults to be familiar with the Biblical text, its historical background, sequence and teaching, as a basis for understanding the historical origins of and background to 'Christianity', rather than seeing the text in any sense as an aspect of 'religion in the modern world'. One of the four sections of the unit, which treats the text thematically, is entitled 'conflict and argument' and four of the eleven topics deal directly with community cohesion. It is worth giving them in full here

- Why disagreements about the Sabbath led to conflict ... and their significance for Christians today, particularly in relation to current issues of social and community cohesion.

- Why disagreements about the meaning of the Law led to conflict ... and their significance for Christians today, particularly in relation to current issues of social and community cohesion.

- Why Jesus' cleansing of the Temple might have caused conflict ... and its significance for Christians today, particularly in relation to current issues of social and community cohesion.

- Why Jesus' answer to the question about Caesar and taxes might have led to conflict ... and its significance for Christians today, particularly in relation to current issues of social and community cohesion.

This part of the specification is unusual. Firstly, it treats the text as a source of inspiration and guidance 'for Christians today', rather than as a historical document. Almost every one of the 44 topics for study includes that phrase. This means that the text is being used as Christians themselves would consider appropriate today, namely that when they hear and read this text they are engaging (though they would not normally use these words) in applied hermeneutics. Secondly, in focusing particularly on conflict in the life of Jesus, this approach raises more profound questions about community cohesion than the process of simply exploring what Christians might be doing about community cohesion. However, working out how these topics should be taught does leave some problems for teachers who must decide what kind of approach is most suitable. Although the context of St Mark's Gospel raises a number of interesting possibilities, one is still left with the impression that it has been seen as more important to have the actual words 'community cohesion' placed prominently and pervasively within the specification, with relatively little thought given to its implications for teaching and learning.

OCR Examination Board

A 'third way' is represented in the OCR specification. There are a number of distinctive features in this approach. As well as the more traditional approaches already mentioned in relation to other boards, OCR has introduced a third component under the title of *Religion and Belief in*

Today's World (Specification C). We are told that courses under this title 'enable candidates to study aspects of two or more religions in an inter-faith framework, community cohesion and valuing diversity' *(sic)*. The specification contains four Units, all of which make up a full course, and two of which comprise a short course. Simply to give an idea of the breadth and scope of this specification, the four Units are:

1. *Religion and Belief in the Modern World*, broken down into Key Areas of Study (religion and secularisation, issues across the faiths, the rise and interest in religious movements);

2. *Religion, Politics and Culture in Britain* (religion and cultural expression, the influence of Christianity on British politics, religion and modern Britain);

3. *The Individual* (religious truth and the individual, religious fundamentalism and the individual, the impact of religion on everyday life);

4. *Community Cohesion and the Individual* (religion and human rights, religion and the influence of technology, religion and citizenship).

The community cohesion section effectively comprises half-a-year's work, as in the Edexcel model, which is a considerable investment of time in this area of study. The preamble to this section suggests that it provides students with an opportunity 'to explore the links between individual identity and community cohesion, religious faith or personal belief and cultural diversity in order to consider the role of religion in the modern world.' A requirement is that a minimum of two religions/secular philosophies are considered in relation to the topic area. The overall section is broken down into three key areas: religion and human rights; religion/secular philosophy and the influence of technology; religion/secular philosophy and citizenship. The detail for each of these is set out under the headings of 'key themes', 'indicative content' and tables of relevant teachings from the main religions and secular philosophies.

The result is a veritable *pot-pourri* of themes, ideas, teachings and perspectives, not all of which can straightforwardly be linked with equal facility to the overall theme of community cohesion in the title. Like the other sections, there is extensive ground to cover, and sceptics will no doubt draw attention to yet another case of 'content overload' – too much information. On the other hand, it is of course, merely an optional course and, significantly, a pilot course. It therefore remains a matter of conjecture as to how far an analysis of the likely entry and an evaluation of its impact on teaching and learning will prompt the designers to retain, adapt or abandon this project.

Northern Ireland Examination Board

In concluding this part of the discussion, it is worth mentioning one aspect of the specification produced by the examination board in Northern Ireland, if only because of the very obvious relevance of issues of community cohesion in that context. Much of it follows a very traditional pattern, and still moves largely in the orbit and context of the Catholic and Protestant communities. Amongst the aims of the overall specification, one is to enhance students' 'personal, social and cultural development, along with their understanding of different cultures locally, nationally and in the wider world, so they may contribute to social and community cohesion.' Without going into the complexity of the differences between short and long courses, or the intricacies of forbidden combinations of units, students can choose one (short course) or two (full course) units from a menu of 9. The result is that, in most cases, students will be expected to deal with the issue of community cohesion, and in some instances to explore 'the contribution of the Christian Churches to peace and reconciliation in a divided society, for example the work of the Corrymeela Community as well as their contribution to the local community and community cohesion.' But, once again, this remains an option only available to those who choose it.

GCE AS AND A LEVEL

As already indicated, the advanced level fraternity has been much more reluctant to move into the field of community cohesion, or even into the wider orbit of the concept of 'religion in the modern world', preferring instead to retain the traditional categories of study such as philosophy and ethics, for which the overwhelming majority enter, plus the areas of history and textual study, together with learning based on the concepts of individual religions. So, for example, none of the English boards refers to religion in its contemporary or modern setting in their 'aims', and neither OCR nor Edexcel include examples from that context in their indicative content. The only possible exception is in the Edexcel Unit 2 (*Investigations*) under a relatively minor topic heading which includes 'religious pluralism, inter-faith dialogue and religious practice in a multicultural society.'

AQA, however, includes at both AS and A2 level a unit on 'religion and contemporary society'. Both include a range of aspects under the broad theme of 'expressions of religion within society' which encompasses such topics as the influence of faith schools or faith community leaders, and specific topics such as 'ways in which buildings, community centres etc. contribute to or detract from community cohesion.' At A2 level these themes are broadened out into areas such as the impact of secularisation, national identity, 'establishment' and civic religion. In this case, therefore, although optional the course does offer opportunities for advanced level students to explore some of the wider issues and ramifications of community cohesion.

WIDER ISSUES

Firstly, one may come to a fairly obvious and straightforward conclusion from the above survey that public examinations in RS do not *adequately* address the issues of social and community cohesion. They are too hit-and-miss because most courses treat the issue as a matter of choice. The issue is, in any case, peripheral at A level. In some GCSE courses it appears to be more important for the words 'community cohesion' to be included like a mantra in a specification, to meet a particular directive, than for a more profound understanding of the issue to inform the material for coherent courses. The issues have not been well thought through in terms of goals and outcomes. This situation is not improved – just the opposite – if we take into account possible implicit opportunities for considering issues of community cohesion through examination courses, rather than simply focusing on the issue only when it is included explicitly in courses. There is further confusion about the possible boundaries between subjects, for example between citizenship and RE. The whole exercise has evolved in a somewhat piecemeal manner.

Secondly, it is not possible or desirable to try to divorce the discussion of whether or to what extent community cohesion should feature in examination courses in RS from the issues about whether or how it should form part of any wider curriculum in RE. Readers might therefore wish to reflect on what has been written elsewhere in this symposium about the place of community cohesion within RE. In that context, it is also worth noting that the view that RS must be distinguished from RE, on the grounds that there are aspects of the latter which cannot or should not be assessed, is now a rather less contentious issue than it used to be. Suffice it to remark that aspects of personal development are aspirational, but that does not mean that the processes of assessment for learning cannot also be congruent with the procedures for assessment of learning, both of which take place throughout all Key Stages.

Thirdly, having said that, and leaving on one side the issue of whether community cohesion should provide a specific focal point in RE courses, there still remains the issue, referred to earlier in this chapter, about the pedagogical processes envisaged in any examination course. To put it more succinctly, what is the balance between what students are intended to learn *about* religion and community cohesion, and what they are supposed to be learning *from* these two aspects? This in turn is not a matter about the content or information that students explore, but about their intended impact on the students themselves as young adults growing up in the modern world. The more significant change, certainly at GCSE level, is the move to a balanced weighting of the assessment objectives.

The implication behind this change in the weighting of objectives is that it places equal emphasis on what students may learn about community cohesion (Assessment Objective 1: Describe, explain and analyse, using knowledge and understanding) and on how they may respond to the issues raised. Assessment Objective 2: Use evidence and reasoned argument to express and evaluate personal responses, informed insights and differing viewpoints). This in turn means that students now need to spend less time accumulating information, and more time on learning how to respond to the issues raised. Examinations in this subject have suffered over the years through a pre-occupation with 'content'. Information overload has simply contributed to the perception of examinations as memory tests. The examination system in RS is now much more closely in line with the growing movement in RE towards recognising the subject as a fundamental part of personal and social education. Religion and religions serve as a means to an end; they are 'instrumental' (as well as 'essential') to the learning process. Community cohesion provides a fitting context for this process, since it invites students to reflect on what is happening around them today. It also invites them to clarify and express their own beliefs and values coherently, through an engagement with religion. How far it is also able to provide a context in which students may actually become more sympathetic to, or engaged in promoting, community cohesion must remain part of the wider debate discussed in this book.

REFERENCES

Assessment & Qualifications Alliance (AQA) www.aqa.org.uk

CCEA: (Council for the Curriculum, Examinations and Assessment – Northern

Ireland) www.ccea.org.uk

Edexcel: www.edexcel.com

QCA,DfES (2004) *Religious Education:The non-statutory national framework*

QCDA (Qualifications and Curriculum Development Agency): www.qcda.gov.uk

OCR (Oxford, Cambridge & RSA): www.ocr.org.uk

WJEC (Welsh Joint Education Committee): www.wjec.co.uk

CHAPTER 16

CONTRIBUTING TO SOCIAL AND COMMUNITY COHESION:
Just another stage in the metamorphosis of RE?

An Extended End Piece

Michael Grimmitt

SUMMARY

THIS EXTENDED CHAPTER traces what it calls the 'metamorphosis' of RE as a curriculum subject within the schools of England and Wales as it continues to accommodate itself to the changing needs and expectations of an increasingly plural and diverse society. It examines some of the obstacles to RE fulfilling its requirement to contribute to social and community cohesion and offers a perspective on government-related initiatives that are related to this. Finally it suggests how RE may need to undergo further changes in its curriculum and pedagogy in order to respond both to the needs of young people and to those of a volatile and unpredictable future society. The focus of the chapter is mainly on RE in the secondary schools of England and Wales, although some implications for RE in primary schools are also identified.

INTRODUCTION

The legal requirement that RE, like all other subjects in the curriculum, should contribute to social and community cohesion is one of the latest challenges to the subject. An ability to re-design itself has been a remarkable feature of RE for at least the last sixty-five years, and even before that. Inevitably within each stage of its metamorphosis some earlier features of the subject have been carried forward and been variously modified, sometimes quite radically. It would be odd if some sense of an enduring underlying identity could not be detected in RE in the English educational system. Certainly there has been an enduring influence, an abiding presence, rather like some persistent environmental feature designed to restrain any tendency towards unfettered and uncharacteristic mutation – I refer to the influence of the religious clauses of Education Acts, especially those of 1944 and 1988. But even within these constraints, the subject has demonstrated enormous resilience and inventiveness in pursuing its commitment to participating effectively within an ever-changing educational enterprise and contributing successfully to an ever-widening curriculum to the benefit of pupils and of society.

The issue which the subject must now address is whether the very different circumstances of a post 9/11 world make it necessary for a new stage in RE's metamorphosis. If so what changes might this involve? For example, can RE contribute to social and community cohesion effectively within the current legislative framework? Are the present two attainment targets fit for purpose? Might it be necessary to add to them or change them? What are the implications for the content of the RE curriculum? Where should the emphasis in RE be placed? – on studying religions or on understanding religion? – on exploring controversial and sensitive issues within and between religions? – or on recognising religion as a 'cultural fact'? What pedagogies of RE are likely to be effective in addressing the new demands made on the subject? How can we know? These are important questions which should be considered thoughtfully by all who value the place of RE in the curriculum. It is my intention in this chapter to elaborate upon these questions as a small, personal contribution to an important, ongoing debate.

However, before coming to these questions, I propose to try and delineate those stages in the metamorphosis of RE which have brought the subject, at least in England and Wales, to its present nature and identity. Having lived through and been professionally engaged in much that has happened to RE in the UK since the middle nineteen-sixties, I can, hopefully, provide student teachers of RE, interested readers from overseas and others less familiar with these events than myself with an insight into how RE has been, and continues to be shaped by a unique combination of pressures which are variously political and religious and, especially through the influence of individual religious educators, are also variously ideological and educational. At the same time I need to state my conviction early on that any changes in RE which are directed towards the encouragement of social and community cohesion, will, like all educational policies, only succeed when those factors which contribute to inequality, discrimination and alienation in society are ameliorated by enlightened political, social and economic policies which can actually deliver equal opportunities for all, especially with regard to employment, housing and education, irrespective of ethnicity, religion, class and gender. At a time of unprecedented economic recession it is too easy for such policies to be relegated and downgraded so that even the most enlightened of educational policies can have little effect.

RE, THE LAW AND THE NATIONAL CURRICULUM

I cannot pretend to be content with the legal framework within which RE is taught in the community schools of this country. I believe that what eventually came into being as Section 8 of the 1988 Education Reform Act was a missed opportunity to realise the subject's undoubted capacity and potential to play a key role in fostering inter-religious and inter-cultural understanding. The proper response to diversity in conditions of post-modernity should aspire to go beyond trying to contain racism, discrimination, inequity and other forms of social injustice by appealing to the law, and to find in diversity itself an intrinsically valuable form of social existence capable of enriching the lives of all citizens.

The basis for constructing the kind of RE which is appropriate in a plural, multi-cultural, multi-faith and democratic society must be one which promotes equality of opportunity, safeguards human rights, builds a positive view of diversity, contributes to social and community cohesion and opposes racial, ethnic, sexual and religious discrimination and prejudice as a matter of principle.

Unfortunately by requiring the RE curriculum to be disproportionately and discriminatingly weighted towards the study of Christianity for all pupils, irrespective of their family backgrounds, the religious clauses of the 1988 Education Act undermine important educational principles and impair the subject's credibility as a vehicle for contributing to inter-religious and inter-cultural understanding and community cohesion.

Sketching the background events to the current legislative arrangements will, hopefully, enable me to substantiate this view and point to those obstacles that I believe the legislation continues to place in the way of RE contributing to this positive vision of diversity. Equally, I hope that offering a critical account of the various ways in which RE has sought to re-define itself in response to Government-related initiatives will enable me to chart its progress towards its present nature and identity and, hopefully, suggest ways in which it can be further enabled to address the present needs of pupils and those of a volatile and unpredictable future society.

How a secular view of education was combined with secular ways of studying religion.

The task of establishing RE on a sound educational footing within a total curriculum which was no longer seen as being rooted in a Christian consensus of beliefs and values took on a new urgency in the early seventies. The period from then through to the late eighties represented, I believe, the most productive period of research and development in RE in the UK that the subject has yet known. Creative and imaginative efforts brought education and religion into a new relationship by combining a secular view of education with secular ways of studying religion. The heady mix of R.S. Peters's *Ethics and Education* (1966) with Ninian Smart's *Secular Education and the Logic of Religion* (1968) and *The Science of Religion and the Sociology of Knowledge* (1973) proved to be decisive in their influence on the reformulation of RE in terms of its aims, methods and content in ways which would finally, at least in theory, enable the subject to be no longer justified by or dependent upon its Christian and Church-related antecedence and so enjoy parity with other subjects within a secular curriculum.

Smart's work through the Schools Council RE Project at the University of Lancaster also provided a huge impetus for other religious educators to refine this new way of creating a proper method for conducting the public study of religion in an open, democratic, plural and increasingly secular society. Although a lively debate about the place or otherwise of theology in the delineation of education and of RE followed, there was a clear consensus among religious educators, teachers and representatives of Local Education Authorities that the combination of analytical educational philosophy and the methodology of the phenomenology of religion provided a basis for the study of religion in schools which would safeguard RE's future.[1]

There was, however – at least on the part of some religious educators – a reluctance to abandon some of the child-centred and experience-related methods in RE which sought to enhance pupils' understanding of religious concepts and make them relevant to exploring issues in their own lives. The creative and imaginative work of the sixties and early seventies designed to promote a form of RE which contributed to pupils' 'personal search for meaning', fully endorsed by the Church of England's Commission on RE in Schools Report, *The Fourth R* (1970), looked to be in danger of being marginalised by the eruption upon the RE scene of what was sometimes called a 'Shap-Shaped' approach to RE dominated by the study of the world's religions.[2] The door was left open for the integration of these pupil-centred concerns with a phenomenological approach within RE by the Lancaster RE Project's distinction between 'Explicit' and 'Implicit' Religion and also its presumption of the centrality of the experiential dimension of religion as a common element of religions and one which is integral to the human experience of religion *per se*. This allowed a new argument for the study of religion in schools to eventually emerge which went beyond the view that it should be studied as an important aspect of human experience, namely that studying religion could also contribute to pupils' human development. Rather than align this approach with any form of theological rationale for RE, my colleague, Garth Read, and I proposed in 1977 that through *learning about religion and learning from religion* RE should contribute to pupils' understanding of the process of humanisation, and especially to the place of 'faith' (in the broadest terms) in human meaning-making.[3] This approach also gave a new basis for the claim – increasingly emphasised in the following years by Government–related agencies like the National Curriculum Council (NCC) and the Qualifications and Curriculum Authority (QCA) – that RE could contribute to pupils' spiritual, moral, cultural, and mental development and thus to society as a whole – as required by both the 1944 and 1988 Education Acts.

A glance at the Contents page of the volumes of the *British Journal of Religious Education* from its inception in 1978 through to Special Issue Vol 13 No 3 in 1991 on *Religious Education After the 1988 Education Act* reveals an extraordinarily rich variety of articles each affirming the necessity of the subject adhering to broadly secular disciplines in order to create a 'multi-faith RE'. In the country as a whole there was also a developing consensus of opinion among RE teachers that the subject had now been invested with a new dynamism and relevance to the changing pattern of religious faith and practice evident in society and among the pupils themselves. In so far as Agreed Syllabuses of RE were still able to reflect in their choice of content any special religious features of the local vicinity and also adapt this to pupils' family backgrounds, this was a period when it was realistic to say that RE, in encouraging pupils to participate in the study of religion and religions in an atmosphere of mutual trust, respect and appreciation, did contribute to social and community cohesion through the positive attitudes to diversity which young people, hopefully, took with them from their experience of RE into society and into their communities.

Had politicians and their advisers been given, during the period of consultation immediately prior to the 1988 Education Reform Act, a greater assurance and understanding of this newly acquired state of RE's educational maturity, of the emerging consensus about the most appropriate content for pupils to study in RE and the subject's capacity for enhancing community relations, they might – just might – have been persuaded to abandon the religious clauses of the 1944 Education Act and allow RE to enter the National Curriculum on the same basis as all other curriculum subjects. This would have meant that the conscience clause and the mechanism for devising a local agreed syllabus would have been no longer required.[4] The same sort of advisory body for RE as for other curriculum subjects would have been established and this body would have set the subject's attainment targets, programmes of study and forms of assessment in a manner common with all other curriculum subjects. It would have done so, however, under the control and influence of the Secretary of State for Education with Local Education Authorities losing this power. Consequently there would have been no question of religious representatives, such as those of the Church of England, having a majority place on the advisory body with other Christian denominations and minority faiths being represented in a more token manner. The much respected and fully representational RE Council of England and Wales with many years of experience working with the faith communities for the improvement of RE could have fulfilled this role with wisdom and equanimity. Thus RE would have come of age and been admitted to the National Curriculum on the basis of a sound educational rationale and with a national curriculum (instead of 172 Local Education Authorities (LEA) being required to create their own Agreed Syllabus of RE or adopt one from another LEA) which would have enabled all pupils to learn about religion and religions in a way which did not compromise the integrity of their own religious or non-religious personal stance nor the integrity of the religious faiths being studied. As an academic and examination subject a multidisciplinary approach to studying religion and religions would have been adopted which embraced description, interpretation, critical analysis and evaluation. Only within schools with a religious foundation or trust deed, or, later, in the newly formed 'faith schools', would RE have been allowed to continue as an uncritical confessional activity, although many 'faith schools', in their concern to extend pupils' knowledge of religion and religions in order to further community understanding, may well have chosen to adopt a broader and more educational approach to how they taught RE.

The unexpected setback to multi-faith RE through opposition by a Christian minority; the questionable educational legacy of the 1988 Education Act

But as is well known, following a powerful and well-orchestrated attack on multi-faith RE by a small but influential group of conservative Christians during the passage of the so-called 'religious clauses' of the Bill through the House of Lords, the 1988 Education Reform Act took a completely different turn and re-asserted the right of Christianity to retain its privileged position in schools and in RE, including retaining daily acts of 'collective' worship which were to be 'wholly or mainly of a broadly Christian character'. (*op.cit*, 7:1) In requiring RE Agreed Syllabuses to 'reflect the fact that the religious traditions in Great Britain are in the main Christian while taking account of the teaching and practices of the other principal religions represented in Great Britain', the 1988 Education Reform Act imposed a religious settlement more assertive of the place of Christianity in RE than the 1944 Education Act, despite 'taking account of' the strong 'multi-faith' identity that RE had acquired by the late eighties and the religiously plural, multicultural and increasingly secularised society that had, by then, come into being. These events have been fully documented, analysed and commented upon elsewhere, and here my concern is only to give some estimate of the long term effects they may have had, and continue to have on the subsequent development of RE and its capacity to address the effects of diversity upon the differently situated religious and ethnic communities in Britain and their relationship to each other within an epoch of globalisation.

The first effect of these events was to throw RE into a state of confusion. There was a presumption that a phrase like 'reflect the fact that' could be quickly and easily translated into how much curriculum time should be divided between the study of Christianity and the study of other religions. The decisions taken have always been contentious and there have been several well publicised court cases where some Christian parents have taken legal action against LEAs and schools for not giving, in their view, a preponderence of time in RE – as much as ninety-percent – to the study of Christianity. Members of other faiths have been rather more circumspect in their response but have exercised their rights within Agreed Syllabus Conferences and SACREs, newly established by the 1988 Education Act, to argue that whatever equation is used in the distribution of time across the religions theirs should be as fully represented as the law allows. Whatever else might be said about the outcome to the legislation there can be no doubt that the religions, other than Christianity, were placed in a position of having to compete with each other for curriculum time and representation in RE. This did not auger well for a future situation when world events would exacerbate a sense of suspicion and even antagonism between faiths, especially between some of the followers of the three Abrahamic religions of Judaism, Christianity and Islam.

Related to this was another effect of the Act upon RE's development, that of giving encouragement to what I will call a 'stratified' approach to the study of religions. If proportions of time are to be allocated to the different faiths the faiths are, presumably, to be taught separately, using a 'systems' approach. I will comment further on the implications of this later, but it is worth noting that the 1975 Birmingham Agreed Syllabus provided a precedent for this approach. However, in my view, the 1988 legislation lacked the sensitivity that was shown by the Birmingham Agreed Syllabus Conference in 1975 to the educational, social, religious and community circumstances of the time. While the syllabus did require all pupils in secondary schools in Birmingham to study Christianity it was to be only one course among four in 'The Direct Study of Religion' which could include, for example, two or three other religions, or a study of themes from several religions or a secular stance for living. Pupils could choose to study their own religion as a 'major course' with the rest, including Christianity (if it was not chosen as the pupil's major course), as minor courses. In addition, all secondary pupils in Birmingham schools were required to follow a course in 'The Indirect Study of Religion' – religious beliefs, values, attitudes and practices relating to problems confronting the individual, such as issues about identity, morality, sexuality, etc, and problems confronting the community, such as race and community relations, war, the use and conservation of resources, etc. The 1975 Birmingham Agreed Syllabus represented, I believe, an ingenious and praiseworthy attempt to create a form of RE which could meet the complex religious and cultural needs of a large, multi-cultural and multi-faith city by relating the study of religion to the lives, communities and families from which the pupils came. While this may still remain a possibility under the 1988 legislation, I believe that, by allowing the RE curriculum to be disproportionately and discriminatingly weighted toward the study of Christianity for all pupils, irrespective of their family backgrounds, important educational principles have been undermined and the potentially valuable social impact of the subject has been seriously weakened.

In response to this continuing situation in which the teaching of Christianity is given pre-eminence, we might ask what relationship is envisaged in the 1988 Education Act (and later in the SCAA *Model Syllabuses* of 1994 and, ten years later, in the QCA/DfES *Non-Statutory National Framework for Religious Education* of 2004) between having more time to devote to the study of one faith – Christianity – and the educational aims of RE? Does having more time enable these aims to be fulfilled more successfully in relation to the teaching of Christianity than in relation to the other faiths? If so, where is the integrity in a process which safeguards Christianity from being understood superficially by pupils at the expense of allowing other faiths to be only superficially understood? If not, then why are all religions represented in Britain not given an equal share of curriculum time in RE? The historical-cultural argument that this country has roots in Christianity and that this provides an acceptable reason for the study of Christianity having a special, privileged and pre-dominant position in the RE curriculum, may have been persuasive twenty or thirty years ago, but this argument is less persuasive in our present social and political climate, both nationally and globally.

What is different about the UK today is that attitudes and aspirations are being shaped by a socio-political culture which sees the values of equality and social justice as having a greater claim on public allegiance than arrangements whereby state institutions, (such as the established Church of England but also, through the controlling influence of the legislation, the nation's schools) are permitted to continue to be the agents of a cultural hegemony in which the vested interests of certain privileged groups in society are preserved while perpetuating unequal and unjust policies towards others. Alas, RE still stands outside the equality agenda that has been such a positive feature of the period of Labour Government in Britain. Unfortunately it is not something that the present government – or, indeed, any future government – is ever likely to consider worth addressing as interfering with the current legislation affecting RE will bring no advantage politically to any of the parties and could work decisively against them. It is, however, clearly anomalous that the government should expect RE to play a significant role in promoting social and community cohesion and, more recently, in combatting religious extremism, when the legislation remains seriously flawed in respect of the very thing which militates against this – the persistence of discrimination against minority ethnic and religious groups and the preservation of privilege and power in the hands of those who are already advantaged.[5]

GOVERNMENT-RELATED INITIATIVES AND THEIR EFFECTS ON THE METAMORPHOSIS OF RE

In 1993, the response of the Conservative government to protracted criticism of the new religious clauses of the 1988 Education Act, especially to the inbalance between Christianity and the other faiths, was for the Minister of State for Education to ask the National Curriculum Council (NCC) and subsequently the School Curriculum and Assessment Authority (SCAA) to produce 'model' syllabuses for RE. Thus began an extensive programme of consultation with representative members of all faiths and of the teaching profession and professional associations of RE. The SCAA *Model Syllabuses for Religious Education* which were produced in 1994 reflected the brief which was given to the six working faith groups, namely that they were to 'set out the key areas of knowledge about their faith which they considered appropriate at different stages of study'. Model One was 'structured around the knowledge and understanding of what it means to be a member of a faith community', and Model Two 'around the knowledge and understanding of the teachings of religions and how these relate to shared human experience'. At the same time the Secretary of State for Education, John Patten, issued Circular 1/94 (1994) which interpreted the 1988 Education Act's statement that the 'religious traditions (in Britain) are in the main Christian' to mean that the teaching of Christianity should predominate at each of the Key Stages – a view that has remained in force until the very slightly more flexible interpretation provided by the non-statutory guidance issued in February 2010 by the DCSF under the title *Religious Education in English Schools*.[6]

How the Model Syllabuses limited the educational potential of RE to contribute to social and community cohesion.

Although having no legal status and intended only to provide Local Education Authorities with guidelines for revising their Agreed Syllabus of RE in line with the requirements of the 1988 Education Act, the publication of the *Model Syllabuses* proved to have an influence on the direction of RE's development which was quite disproportionate to their advisory status. This influence was greatly strengthened by the eventual incorporation of knowledge of the religious content of the *Model Syllabuses* as a 'Standards' requirement by the Teacher Training Agency (TTA) and the Office for Standards in Education (OfSTED) for teacher trainees in RE. While, as we shall see, the Model Syllabuses have some positive features there are also negative ones which, unfortunately, have only served to create a number of weaknesses in the subject during its subsequent stages of metamorphosis. These derive from the limited educational vision that the Model Syllabuses convey about the use and function of the study of religion in enhancing pupils' spiritual, moral, cultural, social and personal development by their implied preference for a 'systems' approach to studying individual religions as a basis for the RE curriculum. They also derive from a negative feature of the national curriculum as a whole, namely a complete disregard for incorporating within curriculum planning any reference to theories of learning or human development which might influence decision-making in relation to programmes of study and forms of assessment appropriate to pupil attainment. As these weaknesses have been replicated to some extent in most if not all agreed syllabuses and non-statutory guidance for RE which have followed from them it is worth indicating why some of these aspects are problematic, especially in their impact upon the subject's capacity to contribute to social and community cohesion.

An aspect which is problematic is the priority given to faith communities in determining what it is they wish to have taught in RE. It is inevitable that what faith communities wish to see taught about in RE are those beliefs which they regard as being central to their faith. But the question is, does this provide a proper basis for deciding upon the religious content that all pupils should study in RE? What may be regarded by adherents as central to their faith does not necessarily result in the identification of religious content which is appropriate for addressing the wider educational concerns of the subject. For example, adherents may not be well placed to identify those aspects of their own faith which best enable pupils to understand what is distinctive about 'religion' as a way of giving meaning to human experience. Neither may they easily identify content from their faith which can engage pupils in the important educational task of understanding how religious beliefs and practices impact upon and contribute to the controversial nature of many social and moral issues in contemporary society. The problem here is for adherents to appreciate that those religious beliefs which may have the status of categorical imperatives or act as religious and moral absolutes within a faith are inevitably subjected to a relativising process within RE whereby each religion is understood to make its own claim to truth.[7] Recognising that in RE religious beliefs and practices fulfil an *instrumental* function which is distinct from the *intrinsic* worth and status which they enjoy within faith communities remains a significant obstacle which can prevent religious educators and religious adherents from agreeing about the nature of RE. Indeed it is the same obstacle which causes many to question whether religious faiths and the concept of religion itself can ever contribute to social and community cohesion but must always be seen as being divisive.[8]

Raising questions about how much curriculum time should be given to each faith as required by the 1988 Education Act will continue while the current legislation remains, but, more to the point, we should ask: is it the purpose of RE to give all pupils in community schools the same understanding of a faith as those who are adherents? Similarly, are pupils from many different religious backgrounds and of none who attend community schools to be expected to have the same understanding of a faith as those pupils who attend, as a result of parental choice, a faith school where the teaching of one particular faith is given pre-eminence ? And – more problematically – what methods of teaching are available to the RE teacher in community schools if this is the expectation? Are all inter-disciplinary methods of studying religion which contribute to its proper study within a secular curriculum to be regarded as equally applicable in teaching about all faiths? Or are methods of study to be restricted in accordance with whichever views members of a faith may have about what are considered to be the proper approaches to understanding their faith? What is at stake here is whether RE teachers should, because of a tradition's opposition, for example, to any form of academic criticism of what it regards as authoritative, such as its scriptures, its tenets of faith, or the special authority invested in a religious leader, etc., revert in their teaching of that faith to an approach which is uncritically instructional, even confessional? Equally, in teaching about

Christianity, whether RE teachers should stress its past and continuing influence upon Britain's cultural identity and values as an explanation to pupils for why they are required to spend more time studying it than any other faith? – thus implying that Christian beliefs must continue to have more significance than the beliefs of other faiths in the life of contemporary British society. And finally, whether RE teachers should be responsive to the highly critical treatment which is often given to religions, especially Christianity and Islam, in the popular press and seek in their lessons to attempt some form of apologetic against the political, ideological and social agendas which exert such a powerful influence on people's views of, and attitudes towards religion and to RE? As far as I am aware, these are not questions which an RE teacher will find, as yet, addressed in statutory or non-statutory guidelines or Agreed Syllabuses of RE.

Given the complexities of dealing equitably with the different expectations that arise in the teaching of RE, the place of the individual teacher of RE has become increasingly vulnerable. To what extent is the RE teacher free to respond to such complexities by exercising a personal judgement? Although there has always been a deep concern among liberal educators for RE teachers to retain a degree of personal and professional autonomy in how they fulfil the educational aims of RE, in circumstances where the law allows the rights of parents and the expectations of faith communities to be paramount, RE teachers, in exercising a personal judgement in their teaching, may find themselves in conflict with both. In recent years we have seen how the RE enterprise can be easily undermined if the personal perspectives and views of the individual RE teacher are allowed to determine how religious content is treated or taught within the particularities of the school in which they are teaching. This has reinforced the necessity of asserting that the integrity of the whole educational enterprise of teaching about religion and religions in community schools can never depend on an individual teacher's perception of how this should be conducted. More to the point, in a world in which religious, ideological and cultural perspectives can be difficult to disentangle, it is wholly undesirable for individual RE teachers to exercise personal judgements about how best to teach about religion and religions without being fully supported and protected by statutory (as opposed to non-statutory) guidelines. And now, when, in employment, the expression of personal religious beliefs by employees is increasingly prone to being seen to contravene policies of political correctness, how long will it be before RE teachers are unable to make any reference to their own personal religious or non-religious stance when teaching RE?[9] These are difficult and potentially dangerous times for RE teachers, especially given, until recently, the reduction in the number of professional advisers and in-service courses by Local Authorities and professional development opportunities provided by training institutions such as University Departments of Education.[10]

Learning about and from religion(s): how RE's field of enquiry was reduced and its potential contribution to social and community cohesion further curtailed

One positive feature of the Model Syllabuses was the adoption and advocacy of *learning about religion* and *learning from religion* as the two attainment targets for RE. How these targets were presented in the syllabuses, however, neglected the much broader theoretical framework of which this concept of interactional learning in RE was originally seen to be a part. The field of study for RE which I identified in my book *Religious Education and Human Development* (1987) comprised five parts – 'Human Givens', 'Core Human Values', 'Substantive Religious Categories', 'Shared Human Experience' and 'Traditional Belief Systems'. Only the latter two were included in the *Model Syllabuses*, with 'Traditional Belief Systems' becoming 'World Religions'. In removing these from their place within this wider context, important criteria influencing the choice and treatment of religious content and its relationship to the educational aims and humanising concerns of RE were lost. For example, my identification of seven core human values and their potential relationship to seven substantive religious categories was an attempt to reduce the religious content of RE to what I called 'essential minimum key-concepts' which would enable pupils to study religious content in a way which related it to the interpretation of core values and as responses to those ultimate questions which are an important stimulus to human meaning-making.[11] This process of *learning about religion* was intended to contribute to pupils' understanding of how human beings develop as a result of their interaction with each other in communities and societies, and also how their 'faith responses' to life's questions and dilemmas and the beliefs they hold and the values they adopt have a shaping influence on their own identities and how they perceive the identities of others. In abandoning this theoretical framework, which is admittedly complex, the model syllabuses fell victim to allowing the religious content of RE to be decided mainly on the basis of what adherents of a faith want pupils to learn about their faith, which, as we have seen, is not always well suited to the task of matching content with the wider educational aims of the subject.

But if the potential for *learning about religion* (which, not surprisingly, given the stress on a 'systems approach', became *learning about religions*) was truncated within the *Model Syllabuses*, how *learning from religion* was applied there curtailed its educational potential even more severely. In its original form *learning from religion* was intended to fulfil several important educational functions, not least in encouraging pupils to think through their own beliefs, values and attitudes and to examine and clarify these (and, possibly, affirm or reject them) in the light of the beliefs and values they had been learning about in the religious traditions they had studied.

> 'The value of studying religions is not merely to be found in the understanding of religious meaning that it promotes, but in what understanding of religious meaning contributes to the pupil's understanding of self.' (Grimmitt 1987,165)

It is the contribution which *learning from religion* makes to encouraging pupils to empathise with belief and value perspectives other than their own which makes it a significant way of enabling RE to contribute to an appreciation of diversity and to social and community cohesion. As a method of reflection it owes much to the sort of dynamic which is a necessary part of inter-faith dialogue. Pupils are to be encouraged to:

> 'Evaluate their understanding of religion in personal terms and evaluate their understanding of self in religious terms (i.e. in terms of the religious beliefs they have learned about).' (*ibid.*, 213)

As result, pupils should:

> 'be able to describe what is would mean *to them* to be a Christian, Hindu, Jew, Muslim, Sikh, etc. We should note that this requirement applies to all pupils, irrespective of whether or not they are practising members of a religious faith.....and indeed an important variant would be that those who are members of a religious faith to be able to describe what it would mean to them not to have a religious faith, or to adopt a naturalistic stance.' (*ibid.*, 213)

The need to help pupils to develop their capacities to empathise with people whose beliefs and values may be different from and in conflict with their own is an essential step in helping them to live with, and participate within a diverse society and to recognise and accept the claim that this makes on individuals to respect the right of others to adopt different value positions on significant issues within a pluralist society. The interdependent process of *learning about religion* and *learning from religion* is thus essential in enabling pupils to understand how religion works, especially how it affects the ways in which some human beings respond to life's exigencies, find meaning and purpose in both positive and negative experiences and adopt a particular ethical perspective on fundamental human issues. Ideally pupils should be able to have an imaginative appreciation of the power of religion to exert an influence on how they might understand their own life experiences if they choose to interpret them within a religious framework, and also, of course, to have an informed understanding of how adopting a religious interpretation can have a decisive impact upon the lives of others whose religious and cultural histories are different from their own. It is regrettable that rather than being an ever-present process of reflective, critically-evaluative interaction between what is *learned about religion* and how that learning may impact upon pupils' self-awareness and self-understanding, *learning from religion* in practice is often reduced to a short and superficial plenary reflection at the end of a lesson. This is far from adequate as the evaluative process of *learning from religion(s)* should be fully integrated with how pupils are *learning about religion(s)* in the first place. Indeed the choice of religious content should, in the first instance, be made with a conscious awareness of what it is able to contribute to the process of *learning from religion*.[12]

Has the publication of the Non-Statutory National Framework for Religious Education (2004) improved the subject's capacity to contribute to social and community cohesion?

Attempts in recent years to provide a non-statutory national framework for RE have built on the *Model Syllabuses* but modified them in ways which, in small measure, have restored some of the earlier theoretical underpinnings to the terms *learning about religion* and *learning from religion* and have introduced new ways of applying them to the RE curriculum. In the *Non-Statutory National Framework for Religious Education* issued by the QCA/DfES in 2004, these terms are used consistently in the generic form; there are no references to *learning about religions* or *learning from religions*. This usage is much closer to how I originally conceived these terms and applied them within the context of learning and teaching in RE. *Learning about religion* (as the singular, generic use of 'religion' implies) gives importance to pupils understanding how 'religion', as a mode of categorising human thought and experience, or as a distinctive form of knowledge, is conceptualised and expressed. This involves recognising and being able to use the substantive categories that religion uses to identify and express the central concepts that provide it with a theoretical structure which distinguishes it from other ways of interpreting human experience (such as one which, for example, uses scientific categories and concepts). There is still much more work to be done to identify such categories and apply them to the RE curriculum. Such work would, I believe, enable the RE curriculum to be organised in a way which is more conducive to encouraging honest engagement with the difficult issues of conflict within and between religions than can ever be the case when each religion is studied separately and in isolation from the others. It is where the much-needed but rarely achieved collaboration between religious educators and academics working in theology and religious studies could begin to occur.[13]

The Non-Statutory National Framework for Religious Education: (QCA/DfES, 2004) makes a modest contribution to this sort of thinking by introducing a taxonomic list of 'knowledge, skills and understanding' that pupils 'should be taught' at each Key Stage under *learning about religion* and *learning from religion*. Explicit religious content is avoided (this being the responsibility of Agreed Syllabus Committees) but broad areas in which religious belief and practice interface with contemporary life and experience are identified. For example, pupils at Key Stage 2 are expected to 'identify and begin to describe the similarities and differences within and between religions',(*op.cit.*, 26) and at Key Stage 3 to 'investigate why people belong to faith communities and explain the reasons for diversity in religion'. (*op.cit.*, 28) Grounding RE in the study of a generic understanding of religion within its social context and how it works would, I believe, enable pupils to achieve such understanding more easily. It would also enable RE to give pupils a better appreciation of how religion can contribute to social and community cohesion as well as understand why it can also be an obstacle to it. Such an arrangement, in which illustrations can be drawn from several religions, (for example, of beliefs which favour exclusivism or inclusivism, orthodoxy or liberalism, patriarchy or gender equality, the absolute authority of scripture or the rights of individual conscience, etc.,) discourages the tendency for any one particular religion's interpretation of substantive religious categories to be seen as normative. The educational task is for pupils to understand how such interpretations can arise and to consider the implications that these may have for intercultural understanding and relationships within a society accepting of diversity and, with difficulty and reluctance, the necessary co-existence of plural realities, including those of an ultimate nature. It may also enable the important question of the multiple identities of young people, and, in some cases, their relationship to religion, to be addressed in RE.

Because RE, unfortunately, must continue to meet the requirements of the religious clauses of the 1988 Education Act, *The Non-Statutory National Framework for Religious Education* includes, *religions and beliefs* as one of three compulsory areas of study. Thus, pupils at Key Stage One, Two and Three are to study: Christianity (always), at least one other principal religion (two at Key Stages Two and Three), a religious community with a significant local presence where appropriate, and a secular world view, where appropriate. It is also recommended that opportunities for pupils should be given to study the Baha'i Faith, Jainism and Zoroastrianism. But here we find ourselves facing the same problems as those I previously identified in relation to the model syllabuses. On what basis will decisions about content in the section *'religions and belief'* be made? Quite simply, there is, at present, no agreed basis other than what faith groups may wish to see included – something which is acknowledged in the *Non-Statutory National Framework* (*op.cit.*,12). The innovative inclusion of a secular world view is about maintaining a 'broad and balanced curriculum', and in recognition that 'many pupils come from religious backgrounds but others have no attachment to religious beliefs and practices'. (*op.cit.*,12). But informing pupils about the beliefs that others hold without encouraging them to engage in a critical exploration of how they think these beliefs may impact locally and globally upon matters of personal, social and political concern is unlikely to further the cause of social and community cohesion.

Much more helpful and having greater future potential for encouraging RE to contribute to social and community cohesion are the two other areas of study identified in the document – *themes* and *experiences* and *opportunities*. It is under *themes* that we encounter at least some religious categories being used to enable religious content to be chosen which relates to what pupils should be taught under the heading *learning about religion*. Gratifyingly the focus of some of the themes is on promoting understanding of the impact that holding certain religious beliefs may have upon life in the local community and wider society, and globally. For example, pupils at Key Stage 2 are to explore ways in which 'religions and beliefs respond to global issues of human rights, fairness, social justice and the importance of the environment' (*op.cit.*, 27); and at Key Stage 3 a study of interfaith dialogue includes 'a study of relationships, conflicts and collaboration with and between religions and beliefs'. (*op.cit.*, 29) Similarly, under *experiences and opportunities* the focus of the curriculum is to be on helping pupils to understand the impact and influence of religious belief and practice upon the local and global community, not just upon their significance within the confines of particular faith communities. In illustration, at Key Stage 2 the popular use of visitors in RE classrooms and class visits to places of worship is seen as having its focus on pupils both 'encountering religion' and recognising 'the impact and reality of religion on (sic and in?) the local and global community'. (*op.cit.*, 27) The educational value of these two sections and their potential to contribute to social and community cohesion is high and could, in their own right provide a sufficient basis for RE without the need for *religions and beliefs* to be studied separately. But that would not, unfortunately, meet the requirements of the 1988 Education Act.

Another important feature of the *Non-Statutory National Framework for Religious Education* is its attempt to bring greater clarity to the important activity of assessment in RE, which should always be seen as having a participatory function within the process of learning and teaching, not something separate and later. In determining levels of attainment in RE it categorises the 'knowledge, skills and understanding' that pupils should be taught' at each Key Stage under *learning about religion* and *learning from religion* by using three strands for each Attainment Target. The strands for AT1 (*learning about religion*) are: *beliefs, teachings and sources; practices and ways of life; forms of expression*. The strands for AT2 (*learning from religion*) are: *identity and belonging; meaning, purpose and truth; values and commitments*. These then inform the descriptors provided at each of the eight levels which each AT encompasses. It is odd that this helpful categorisation is not used earlier in the document when first introducing the taxonomic lists of 'knowledge, skills and understanding' that pupils are to be taught at each Key Stage.

The QCA's non-statutory guidance on RE in the new national curriculum: a pattern for the future?

The approach taken by the *Non-Statutory National Framework for Religious Education* (2004) to enhancing ways in which RE may contribute to social and community cohesion has recently been taken up under the auspices of the QCA in response to the new national secondary curriculum introduced in 2008 as part of major reforms of education and qualifications, as set out in *The Children's Plan* (2007). Irrespective of the undoubted advantages of ensuring that developments in RE are in line with those of the rest of the curriculum, the participation of the QCA in providing a 'non-statutory' programme of study for a 'statutory subject' which, theoretically, could be rejected by Agreed Syllabuses Conferences within each Local Authority – but will not be – further reflects the anomolous relationship of RE to the national curriculum and the negative effects of the religious clauses of the 1988 Education Act upon the subject's development. The proposals for RE's programmes of study issued by the QCA under the heading 'National Curriculum', while having no legal authority, are, therefore, likely to exercise the same effect and influence on the metamorphosis of RE as did the contents of the *Model Syllabuses* fifteen years earlier, but in a very different social and political climate more attuned to the implementation of an equality agenda and therefore, hopefully, with better results.[14]

It is immediately apparent, however, in looking at the new programmes of study for RE at Key Stages 3 and 4, that the QCA architects have been influenced by the OfSTED report *Making sense of religion – a report on religious education in schools and the impact of locally agreed syllabuses.* (2007). This report – which, as indicated in its title, consistently uses the generic form of 'religion' – highlights the significance of RE contributing to social and community cohesion in accordance with the Education and Inspections Act (2006), as may be seen from the following statements taken from its first and subsequent pages:

'Recent world events have raised the profile of religious education significantly and schools have new responsibilities to promote community cohesion. Those with responsibility for RE therefore have the task of ensuring that children and young people are able to make sense of religion in the modern world and issues of identity and diversity. (*op.cit.*,1)

It asserts:

'At its best RE equips pupils very well to consider issues of community cohesion, diversity and religious understanding.' (*op.cit.*,5)

But later it admits:

'The curriculum and teaching in RE do not place sufficient emphasis on exploring the changing political and social significance of religion in the modern world. As a result, the subject's potential to contribute to community cohesion, education for diversity and citizenship is not fully realised.' (*op.cit.*, 7)

The Report's recommendations include the following:

'Local authorities, in partnership with their SACREs, need to:

- consider how the work of SACREs might support further the promotion of community cohesion and educating for diversity.' (*op.cit*, 8)

'All schools should:

- ensure that RE contributes strongly to pupils' understanding of the changing role of religion, diversity and social cohesion.' (*op.cit.*,9)

Later, in a section dealing with RE and pupils' personal development, it includes the following quotation from Inter Faith Network: *Faith, Identity and Belonging*: *Educating for Shared Citizenship (2006)*:

'A particular issue emerges about schools' contribution to promoting community cohesion....There are many existing resources dealing with individual religious traditions but few examples of good resources which help in teaching about the faith and inter-faith dimensions of citizenship or about issues of belonging, coping with difference and respecting other people's beliefs and values.' (*op.cit.*,18)

and adds:

'The changing and controversial role of religion in contemporary society is not given sufficient attention in most agreed syllabuses and examination courses.' (*op.cit.*,27)

Finally, the report identifies four key points upon which RE should focus:

- 'RE cannot ignore diversity within each religion...;'
- 'RE cannot ignore controversy. We should dispense with the notion that we should encourage pupils to think uncritically of religion as a 'good thing'.
- 'RE cannot ignore the social reality of religion....It now needs to embrace the study of religion and society.'
- 'RE cannot ignore its role in fostering community cohesion and in educating for diversity......Developing respect for the commitments of others while retaining the right to question, criticise and evaluate different viewpoints is not just an academic exercise: it involves creating opportunities for children and young people to meet those with different viewpoints. They need to grasp how powerful religion is in people's lives. RE should engage pupils' feelings and emotions, as well as their intellect.' (*op.cit.*, 40-41)

The report, typically of OfSTED, does not attempt to suggest ways in which these important recommendations should be operationalised. It is, therefore, primarily an expression of hope that future planning and development in RE will take them seriously, as indeed they must if the report's confidence that RE can contribute to social and community cohesion is to be justified.

The QCA programmes of study for RE identify with this view and, therefore, serve to reinforce pressure on the subject to respond to the challenges of contemporary social, political, and cultural agendas and of the new Government-related initiatives intended to improve the learning experiences of pupils within schools as a whole. (See the section which follows.) Significantly, in keeping with the *Non-Statutory National Framework*, *learning about religion* and *learning from religion* are recognised as an essential process of *how* learning takes place in RE, not merely as learning outcomes to be achieved.[15] The 'skills and processes in RE' which are part of this represent a conflation of those identified in the taxonomic lists of the *Non-Statutory National Framework* under 'knowledge, skills and understanding'. But there is also an additional and helpful innovation in transforming the six strands previously restricted to categorising 'knowledge, skills and understanding' for the purposes of attainment into 'a number of key concepts that underpin the study of RE and which pupils need to understand in order to deepen and broaden their knowledge, skills and understanding.' (QCA National Curriculum; RE key stage 3, 1) These key concepts are now re-stated as: *beliefs, teachings and sources; practices and ways of life; expressing meaning; identity, diversity and belonging; meaning, purpose and truth; and values and commitments.*

Even though they may, in the future, play an important part in identifying religious content which is to be incorporated within the RE curriculum, there is, at this stage, something fairly arbitrary about the choice of these concepts; substantive religious categories to which they might be related are not suggested, neither is illustrative content. The introduction of 'key concepts' here (in accordance with their use in the new programmes of study for all other curriculum subjects coming from QCA) does, however, signal the all important recognition that there is a need in RE curriculum planning for some device to be introduced which enables appropriate religious content which contributes to the educational purposes of RE and the needs of the pupils to be distinguished from that which does not. Although insufficient in themselves to do this, the key concepts identified could be helpful in ensuring that teaching and learning and assessment in RE at least focuses upon enabling pupils to understand and respond critically to the impact of religion upon issues within contemporary society which connect with their own experiences and prompt them to be reflective about their own identify, values and commitments, whatever their family background. This is a welcome advance in the re-shaping of RE in a manner which enhances its ability to contribute to social and community cohesion. So too is the recognition, at both Key Stage Three and Four, that the statutory requirement to study Christianity and other principal religions can be met by using themes (such as 'issues related to God, truth, the world, human life, and life after death' – another fairly arbitrary list) or by teaching them 'either directly as a religion or indirectly through philosophical or ethical issues.' There are, however, other factors emerging which may play an even more decisive part in the future metamorphosis of RE, and it to a consideration of these that I now turn.

THE 'BIG PICTURE OF THE CURRICULUM' AND THE PLACE OF RE WITHIN IT

There have been some very significant developments in thinking about the National Curriculum in the last three years and, although remaining technically outside it, RE will need to respond positively to these and be seen to make a distinctive contribution to the 'joined up' vision of education that is fast emerging. These developments have been heralded by a proliferation of new acronyms, such as ECM ('Every Child Matters'), SEAL ('Social and Emotional Aspects of Learning'), PLTS ('Personal, Learning and Thinking Skills'), PL ('Personalised Learning') and PV ('Pupil Voice'), and re-worked ones like PSHE ('Personal, Social, Health and Economic Education), SMD ('Spiritual and Moral Development') and some yet to be acronymed, such as 'Education for Personal Well Being (usually spelled 'wellbeing') and for Happiness'! And, of course, since 2002, Citizenship has been a compulsory part of the secondary school National Curriculum.

In almost every aspect of these developments RE might be thought to have been a forerunner, not of course, in terms of the more precise applications that each of these areas of concern are now being given within the wider curriculum and the whole-school framework, but in the way in which some proponents of RE have sought to accommodate a holistic, experiential and humanising approach to pupils' development and well being within and through the RE curriculum. There was a time when RE was criticised for taking on too wide an educational brief, enveloping – because they were neglected elsewhere – sex education, personal, social and moral education, and multicultural and anti-racist education. When 'citizenship education' emerged as a strong contender for a compulsory 5% place in the secondary school curriculum some religious educators – like they had done previously with PSME – were prepared to look for ways in which RE could collaborate in its delivery. In these different ways RE has sought to fill a vacuum in the educational experience of pupils. This has led to the subject being in the vanguard of promoting an underlying rationale for education which goes beyond dependence upon and adherence to taxonomies of knowledge or on checking outcomes against lists of competences or of applying levels of attainment to everything that is learnt or taught. As so many of the Agreed Syllabuses of RE demonstrate, the subject has consistently aligned itself with a determination to provide a vision of the highest aspirations and achievements of human beings and their necessary engagement with ethical issues and moral ideals which would challenge and inspire pupils to seek self-fulfilment through participating actively and responsibly as citizens within a complex, plural and culturally diverse society.

With the emergence, at last, of the possibility of a National Curriculum which is based on a commonly agreed set of aims (to which each subject contributes) and, more importantly, is conceived of as 'an entire planned learning experience underpinned by a broad set of common values and purposes' (QCA Big Picture chart), RE is in a strong position to collaborate by identifying what its distinctive *educational* contribution to this process may be. Furthermore, because the total curriculum now embraces, at last, some semblance of theory drawing upon insights from studies in human development, approaches to learning and teaching (i.e. pedagogy), social psychology, ethnography and political theory, RE, while not abandoning its past identity, can re-define itself in terms of what it is best able to contribute, in the language of today, to the 'big picture' of the curriculum. In this sense, another stage in RE's metamorphosis is about to emerge which, hopefully, will not only enable the subject to embrace the challenge of ensuring that the study of religion contributes to social and cultural cohesion, although that remains controversial, but also that RE makes its own distinctive contribution to young people becoming successful learners, confident individuals and responsible citizens. (QCA (2009))

It is appropriate to give due recognition to the part played by the Religious Education Council of England and Wales in steering RE towards this new goal. Its timely production and presentation in March 2007 of *A National Strategy for Religious Education* to Lord Adonis, the Parliamentary Under-

Secretary of State with responsibility for RE, has not only enabled the subject to be brought into greater prominence in the recent consultation about the new national curriculum but has also signalled important new directions and emphases that the subject must encompass. viz:

> 'RE should be aligned more closely with other related developments in education, particularly citizenship, personal, social, health education with its significance for moral education, diversity and community cohesion, and the personalisation of learning, to ensure a synergetic approach to the contribution of education to social and community issues.' (Summary of the Report, 7)

It is gratifying that this initiative has also resulted in the award of Government grants of a little over a million pounds for research and development in RE, much of which is currently being used in ways which have a direct bearing on this task.[16] It is not for me, however, to pre-empt the eventual outcomes by commenting on them here. Rather, my final task in this chapter is to return to the questions I raised in my introduction and, in the light of the account of RE's metamorphosis that I have offered, to reflect on how they might now be addressed.

MAPPING OUT A NEW GROUNDPLAN FOR RE IN WHICH THE STUDY OF RELIGION CONTRIBUTES TO SOCIAL AND COMMUNITY COHESION

Can RE contribute to social and community cohesion effectively within the current legislative framework?

Any system of legislation today, whatever its focus – social welfare, education, health, housing, employment, etc., – and however deeply rooted in a nation's historical and cultural tradition, which fails the test of even-handedness with regard to equality of opportunity and social justice cannot, in my view, be a vehicle for social reconciliation or community cohesion. This means that the capacity of RE to contribute effectively to social and community cohesion has been, and continues to be seriously undermined by being based on legislation which so clearly fails this test. If faith groups are to be encouraged to support an educational enterprise which sets the study of religion and religions within a framework of critical understanding it is essential that all religions are given, and are seen to be given, parity of status and esteem within that enterprise. In my view, it is only when the legislation addressing the provision of RE in community schools actively serves to reduce the potential for conflict and competition between faiths that RE will be able to play its part in encouraging moderation and greater inter-faith co-operation within society as a whole. It is also to be hoped that 'faith schools' may also feel able to address this agenda through the sort of RE they adopt and support.[17]

It is not surprising, therefore, that the legislation has hindered rather than encouraged a model of RE to emerge which is well-suited to addressing the additional social and political expectations that are now being placed on the subject. In my view such a model would be one that:

- allows the strengths and weakness of religion and ideology as agents of social and community cohesion to be explored dispassionately;

- enables the nature of faith and the positive and negative influences of religious belief on human development and human aspiration to be critically understood;

- explains how religions may contribute to individual, group and ethnic identity but in so doing can also cause profound and irreconcilable divisions between people both individually and collectively;

- encourages understanding of how inter-religious conflict can and does arise in the interpretation of core human values and human rights;

- demonstrates how religions contain within themselves a considerable diversity of belief and practice which, while being a strength in responding to the varieties of human experience and need, can also contribute to tensions within and between faiths leading to divisions, schisms, acts of violence, persecution and genocide;

- encourages the recognition of how religions may share common aspirations and hopes for human well-being and can participate co-operatively in humanitarian projects in which religious differences are transcended for the common good.

As I hope to show, a model of RE that can contribute effectively to the new educational and social expectations which are now being attached to the curriculum as a whole, will need to be rather more sophisticated pedagogically than anything which has so far emerged in the subject's history. For example, as previously indicated, the model will need to combine an approach to the study of religion and religions which balances exploring both negative and positive influences that they exert upon the quality of social and community relationships. The successful formulation of such an approach is difficult to imagine within a legislative framework in which the different religions are not given equal opportunities for their perspectives to be represented within the RE curriculum. But equally, there may be strong grounds for the difficult issue of conflict within and between religions to be approached in RE, not through studying religions separately, (which can over-expose individual religions to the critical process with unfortunate results), but rather by selecting from them for critical study examples of how the substantive concepts of religion are interpreted and expressed within different religious traditions. There is a considerable danger that in bringing the study of religion and religions within a process which is designed to promote certain social and political outcomes that pupils are given a distorted view of religion as well as of the individual religions. The debate about whether or not religion and religions contribute positively to social and community cohesion is not over and has not reached a conclusion.[18] We must avoid trying to find a model of RE which closes down this debate or suggests otherwise.

Are the present two attainment targets for RE fit for purpose? Might it be necessary to add to them or change them?

The widespread use of *learning about religion* and *learning from religion* as the two *attainment* targets for RE followed from their use in this way in the SCAA *Model Syllabuses* of 1994. However, as previously indicated, these two terms did not originate as attainment targets but as descriptions of an essential *pedagogical procedure or strategy* within a human development model of RE which stressed the instrumental value that the study of religion and religions can make to pupils' human/personal development. In introducing the model I wrote:

> 'If religions are studied in such as way as to juxtapose the 'content' of the religious life-worlds of adherents with the 'content' of the pupils' life-worlds, pupils become informed about religious beliefs and values and are able to use them as instruments for the critical evaluation of their own beliefs and values.' (Grimmitt 1987, 141)

Thus the relationship between *learning about religion* and *learning from religion* is a symbiotic or a synergetic one; taken together – and they must always be taken together – they represent a *dialogical* way of learning and teaching in RE. It is this type of learning which delivers the human development outcomes of this model of RE.

It is, of course, possible to translate this *pedagogical procedure* into the educational outcomes that are intended to be achieved as a result of its application. For example, it is possible to identify and describe what pupils need to *know, understand and be able to do* in order to demonstrate that they have indeed learned how to learn about religion (Attainment Target One). Similarly, but with rather more difficulty, it may be possible to identify and describe what pupils need to *know, understand and be able to do* in order to demonstrate that they have also learned how to apply what they have learned from religion in a reflective and critical manner to issues and concerns which may affect their own lives (Attainment Target Two). Alternatively, as in the *Non-Statutory National Framework for Religious Education*, each of the two attainment targets can be further amplified by listing beneath each one the *knowledge, skills and understanding* which contribute to pupils attaining them and by arranging these in a speculative hierarchy of their complexity across eight levels of attainment (plus one of exceptional performance) with guidance on the expected level of attainment for the majority of pupils at the end of each key stage (e.g. Level 4 at age 11 or Level 5 or 6 at age 14.)

The danger of linking the two terms with lists of separate outcomes (even if they are intended to be complimentary) is that the *dialogical* nature of the process is lost sight of and they are treated independently. For example, it might be thought that the *learning about* outcomes and the levels of attainment related to these should first be met, followed by the *learning from* outcomes and the levels of attainment related to these. While this is a possibility, as reflected in common classroom practice, the educational benefits derived from the strategy are much greater if the nature of the interdependence of *learning about* and *learning from religion* is better understood in both teaching and learning and in assessment. Indeed there is a burgeoning academic and professional literature in RE exploring and refining their relationship – almost thirty-five years after the terms were first introduced. (Attfield 1996; Attfield 1997; Ellis 1997; Grimmitt 1987; Grimmitt 2000; Maybury and Teece 2005; Fancourt 2005; Engebretson 2006; Teece 2008; Dossett 2008; Hella and Wright 2009; Baumfield 2009; Blaylock 2009; Teece 2010.) As a result, 'the unity of learning about and learning from' (Hella and Wright, 2009, 57) is being variously interpreted and used within newly emerging pedagogical perspectives within RE, so clearly the dialogical style of interaction that is envisaged as a basis for learning in RE continues to be seen as having both viability and vitality as a way of addressing the learning needs of the pupils and the concerns of the subject.

It is particularly interesting to see how the relationship between *learning about* and *learning from religion* can be variously described, on the one hand, as 'ambiguous' or 'confusing' by some religious educators yet, on the other hand, still be used by them to further the aims and objectives of quite different pedagogies from the human development model related to the process of humanisation with which it originated A good example of this is how Hella and Wright (2009) can incorporate *learning about* and *learning from religion* within a critical realist view of RE:

> 'Our alternative proposal is that the unity of religious education is to be found in the notion of the good life. We suggest that the desire to live a good or fruitful life is shared by most human beings including students themselves and the religious and secular traditions they engage with.

> Since we are relational creatures whose identities flow not just from introspective self-awareness but also from our relationships with other human beings, the natural world, and the presence or absence of God or some transcendent reality in our lives – our understanding of the good life is intrinsically linked to the realistic question of the ultimate order-of-things. In traditional philosophical language, the quest for truthful living is bound up with the pursuit of truth (Wright, 2007).'

> 'Different religious and secular traditions offer contested accounts of the good life which are inextricably linked to contested accounts of reality. Hence the basic unity of learning about and learning from religion is ontological: the personal and spiritual development of pupils is dependent on their understanding of the good life, and hence their understanding of ultimate reality. Since, in a plural context, such understandings are contested, the unity of the twin dimensions of religious education lies specifically in the *pursuit* of truth and truthfulness.' (Hella and Wright, 2009, 57-58)

Hella and Wright's view of how *learning about* and *learning from religion* can be incorporated within a critical realist view of RE is consequently expressed as follows:

> '....by cultivating a deep understanding of students' horizons of meaning and the horizons of various religious and secular traditions, religious education should aim to empower students to make informed judgements about the ultimate nature of reality and the implications of this for the way in which they choose to live their lives. Such a critical religious education, we suggest, assumes the unity of learning about and learning from religion.

Students can only make informed judgements about their beliefs and values (learning from religion) by engaging with the truth claims of various religious and secular traditions (learning about religion). Similarly, students can only achieve a deep understanding of religion (learning about religion) by relating such understanding to their own belief system (learning from religion).' (*ibid.*,62)

Geoff Teece also incorporates the principle successfully within a view of RE which is influenced by John Hick's view of religion:

'I have been interested in writing about religion as a distinctive phenomenon with its overriding characteristic being its spiritual dimension as understood as human transformation in the context of responses to the transcendent (Maybury and Teece, 2005: Teece, 2008: 2009). However in interpreting religion with the aid of this particular second order framework the intention is not to learn about and from the framework but to enable teachers and syllabus compilers to select appropriate content from the religions that pupils could beneficially learn about and from.' (Teece, 2010, 99)

'What I have been concerned with here is an attempt to clarify how we might best understand the pedagogical strategy of *learning about religion* and *learning from religion* that presents religion as a distinct phenomenon that does justice to the transformative qualities of the religious traditions in a way that may enable pupils to widen and deepen their understanding of both what lies at the heart of the religions and their interpretation of the human condition. In this sense learning about and from *religions* can be said to be a dialogue between the pupils' life worlds and the worlds of the religions. I have suggested elsewhere (Teece 2008) that such a dialogue can be understood as *upayic* as in the Mahayanan Buddhist concept of 'skilful means'.' (*ibid.*, 101)

In this article Teece makes some very significant remarks about the importance of teachers concentrating on 'the concepts and values that are inherent in the spirituality of religious traditions', especially in making decisions about the choice and treatment of curriculum content. In the light of my earlier commendation of the emphasis that the *Non-Statutory National Framework for Religious Education* and the QCA's *non-statutory guidance on RE in the new national curriculum* have placed on identifying key concepts as a device for choosing content, it is of benefit to note Teece's observations of how this contributes to 'a proper understanding of the terms *learning about religion* and *learning from religion.*' (*ibid.*101)

'As concepts provide a framework for human beings to interpret and understand human experience, the Hampshire syllabus (as does the Westhill

Project, see Read et al. [1986] 1992, 27–9) divides concepts into three categories, namely concepts that are common to religious and secular experience such as celebration, community, justice, relationship; concepts that are common to many religions and the study of religion such as God, worship, myth; and concepts that are distinctive of particular religions such as *sewa* (selfless service) in Sikhism, *ibadah* (worship) in Islam, *kedusha* (God's holiness) in Judaism, etc.' (*ibid*.101)

This indicates a rather less arbitrary basis for choosing key concepts in the study of religion and religions that can be applied to the process of curriculum decision-making in RE than the one used by QCA. Teece also sets out clearly the rationale for using the three different categories of concepts.

'...the second category of concepts is common to many religions and the study of religion can facilitate a broad understanding of religion. But it is a deep understanding of the relationship between the other two categories of concepts, those common to religious and secular experience and concepts that are distinctive of particular religions that hold the key to a conceptual approach and, in my opinion, to a proper understanding of the terms *learning about religion* and *learning from religion*. But unless teachers really understand this then it's expecting a lot to expect them to enable pupils to use such concepts as interpretive tools when applying what they have learned about these concepts to their own and other peoples' lives, and to the world at large.' (*ibid*.101)

Teece's writings do much to counter those facile interpretations of learning from religion in which there is no apparent link made with the religious or theological content which has been explored through *learning about religion*. His comments provide a useful antidote to the widespread misunderstanding that exists about the nature of their interdependence and which leads to the inadequate and questionable practices in schools which prompt the OfSTED Report (2007), *Making Sense of Religion*: to conclude, that:

'Schools, however, find it difficult to provide a coherent RE curriculum which enables pupils to make progress and achieve their potential. The two attainment targets give rise to particular difficulties. They have helped teachers to remember the importance of balancing an academic approach to studying religion with one that fosters pupils' wider personal development. The model has commanded considerable, but not universal, support for some years. However, it has proved problematic as a basis for planning and assessment.' (38)

Blaylock (2009) in addressing the question 'Does 'learning from religion' make a wise depiction of half of RE's field of enquiry?', provides a spirited defence of the pedagogical strategy which concludes with his suggesting that *learning from religion* could become the sole attainment target of RE. He begins by recalling the original concept of *learning from religion*:

> '...pupils should evaluate their understanding of self in religious terms... the evaluative process of learning from religion(s) should be fully integrated into how, within a secular educational context, pupils are learning about religion(s) in the first place." (Grimmitt (2000),15)

He then comments:

> 'This kind of integrated vision is not actually of what the National Curriculum calls an 'attainment target' but is instead a vision of purpose for the subject. This vision, often expressed in the context of attainment by government documentation, is often highly valued by teachers, who acknowledge very largely that 'AT2' is the part of RE that carries inspiration for teachers and pupils. The current description of appropriate achievement for 14 years olds requires that:

> "Pupils use reasoning and examples to express insights into the relationship between beliefs, teachings and world issues. They express insights into their own and others' views on questions of identity and belonging, meaning, purpose and truth. They consider the challenges of belonging to a religion in the contemporary world, focusing on values and commitments." (*National Non-Statutory Framework for RE*, level 6 AT2 descriptor, QCA 2004)

However he agrees with the OfSTED report's comment that:

> 'Unevenness in the progress that pupils make across the two attainment targets of 'learning about' and 'learning from' religion reflects the continuing emphasis that many schools place on 'learning about' religion. Where provision is particularly weak, pupils learn about only superficial features of the religion, rather than deepening their understanding through investigation. This tends to happen when teachers assume that more analytical and reflective tasks are linked predominantly to attainment target 2, 'learning from' religion; as a result, they do not include challenging tasks in work related to 'learning about' religion." (OfSTED (2007),10)

In 2006, one of my research students, Michelle Lucas (née Chatterley), began extensive trials of the three-fold strategy of my 'Constructivist RE Pedagogy' in her classroom.[19] Her introductory comments on the investigative and action research she undertook exactly parallel the criticisms that have been made by OfSTED about superficial and unchallenging tasks being set in RE and their failure to deepen pupils' understanding of religion.

'The AT2 element in lessons was usually added on as a quick plenary or starter and was often a rather rushed attempt at evaluating the content or asking pupils to reflect upon it. *Furthermore, the reflective aspect usually attempted to make a somewhat tenuous link between the religious content and pupils' experience. This often had the effect of trivialising the religious content and the deeper, more spiritual aspect that the teacher was trying so hard to bring alive for the pupils was often lost.*' (my emphasis)

Through working with pupils on many different topics in RE she was able to identify important ways in which the quality of their learning could be greatly improved by the teacher giving very careful attention to the relationship between the learning outcomes of *learning about* and those of *learning from*. These included:

- The teacher always ensuring that the *learning from* outcome '*is related to the meaning that the religious belief or practice has for the believer, while also addressing the experiences of pupils far removed from the particular religious tradition being studied.*'

- The teacher always discerning the questions and themes of human experience which are addressed by the religious content before making any decisions about the learning outcomes of either *learning about* or *learning from*. In illustration, preparing for a series of lessons on The Five Pillars of Faith of Islam, she comments:

  'For the preparatory stage, I posed the question 'what makes a good person?' A variety of answers were suggested, including: kindness, patience, discipline and consideration of other people. I continued to ask 'what influences someone to be a good person?' Suggestions included: parents, the people you spend time with, teachers and religion. I then devised a set of themes which were closely linked to the answers of the pupils, but would also prepare them for the work on the Five Pillars. The themes were: spending time away from everyday life; walking in the steps of somebody else; assessing your life; being part of a community; discipline; being sure of your beliefs, and coping with physically testing times. I devised a set of group tasks to allow small groups to each reflect upon one of the themes.'

- The teacher always being clear about the function of such preparatory work and its relationship to the teaching and learning strategies that are then adopted:

  'It is through this process that pupils are able to reflect upon the material which is to be studied and discern meaning within it. The links that pupils make from the outset are not tenuous, trivial ones because their thinking has been carefully guided by the themes originally devised by the teacher. Through applying this principle of planning by outcomes, a dialogue is opened up at the outset between the pupils' experience and the content to be studied. This is due to the fact that pupils are given the opportunity to form a very early link between their own experiences and those of the members of the faith community in question. Pupils are subsequently more able to discern meaning in the religious practices that they are studying and link them with their own questions and experiences.'

- The teacher always planning for the item of religious content to become the stimulus for pupils to construct their own meaning and understanding of it by using observation, formulating hypotheses, and drawing upon their own experience and that represented in the group.' (Grimmitt 2000, 216).

  'For this stage, pupils were given a diagram of the Five Pillars and asked to colour-code it according to the six themes previously explored. This allowed them to make a close link between the Five Pillars and their own experiences of the themes.'

- The teacher always ensuring that both *learning about* and *learning from* outcomes are engaged together in pupils' evaluation of their learning.

  'Pupils taught by this pedagogy are more engaged with the content of the lessons as the Five Pillars begin to hold more meaning for them because the content has been approached at the outset from their reflections on their own personal experiences. Pupils taught in this way are able to see more clearly why Muslims carry out the Five Pillars and, by the end of the unit, they are able to give articulate, well informed evaluative judgements about the beliefs and practices underlying the Five Pillars of Islam. It was also obvious that pupils enjoy this type of work as they have been able to discern meaning in the practice of the Five Pillars of Islam which has meaning to them.'

While this is an account of how the relationship between *learning about* and *learning from religion* can be strengthened within an application of a constructivist pedagogy, it remains the case that as a method of dialogical learning it can be applied in similar manner within other pedagogies just as successfully. But the success of the strategy depends on the teacher discerning the potential that the choice of religious content has for achieving the dialogical cross-over to, and application within the life-worlds of the pupils. It is not just a matter of them requiring pupils to *learn about something from religion* and then, almost as an afterthought, wondering what pupils might *learn from* it – as if by chance. This is a teaching and learning strategy which demands careful planning; worthwhile educational outcomes do not just happen. The connections that are to be made do, at least, have to be seen as a successful outcome to pupils applying their understanding of a religious or theological concept (probably explored initially within the context of a particular religion) in the interpretation of issues, experiences and questions which arise within shared human experience and, more specifically, in their own experience. In such circumstances they are truly *learning from religion.*

In terms of my concern to consider how RE may contribute to social and cultural cohesion, is this learning and teaching strategy – learning about and from religion – one that can be used in RE to address the need for a reflective and critical response to issues which influence pupils' attitudes towards cultural and religious diversity? To be more precise, can this pedagogical strategy be used to help pupils understand how tensions and differences arise both within faiths and between faiths over personal, social, moral, political and religious issues and how these differences can easily create flash points for conflict and antagonism both between local communities and within society?'.[20] Can it make pupils more sympathetic to the need for such issues to be resolved through further dialogue in which all viewpoints are treated with respect and understanding? Because the strategy supports a process of learning about religious beliefs and values within a critical and evaluative framework which encourages pupils' learning to be applied existentially to their understanding of other personal and social issues, it is, in my view, eminently more suited to the task than, for example, a teaching process which is merely instructional or descriptive, informing pupils of the different religious beliefs that are held by religious adherents and why. This latter approach, regrettably still so apparent in some RE classrooms, is unlikely to provide pupils with either the skills or the determination to grapple with the complex process of understanding the interface between religion and social and political issues and how religion may or may not contribute to social and community cohesion.

As Blaylock observes, we are not here talking about RE's 'attainment targets' so much as about ways in which RE's educational vision can be realized. Adding further attainment targets to the current AT1 and AT2, whatever they might be, will not improve the educational outcomes that this pedagogical strategy is designed to produce. Indeed, the learning process that we have been considering is, I think, able to address all forms of learning and to engage successfully with most religious, cultural, moral, social, and political content. To this extent the question whether the two attainment targets in RE are fit for purpose is answered not by adding more but by ensuring the two that we already have are applied successfully.[21] The process of *learning about religion* is well suited to encouraging pupils to learn about religion's contribution to social and community cohesion, just as *learning from religion* is well suited to encouraging them to reflect critically on whether that contribution is to be regarded as a help or a hinderance.

What are the implications for the content of the RE curriculum?
Where should the emphasis in RE be placed? – on studying religions or on understanding religion? – on exploring issues within and between religions which divide them? – or on recognising religion as a 'cultural fact'?

Ironically the 'Big Picture of the Curriculum' avoids the problem of what we are to understand by attainment targets by providing three over-arching educational aims which should apply to all subjects. A statement on 'RE and the national curriculum aims' is provided by the Qualifications and Curriculum Development Agency (QCDA) on its website. The three aims are, as previously noted, to develop *successful learners*, create *confident individuals* and prepare pupils to become *responsible citizens*. The statement details how RE can contribute to these aims without actually describing a pedagogical strategy for doing so. It is, therefore, fortunate, that RE has retained its current AT1 and AT2 which, I have argued, provide the pedagogical strategy which is omitted here. But there is more to what the curriculum (and all subjects) should aim to achieve, namely, the requirements of ECM (*to be healthy, stay safe, enjoy and achieve, make a positive contribution, and achieve economic wellbeing*) and, by focusing on learning, certain *attitudes and attributes, skills, and knowledge and understanding*. Concerning the latter we might pick out for consideration how RE can contribute to '*personal, learning and thinking skills*' and, rather more ominously, to understanding '*big ideas that shape the world*'. If we look ahead we see that we are to organize this learning in ways which, among others, provide opportunities for *spiritual, moral, social, cultural, emotional and intellectual development*, and are *in tune with human development*. Gratifyingly we are given whole curriculum dimensions within which to do this which are defined as '*overarching themes that have significance for individuals and society, and provide relevant learning contexts*'. These include, among others:

identity and cultural diversity, healthy lifestyles, community participation, global dimension, and critical thinking. All of this appears to set an agenda to which RE may respond significantly, but the unanswered question is, how? It is a question, which highlights the problematic nature of how we decide on what is appropriate content for the RE curriculum and which pedagogies are best suited to its treatment.

There is no doubt that 'The Big Picture of the Curriculum' takes the view that pupils' needs are to be taken very seriously indeed in constructing the new national curriculum. At the same time their learning is still to result from their encounter with the content of curriculum subjects, described as 'statutory expectations'. The study of Christianity and the other principal religious traditions represented in Britain, as defined by the 1988 Education Act is, therefore, also to continue to be taken very seriously. But there is a new, additional agenda to address which is social and political. There is no doubt that when the DCSF introduced its guidance on the duty of schools to promote community cohesion in July 2007 it changed the parameters within which curriculum decision-making in a subject like RE would need to occur. From September 2008 RE in England and Wales has been required to address the following requirement and align itself with the realization of the vision of society which lies behind it.

> 'By community cohesion, we mean working towards a society in which there is a common vision and sense of belonging by all communities; a society in which the diversity of people's backgrounds and circumstances is appreciated and valued; a society in which similar life opportunities are available to all; and a society in which strong and positive relationships exist and continue to be developed in the workplace, in schools and in the wider community'. (DCSF 2007)

The new-statutory guidance of 2010 amplifies this as follows:

> 'The breadth of study should take account of the four levels of community cohesion which all maintained schools are now obliged to promote. Decisions by SACREs and ASCs about the religions, other than Christianity, to be studied should take account of the balance of religion within: the school community, the community within which the school is located, the UK community, the global community. (DCSF 2010, 23)

In these changed circumstances, what religious content would need to be included in order to enable the subject to address both the needs of the pupils and those of the wider community? Without doubt the inclusion of, and attention to the interface between religion and society is a necessary part of understanding religion and would need to feature in the RE curriculum.

Pupils today should, therefore, investigate how religion impacts, both positively and negatively, upon aspects of public and private life within contemporary society and, indeed, world-wide. Exploring the ways in which religion can enrich the experience of diversity but may also undermine it should enable pupils to make a more informed assessment of the complex relationship that religion has to everyday events today. This considered view is just as difficult to extrapolate from the systematic study of a religion as it is from an uncritical reading of the popular press. It is important, therefore, that part of the process of helping pupils to learn how to understand the reasons for inter-religious and inter-cultural conflicts should involve helping them to disentangle these from the social and political factors which contribute to them. From an educational and pedagogical viewpoint, there is value in setting such an exploration within the context of *'overarching themes that have significance for individuals and society.'* (QCA 2008). These themes are likely to be those which have already captured the attention of the centre ground of politics and feature prominently in social and welfare policies in this country and world-wide, namely human rights, child protection, equality and social justice, citizenship, immigration, world poverty, conservation, climate change, etc.

While some RE teachers may not wish to encourage a closer relationship between RE and citizenship education in schools, the fact cannot be denied that any attempt to incorporate the study of religion within a contemporary, social context will involve the investigation of topics which are already significant themes within citizenship education. The decision by the DfCSF in 2007, as recommended by the *Curriculum review: diversity and citizenship* – the Ajegbo report – to introduce an additional strand to the citizenship education framework on *'identity and diversity: living together in the UK'* could easily have also been applied to RE with an expectation that pupils would be helped to understand how religious beliefs and values contribute, both positively and negatively, to the experience of diversity and exercise an influence on social and community cohesion. It is surely now time for this to be implemented in RE, certainly within work at Key Stage Four but also earlier at Key Stage Three.

A new model of RE would also need to provide the appropriate means of exploring those points of conflict which exist between traditional values within religion and changing values in a post-modern world. There is, in my view, need for a much more deliberate policy for RE to provide the arena within which young people can explore social issues which are controversial within and between the religions because of unresolved tensions between, for example, equal opportunities legislation and some traditional values which the religions are unprepared to relinquish.[22] These issues would include the conflict between different forms of sexual and cultural identity and the experience of divided loyalties in matters of national and cultural or religious identity. Equally, significant themes would also include the conflict that some young people may be experiencing between being loyal to traditional values within their community and being loyal to themselves in aspiring towards different models of identity. Because a subject is politically and religiously sensitive is not an adequate reason for excluding it from exploration within an educational context. For example, it is unrealistic to try and exclude from exploration in RE a consideration of those factors which may cause some young people to find radical stances towards the achievement of some social, political and religious goals more compelling than depending upon such outcomes to be achieved by means of more conventional, democratic processes. The media is given to sensationalist reporting of many local and world events in ways which polarize public opinion and affect the attitudes of young people. In these circumstances I find myself persuaded that the RE classroom has the important potential for being a 'space for conflict' in which issues which affect social, community and personal well-being are discussed in a 'cool' and 'safe' environment, provided adequate safeguards for the teacher are in place.[23]

Making RE more 'issues-based" or 'issues-related' would, I believe, serve to improve pupils' inter-cultural and inter-religious understanding *within their own situated social, community, religious and cultural contexts*. Such a view is in keeping with the emphasis in the 'Big Picture of the Curriculum' on an education which contributes to the personal, social, economic and political thinking skills and capacities of young people and where the 'statutory expectations' of curriculum subjects, like RE, are shaped in such a manner as to facilitate the acquisition and development of these skills and capacities. The expectation is, of course, that having achieved these, young people, as they mature, are better able to play their part in the development of a society in which diversity provides the conditions which contribute positively to human well-being and fulfilment. I have long believed that the RE curriculum has suffered from being encumbered by far too much religious content which is irrelevant to fulfilling such a purpose, or which, at best, can contribute only very marginally to its stated educational concern. One reason for this is because the subject continues to be haunted by the entirely worthy, brilliantly-conceived but totally unrealistic expectation that RE can and should deliver the sort of understanding of religion set out in the Schools Council Religious Education Committee publication, *A Groundplan for the Study of Religion* (1977). This remarkable document drew heavily but not exclusively on phenomenology to provide a method of investigating religion which would lead to an understanding of central religious concepts, feelings and actions, knowledge of individual religious traditions and an opportunity for pupils to evaluate a tradition's truth claims, self-understanding and values, and to do so in a way which encouraged them to also consider the personal relevance of what they were studying.

> 'The question we are seeking to answer, in however preliminary a way, concerns *what* one needs to understand in order to understand religion.' (Groundplan, 19)

To their credit the authors acknowledged the intellectual demands that their recommended approach made and were tentative about its application with all pupils. But it set in trend a view of RE which has been reinforced by the 1988 legislation, the *Model Syllabuses* and the *Non-Statutory National Framework for Religious Education*, namely that RE consists primarily of the study of religions, and at the latest estimate ten of them![(24)] This emphasis on applying a 'systems' approach to the study of religious content has tended to 'stratify' religions in a manner which does not encourage the sort of issues I have identified as central to our present social and political circumstances to be easily addressed. For example, how would a systems approach deal with issues such as ; 'Religion and Violence'; 'Religion and Human Rights'; 'Religion and Gender Equality'; 'Religion and Assisted Suicide' – to pick up four issues which have all recently appeared in the press in a single week? In the cause of connecting with the needs of young people and of society should we not be reducing the time spent on learning about religions in isolation from each other and concentrate instead on investigating how religious beliefs, of whatever origin, impact upon and shape people's understanding of and reactions to daily events within both local, national and global contexts? It may well be a surprise to discover how the careful analysis of a single issue – examining what we might call a *microcosm of religion* – can lead into a much more purposeful investigation of the *macrocosm of religion* and *religions*, especially of *theological concepts* underlying the issue, than was previously the case.[25] There is, I believe, a much greater possibility that this mode of investigation can have a transforming effect upon pupils' understanding of and attitudes towards such issues and in so doing enable them to be better placed to become *successful learners, confident individuals and responsible citizens.*

In support of this strategy I wish to refer again to several statements in the OfSTED Report, *Making Sense of Religion* (2007).

On the basis of inspection evidence at Key Stage 3 it comments:

'Pupils' achievement has improved where teaching incorporates a more issues-based approach to the subject.' (*op.cit.*,11)

'All the boys interviewed preferred work which discussed issues rather than gathering information about religions;' (*op.cit.*,15)

'Schools with the most effective provision have made the relevance and interest of the RE curriculum a priority by combining the investigation of religion with opportunities for pupils to discuss ideas and reflect on profound aspects of human experience.' (*op.cit.*,25)

But, quoting the *Diversity and Citizenship Curriculum Review* (DfES 00045 – 2007) it notes:

'There is a widespread perception that issues of ethnicity and 'race', whilst often controversial, are more often addressed than issues relating to religion.' (*op.cit.*,27)

and then adds, later:

'The changing and controversial role of religion in contemporary society is not given sufficient attention in most agreed syllabuses and examination courses.' (*op.cit.*,27)

Also in support of my proposed strategy, I want to refer to the very interesting events that have been taking place in Europe concerning the value of introducing the study of religions and beliefs into the school curricula of countries that have previously been reluctant to countenance having any form of RE. Following the experience and findings of the European Commission Framework 6 Project, the publication in 2007 of the *REDCo* Project, and the *Toledo Guiding Principles on Teaching about Religions and Beliefs* by The Office for Democratic Institutions and Human Rights, it was agreed that the basis upon which the study of religion could be included in schools and educational institutions is that religion is a 'cultural fact'.[26]

300

'The key condition for including religion as a pan-European topic in education was that, despite different views on religion at the personal and societal levels, all could agree that religion is a 'cultural fact' and that knowledge and understanding of religion at this level is highly relevant to good community and personal relations and is therefore a legitimate concern of public policy. This was not a form of intellectual reductionism, but a pragmatic recognition that the fact of the presence of religions in society was a cultural reality – religion was out there as part of human social life.'[27]

Although I would prefer to speak of religion as a 'social' rather than a 'cultural' fact, this argument for the study of religion and religions makes it clear that the emphasis in the curricula will be on exploring how religion manifests itself in society. *The Toledo Guiding Principles on Teaching About Religions and Beliefs*, with which I agree and from which we can learn, express the point succinctly and well.

'...such curricula should, as much as possible, be comprehensive and pay particular attention to key historical and contemporary developments pertaining to issues of religion and belief. Societies are not static and all communities undergo change. Far reaching change can occur because of processes such as migration, environmental degradation, contacts with other cultures, new interpretations of holy texts, scientific developments, as well as wars and conflicts. These global and local processes have an impact on the manner in which religions and beliefs manifest themselves in states and in local communities. Individuals and communities often view history and contemporary society differently (for instance, depending on whether they were targets of persecution, or if they speak the dominant language or adhere to the dominant belief system) and this gives rise to varying views and perspectives. Thus, curricula should be sensitive to different interpretations of reality. This is often referred to in education as the principle of multi-perspectivity.' (41) [28]

What pedagogies of RE are likely to be effective in addressing the new demands made on the subject? How can we know?

It is interesting to note how much of contemporary discussion in RE is now focused on 'pedagogy' and 'pedagogies'. Despite its illustrious history in educational thinking in continental Europe since the eighteenth century and later in the USA, for example, by Dewey and, towards the end of the twentieth century, by radical educators, such as Giroux, prior to the publication of my edited book, *Pedagogies of Religious Education* in 2000, the term 'pedagogy' was rarely if ever used in British RE.[29] Now no discussion of learning and teaching in RE is complete without some reference to 'pedagogy'.[30]

However, the term is often used without the precision that I tried to apply to it when, following Simon (1981), I defined a pedagogy as:

> '...a theory of teaching and learning encompassing aims, curriculum content and methodology... Whatever the definition, the fundamental concern of pedagogy is to relate the process of teaching to that of learning on the part of the child.' (Grimmitt (2000), 16)

For example, 'pedagogy' is sometimes used as if it is equivalent to a 'method of teaching'.[31] This is unfortunate because a 'pedagogy', as indicated above, brings theory and practice into a coherent whole and articulates how this combination results in the process of teaching and learning achieving particular aims and outcomes. 'Methods' of teaching can exist quite independently of a pedagogy and, therefore, is better used as a term which refers, for example, to the use of worksheets, or organizing learning in groups or showing a video to stimulate discussion, etc,. On the positive side, this means that different 'pedagogies' may draw upon a common pool of 'methods of teaching' while retaining their own distinctive combination of theory and practice.

There has been reluctance, possibly even resistance, in the UK to a distinctive pedagogy of RE being incorporated, for example, within Agreed Syllabuses of RE and Government-related initiatives such as the *Non-Statutory National Framework for Religious Education*. This may reflect the fact that different pedagogies of RE have been developed mainly by individual religious educators developing theories for the subject's development in accordance with their own ideological and educational perspectives. This is both a strength and a weakness. The strength is to be found in the stimulus that it has given to the subject to respond in a variety of ways to changing political, social, cultural, religious and educational circumstances. The weakness is to be found in the 'pick and mix' response to pedagogy which is now a common feature of classroom practice – something which, in publishing *Pedagogies of RE* in 2000, I originally thought to be a strength. Ironically, as indicated earlier, the persistence of *learning about* and *learning from religion* has united a number of pedagogies which otherwise could have been seen as being partisan and competitive.[32] But I am now persuaded that the weakness of a 'pick and mix' approach to choosing pedagogies of RE and applying them indiscriminately in the classroom is that it greatly diminishes the possibility of achieving the stated aims and outcomes of any one pedagogy.

There is, I think, a reasonably strong argument for primary schools to tend more towards teaching RE at Key Stages One and Two through a pedagogy which draws on accurate phenomenological description of the features of different religions, tempered with some engagement with the religious content from a personal perspective.[33] But at Key Stage Three, and certainly at Key Stage Four, this approach is insufficiently challenging to pupils who need to be fully engaged in not only knowing more about religion but being able to critique it. If RE is to implement a policy which is progressive and developmental, moving pupils from knowing about, understanding and being able to evaluate religion and the effects of religious belief upon individuals and upon society as a whole, it needs to adopt a pedagogy which does this effectively. Especially in an age when it is essential that those pupils who have no direct links with, or interest in religion are fully engaged in RE, it is important that whatever pedagogy is adopted it enables their experiences, attitudes and questions to be fully accommodated and drawn upon. Knowing what religious people believe is only a very small part of this process. The new secondary national curriculum, as we have seen, places an emphasis on all curriculum subjects contributing to developing pupils' *personal, learning and thinking skills* and it is important to recognize that some pedagogies of RE are better equipped to do this than others.

Despite these observations, however, I will be brief in addressing the two questions, *'What pedagogies of RE are likely to be effective in addressing the new demands made on the subject? How can we know?* as they are already extensively and expertly addressed by Baumfield in her chapter in this book (Chap 11). Like her, I would advocate that those pedagogies which apply a constructivist dialogical pedagogy to learning and teaching are best suited to enabling RE to produce educational outcomes which contribute to social and community cohesion. What follows are my reasons for believing this to be the case.

The significant factors that enable a constructivist pedagogy to produce learning outcomes which can contribute to social and community cohesion are to be found in the way in which the pedagogy *helps to challenge and develop pupils' perceptions of and attitudes towards the subject matter being studied.* This is a direct result of the dialectical learning strategies which a constructivist pedagogy employs to encourage pupils, both as individuals and as group members, to be responsible for their own learning and the learning outcomes which the group achieves. A vital component in this process is the intention to encourage pupils to draw upon their situated place within families, groups and communities (cultural, ethnic and religious) and upon the shared repository of experiences and values which such membership provides and to apply this to their understanding of the subject or topic being explored. Although the teacher may, of course, contribute knowledge and information to this process a dialogical pedagogy aims at enabling knowledge to be co-constructed between pupils and teachers. There are certain optimum conditions under which this takes place.

Firstly, the pedagogy places a considerable value on encouraging pupils to express their views and experiences orally to each other in their groups, to the teacher and to the class as a whole. Classroom dialogue and conversation is the essence of the pedagogy. However, this is not to be unstructured or unguided. It is essential that such dialogue and conversation is purposeful and productive. It is here that the teacher's role is decisive. It is the teacher who determines, at least initially, the questions which will act as the stimulus for conversation and research (i.e. hypothesis testing) within the groups.

Secondly, as demonstrated in the earlier description of Lucas' work, considerable preparation on the part of the teacher is needed to ensure the success of this pedagogy. It is the teacher, for example, who ensures that the activities of the groups, including their conversations, focus on deepening their understanding of the topic of the lesson in order to learn about and from religion. It is the teacher, too, who ensures that the goals of group work are clearly specified and that each group is given a task, preferably a different task, which encourages them to work together collaboratively to achieve the outcome.

Thirdly, as the theoretical work of Wells (1999) has indicated, there is more educational potential in an enquiry-oriented or issue-related curriculum than one where teachers feel constrained to 'deliver' a centrally-prescribed curriculum which is dominated by high concentrations of content. Alexander (2000) shows from his large-scale comparative study of primary teaching (but not of RE) in five countries that whole-class directed instruction 'is probably the dominant teaching method internationally'. (Alexander (2000), 516) His proposed use of 'scaffolded dialogue' (op.cit., 527), applied within 'communities of enquiries', is designed to foster a 'pedagogy of mutuality' in which pupils take responsibility for engaging with their peers in thinking through questions and issues for themselves and justifying their conclusions.[34]

Fourthly, the experience of negotiating meaning in a co-operative manner can be transformational of pupils' attitudes not only to learning itself but to how issues of conflict may be resolved both personally and more widely within a plural society. Providing young people with an experience of addressing divisive issues in a reflective manner and taking some responsibility for the solutions they propose must, at least marginally, build up some critical resistance on their part to accepting the simplistic, sloganising approaches to matters of conflict which are characteristic of the popular press. In seeking to encourage a thoughtful and considered approach to issues of conflict a constructivist pedagogy might, therefore, be expected to make a significant contribution to the development of social mores which are compatible with valuing diversity and appreciating those social forms of life which can assist social and community cohesion.

CONCLUSION

I conclude by returning to a point that I stressed in *Pedagogies of RE* (2000, 22): there remains a considerable deficit in the research base of RE of studies which provide insight into whether the intended outcomes of different pedagogies of RE are realized or not. Until this work is undertaken, questions about the efficacy of RE with regard to its personal and social impact, especially with regard to social and community cohesion, will remain unanswered and proposals for new developments in curriculum and pedagogy will remain speculative. It behoves those who support the subject – government, faith communities and educational charitable trusts – to provide much needed financial resources for this issue to be thoroughly investigated as a preliminary step to embarking upon a further stage in RE's metamorphosis. Without this the subject may lack the confidence to identify with the personal, social, political and educational agenda of the new national curriculum and play its part in its realization as vigorously as it should.

NOTES

1. For example, John Hull offered courses in the 'Theology of Education' in the University of Birmingham, mainly from a Christian perspective, from 1977 until the mid nineties. His robust defence against Paul Hirst's assertion that there can be no useful and coherent relations between theology and educational theory can be found in a series of articles reprinted in Hull, J.M. (1984). See also Islamic and Christian approaches to this issue in Asraf, S.A. and Hirst, P. (1994) and Christian approaches in Astley, J. (1994), Cooling, T. (1994) and Hart, C.J. (1994).

2. SHAP is not an acronym, it is the name of a village in Cumbria. In the spring of 1969 a conference on 'Comparative Religion in Education' was held at a hotel in Shap. Arising out of that conference came the decision by the participants to set-up a working party to campaign for and support the development of teaching about the world's religions in schools and other educational settings. Shap produces an annual Calendar detailing the festival dates of many world religions and a Journal, the back catalogue of which is available from:
   http://www.shapworkingparty.org.uk/journals.html

3. See Grimmitt, M.H. & Read G.T. (1977, 7-8).

4. Of the conscience clause, Ninian Smart wrote in 1970, 'It must be bad education if there is a conscience clause. It must presume bias and unfairness....If there is one it means that teachers are singularly lacking in objectivity. I count myself a Christian but it worries me that Christians concerned with religious education should support the conscience clause, for such support betrays a secret aim. Or do they recognise that indoctrination is actually going on? It should be denounced daily by bishops, priests, evangelical laity and the ordinary man.' (Smart, N. 1970)

   In 2010, forty years later, The Revd Dr. John Gay, spokesperson for RE on behalf of the Church of England, wrote, 'This clause is a relic of a bygone times, when the subject, then known as Religious Instruction, had a more catechetical hue. Today's RE is a fully educational subject, and no teacher or parent should feel uncomfortable with its content. Keeping the opt-out clause gives the impression that there might still be something dodgy lurking in the undergrowth.' (Gay, J. 2010)

5. In 2010 the RE Council of England and Wales was successful in bidding for funding from the DCSF to develop a training programme for religious education teachers on community cohesion and preventing violent extremism. This is known as the 'Resilience Project'. It is scheduled to last until 31 March 2011. Further details may be downloaded from http://www.religiouseducationcouncil.org/
   See also HM Government (2008) *The Prevent Strategy: A Guide for Local*

Partners in England: stopping people becoming or supporting terrorists and violent extremists (jointly issued and supported by the Lord Chancellor and Secretary of State for Justice, the Home Secretary and the Secretaries of State for Communities and Local Government, for Children, Schools and Families, for Innovation, Universities and Skills, and for Culture, Media and Sport.) *The Prevent Strategy* can be downloaded from www.dcsf.gov.uk/violentextremism/downloads

6. DCSF (2010) *Religious Education in English Schools: Non-statutory guidance 2010* does not change the legal basis of RE with Christianity still continuing to predominate. However, as the following statements indicate, 'the curriculum is less prescriptive as to content than it was.......subjects such as RE, history and citizenship might be taught discretely but also together within a humanities framework.' (5) The possibility of varying which religions are studied, other than Christianity, is indicated by the statement, 'The law does not define what the principal religions represented in Great Britain are. ASCs (Agreed Syllabus Conferences) can decide which are the principal religions represented in Great Britain, other than Christianity, to be included in their agreed syllabus.' (14).

7. It is because the RE curriculum requires pupils to study religions separately that the religions are subjected to a relativising process, not because any of the chosen pedagogies of RE deliberately seek to relativise the religions in their treatment of them.

8. See Barnes, L. P. (2006) for a powerfully argued exposition of the case that British RE has misrepresented the nature of religion in efforts to commend itself as contributing to the social aims of education, as these are typically framed in liberal democratic societies. Consequently current representations of religion in 'British RE are limited in their capacity to challenge racism and religious intolerance, chiefly because they are conceptually ill equipped to develop respect for difference.'

9. See, for example, P. Hitchens' observation in his column in *The Mail on Sunday*, 27 December, 2009, 29: 'I believe in a pretty reserved sort of religion myself, and wouldn't necessarily welcome it if a nurse or a teacher offered to pray for me. But I think I would make the point politely myself. What is actively sinister is the way that such people are now threatened with disciplinary action...the binding conduct and practice of many trades and professions contain the same little provision... Equality and diversity are codewords for political correctness, and these codes make it compulsory.' See *The Sunday Telegraph*, 20 September, 2009: 'NHS nurse faces sack for wearing her cross'. Also *The Mail of Sunday* 27 December, 2009, 'Christian teacher's sacking is so unjust' (A Maths supply teacher was initially dismissed from her part time post with North Somerset Tuition Service for offering to pray for a sick child. She was later reinstated and, according to The Mail on Sunday (31 January

2010), 'North Somerset Council agreed it could be appropriate for a teacher to share his or her faith, but in offering the teacher further work, a spokesman added: 'A careful judgment has to be made.')

10. Through the RE action plan introduced in 2009 the DCSF is working with partners to identify how continuing teacher recruitment and professional development and initial teacher training in RE can be improved. In conjunction with this, the DCSF have commissioned the development of a Continuing Professional Development (CPD) Handbook, which will include a chapter on dealing with controversial issues in the classroom.

11. The seven core human values related to substantive religious categories which I proposed in 1987 are:

    a. Order, purpose and meaning – providence
    b. Human life and human beings – the sacred
    c. A just society – law
    d. The individual's right to self-fulfilment – soul
    e. Ethical endeavour and the exercise of moral responsibility – discipleship
    f. commitment to inter-personal relationships and to the notions of 'family' and 'community' – priesthood/community of faith
    g. Human spirituality and the desirability of spiritual development – revelation/worship (Grimmitt 1987, 21-132)

12. See Maybury, J. and Teece, G, (2005) 'Learning from what? A question of subject focus in religious education in England and Wales', *Journal of Beliefs and Values*, 26:2, 179-190, for good examples of how these choices should be made and the weakness of much current practice where this is not applied.

13. 'A common question from teachers is, 'Why don't academics care about what goes on in schools and the threats to RE from all directions? Why are there no figures like Ninian Smart, Geoffrey Parrinder, Cyril Williams anymore?' (Dossett, W. (2008, 309). See her argument that a lack of intellectual investment in all levels of education is to the detriment of both academic theology and religious studies at university level and to religious education at school level.

14. The new non-statutory guidance for RE issued by the DCSF in February 2010 is unlikely to add significantly to the QCA proposals. Such a statement as the one which follows can hardly be said to provide a stimulus for change and development:

    'The study of religion should be based on the legal requirements and provide an appropriate balance between and within Christianity, other principal religions, and, where appropriate, other religious traditions and worldviews, across the key stages as a whole, making appropriate links with other parts of the curriculum and its cross-curricular dimensions.'(23)

However, in summarizing the contribution of RE to the total curriculum experience of children and young people the guidelines do place a new emphasis on it contributing to both personal and social agendas within a diverse society. viz:

- RE provokes challenging questions about the meaning and purpose of life, beliefs, the self, issues of right and wrong, and what it means to be human. It develops pupils' knowledge and understanding of Christianity, other principal religions, and religious traditions that examine these questions, fostering personal reflection and spiritual development

- RE encourages pupils to explore their own beliefs (whether they are religious or non-religious), in the light of what they learn, as they examine issues of religious belief and faith and how these impact on personal, institutional and social ethics; and to express their responses. This also builds resilience to anti-democratic or extremist narratives

- RE enables pupils to build their sense of identity and belonging, which helps them flourish within their communities and as citizens in a diverse society

- RE teaches pupils to develop respect for others, including people with different faiths and beliefs, and helps to challenge prejudice RE prompts pupils to consider their responsibilities to others, and to explore how they might contribute to their communities and to wider society. It encourages empathy, generosity and compassion.(8)

My own view is that the successful realization of this agenda is, however, heavily dependent upon devising an RE curriculum which is designed, through its choice of content and learning experiences and its application of an appropriate pedagogy, to produce these outcomes. They will not just happen.

15. I prefer to see *learning about* and *from religion* as a *pedagogical procedure* or *strategy* which enables certain pedagogical principles to be implemented in RE. (Grimmitt, 2000, 20)

16. The DCSF has recently funded by £1m the RE action plan – a range of initiatives, designed to improve teaching and learning in RE. Through this action plan, the DCSF has made a commitment to support the work of key stakeholders including the Religious Education Council, the National Association of Teachers of RE (NATRE) and the National Association of SACREs (NASACRE). The funding provided to NATRE will strengthen their capacity to support teachers in primary and secondary schools, including the development of web-based resources for teachers and the development of local network groups of teachers. Research into 'Materials used to Teach about World Religions in Schools of England' WRERU/DCSF (2010) WRERU has now been completed and can be downloaded from www.dcsf.gov.uk/research

17. 'Faith' schools are currently not required to offer a 'multi-faith' Religious Education in accordance with the 1988 Education Act, and may restrict their religious teaching to the school's founding faith.

18. A significant contribution to the discussion of this question was made by Rowan Williams, Archbishop of Canterbury, in his address entitled 'Why cohesion needs religion' to the Building Bridges Conference in Singapore, December 2007. The full text can be downloaded from Network for Interfaith Concerns. http://nifcon.anglicancommunion.org/index.cfm Evidence for the positive contribution of religion, through faith-communities and inter-faith groups, to social and community cohesion is to be found in the report, *Face to Face and Side by Side: a framework for partnership in our multi-faith society* (2008) published by the Department for Communities and Local Government, which can be downloaded from www.communities.gov.uk

19. The article by Michelle Lucas' (née Chatterley) is downloadable from http://www.shapworkingparty.org.uk/journals.html The extracts in this chapter are included with her kind permission.

20. For example. 'Extreme Muslim protestors in Luton about British troops in Afghanistan' (May 2009). 'Threat from the radical group *Islam4UK* to parade through Wootton Bassett in Wiltshire with empty coffins to symbolize Muslims 'mercilessly murdered' in Iraq and Afghanistan' (January 2010). (Various press headlines and reports).

21. The Hampshire Agreed Syllabus of RE, '*Living difference: The agreed syllabus for Hampshire, Portsmouth and Southampton*' has only one attainment target – 'interpreting religion in relation to human experience'. Teece comments, in a way which is consistent with my own argument in this chapter, that 'In having only one attainment target, 'interpreting religion in relation to human experience' it begs the question as to whether the terms *learning about religion* and *learning from religion* should be retired gracefully. For this to happen the RE profession would have to agree a commonly understood teaching and learning process, in the way that Hampshire does, to ensure that the kind of learning about and from *religions*, that I have attempted to outline here, actually takes place.' (Teece, 2010, 101)

22. The passage of the Equality Bill through the House of Lords in January and February of 2010 (especially a consideration of the amendments proposed by the Bishops of the Church of England) and the evidence collected before then by the Parliamentary Committee, provide the sort of 'issue' which could enable pupils in RE to consider how theological concepts can be used to resist equal opportunities legislation and to come to an informed views of their own on the matter. Opponents to clauses of the Bill, which would have an effect on current employment practices in the churches, included the Archbishop of York and the Pope, Benedict XVI, who declared the proposed

legislation as 'unjust' because it restricted religious freedom and violated 'the natural law'. The popular press's headlines at the time included: 'Equality law could ruin Christmas, warn bishops' (*Daily Mail*, 18 November, 2009), 'Churches win fight over discrimination – Harman abandons equality moves after Pope's attack' (*The Times*, 3 February, 2010), and 'Christianity being squeezed out in the name of 'equality'' (*Daily Mail*, 4 Feb, 2010).

23. See, for example, K.H. Ina ter Avest (2009) 'Education in Conflict', *Panorama* 21, Summer/Winter 2009, 13-23. The Department for Communities and Local Government (CLG) Report of 2008, *Face to face and side by side: A framework for partnership in our multi-faith society* comments: 'Effective RE can play a key part in promoting inter-faith understanding and dialogue and can address the prejudices brought about by a shallow knowledge of world religions and provides pupils with a safe forum for the discussion of controversial issues. This is an essential part of RE's contribution to community cohesion.' (96)

24. *The Non-Statutory National Framework for Religious Education* (2004) and *Religious Education in English Schools: Non-statutory guidance* (2010) both recognise the possibility of ten world 'faiths' being included in RE. In addition to content from Buddhism, Christianity, Hinduism, Islam, Judaism, and Sikhism, the *Non-statutory guidance* acknowledges that, under appropriate circumstances, content may also be drawn from the Bah'ai Faith, Jainism, Zoroastrianism and traditional African religions, as well as from 'secular beliefs such as atheism and humanism'.

25. There are few classroom or pedagogical studies available which offer, firstly, a way of identifying those theological concepts and their interpretation which may contribute to issues of conflict and tension within a society and between its different communities and, secondly, provide a way of analyzing them in a dispassionate manner to create at least a respectful appreciation of differences if not an actual reconciliation of those differences. In an interesting article which draws on hermeneutical theory to suggest ways of lessening the force of scriptural justifications for violence in three religious traditions – Judaism, Christianity and Islam – Schmidt, G.R. and Barnes, L.P. (2009) provide the beginnings of a pedagogy in which critical openness can harness the positive aspects of religion with its negative aspects and so make a contribution to education for peace.

26. *REDCo* is an acronym for 'Religion in Education: a Contribution to Dialogue or a Factor of Conflict in Transforming Societies of European Countries'. See Weisse, W. (2007) in Jackson, R. *et al* (2007, 9-25)

27. Taken from the inaugural speech given in May 2009 by Robert Jackson at the opening of European Wergeland Centre (EWC) for Intercultural Education, Human Rights and Education for Democratic Citizenship, Norway. More information about the Centre may be downloaded from www.thecwc.org

28. *The Toledo Guiding Principles on Teaching About Religions and Beliefs*, (2007), 41. See also, Joyce Miller (2009).

29. An exception is Wright's Spiritual Pedagogy (1998) but there is no mention of it in Jackson's influential book *Religious Education: An Interpretive Approach* (1997) or in Hull's *Utopian Whispers* (1998).

30. See, for example, Stern J. (2006) pp.63-79, and Blaylock, L. (2004).

31. For example, the recently published research report by The Warwick Religions and Education Research Unit for the DCSF entitled *Materials for Teaching about World Religions in Schools in England* (2010): uses the term 'Pedagogy of RE' to describe what it calls 'world religions approaches, scriptural approaches, experiential approaches, philosophical and ethical approaches'. (136-146)

32. The concept of 'edification' in Jackson's *Interpretive Approach* (1997) has a close approximation with this concept, and, as we have seen, it is also consistent with the process of learning envisaged by the *Critical Realist* pedagogy of Wright.

33. 'The Gift to the Child Approach' pedagogy combines this very successfully. See Grimmitt, M. H. et al (1991) and (2006)

34. I have drawn here on Skidmore, D. & Gallagher D, (2005) 'A Dialogical Pedagogy for Inclusive Education', a paper presented to Inclusive and Supportive Education Congress and International Special Education Conference, on Inclusion: Celebrating Diversity? 1st - 4th August 2005. Glasgow, Scotland, downloadable from www.isec2005.org.uk/isec/abstracts/papers_s/skidmore_d.shtml

REFERENCES

Alexander, R.J. (2000) *Culture and Pedagogy: International Comparisons in Primary Education*, Oxford: Blackwell.

Alexander, R.J. (2004) *Towards Dialogic Teaching: Rethinking Classroom Talk*, Cambridge: Dialogos.

Ashraf, S.A. & Hirst, P.H. (eds) (1994) *Religion and Education: Islamic and Christian Approaches*, Cambridge: The Islamic Academy.

Astley, J. (1994) *The Philosophy of Christian Religious Education*, Birmingham, Alabama: Religious Education Press.

Attfield, D.G. (1996) 'Learning From Religion', *British Journal of Religious Education*, 18:2, 78 – 84.

Attfield, D.G. (1997) 'A Response to Robert Ellis', *British Journal of Religious Education* 19:3, 133.

Barnes, L. P. (2006) 'The Misrepresentation of Religion in Modern British (Religious) Education', *British Journal of Educational Studies*, 54:4, 395-411.

Baumfield, V. (2009) 'Learning about and learning from religion', Editorial, *British Journal of Religious Education*, 31:1, 1 -2.

Baumfield, V. (2010) 'Pedagogies of Religious Education for inter-communication and inter-cultural understanding: what are they? do they work', in Grimmitt, M.H. (ed) (2010) *Religious Education and Social and Community Cohesion: Challenges and Opportunities*, Great Wakering: McCrimmon Publishing Co. Ltd.

Blaylock, L. (2004) 'Six Schools of Thought in RE', *REsource*, 27:1.

Blaylock, L. (2009) 'Learning from religion: a very short history', *REsource*, 31:2,10-13.

City of Birmingham Education Committee (1975), *Agreed Syllabus of Religious Instruction*

Cooling, T. (1994) *A Christian Vision for State Education*, London: SPCK

DCSF (2007) *Guidance on the duty to promote community cohesion*. Download from www.dfcsf.gov.uk

DCFS (2007) *Curriculum Review: Diversity and Citizenship* (The Ajegbo Report) Download from www.dfcsf.gov.uk

DCSF/RE Council for England and Wales,(2010) *REsilience Project*, http://www.religiouseducationcouncil.org/

DCSF (2010) *Religious Education in English Schools: Non-statutory guidance 2010* Download from www.teachernet.gov.uk/

Dossett, W. (2008) 'Learning About and Learning From': Reflections of the significance of Theology/Religious Studies method debates for modern Religious Education', in Warrier, M. & Oliver, S. (eds) (2008) *Theology and Religious Studies: The Disciplines and Their Boundaries*, Edinburgh: T & T Clark, 308-327.

Durham Commission on Religious Education in Schools (1970) *The Fourth 'R'*, London: National Society/SPCK.

Ellis, R. (1997) 'Revelation, Wisdom and Learning From Religions: A Response to D.G. Attfield', *British Journal of Religious Education*, 19:2, 95 -103.

Eriksson, K. (2000) 'In Search of the Meaning of Life: A Study of the Ideas of Senior Compulsory School Pupils on Life and its Meaning in an Experiential Learning Context', *British Journal of Religious Education*, 22:2,115-127.

313

Engebretson, K. (2006) 'Learning about and learning from religion. The pedagogical theory of Michael Grimmitt' in M. de Souza, K. Engebretson, G. Durka, A. McGrady, and R. Jackson (eds) *Springer International Handbook of the Religious, Spiritual and Moral Dimensions of Education*, The Netherlands: Springer Academic Publishers, 667-678.

European Union (2009) REDCo Research Project ('Religion in Education. A Contribution to Dialogue or a Factor of Conflict in transforming Societies of European Countries'). Download the Research Project's Policy Recommendations from http://www5.quvion.net/cosmea/core/corebase/mediabase/awr/redco/research_findings/REDCo_policy_rec_eng.pdf

Gay, J. (2010) 'At last – a proper curriculum for RE', London, *Church Times* No 7665, 12 February 2010, 29 – 30.

Grimmitt M.H. & Read G.T. (1977) *Teaching Christianity in RE*, Leigh-on-Sea, Essex: Kevin Mayhew Ltd.

Grimmitt, M.H. (1987) *Religious Education and Human Development*, Great Wakering: McCrimmon Publishing Co. Ltd.

Grimmitt, M.H., J.E. Grove, J.M. Hull, and L.M. Spencer. (1991) *A Gift to the Child: Religious Education in the Primary School: Teachers' Source Book*. London: Simon & Schuster Education.

Grimmitt, M.H. (ed.) (2000) *Pedagogies of Religious Education: Case Studies in the Research and Development of Good Pedagogic Practice in RE*, Great Wakering: McCrimmon Publishing Co. Ltd.

Grimmitt, M.H., J.E. Grove, J.M. Hull, and L.M. Tellam. (2006) *A Gift to the Child: Series One and Two: Religious Education in the Primary School: Teachers' Source Book*. Bury, UK: Articles of Faith.

Hampshire County Council/Portsmouth City Council/Southampton City Council. 2004. *Living difference: The agreed syllabus for Hampshire, Portsmouth and Southampton*. Winchester: Hampshire County Council/Portsmouth City Council/Southampton City Council.

HM Government (2008) *The Prevent Strategy: A Guide for Local Partners in England: stopping people becoming or supporting terrorists and violent extremists*, www.dcsf.gov.uk/violentextremism/downloads

Hart, C.J. (1994) *RE: Changing the agenda.*, Newcastle: The Christian Institute.

Hella, E. and Wright, A. (2009) 'Learning 'about' and 'from' religion: phenomenography, the Variation Theory of Learning and religious education in Finland and the UK', *British Journal of Religious Education*, 31:1, 53-64

Hull, J.M. (1984) *Studies in Religion and Education*, Lewes: The Falmer Press.

Hull, J.M. (1998) *Utopian Whispers*, Norwich: Religious and Moral Education Press.

Ina ter Avest, K.H. (2009) 'Education in Conflict', *Panorama: Intercultural Journal of Interdisciplinary Ethical and Religious Studies for Responsible Research*, 21, 13-23.

Jackson, R. (1997) *Religious Education: An Interpretive Approach*, London: Hodder & Stoughton.

Jackson, R. (2004) 'Intercultural education and recent pedagogies of religious education', *Journal of Intercultural Education*, 15:1, 3-14.

Jackson, R. et al. (eds) (2007) *Religion and Education in Europe: Developments, Contexts and Debates*, Münster and New York: Waxmann,

Jackson, R. (2009) Inaugural speech at the opening of the European Wergeland Centre (Norway) for Intercultural Education, Human Rights and Education for Democratic Citizenship. Download from http://www2.warwick.ac.uk/fac/soc/wie/research/wreru/development projects/ewc/

Kalve, P. (1996) 'Some Aspects of the Work of Michael Grimmitt' *British Journal of Religious Education*, 18:3, 181-190.

Lucas, M. (née Chatterley), (2005) 'Constructivism Revisited: The Theory in Practice', in *World Religions in Education – Reflecting on Learning and Teaching*, SHAP Working Party. Download from http://www.shapworkingparty.org.uk/journals.html

Maybury, J. and Teece, G. (2005) 'Learning from what? A question of subject focus in religious education in England and Wales', *Journal of Beliefs and Values*, 26:2, 179-190.

Miller, J. (2009) 'So, what do the Toledo Guiding Principles have to do with me?', *REsource*, 31:2, 6-9.

Office for Democratic Institutions and Human Rights (OSCE) *The Toledo Guiding Principles on Teaching About Religions and Beliefs* (2007) Download from www.osce.org/odihr/item_11_28314.html

Ofsted (2007) *Making Sense of Religion: A report on religious education in schools and the impact of locally agreed syllabuses*. Download from www.ofsted.gov.uk

Peters, R.S. (1966) *Ethics and Education*, London: George Allen & Unwin

Puolimatka, T & Tirri, K (2000) 'Religious Education in Finland: Promoting Intelligent Belief?', *British Journal of Religious Education*, 23: 1, 38-44

QCA/DfES (2004) *The Non-Statutory National Framework for Religious Education*: Download from http://www.qcda.gov.uk/libraryAssets/media/9817_re_national_framew ork_04.pdf

QCDA (2008) *A big picture of the curriculum*. Download from http://www.qcda.gov.uk/libraryAssets/media/Big_Picture_2008.pdf

QCDA (2009) *National Curriculum/RE and the national curriculum aims*. Download from http:// curriculum.qcda.gov.uk/

Read, G., Rudge, J., Teece, G., and Howarth, R. (1992) *How do I teach RE? The Westhill Project RE 5-16*. 2nd ed. Cheltenham: Stanley Thornes. (Originally published 1986)

Religious Education Council of England and Wales (2007) *A National Strategy for Religious Education*. Download from http://www.saled.org/what-we-offer/Schools/religious-education/resources/national-strategy-for-re

School Curriculum and Assessment Authority (SCAA) (1994) *Model Syllabuses for Religious Education*, Model 1, *Living Faiths Today*, pp.68, Model 2, *Questions and Teachings*, pp.60, London, SCAA.

Schmidt, G.R. & Barnes L.P, (2009) 'Educating for Peace and the Problem of Violence in the Bible and in the Qur'an', *Panorama: Intercultural Journal of Interdisciplinary Ethical and Religious Studies for Responsible Research*, 21, 111-121

Schools Council Religious Education Committee (1977) *A Groundplan for the Study of Religion*.

Shap Working Party on World Religions: http://www.shapworkingparty.org.uk/

Simon, B. (1981) 'Why no pedagogy in Britain?' in Simon, B (ed) 1981, *Education in the Eighties: the central issues*, London: Batsford.

Smart, N. (1970) 'What is Truth in RE?', *Learning for Living*, 10:1,13-15

Smart, N. (1968) *Secular Education and the Logic of Religion*, London: Faber

Smart, N. (1973) *The Science of Religion and the Sociology of Knowledge*, New Jersey: Princeton University Press

Skidmore, D. & Gallagher D, (2005) 'A Dialogical Pedagogy for Inclusive Education', a paper presented to Inclusive and Supportive Education Congress and International Special Education Conference, on Inclusion: Celebrating Diversity? 1st - 4th August 2005. Glasgow, Scotland.

Stern, J. (2006), *Teaching Religious Education*, London, New York: Continuum.

Teece, G. (2008) 'Learning from religions as 'skilful means'; a contribution to the debate about the identity of religious education', British Journal of Religious Education, 30:3,187-198

Teece, G. (2010) 'Is it learning about and from religions, religion or religious education? And is it any wonder some teachers don't get it?' *British Journal of Religious Education* 32: 2, 93-103.

Weisse, W. (2007) 'The European Research Project on Religion and Education, REDCo'; An Introduction' in Jackson R. et al (eds) (2007) 9-25

Wells, G. (1999) *Dialogic Inquiry: Towards a Socio-cultural Practice and Theory of Education*, Cambridge: Cambridge University Press.

Williams, R. (2007) 'Why cohesion needs religion' an address to the Building Bridges Conference in Singapore, December 2007. The full text can be downloaded from Network for Interfaith Concerns. http://nifcon.anglicancommunion.org/index.cfm

WRERU/DCSF (2010), *Materials for Teaching World Religions in Schools in England*, University of Warwick, Research Report – DCSF-RR197, download from www.dcsf.gov.uk/research

Wright, A. (1998), *Spiritual Pedagogy. A Survey, Critique and Reconstruction of Contemporary Spiritual Education in England and Wales*, Abingdon, Oxford: Culham College Institute

Wright, A. (2007), *Critical Religious Education, Multiculturalism and the Pursuit of Truth*, Cardiff: University of Wales Press.

CONTRIBUTORS

❖ PROFESSOR VIVIENNE BAUMFIELD is Professor of Pedagogy in the Faculty of Education at the University of Glasgow, prior to which she was Reader in Pedagogy in the London Institute of Education and Senior Lecturer with responsibility for PGCE RE in the University of Newcastle. For many years Associate Editor she will take over as Editor of the *British Journal of Religious Education* in 2011. She is also currently one of the editorial team for the *British Educational Research Journal*. Having spent 12 years as a teacher of Religious Education in inner city secondary schools, she combines an interest in the practicalities of teaching in the classroom with research into how inquiry supports learning for teachers and their students. Recently, she has been working on cross-cultural approaches to inquiry based learning and is supervising PhD students from Pakistan and Libya interested in the relationship between tradition and modernity in educational reform.

❖ PROFESSOR CLYDE CHIITY has recently retired from Goldsmiths College, University of London, where he was Head of the Department of Educational Studies for eight of the past twelve years. He is now Visiting Professor of the Institute of Education, University of London. He is the author, co-author or editor of over forty books and reports on education, including *Thirty Years On* (with Caroline Benn) (1996, 1997), *Eugenics, Race and Intelligence in Education* (2007, 2009) and *Education Policy in Britain* (2004, 2009). He is the editor of the independent journal *Forum*: for promoting 3-19 comprehensive education, which has appeared three times a year without a break since 1958.

❖ PROFESSOR TERENCE COPLEY is Emeritus Professor of Religious Education at Oxford University and Emeritus Professor of Religious Education at the University of Exeter. He is a Senior Research Fellow at Harris Manchester College, Oxford and at the Oxford University Department of Education. His current research interests include the history of RE, the nature and role of indoctrination and the implications of global warming and climate change for religious education.

❖ PROFESSOR LIAM GEARON has recently been appointed to a University Lectureship in Religious Education at the Oxford University Department of Education in association with a Senior Research Fellowship at Harris Manchester College. He was previously Professor of Lifelong Learning and Participative Pedagogy in the Faculty of Education at the University of Plymouth. With a background in the study of religion and literature, he is widely published in religious education as well as citizenship. Recent major publications include the co-authored Arthur (UK), Gearon (UK), and Sears (Canada) (2010) *Education, Politics and Religion: Reconciling the Civil and the Sacred in Education* (London and New York: Routledge) and the co-edited Engebretson (Australia), De Souza (Australia), Durka (USA), and Gearon (UK) (2010) *International Handbook for Inter-Religious Education* (Dordrecht, Heidelberg, London and New York: Springer). A former chair of the Association of University Lecturers in Religion and Education, he is also editor of the *Religious Education Handbook*, an online resource for teachers funded by the DCSF and the Religious Education Council of England and Wales (www.re-handbook.org.uk) launched in the summer of 2010. He has held research grants from the British Academy (2008-09) and (currently) the Arts and Humanities Research Council (2010-2011) He is also presently a recipient of a Leverhulme Research Fellowship (2011-2012) for research on 'Writers and their Dictators'.

❖ DR MARIUS FELDERHOF is a Senior Lecturer in Systematic and Philosophical Theology in the School of Philosophy, Theology and Religion of the University of Birmingham. Previously he taught Christian Theology, Ethics and the Philosophy at St. Andrews University, Scotland and at Westhill College, Birmingham. It was his time at Westhill, a mainly teacher training institution, that sparked his research interest in Religious Education and its theological and philosophical dimensions. From 2005 to 2007 he was seconded to the City of Birmingham to act as the drafting secretary to the Agreed Syllabus Conference that led to the City's most recent and acclaimed RE syllabus. He continues to advise the City's Cabinet Member for Children, Young People and Families on matters relating to Religious Education. In addition to his teaching and research, he is currently promoting the active collaboration between the City, Faith Leaders and the Academy through the *Faiths for the City Initiative*. A recent contribution to the debates in RE is his jointly edited book, *Inspiring Faith in Schools: Studies in Religious Education*, 2007 (Ashgate).

❖ DR MICHAEL GRIMMITT is the Dr David H. Lee Senior Research Fellow in Religious Education in the Oxford University Department of Education and a Senior Research Fellow of Harris Manchester College, Oxford. He is also a member of the Oxford University Faculty of Theology. He was previously Reader in Religion in Education in the University of Birmingham where for many years he was responsible for the PGCE Initial Teacher Training course in Religious Education. After 45 years teaching and writing about RE he will retire this year and intends to devote the remainder of his life to music and dog-walking.

❖ DR JOYCE MILLER is the former Head of Diversity and Cohesion at Education Bradford. Prior to that she taught at schools in Northumberland and Coventry and was a Senior Lecturer in Religious Studies at the University of Wolverhampton from 1992-2000. She is the deputy chair of the RE Council of England and Wales and Vice Chair of the Schools Linking Network. Until July 2008, she was the Chair of the Association of RE Inspectors, Advisers and Consultants. She has recently completed doctoral research on community cohesion and religion at the University of Warwick where she is an Associate Fellow.

❖ PROFESSOR AUDREY OSLER is Visiting Professor at Birkbeck College, University of London and the University of Leeds, where she was founding director of the interdisciplinary Centre for Citizenship and Human Rights Education. She has also held academic posts at the universities of Birmingham and Leicester, where she was, until 2004, Chair in Education. Audrey has experience as consultant to a number of international agencies, including the Council of Europe, the European Commission, and UNESCO, engaging in both research and consultancy in Europe, East Asia and sub-Saharan Africa. In 2007 she was Visiting Scholar at the University of Washington in Seattle. She has published widely, including 18 books, and her work translated into various languages, including Japanese and Chinese. She has a long-standing interest in faith schooling, diversity and children's human rights. Her most recent books are *Students' Perspectives on Schooling* (2010, Open University Press) and *Teachers and Human Rights Education* (2010, Trentham, with Hugh Starkey).

❖ PROFESSOR RICHARD PRING retired after 14 years as Director of the Department of Educational Studies at Oxford University in May 2003. Since 2003, he was Lead Director of the Nuffield Review of 14-19 Education and Training. This was a £1,000,000 six year project, funded by the Nuffield Foundation. He has published widely on many educational subjects, especially in the philosophy of education (pertinent to his chapter in this book is his book *John Dewey: the Philosopher of Education for the 21st century*, London, Continuum (2006)) Arising from a Leverhulme Fellowship, 2003/4, and from his work with the Aga Khan University's Institute for the Study of Muslim Civilisations he has a strong interest in faith based schools. He has recently completed his 27th London marathon and is working on the *Runners' Guide to Oxford*.

❖ NORMAN RICHARDSON is a lecturer in teacher education programmes at Stranmillis University College, Belfast, specialising in religious and cultural diversity and inclusive approaches to Religious Education. A former teacher, he has also worked as an ecumenical peace education officer for the Irish Churches. He is an executive committee member of the Northern Ireland Inter-Faith Forum and the UK Inter-Faith Network, and serves on a number of local, national and international Religious Education bodies.

❖ DR JOHN RUDGE taught in schools in Manchester before joining the staff of the RE Centre at Westhill College, Birmingham, in 1980 where he was later appointed Director. He was involved in the development of the Westhill Project RE 5-16 and made a specialist contribution to the development of assessment in RE and RS. Since taking early retirement, he continues to be involved in RE through the inspection of Initial Teacher Education, and as Chair of Examiners for RS with Edexcel.

❖ DR ABDULLAH SAHIN is a Muslim educator and comes from an interdisciplinary educational background that consists of classical Islamic studies, theology and educational studies. He is Head of Research at Markfield Institute of Higher Education affiliated with the University of Gloucestershire where he coordinates the PG research programme and teaches the newly developed MEd programme; 'Islamic Education: *new perspectives*'. He is interested in exploring diverse issues informing the learning and teaching of Islam in the mainly secular, culturally and religiously plural contemporary societies in Europe. He has conducted research on religious identity formation amongst British Muslim youth and worked on educational strategies to address the impact of religious extremism in their lives. He has completed an international research project on Religious Extremism and Muslim Youth (2004-2006) and is currently completing a book, *Pedagogy and Identity Formation: New Directions in Islamic Education*, (Kube Publications). He has taught at the Universities of Birmingham, Aberdeen and Gulf University for Science and Technology, Kuwait. He is a member of the International Seminar on Religious Education and Values (ISREV) and is currently Visiting Professor at the Institut d'Etudes de l'Islam et des Sociétés du Monde Musulman at the EHESS, Paris.

❖ DR MATTHEW THOMPSON is the founder director of Liverpool Community Spirit (LCS) a grass-roots community education partnership. Over the last decade, LCS has been developing and delivering innovative community education programmes, projects and resources engaging both young people and adults in promoting enduring community spirit and tackling fear and prejudice with respect to faiths. In recent years he has been pioneering Community Spirit courses for offenders which draw upon the wisdom of faith traditions to engage learners in the promotion of both their personal and their community's welfare. He is also a part-time Senior Lecturer in Religious Education at Liverpool Hope University.

❖ PROFESSOR GEOFFREY WALFORD is Emeritus Professor of Education Policy and an Emeritus Fellow of Green Templeton College at the University of Oxford. He was previously Reader in Education Policy at Oxford, and Senior Lecturer in Sociology and Education Policy at Aston Business School, Aston University, Birmingham. He has academic degrees from Oxford, Kent, London and the Open Universities, and is author of more than 150 academic articles and book chapters. He was Joint Editor of the *British Journal of Educational Studies* from 1999 to 2002, and is Editor of the annual volume, *Studies in Educational Ethnography*. He has been Editor of the *Oxford Review of Education* since 2004.

❖ SIMONE WHITEHOUSE studied Theology, gained a Master's degree in Philosophy and took her PGCE in RE at the University of Birmingham before embarking on her teaching career. For ten years she was Head of RE in two very different secondary schools within Birmingham which gave her wide ranging and practical experience in the delivery of quality RE. Whilst working in school she became an associate adviser for RE to the City. For the last five years she has been the Adviser with Responsibility for RE in Birmingham, the largest education authority in the country, and has shared her experience with the Agreed Syllabus Conference which produced the groundbreaking 2007 Syllabus. Currently she is working collaboratively with the Standing Advisory Council for Religious Education (SACRE), on designing, implementing and supporting the development of the Syllabus with resources, schemes of work, lesson plans and CPD. She is also involved in leading and training Birmingham schools in implementing the SEAL (Social and Emotional Aspects of Learning) programme. She has research interests in values and spirituality and, in her leisure time, enjoys reading and practices yoga.

❖ PROFESSOR ANDREW WRIGHT is Professor of Religious and Theological Education at King's College London. His academic research focuses on the interface between theology, philosophy and education, with particular reference to Trinitarian theology, critical realism, ontology, epistemology, hermeneutics, spirituality and pedagogy. A former chair of the Association of University Lecturers in Religion and Education, he was a member of the writing group that produced the *Non-Statutory National Framework for Religious Education* (2004). His books include *Spirituality and Education* (RoutledgeFalmer 2002), *Religion, Education and Post-modernity* (RoutledgeFalmer 2004) and *Critical Religious Education, Multiculturalism and the Pursuit of Truth* (University of Wales Press 2007). He is currently writing a book on critical realism and religious education, to be published by Routledge in 2011.

Author Index

Subject Index